Economic Diplomacy and the Origins of the Second World War

ECONOMIC DIPLOMACY AND THE ORIGINS OF THE SECOND WORLD WAR

Germany, Britain, France, and Eastern Europe, 1930-1939

David E. Kaiser

Princeton University Press, Princeton, New Jersey

Contents

List of Tables

Preface

During the interwar period, Eastern Europe was the scene of violent international political struggles.[1] The chronic backwardness and instability of the region had helped to precipitate the First World War; the war and the Paris peace treaties of 1919 transformed the area. The survival of the postwar European order depended on maintaining the new Eastern European status quo. In the following two decades the German government schemed to overturn the new settlement, the French officially defended it, and the British took no firm stand. Under pressure from Hitler, the settlement finally collapsed in 1938. A general European war, in which Germany defeated France and drove Britain from the European continent, followed one year later.

Although the political and military aspects of the struggle for Eastern Europe among Germany, Britain, and France during the interwar period have been the subject of many studies, the economic aspects of this struggle have received much less attention. This book has been written to fill this gap. A relatively backward and undeveloped region, Eastern Europe offered economic as well as political opportunities to the great powers. Its new states, most of them agricultural, needed loans from the western powers to develop their economies and markets in which to sell their agricultural surplus. Beginning in 1930, the

[1] As used herein, "Eastern Europe" includes Poland, the three Baltic states of Estonia, Latvia, and Lithuania, Austria, Czechoslovakia, Hungary, Rumania, and Yugoslavia. "Northeastern Europe" refers to the first four of these countries, and "Southeastern Europe" to the last five. Other writers have used the term "Southeastern Europe" to include Albania, Bulgaria, Greece, and Turkey; however, the five successor states of the Austro-Hungarian monarchy—Austria, Czechoslovakia, Hungary, Rumania, and Yugoslavia—form a more compact, homogeneous unit. Furthermore, during the 1930s they were often grouped together as the "Danubian states." A discussion of great-power diplomacy in Albania, Bulgaria, Greece, and Turkey would also involve a host of Mediterranean questions irrelevant to the Danubian states. Finland might arguably be included in Northeastern Europe, but observers during the 1930s tended to group it with the Scandinavian countries rather than with Poland and the Baltic states.

Great Depression and the worldwide fall in agricultural prices made economic help for Eastern Europe a matter of general international concern.

The economic crisis within the region opened up opportunities for the great powers to extend their political influence. The German Foreign Office immediately tried to exploit Eastern Europe's weakness for its own ends. Berlin undertook several major economic initiatives in Southeastern Europe during 1931 with the avowed goal of increasing German political influence. For various reasons, including the determined opposition of the French government, these initiatives failed. Under Hitler, however, the Wilhelmstrasse concluded important new trade treaties with Southeastern European states in 1934 and 1935. Beginning in 1937, the importance of German trade with Eastern Europe increased dramatically; imports from the region played a vital role in feeding the German people while Hitler prepared for war. In contrast, Britain and France gave virtually no economic help to Eastern Europe. Their commercial policies favored their colonial empires, and their imports from Eastern Europe remained extremely low. In 1938 the Munich agreement, which removed the last effective barrier to German military expansion eastward, also laid the region's economic resources at Hitler's feet. This peaceful triumph enabled Hitler to begin war one year later and to defeat the western powers in 1940.

The principal sources for economic diplomacy in Eastern Europe during the 1930s include the archives of the German cabinet, Foreign Office, Economics Ministry, and War Ministry; the British Cabinet, Foreign Office, Board of Trade, and Treasury; and the French Finance and Agriculture ministries. Most of these archives have only recently been opened. The story they tell is one of great interest to any student of the origins of the Second World War and to anyone who wishes to understand the interaction between foreign trade and foreign policy.

Many people gave me invaluable assistance in preparing this book. Ernest May, my dissertation adviser at Harvard, helped to define the topic and provided incisive editorial criticism and generous encouragement throughout. Stephen Schuker, now of Brandeis University, gave me superb advice with respect to sources; his knowledge of European archives can benefit any student of interwar diplomacy. While preparing the manuscript I also received very valuable advice from Hans-Jürgen Schröder of the Institut für Zeitgeschichte in Mainz and Timothy W. Mason of St. Peter's College, Oxford. Others who made useful suggestions include Brad Lee, Thomas Childers, Charles Maier, and the late Sir John Wheeler-Bennett, who shared some of his vast firsthand knowledge of interwar Europe. Keith Eubank of Queens College and Anna Cienciala of the University of Kansas, who both read the manuscript for Princeton University Press, made suggestions that improved the work very much indeed. Joanna Hitchcock, who first read the book at Princeton University Press and has guided it to publication, was also most helpful. Lastly, I was also assisted by Sir Laurence Collier. It was gratifying to correspond with one of the few characters in the book who plays a truly heroic role.

The generous assistance of the Harvard Center for European studies enabled me to spend valuable time in London, Paris, Koblenz, and Bonn. I greatly appreciated the cooperation of the staff of the Public Record Office in London, and I thank the Controller of Her Majesty's Stationery Office for permission to cite unpublished Crown copyright material in that office. I must also thank Mme Alice Guillemain of the French Finance Ministry, and the staffs of the Archives Nationales in Paris, the Politisches Archiv in Bonn, the Bundesarchiv in Koblenz, and the University of Birmingham Library. My work was enormously facilitated by the staff of Widener Library; in particular, the Documents Division generously agreed to purchase some important material available on microfilm. An earlier decision by the Boston Public Library to purchase the entire T-120 series of German Foreign Office microfilms also simplified my task. Naturally I have also incurred many more personal debts, but these I prefer to acknowledge personally.

Abbreviations

AA	Auswärtiges Amt, Berlin
AE	Ministère des Affaires Etrangères, Paris
AGK	Ausfuhrgemeinschaft für Kriegsgerät, Berlin
AN	Archives Nationales, Paris
APA	Aussenpolitisches Amt, Berlin
BT	Board of Trade, London
DBFP	*Documents on British Foreign Policy, 1919-1939*, ed. E. L. Woodward et al., series 2 and 3 (London, 1946-1970)
DDF	Ministère des Affaires Etrangères, Commission de publication des documents relatifs aux origines de la guerre 1939-1945, *Documents diplomatiques français (1932-1939)*, series 1 and 2 (Paris, 1963-1977)
DGFP	U.S. Department of State, *Documents on German Foreign Policy, 1918-1945, from the Archives of the German Foreign Ministry*, ed. Raymond Sontag et al., series C and D (Washington, D.C., 1949-1966)
ECGD	Export Credits Guarantee Department, London
FO	Foreign Office, London
HPA	Handelspolitisches Ausschuss, Berlin
ITS	League of Nations, *Publications, International Trade Statistics* (Geneva, various years)
LN	League of Nations
LNP	League of Nations, *Publications*
OKW	Oberkommando der Wehrmacht
PA	Politisches Archiv, Bonn
PD	Great Britain, *Parliamentary Debates*, House of Commons, House of Lords, 5th series (London, various years)
PRO	Public Record Office, London
SAUK	Great Britain, Board of Trade, *Statistical Abstract of the United Kingdom* (London, various years)

SJB   Kaiserliches Statistisches Amt (later Statistisches
           Reichsamt), *Statistisches Jahrbuch* (Berlin, various
           years)

SMCF   Ministère des Finances, Direction Générale des
           Douanes, *Statistique mensuelle du commerce extérieur de
           la France* (Paris, various years)

TUK   Great Britain, Customs and Excise Department,
           Statistical Office, *Trade of the United Kingdom with
           Foreign Countries and British Possessions* (London,
           various years)

Economic Diplomacy and the Origins of the Second World War

I.

Eastern Europe and the Western Powers, 1871-1930

Ever since the beginning of the industrial and democratic revolutions in the late eighteenth century, the failure of Eastern Europe to follow western models of political and economic development has been a major theme in European history and a major factor in international relations. Between 1789 and 1871, Britain, France, and Germany all grew into unified, industrialized national states, and, despite the failure of parliamentary democracy completely to overcome the authoritarian political structure in Germany, their political development seemed to be following an essentially common course as well. Eastern Europe, however, remained relatively untouched by the industrial and democratic revolutions, and during the nineteenth century its inability to follow western patterns of development became more and more apparent. The development of national states was almost impossible to the east and southeast of Germany, where the Russian and Austro-Hungarian empires ruled numerous subject nationalities. The emergence of Balkan nationalism in the late nineteenth and early twentieth centuries threatened to disrupt Europe by eliminating the Dual Monarchy as a great power.

The east lagged behind economically as well. Industrialization took place only in the Austrian provinces of the Hapsburg Empire until the late nineteenth century, when the Russian government began a frantic attempt to catch up with the west. Agriculture remained backward; in many areas, techniques had progressed little since the Middle Ages. Europe remained a diplomatic and strategic entity; economically and politically, however, it was increasingly divided into more and less developed regions.[1]

[1] The best survey of economic development in Eastern Europe is Ivan T. Berend and György Ránki, *Economic Development in East-Central Europe in the 19th and 20th Centuries* (New York, 1974).

In the late nineteenth century the development of worldwide patterns of trade and finance tightened British, French, and German ties to other parts of the world at the expense of their Eastern European neighbors. Industrialization and the population explosion in Western Europe had created an enormous need for imported foodstuffs, especially grain. Increasingly during the nineteenth century, climate, large-scale production, and low-cost sea transportation gave the United States, Argentina, and the British Empire advantages in the grain trade that far outweighed the geographical proximity of Austria-Hungary, the Balkans, and Russia. Although the tsarist regime exported large quantities of cereals, it lagged far behind the United States and Argentina as a supplier of Britain, Germany, and France. Russia also exported large quantities of butter, eggs, and timber to Western Europe, but, on the whole, the Eastern European market was relatively insignificant to the western powers. On the eve of the First World War both Britain and France bought only 7 percent of their imports from Russia, Austria-Hungary, and the Balkans and sold even less of their exports there. Germany took 22 percent of its imports from Eastern Europe—13 percent from Russia—and sold 21 percent of its exports there.[2]

Western European capital flowed in the same overseas channels. Britain, the largest foreign investor during the nineteenth century, had less than 4 percent of its overseas investments in Russia, Austria-Hungary, or the Balkans by 1914. Furthermore, despite Berlin's and Paris's much greater political interests in Eastern Europe, the corresponding figures for German and French capital were 28 percent and 35 percent, respectively. Left to its own devices, capital inevitably sought more profitable opportunities in the Western Hemisphere. Thus, despite the French government's sponsorship of investments in its ally's economy, loans to Russia amounted to just 25 percent of French foreign investment.[3]

---

[2] These figures have been compiled from: Kaiserliches Statistisches Amt (later Statistisches Reichsamt), *Statistisches Jahrbuch* (Berlin, various years) (hereafter *SJB*); Statistique Générale de la France, *Annuaire Statistique* (Paris, various years); and Great Britain, Customs and Excise Department, *Trade of the United Kingdom with Foreign Countries and British Possessions* (London, various years) (hereafter *TUK*).

[3] Herbert Feis, *Europe, the World's Banker, 1871-1914* (New Haven, 1930), pp. 23, 51, 74.

Despite the economic backwardness of Eastern Europe, the German government and important segments of German public opinion showed a healthy interest in the region in the years before 1914. In 1879 Chancellor Otto von Bismarck decided to base his diplomacy upon an alliance with Austria-Hungary, an alliance that ultimately drew Germany into war in 1914. Bismarck also proposed a customs union with the Hapsburg monarchy in 1879, but the Vienna government, fearing that such a plan would destroy Austrian independence, turned him down. Later, in Wilhelmine Germany, various pressure groups and publicists, led by the Alldeutscher Verband, or Pan-German League, loudly campaigned for German expansion to the east. German and Austrian elements of the Pan-German League called for the incorporation of the German-speaking provinces of the Hapsburg Empire into the German Empire, while Baltic German publicists advocated expansion into the Baltic provinces of the Russian Empire. Economic theorists proposed a Central European customs union, often called Mitteleuropa, which would provide Germany with a protected market sufficiently large to compete economically with the British Empire, the United States, and Russia—an idea that even Emperor William II sometimes discussed. Although the German government did not commit itself to territorial expansion in Eastern Europe before 1914, interest groups and publicists had their own reasons for encouraging eastward expansion, just as the Junker ruling class, for its own reasons, fostered the climate of aggressive international competition that helped to lead to the catastrophe of 1914-1918.[4]

The First World War destroyed normal patterns of international trade and changed the role of Eastern Europe in the international order. During the conflict, Germany tried to consolidate its strategic and economic position by economic and territorial expansion in Eastern Europe. Most German government, military, political, and business leaders assumed that the war would ultimately partition the world into a few enormous political and economic blocs. To survive as a world power, Germany would have to establish secure new frontiers and

[4] Helmut Boehme, *Deutschlands Weg zur Grossmacht* (Cologne and Berlin, 1966), pp. 587-604; Henry Cord Meyer, *Mitteleuropa in German Thought and Action, 1815-1945* (The Hague, 1955), pp. 30-56; Fritz Fischer, *War of Illusions: German Policies from 1911 to 1914* (London, 1975), pp. 6-43.

monopolize the Central European industrial market to compensate for the loss of exports overseas. In public, Germany's eastern war aims came to center around the concept of Mitteleuropa, a German-dominated Central European federation based on a customs union between the German and Austro-Hungarian empires. Friedrich Naumann popularized the concept in his sensational 1916 best seller, *Mitteleuropa*, and it attracted enormous support throughout German society. The Arbeitsausschuss für Mitteleuropa (Working Committee for Mitteleuropa), founded by Naumann in early 1916, included representatives of virtually every major segment and shade of opinion in German public life: industrialists Albert Ballin and Hugo Stinnes; banker Hjalmar Schacht; economist Gustav Schmoller; sociologist Max Weber; and such political leaders as Matthias Erzberger of the Catholic Center party, Gustav Noske of the Social Democrats, and Cuno von Westarp of the Conservatives. Naumann and his disciples characterized Mitteleuropa as a free federation of all Central European peoples, chiefly with an eye toward maintaining the loyalty of the subject nationalities of the Hapsburg Empire.[5]

By 1916, however, a split developed between two alternative German eastern policies. Mitteleuropa occupied the public eye, but during the first three years of war the German General Staff and the Foreign Office decided that German expansion should proceed principally on an eastern rather than a southeastern axis and that it should be based on territorial annexations, Germanization, and resettlement rather than on federation. By early 1917 the German government intended to annex a "frontier strip" along the Polish border and the Baltic provinces of Russia (the future Baltic states). General Erich Ludendorff had already begun resettling Lithuania and Courland with German peasants and Germanizing the Baltic population in 1916. Ludendorff opposed closer German-Austrian relations—in fact, he was convinced that a new war with Austria was inevitable— and he was generally successful in shifting German expansion to an eastern axis, in spite of the Salzburg agreement of October 1917, by which Berlin and Vienna agreed in principle to a customs union. The Bolshevik revolution and Russia's collapse en-

---

[5] Meyer, *Mitteleuropa*, pp. 230-31; Fritz Fischer, *Germany's Aims in the First World War* (London, 1967).

abled Ludendorff, the Foreign Office, and German industrial interests to expand even further east. In April 1918 the Treaty of Brest-Litovsk effectively established German domination of the Baltic provinces, Poland, and the Ukraine. The Germans immediately began organizing the exploitation of Ukrainian grain, coal, and iron; one month later a peace treaty with defeated Rumania assured German control of the Rumanian oil fields. German policy concentrated on monopolizing Europe's vital raw materials to put postwar France and the Hapsburg Empire at its mercy.[6]

The defeat of Germany and the collapse of Austria-Hungary in November 1918 bankrupted all of Germany's schemes for expansion. During the war the Allies had tried to secure the support of the Eastern European nationalities by promising them autonomy or self-determination. The Allied victory transformed the map of Europe. Within a few years Poland had been reborn as an independent state, Czechoslovakia newly created, and the Baltic states established, and Rumania and Yugoslavia (the former Serbia) both had more than doubled in size. These territorial changes did not necessarily reflect the long-term balance of power in Europe; they occurred largely because of the successive defeats of Russia, Austria-Hungary, and Germany. The survival of the new order would depend upon the new balance of power that would emerge in Europe and the world as a whole.

New relationships between the three western powers and the new Eastern European states reflected the vastly altered circumstances of the postwar world. German dreams of a great eastern empire lay in ruins; instead, Germany had to endure the humiliating loss of the Polish Corridor, the province of Posen, and parts of Upper Silesia to Poland, of Memel to Lithuania, and of Danzig, which became a free city under League of Nations authority and entered into a customs union with Poland. The Allies confiscated German investments in Eastern Europe, apportioning them among themselves, and the German minorities within the new eastern states suffered from the pressure of aggressive nationalities policies. During the 1920s the revision of Germany's eastern frontiers and the Anschluss with Austria remained major long-term objectives of German foreign policy,

[6] Fischer, *Germany's Aims*, pp. 271-79, 375-79, 437, 512-13, 523-33.

but Berlin had to concentrate on the issue of reparations, the securing of foreign capital, attempts to end the occupation of the Rhineland, and the cultivation of good relations with the other outcast power of Europe, the Soviet Union.

In the meantime, the German government maintained economic interest in Eastern Europe, viewing the region as a natural market for German products. Only with regard to Poland did the German government try to link commercial policy with political objectives, and here Berlin vacillated between weakening Poland by restricting German-Polish trade, and increasing German influence by stimulating it. In 1928, in an effort to outflank Poland, the German government concluded a generous economic agreement with Lithuania. The Lithuanians also held territorial grievances against Poland, owing to the Polish seizure of the city of Vilnius, and had themselves hinted at possible military collaboration with Germany against Poland. To secure Lithuanian support, Foreign Minister Gustav Stresemann even granted the Lithuanians the right to export live pigs into Germany, a virtually unprecedented concession to an Eastern European state and one that the Prussian bureaucracy promptly blocked. In 1930, after years of tariff war, the German government concluded a far-reaching commercial agreement with Poland, but agricultural protectionists succeeded in blocking its ratification in the Reichstag.[7]

Nevertheless, in spite of the efforts of the Wilhelmstrasse, the new states of Eastern Europe played even less of a role in German foreign trade than the prewar empires had. After the end of the war and the Allied blockade, German grain purchases from North and South America began again. Soviet Russia ended large-scale grain exports, and its share of the German market passed not to Eastern European cereals growers like Yu-

---

[7] See Hans-Adolf Jacobsen, ed., *Missträuische Nachbarn* (Düsseldorf, 1970), pp. 49-54, for an August 1926 Foreign Office Memorandum on policy toward Southeastern Europe. On the German-Lithuanian rapprochement see *Akten zur deutschen Auswärtigen Politik, 1918-1945*, Series B (Göttingen, 1966-), vol. II, pt. 1, nos. 1, 177, pt. 2, nos. 29, 49, 170, vol. 4, no. 76, and the microfilmed German documents, National Archives, Washington, D.C., Foreign Office memorandum, Apr. 11, 1931, T-120/3575/D789146-49 (these documents are cited as series number/serial number/frame numbers). On German-Polish trade relations see Harald von Riekhoff, *German-Polish Relations, 1918-33* (Baltimore, 1971), pp. 161-93.

goslavia, Hungary, Rumania, and Poland, but to the United States, Canada, and Argentina. The Baltic states and Poland exported only a small fraction of Russia's prewar exports of butter and eggs to Germany; Denmark and the Netherlands picked up the slack. Never during the 1920s did total German trade with Eastern Europe reach prewar levels. In 1913 German imports from Austria-Hungary, Serbia, Montenegro, and Rumania amounted to 8.5 percent of its total imports; in 1928 Austria, Hungary, Czechoslovakia, Rumania, and Yugoslavia supplied just 7.7 percent of German imports. The area's share of German exports remained virtually constant, totaling 12.5 percent in 1913 and 12.6 percent in 1928. At constant prices, these figures indicate a 12.0 percent decline in the value of German imports from the Danubian basin and a 13.6 percent decline in its exports there. Similarly, with regard to the former Russian Empire, Germany bought 13.2 percent of its imports from Russia in 1913 and sold 8.7 percent of its exports there. The corresponding 1928 figures for Poland, the Baltic states, and the Soviet Union were 6.3 percent and 8.0 percent.[8] As in the prewar period, the prevailing patterns of German trade did not reflect German political interest in Eastern Europe.

The French and British had won a common victory over Germany in 1918, but in the following decade they differed sharply over many questions relating to the future of Europe, including policy toward the new states of Eastern Europe. The French government tried to make diplomatic and military capital out of the creation of the new states almost from the moment of their inception. French military and political leaders knew that even a truncated Weimar Germany retained far more potential war-making capacity than France. Paris still needed an eastern ally to balance German power, and the Soviet Union, which had turned its back on European diplomacy and defaulted on enormous French loans, was clearly unsuited to the role. Prodded by the military, the French government first approached Poland, the largest and most strategically located of the new states and itself in need of an ally against Germany. On February 19, 1921, French President Alexandre Millerand and Marshal Józef Piłsudski of Poland concluded a defensive al-

[8] *SJB, 1914,* pp. 182-83, 257-58, *1929,* pp. 197-98, 234, 238.

liance. The two states also concluded a military convention, a commercial agreement extremely favorable to France, and a 400-million-franc loan to build up Polish armaments.[9]

Paris subsequently concluded an alliance with Czechoslovakia and treaties of friendship with Yugoslavia and Rumania. These three states were themselves bound together in the common defense of the territory they had secured from Hungary under the Treaty of Trianon, and in the early 1920s they concluded an anti-Hungarian alliance and became known collectively as the Little Entente. In subsequent years the Little Entente was generally regarded as a French creation, although, ironically, Czech Foreign Minister Eduard Beneš had originally brought it into being in response to rumors that the French government sought close economic and political relations with Hungary. These rumors did not pan out, and the government of Prime Minister Raymond Poincaré concluded an alliance with Czechoslovakia on January 25, 1924. This treaty was a looser document than the Franco-Polish alliance and lacked a military convention. Beneš and Czech President Tomáš Masaryk saw French friendship as a steppingstone to influence in Europe, while Paris wanted to line up a diplomatic coalition in support of the postwar European settlement. The subsequent Franco-Rumanian and Franco-Yugoslavian treaties of friendship of June 10, 1926, and November 11, 1927, did not include obligations of mutual assistance in case of aggression by a third party. They merely provided Belgrade and Bucharest with diplomatic support in their respective disputes with Italy over Dalmatia and Albania and with the Soviets over the province of Bessarabia, but they also contributed to the impression of a vast French system of anti-German alliances in Eastern Europe.[10]

In an effort to consolidate French political influence, the French government encouraged long-term loans to Poland and the Danubian states, sometimes by providing government guarantees. Contemporary and secondary sources indicate that these

[9] Piotr Wandycz, *France and Her Eastern Allies, 1919-1925: French-Czechoslovak-Polish Relations from the Paris Peace Conference to Locarno* (Minneapolis, 1962), pp. 215-17, 220-21.

[10] Ibid., pp. 193-97, 300-302; Günter Reichert, *Das Scheitern der Kleinen Entente, 1933-38* (Munich, 1971), p. 5. For the texts of the Franco-Rumanian and Franco-Yugoslav treaties see League of Nations (hereafter LN), *Treaty Series*, 205 vols. (Geneva, 1920-1946), LVIII, 227-31, LXVIII, 375-79.

loans represented less than 10 percent of total French investments abroad, but they were very important to the five Danubian states and Poland. Paris tied some loans to Poland, Yugoslavia, and Rumania to purchases of French arms. During the 1920s, however, the French government failed to orient French commercial policy so as to enable the eastern states to service their loans out of an active trade balance with France. French exports and imports remained an insignificant entry in the trade balances of the eastern states. France continued to import large quantities of cereals, but, as in the case of Germany, low American prices outweighed the possible political advantages of buying in Eastern Europe. Furthermore, the French tariff structure favored the French Empire at the expense of foreign trading partners.[11] Deprived of exports to France, the eastern states tended to pay the service on their loans by floating new loans—a tactic that led to disaster in 1931.

British financial interests lent more generously in Eastern Europe than did French ones, but the British government viewed French attempts to extend its political influence within the region with extreme distaste. The British wanted to keep the new states independent of all of the great powers; thus, although conscious of the financial needs of Eastern Europe, they encouraged purely private loans or loans administered by the League of Nations rather than credits guaranteed by a single government. During the 1920s the British government seemed more disturbed by the prospect of French hegemony on the Continent than by the more distant possibility of German predominance. From the beginning, the British opposed the French alliances in Eastern Europe as a relic of prewar international diplomacy and an attempt to maintain a permanent division of Europe into victors and vanquished. Nor did the British government regard the new frontiers in Eastern Europe as

[11] On Apr. 18, 1932, when French lending in Southeastern Europe had reached its peak, the British Treasury reported that French long-term loans to the five Danubian states totaled 4.75 billion francs. See Public Record Office, London (PRO), Treasury statement of Apr. 18, 1932, FO 371/15929, C3096/58/62. Alice Teichova, *An Economic Background to Munich* (Cambridge, 1974), p. 6, puts total French long-term foreign holdings at 60 billion francs in 1933. Thus, even allowing for a proportional figure for Poland, the proportion of French foreign investments in Eastern Europe was less than 10%. On French commercial policy see Jacques Fouchet, *La Politique commerciale en France depuis 1930* (Paris, 1938), pp. 156-63.

necessarily final—much less worthy of a British commitment to maintain them. Thus London rejected the Geneva protocol of 1924, by which the French attempted to pledge all League members to defend the frontiers of any European state.[12]

In 1925 the French government began to draw away from its eastern allies. British pressure was partly responsible. In the early 1920s Millerand and Poincaré may have welcomed the new alliances as substitutes for the prewar treaty with Russia, but Aristide Briand, French foreign minister from 1924 to 1931, felt that close relations with Britain and a final reconciliation with Germany offered better guarantees of French security. Thus at Locarno in 1925, when London offered to guarantee the Franco-German frontier but refused to commit itself to the existing German eastern border, the French government, over Polish objections, accepted an implicit distinction between Germany's western and eastern borders. The German government recognized the former in perpetuity while making plain its intention peacefully to seek changes in the latter. Poland and Czechoslovakia had to be content with arbitration treaties with Germany and new treaties with France that tied French military assistance to action by the Council of the League of Nations. The British agreed that French action in fulfillment of these new treaties would not bring into force Britain's obligation to defend *Germany* against *French* aggression. British Foreign Secretary Sir Austen Chamberlain, however, also assured his government colleagues that Britain need not *assist* France in a war arising out of France's obligations to its eastern allies, and he expressed the hope that France would therefore reduce its commitments in Eastern Europe in the future.[13]

In 1929, in response to British pressure, Paris once again disappointed its eastern allies by agreeing to evacuate French troops from the Rhineland as a corollary to the final settlement

[12] For figures on British investments see the Treasury statement of Apr. 18, 1932, FO 371/15929, C3096/58/62. For a thorough and interesting study of British investment policy in Southeastern Europe during the 1920s see Marie-Luise Recker, *England und der Donauraum, 1919-29* (Stuttgart, 1976). On British attitudes toward the French alliances see Wandycz, *France and Her Eastern Allies*, pp. 304-5, and Sir Robert Vansittart's May 1931 memorandum, PRO, CAB 24/221, CP 125 (31).

[13] Steven A. Schuker, *The End of French Predominance in Europe* (Chapel Hill, 1976), pp. 388-90. Chamberlain made these comments at a June 22, 1925, meeting of the Committee of Imperial Defense.

of German reparations under the Young Plan. The Polish government regarded the presence of French troops within Germany as an important guarantee of Polish security and sought a new German commitment to the German-Polish frontier as compensation for the French evacuation. Thus, during 1929 Warsaw tried to persuade Paris to agree to a Polish-Franco-German treaty under which all three signatories would guarantee their common frontiers against "flagrant aggression" without regard to League Council action. The French government never definitely responded to this proposal. Instead, in October 1929 the French ambassador to Poland, Jules Laroche, submitted a new political agreement to the Polish government that would have definitely subordinated French assistance to Poland to a decision by the League Council. The Poles declined the new pact.[14] In theory, France remained bound to Poland and the states of the Little Entente by their common dependence on the postwar peace settlement, especially its territorial and disarmament clauses. In fact, Briand was clearly seeking an alternative to rigid enforcement of the peace treaties in an effort to put Europe on a more stable footing.

Briand unveiled such an alternative in Geneva on September 5, 1929, when he proposed a Pan-European union to the League Assembly. In June 1929 Briand had told Stresemann that he hoped to consummate the Franco-German reconciliation begun at Locarno within the framework of a larger unit. In his September speech he suggested a European economic union leading eventually to a political one. Briand's purpose was clear: economically, a united Europe could compete more effectively with the British Empire and the United States; politically, union would eliminate territorial grievances arising out of the peace treaties by making frontiers meaningless. In response to requests from other League members, Briand submitted a French memorandum embodying his proposals on May 1, 1930. By this time, although Briand remained foreign minister, the far more conservative and anti-German nationalist André Tardieu had replaced him as premier, and the tone of the new memorandum suggests that Tardieu, Quai d'Orsay civil servants, and France's

[14] Anna Cienciala, "The Significance of the Declaration of Non-Aggression of January 26, 1934, in Polish-German and International Relations: A Reappraisal," *East European Quarterly*, I, no. 1 (March 1967), 9-13. This account is based upon Polish archival sources.

eastern allies may have combined to bring the proposal more in line with existing French policy. It reversed Briand's original emphasis, giving priority to political rather than economic union. The "question of security"—in other words, new guarantees of existing frontiers—would have to be dealt with first, lest economically weaker nations be exposed "to the risks of political domination of the most strongly organized states."[15]

Briand's plan provoked an extremely significant discussion within the German government. German foreign policy stood at a crossroads, and the German government's reaction to the Briand plan revealed a tendency toward a more aggressive foreign policy in general and a more active policy in Eastern Europe in particular. Under Stresemann, German foreign policy had concentrated on easing the most onerous provisions of the Treaty of Versailles. Stresemann had just secured the final settlement of reparations and the evacuation of the Rhineland when Briand issued his first call for union in August 1929, but because Stresemann died only two months later we shall never know how he would have responded to it. Since 1923, Stresemann had concentrated on achieving Germany's aims through agreement with France and Britain; had he lived, he might have sought new concessions in return for assent to Briand's proposals. By the time Berlin replied to the French proposals of 1930, however, the Foreign Office was in new hands, and the complexion of the German government had changed.

Stresemann was replaced by Julius Curtius, also a member of the center-right German People's party but, as he later admitted in his memoirs, by no means so set upon agreement with the western powers.[16] Curtius soon replaced Stresemann's longtime state secretary, Karl von Schubert, with Bernhard von Bülow, a

---

[15] The best available short study of the Briand plan is a two-part article by Walter Lipgens, "Europäische Einigungsidee 1923-1930 und Briands Europaplan im Urteil der deutschen Akten," *Historische Zeitschrift*, CCIII (1966), 46-89, 316-63. Wolfgang Ruge and Wolfgang Schumann, "Die Reaktion des deutschen Imperialismus auf Briands Paneuropaplan 1930," *Zeitschrift für Geschichtswissenschaft*, XX, no. 1 (1972), 40-70, is ideologically biased but includes vital documents. For Briand's speech see LN, *Official Journal*, Special Supplement no. 75 (Geneva, 1929), pp. 51-52; for the French memorandum see *Documents on British Foreign Policy, 1919-1939*, ed. E. L. Woodward et al. (London, 1946-1970), series 2, vol. I, no. 186 (hereafter cited *DBFP*, series, volume, number).

[16] Julius Curtius, *Sechs Jahre Minister der deutschen Republik* (Heidelberg, 1948), pp. 153-54.

traditional German nationalist who had little interest in Franco-German reconciliation.[17] Furthermore, Social Democrat Hermann Müller's left-center government collapsed in March 1930 over the issue of unemployment insurance. Heinrich Brüning of the Catholic Center party formed a new center-right government, retaining Curtius as foreign minister.

Both Bülow and Curtius disliked the Briand plan from the outset. They opposed any new political union that would reaffirm Germany's eastern frontiers or prevent it from seeking their revision. On July 8, 1930, the German cabinet decided to return a noncommital reply that would concede nothing. Brüning made it clear that he opposed the French plan partly for domestic political reasons. The government, he said, would resist any plan that did not assure Germany territorial revision and adequate "Lebensraum" (living space), and the cabinet— perhaps with an eye on approaching elections—agreed that the German reply should be drafted so as to have "favorable domestic political consequences" and a properly "national" orientation. The chancellor had decided to court nationalist sentiment. The German reply ruled out any quick breakthrough toward European union; discussion of the Briand plan in Geneva in September led only to the establishment of a Commission of Enquiry for a European Union and subcommittees to discuss economic, financial, and organizational questions. These new institutions soon became a forum for the discussion of agricultural distress in Southeastern Europe.[18]

Simultaneously, Curtius and Bülow planned new German initiatives in Eastern Europe. Curtius raised the question of an Austro-German customs union with Austrian Chancellor Johann Schober in January 1930.[19] Bülow outlined his goals in Southeastern Europe in two memoranda on the Briand plan for Brüning in July and August of 1930. The first argued that Ger-

[17] Hans-Adolf Jacobsen, *Nationalsozialistische Aussenpolitik 1933-1938* (Frankfurt, 1968), p. 33.

[18] Lipgens, "Einigungsidee," pp. 339-40; for the German reply, see *DBFP*, 2, I, 92. See also two memoranda by Bülow and Curtius, August 1929 and May 1930, T-120/L1508/L444661-65, L444822-28. The German government's emerging interest in Southeastern Europe has also been discussed by Hans-Jürgen Schröder, "Deutsche Südosteuropapolitik 1929-1936. Zur Kontinuität deutscher Aussenpolitik in der Weltwirtschaftskrise," *Geschichte und Gesellschaft*, II, no. 1 (1976), 5-32.

[19] Curtius, *Sechs Jahre Minister*, p. 119.

many's "possibilities" in Europe "lie only in the east and south-east," adding that the government must do nothing to foreclose opportunities in these areas. "When Germany is strong and powerful and need not fear other states," Bülow wrote, "she will be, thanks to her political, economic and moral strength, *the* state to which the new small states will look. We must therefore become the point of attraction and the center of gravity for the eastern states." The second memorandum, written for Brüning on August 26 in preparation for the September discussions of Briand's proposals in Geneva, was even more explicit. After citing the need for Germany to secure more effective procedures for revising the peace treaties as a condition of agreement to any European union, Bülow outlined the uses to which such procedures might be put:

> Conditions are in flux and development in the southeast of Europe more than in any other part of Europe. German policy must exert its leverage there because it is there that the possibilities for Germany lie. . . . In connection with the rapid developments in Southeast Europe, the *union with Austria* must be the most urgent task of German diplomacy, for developments in the southeast could be influenced and guided in Germany's interests from an Austria belonging to Germany more than is now possible. . . . Viewed from the standpoint of the greater future possibilities, the solution of the problem of a union with Austria seems even more urgent and important than the question of the Polish Corridor.[20]

Even though it was never implemented, the Briand plan was a milestone in interwar diplomacy. Briand, himself the symbol of European reconciliation, made one last attempt to achieve permanent peace in Europe within the framework of the postwar frontiers. The German government rejected the plan because it refused to accept those frontiers. Led by Curtius, the German Foreign Office abandoned Stresemann's policy of agreement with the British and French and moved independently to extend its influence. For the next two years Berlin tried to exploit both the Briand plan and the emerging economic crisis in Southeastern Europe in furtherance of its aims.

[20] For these two memoranda see Ruge and Schumann, "Reaktion," pp. 64-65, 69-70.

II.

The German Foreign Office and Southeastern Europe,
1930-1932

Beginning in 1930, a severe agricultural and financial crisis crippled Southeastern Europe. When the cereals-growing states of Southeastern Europe called for help, the German Foreign Office responded in an attempt to extend its influence. During 1931 Berlin concluded preferential tariff treaties with Rumania and Hungary, and the Wilhelmstrasse also tried to increase German power in Eastern Europe by proposing a customs union with Austria. The economic situation in Southeastern Europe and the German attempts to exploit it became matters of serious international concern; the French and Italian governments also tried to step in, and several international conferences discussed this issue. But during 1931 and 1932 the western powers fought their way to a stalemate. None of their initiatives provided effective help, and none of them benefited significantly from the Southeastern European crisis.

In the long run, the agricultural crisis that devastated the states of Southeastern Europe in the early 1930s grew out of the conflicting political and economic needs of the new states; in the short run, it stemmed from the worldwide fall in the prices of primary products at the outset of the depression. Of all the successor states of the Austro-Hungarian and Russian empires, only Austria and Czechoslovakia were predominantly industrial. Poland, the Baltic states, Rumania, Yugoslavia, and Hungary remained largely agricultural, and in the 1920s all but Poland depended on exports of foodstuffs to obtain vital foreign exchange. The Southeastern European states depended especially on the export of cereals. The difficulties these states faced in meeting overseas competition have already been noted. In the 1920s extensive land reforms in nearly all the new agrarian nations further aggravated these problems. Reforms in Rumania, Yugoslavia, Czechoslovakia, Poland, and the Baltic states dispossessed large landowners—many of them Germans and Hungarians—and parceled out their estates among the native peasantry, which constituted the political basis of the new regimes. The most radical reforms occurred in Rumania, Yugoslavia, and the Baltic states; land redistribution in Czechoslovakia and Poland was less extensive. Only in Hungary, whose native aristocracy remained strong, did land distribution remain largely unaltered.[1]

Whatever their social and political benefits, the economic effects of these reforms were serious. The new peasant proprietors emphasized small-scale subsistence farming and animal husbandry rather than the large-scale cultivation of cereals that had dominated the large prewar estates. By the late 1920s this change was reflected in sharply lower average crop yields and much-reduced grain exports in comparison to the prewar period. From 1909 to 1913 the average Rumanian wheat and corn yields per hectare of land were 12.9 and 13.1 quintals, respectively; the corresponding figures for the period 1925-1929 were 9.3 and 10.6 quintals. Rumanian wheat exports had averaged 1,330,000 metric tons annually from 1909 through 1913; during the 1920s they never exceeded 270,000 tons, despite a substantial increase in land area and population. Yugoslavia, more than double the size of Serbia, improved upon prewar Serbian grain exports only in bumper years. The breakup of large estates also led to a decline in the quality of wheat and to breakdowns in the standardization and organization of grain exports. Only the Baltic states of Lithuania, Latvia, and Estonia successfully reconciled land reform with the needs of their national economies. Following the Danish model, they concentrated on pig and dairy production for export, and by the late 1920s all three states had developed stable and substantial exports of butter, eggs, and bacon to Britain and Germany.[2]

The southeastern states' problems reflected the difficulty of

---

[1] For the best survey of these land reforms and of the economic development of Eastern Europe during the 1920s, see Berend and Ránki, *Economic Development*, pp. 186-212, 288-97. See also Hugh Seton-Watson, *Eastern Europe between the Wars, 1918-41*, 3d ed. (New York, 1962), pp. 77-80, and Max Sering, ed., *Die agrarischen Umwälzungen im ausserrussischen Osteuropa* (Berlin, 1930).

[2] Sering, *Agrarischen Umwälzungen*, pp. 121-23; A. H. Hollman, "Die Agrarkrise der Ost- und Südosteuropäischen Staaten," and Rheingold Brenneisen, "Landwirtschaft und Agrarpolitik der baltischen Staaten," in Fritz Beckmann et al., eds., *Deutsche Agrarpolitik*, III (Berlin, 1932), 154-56, 161-85.

telescoping centuries of political and economic development into a few short years. The growth of protective and autarkic tendencies within the former Austro-Hungarian Empire further aggravated these problems. Agrarian interests forced the Austrian and Czechoslovak governments to protect their agriculture against competition from their neighbors, while Rumania, Hungary, and, to a lesser extent, Yugoslavia embarked upon ambitious programs of industrialization. As a result, all these states lost export markets within their neighbors' economies.

A large worldwide harvest in 1929 led to a sudden collapse in world cereals prices that was especially severe in Eastern Europe. Within a year the export price of Rumanian wheat dropped by 50 percent. As agricultural prices fell, the industrial-agricultural price differential widened. In Rumania, the index of agricultural prices, pegged at 1929 = 100, fell to 68.2 in 1930, 50.8 in 1931, and 44.7 in 1932. The index of prices for industrial goods used in agriculture fell only about half as rapidly, reaching a low of only 80.9 in 1932.[3] The introduction of new grain tariffs in Germany in late 1929 dealt a further blow to the eastern states. By 1930, peasant distress was widespread and foreign exchange reserves were shrinking.

In mid-1930 the agrarian states decided to press for international action to ease their plight. They attempted to take advantage of a League of Nations initiative designed to increase international trade. In March 1930 a League Conference on Concerted Economic Action had asked for recommendations for the disposition of the international agricultural surplus. Representatives of the Yugoslav, Rumanian, and Hungarian governments met in Bucharest in late July and agreed jointly to recommend that the European industrial states help to alleviate their agricultural distress by admitting European cereals at preferential tariff rates. This proposal had potentially revolutionary implications: in the name of European solidarity, it would contravene the most-favored-nation clauses of commercial treaties between the European industrial states and overseas cereals suppliers. The idea found favor in Eastern Europe, and a broader conference of all the successor states discussed it in Warsaw in August. The Baltic states, themselves net importers

[3] Hollman, "Agrarkrise," p. 148; Seton-Watson, *Eastern Europe,* p. 122. See Berend and Ránki, *Economic Development,* pp. 242-49, for further price statistics on all the countries involved.

of cereals, disliked the proposal, but the Polish government endorsed it. The preference plan was placed on the agenda of a new League Conference on Concerted Economic Action scheduled to meet in November; in the meantime, a committee of the League Assembly discussed it in September. Although the cereals-growing nations of the British Empire opposed the Warsaw proposals and insisted on the maintenance of their most-favored-nation rights, the committee recommended those proposals as a basis for future discussion.[4]

The industrial nations now had to respond. The British government generally sympathized with the objections of the British Dominions, but since Britain still maintained free trade in foodstuffs in 1930, it did not have to take any specific action in response to the new proposals. The French government faced a dilemma: to maintain its influence in Eastern Europe it would have to respond to this call for help, but the crisis in wheat prices that was facing French peasants made increased imports of cereals impossible. The government initially decided to make a counterproposal: Commerce Minister Pierre-Etienne Flandin toured the southeastern capitals in October with a proposal that France provide financing for Eastern European cereals exports rather than preferential tariff rates.[5]

The German Foreign Office and Economics Ministry immediately decided to exploit this initiative; to them, it was a useful opportunity to extend economic and political influence in Southeastern Europe. Eventually, in the summer of 1931, they concluded preferential tariff treaties with Rumania and Hungary. Coincidentally, German-Rumanian negotiations for a new commercial treaty had begun in early 1930, and after the Warsaw conference the Wilhelmstrasse decided to offer Bucharest preferential tariffs on cereals.[6] Two major obstacles to this policy quickly emerged, however. First, Berlin had to secure international sanction for the principle of preferences in order not to

[4] On the March conference see League of Nations, *Publications* (Geneva, various years) (hereafter LNP), 1930.II.17; for German diplomatic reports of the Bucharest and Warsaw conferences see T-120/K2103/K572711 ff.; on the League Assembly discussion see the report of the Economic Committee, Nov. 4, 1930, LNP 1930.II.51, and T-120/K2103/K572928-33.

[5] German Foreign Office (Auswärtiges Amt; hereafter AA) circular of Oct. 9, 1930, T-120/K2103/K572913-16.

[6] On these conversations see T-120/K2105/K575174-75, 202.

violate its most-favored-nation obligations toward much more important trading partners. Second, the Foreign Office had to overcome strong pressure for increased protection for German agriculture—pressure powerfully exerted within the Brüning government by Agriculture Minister Walter Schiele. Although the Wilhelmstrasse succeeded in concluding preferential treaties with Rumania and Hungary in June and July of 1931, continuing international difficulties ultimately prevented their implementation, and domestic pressure prevented any increases in German agricultural imports from Eastern Europe.

The process of securing international sanction for preferences was relatively simple; various international bodies soon approved preferences during 1930-1931, albeit with safeguards that deprived the preferential concessions of much of their potential significance. The League Conference on Concerted Economic action that met on November 17-28, 1931, approved preferences for Eastern European cereals as a "conditional, exceptional and limited derogation" of the most-favored-nation principle, but added three conditions: preferences must not seriously harm the interests of overseas exporting nations; none must be granted without the consent of all other nations enjoying most-favored-nation rights in the grantor country; and agricultural countries receiving preferences must not grant preferences for industrial products in return. The Italian government, fearing overseas retaliation, opposed preferences, but Germany and France endorsed them, and Britain expressed no definite opposition. German delegates committed themselves to negotiate preference treaties with Rumania, Hungary, Yugoslavia, and Bulgaria. At a meeting of the Commission of Enquiry for a European Union in January 1931, however, the British opposed preferences for Eastern Europe on behalf of their Dominions, and a commission resolution recommended only "concerted action" to dispose of the Eastern European cereals surplus. At a further meeting in late May—a meeting that discussed French plans for preferences and the Austro-German customs union as well—the commission endorsed preferential tariffs for Southeastern Europe as an emergency measure, subject to the restrictions stated at the November conference.[7]

[7] For the November conference see LNP, *Final Act of the Second International Conference with a View to Concerted Economic Action* (1930.II.52), Report of the Sub-Committee Appointed to Examine the Question of the Negotiations con-

The situation within the German government was more difficult. While the Wilhelmstrasse and the Economics Ministry favored preferential treaties as a means of extending German influence, the Agriculture and Interior ministries and many German state governments opposed them as threats to German agriculture, and leading German industrialists feared their effects on vital overseas markets. Karl Ritter and Emil Wiehl of the Economic Department of the Foreign Office, Curtius, and Hans Posse of the Economics Ministry fought for preferences in the Handelspolitische Ausschuss (Commercial Policy Committee; HPA)—a standing committee of civil servants from the Foreign Office and the Finance, Economic, and Agriculture ministries, responsible for foreign-trade policy—in the cabinet, and in meetings with private interest groups.

Most of the argument revolved around the German negotiations with Rumania, the first state to which Berlin offered preferences. Conflicts between Rumanian desires and German protectionism had already emerged in talks early in 1930. The Rumanians wanted lower barley and corn tariffs and permission to export meat and live animals to Germany; the Germans had raised the barley tariff and created a corn monopoly in December 1929 to control foreign purchases, and provincial German veterinary regulations had effectively barred imports of Eastern European meat and animals for many decades.[8] In October and November 1930 Ritter and Posse persuaded the HPA to agree in principle to cereals preferences for Rumania, in part by citing Eastern European threats to retaliate against industrial nations that did not provide help. Two small subcommittees of ministers approved this proposal a few days later. In February 1931, however, the Agriculture Ministry successfully deprived this concession of any practical effect. A domestic German cereals crisis had arisen despite a fall in cereals imports from 7.5 million tons in 1927 to 2.8 million in 1928, and the Agriculture Ministry per-

---

cerning the Trade of the Agricultural States of Central and Eastern Europe; AA circular, Dec. 5, 1930, T-120/L1508/L445199-208. On the Commission of Enquiry meeting see German delegation Geneva to AA, Jan. 20, 21, 1931, ibid., L445373-75, 427-34; for the May meeting see LNP, *Proceedings of the 3rd session of the Commission of Enquiry* (1930.VII.7), pp. 190-93.

[8] For German reports on the Rumanian demands see T-120/7156/H152670 ff.; on veterinary restrictions see Alexander Gerschenkron, *Bread and Democracy in Germany* (Berkeley, 1943), pp. 62, 137-38.

suaded the HPA that Germany could not promise to buy any specific quantities of Eastern European cereals from the 1930 harvest, its offer of preferences notwithstanding. Then, at Schiele's urging, the German government issued a decree on March 28, empowering itself to raise tariffs almost at will—a step that could quickly destroy the effect of any preferential concession.[9]

Leaders of the Reichsverband deutscher Industrie (Association of German Industry) expressed their opposition to preferences at a February meeting with Foreign Office and Economics Ministry officials. Noting that the Southeastern European states took just 5 percent of German exports, these industrialists argued that long-term prospects for these markets were equally meager and must not be allowed to jeopardize vital overseas markets in the United States and Argentina, where preferences for Southeastern Europe might be resented. German industry was apparently not unanimous in this view; during 1931 certain Ruhr, chemical, and electrical industries helped to found the Mitteleuropäische Wirtschaftstag, a private organization to encourage trade with Eastern Europe. But the Reichsverband probably represented the majority view, and, economically, its arguments were logical. Wiehl assured the Reichsverband that preferences would not be granted without the assent of Germany's overseas trading partners, but he added that "the Southeastern European problem has a political as well as an economic side" and maintained that Germany must do something to offset French offers of credits in the region.[10]

In fact, the Foreign Office was determined to extend German influence in Southeastern Europe with or without any clear economic rationale, as we shall see with respect to the Austro-German customs union proposals. Moreover, because the German government generally accepted the primacy of foreign pol-

[9] HPA meetings of Nov. 6, 10, 11, 1930, T-120/K2105/K575283, 290-91; AA memorandum, Nov. 15, 1930, T-120/K2105/K572974-80; HPA meeting and AA instructions for a conference in Paris, Feb. 20, 1931, T-120/7165/ H153842-43, L1508/L445540-50; AA memorandum of Apr. 4, 1931, T-120/ K2105/K575580-81.

[10] For the Feb. 13, 1931, Reichsverband deutscher Industrie memorandum on this subject and discussion of it among German officials see T-120/L1508/ L445553-74. On the Mitteleuropäische Wirtschaftstag see the Nov. 22, 1938, memorandum on its origins and development in the records of the German high command, T-77/174/908653-77 (T-77 records are cited series/serial/frames).

icy, the Wilhelmstrasse eventually won another difficult battle over the import of live animals from Rumania. When German-Rumanian talks began in March 1931, the Rumanians made it clear that any new treaty must guarantee them exports of cattle to Germany. At a March meeting of interested ministers, Curtius's proposal to allow annual imports of 6,000 Rumanian cattle met opposition from the Agriculture and Interior ministers (the latter responsible for the veterinary regulations prohibiting such imports). Curtius argued, however, that the cattle would come almost exclusively from German-populated Transylvania, and Economics and Finance ministry representatives joined him in insisting that veterinary regulations should not be allowed to determine German trade policy. Although Curtius carried the day, representatives of the various German state governments refused on April 14 to agree to import Rumanian cattle.[11]

Curtius brought Karl Ritter to a full cabinet meeting on April 28 in an effort to resolve this issue. Ritter argued that increases in German agricultural tariffs had disturbed the southeastern states but that German industry could still secure concessions if Germany now offered preferences. No active policy in the southeast would be possible, however, if current veterinary restrictions remained in force. Germany must agree to import cattle from Transylvania under appropriate veterinary safeguards and agree to import pigs from Hungary and Yugoslavia as well. The cabinet sided with Curtius and agreed to these concessions.[12]

The German-Rumanian talks finally led to agreement to a new treaty in June 1931. Twice the talks had been interrupted for political reasons. On April 10 the Rumanians broke off talks, reportedly under pressure from the French government, which was trying to get Berlin to abandon its plan for an Austro-German customs union. On May 1 the Germans canceled a scheduled meeting in Bucharest after the Rumanians asked the German delegation to delay its arrival until a meeting of Little Entente ministers was over. New talks were scheduled for June, but at a German cabinet meeting on May 27 several ministers argued that since France's southeastern allies had given Germany no support in the dispute over the customs union, Ger-

[11] Curtius circular of Mar. 26, 1931, and meeting of Mar. 28, T-120/K2105/K575563-66; state government meeting, ibid., K575640-51.
[12] T-120/3575/D786416-22.

many should not favor them with preferences. Curtius replied that negotiations should continue, and Brüning argued that Germany should exploit its position as an agricultural importer—one of its biggest diplomatic weapons.[13]

The Germans and Rumanians reached agreement in late June amid a storm of protests from German domestic interests. On June 26, one day before the treaty was finally signed, the Landbund, the principal pressure group representing Junker agricultural interests, wrote a bitter letter to Brüning protesting German preferences for Rumanian barley and import quotas for Rumanian cattle. At the same time, German industry, which still feared the treaty's effects on overseas markets, tried to assure itself of some definite benefit from the new agreement. Under pressure from German exporters, the German and Rumanian negotiators spent several days trying to find a formula that would commit the Rumanians to purchase German industrial goods without violating the most-favored-nation principle. Ultimately, this proved impossible; the Germans had to be content with verbal commitments, combined with Rumanian tariff reductions tailored to German needs.[14]

The treaty that was finally concluded reflected the difficulty of reconciling concessions to the Rumanians with German domestic interests and international strictures regarding the most-favored-nation principle. It gave the Rumanians a 50 percent tariff preference on fodder barley, a 40 percent preference for corn, and a yearly import quota of 6,000 head of cattle. Imports of slaughtered pigs were conceded in principle, but procedures remained to be worked out. The preferences, however, were hedged about with safeguards reducing their potential effects. First, the Germans reserved the right to raise their base tariffs on barley and corn or otherwise to restrict imports; should they do so, the Rumanians could only demand new negotiations. Second, citing the Final Act of the Second Conference on Concerted Economic Action of November 1930, the treaty stated that the preferences should not be applied to abnormally large quantities of Rumanian cereals. Thus the preferences could not

[13] For German diplomatic correspondence on these delays see T-120/K2105/K575605-7, 708-826; for the cabinet of May 27, T-120/3575/D786500-503.

[14] Landbund letter of June 26, 1931, T-120/K2105/K575894-96; German legation Bucharest to AA, June 25, ibid., K575878-80; German legation Bucharest to AA, June 27, ibid., K575883-85.

sharply increase Rumanian cereals exports to Germany; they could only slightly increase the exporters' return. For their part, the Rumanians reduced duties on many products of special interest to Germany, including iron and steel products, textiles, chemicals and pharmaceuticals, and electrical goods. The two governments agreed jointly to seek the sanction of those countries enjoying most-favored-nation status vis-à-vis Germany before putting the treaty into effect.[15]

During May and June the German government prepared for talks with the Hungarian government, and brief negotiations led to the signing of a similar German-Hungarian treaty on July 18. Hungary received a 25 percent tariff preference on wheat, its principal cereals export, a cattle import quota of 6,000 head, giving Hungary equality with Rumania and Sweden, and a further import quota of 80,000 pigs. However, a clause reminiscent of the German-Rumanian treaty effectively limited the quantity to which the wheat preference could be applied.[16]

The German government intended to offer similar preferences to Yugoslavia and Bulgaria, but Berlin delayed talks with these states while it undertook the slow process of obtaining international consent to the violation of the most-favored-nation principle embodied in the treaties with Rumania and Hungary.[17] In the meantime, the issue of preferences had been thrust into the background by a new German initiative in Southeastern Europe. The Austro-German customs union proposal represented a more dramatic attempt to extend German economic and political power in the southeast and provoked far more reaction on the part of the other great powers of Western Europe.

The announcement in March 1931 that Germany and Austria intended to conclude a customs union created a sensation in Europe. To many, the plan could only be intended as a first step

---

[15] A secret protocol weakened the cattle concession by stating that it would lapse should Germany be forced to extend the same right to any other nation to which it had extended most-favored-nation treatment, except Hungary; see T-120/6120/E456254-56. For the text of the treaty see T-120/K2107/K576027-104.

[16] For an English translation of the German-Hungarian Treaty see LN, *Treaty Series*, CL, 181-245.

[17] HPA meeting, July 15, 1931, T-120/7156/H152902.

toward the political union of Germany and Austria—a step expressly prohibited by the Treaties of Versailles and Saint-Germain. In addition, as a condition for receiving a reconstruction loan from the western powers, the Austrian government had promised in the Geneva Protocol of 1922 to take no action that might tend to alienate its economic independence—a promise that seemed to be broken by the new plan. German foreign-policy makers recognized the importance of this new step. The proposal for a customs union was not, as the Germans claimed, a measure designed to alleviate Austria's postwar economic distress or to provide Germany with an enlarged market to combat the depression. Nor was it merely, as some thought, a desperate attempt by the Brüning government to score a political success in the wake of the disastrous Reichstag elections of September 1930, in which the Nazis had scored their first great success. The proposal was rather the centerpiece of a carefully elaborated policy of penetration of Southeastern Europe conceived principally by State Secretary Bülow and Foreign Minister Curtius. They hoped to restore Germany's status as a great power by creating a German-dominated economic and political bloc in Southeastern Europe—in essence, a return to the Mitteleuropa scheme of the First World War.

The idea of a German-Austrian customs union was not new; Stresemann and Wilhelm Marx, the German chancellor, had discussed the idea with Austrian Chancellor Ignaz Seipel as early as November 1927. Nor was Curtius a stranger to the idea; as he stated in his memoirs, he had discussed it with subordinates in 1927, while serving as minister of economics. These subordinates almost certainly included Hans Posse, then director of the Foreign Trade Department of the Economics Ministry and state secretary of the ministry during the 1930s. Throughout the 1930s Posse remained a staunch advocate of closer economic relations between Germany and its southeastern neighbors. "Making headway in the Central European area," he wrote a German industrialist in December 1930, "seems to me to be at the moment Germany's chief problem in economic policy." In 1933 he was principally responsible for new Nazi initiatives in the southeast. Presumably he influenced Curtius in the direction of an Austro-German customs union in 1927.[18]

[18] Conversation of Nov. 14, 1927, *Akten zur deutschen Auswärtigen Politik*, B. IV, 106; Posse's letter, T-120/L1508/L445235-39; Curtius, *Sechs Jahre Minister*, p. 119.

As foreign minister, Curtius immediately took steps to put the idea into effect. In February 1930 Berlin and Vienna signed a new commercial treaty, and Austrian Chancellor Schober agreed to examine the possibility of a customs union. Work proceeded during the summer, and the language of Bülow's August 26 memorandum to Brüning on the Briand plan, arguing for a customs union with Austria to turn the situation in Southeastern Europe to Germany's advantage, suggests that the time for a decision was drawing near. The momentum was checked when Schober's government fell in late September, but a customs union once again became a possibility when Schober returned to office as vice-chancellor and foreign minister in December 1930. After new discussions, Curtius and Schober agreed on a plan in Vienna in February 1931.[19]

A German-Austrian customs union clearly represented a step toward Anschluss, or union of the two German-speaking states. Although the Treaties of Versailles and Saint-Germain explicitly forbade such a union, it was generally assumed to reflect the will of the peoples of the two states involved, and it enjoyed widespread sympathy in the world at large, particularly in Great Britain. Diplomatic circles generally recognized it as one of Berlin's long-range goals. State Secretary Bülow, however, hoped that the customs union would have even greater consequences. By extending it beyond its original members, he planned to fulfill broader German aims in Eastern Europe. Thus, in January 1931, when he informed Friedrich von Prittwitz und Gaffron, the German ambassador in Washington, that a plan for an Austro-German customs union existed, he intimated that Czechoslovakia and Hungary might also accede to it. He was even more explicit when Walter Koch, the German minister in Prague, subsequently reported the Czechoslovak government's opposition to the plan. Once the customs union was created, Bülow argued, economic necessity would force the Czechs to

---

[19] Curtius, *Sechs Jahre Minister,* pp. 119-20, 188-89, 192-93; F. G. Stambrook, "The German-Austrian Customs Union of 1931: A Study of German Methods and Motives," *Journal of Central European Affairs,* XXI, no. 1 (1961), 15-44. The most thorough account of the customs union project and the subsequent Creditanstalt crisis will be found in Edward W. Bennett, *Germany and the Diplomacy of the Financial Crisis, 1931* (Cambridge, Mass., 1962), pp. 40-113, 286-315. I have treated the episode as briefly as possible, except where differences in emphasis or the availability of new sources require a more detailed discussion.

join it, leading eventually to new, even more favorable developments for German foreign policy:

> The inclusion of Czechoslovakia in our economic system is
> entirely in line with the long-term foreign policy of the Reich
> as I visualize it. Once the German-Austrian customs union has
> become a reality I calculate that the pressure of economic
> necessity will within a few years compel Czechoslovakia to
> adhere to it in one way or another. I would see in this the be-
> ginning of a development which would be likely to lead to a
> solution, scarcely conceivable by other means, of vital political
> interests of the Reich. In this I am thinking of the German-
> Polish frontier problem. If we should succeed in incorporat-
> ing Czechoslovakia in our economic bloc, and if meanwhile we
> should also have established closer economic relations with the
> Baltic States, then Poland with her unstable economic struc-
> ture would be surrounded and exposed to all kinds of dan-
> gers; we should have her in a vise which could perhaps in the
> short or long run make her willing to consider further the
> idea of exchanging political concessions for tangible economic
> advantages.[20]

In a July 1930 memorandum for Brüning, Bülow had referred to the need for "new methods" of realizing German
foreign-policy goals.[21] He evidently saw German economic
power as one of these methods and hoped to use it to solve Germany's most pressing diplomatic problem, the Polish frontier.
Apparently Bülow did not expect France and Britain to help
Germany to secure the revision of that frontier, and German
military weakness ruled out war for some time to come. Direct
economic pressure during the German-Polish customs war of
1925-1930 had failed to force Poland to submit; Bülow now
planned to try economic encirclement. He ignored many economic obstacles to his plan, such as the problem of competition
among German, Austrian, and Czech industries, and, above all,
the tendency of German trade to follow worldwide rather than
Continental patterns. Clearly he expected economics to respond
to the needs of politics—in this case, the establishment of German hegemony in Central Europe.

---

[20] Quoted in Bennett, *Financial Crisis*, p. 48. See also Stambrook, "German-
Austrian Customs Union," pp. 43-44.

[21] See above, Chapter I.

Although Gerhard Köpke, the director of the Western and Southern European Department of the Foreign Office, suggested that French and Czechoslovak opposition would probably defeat the plan and turn Austria away from the idea of Anschluss for some time, Curtius and Brüning decided to go ahead. Brüning's role in the episode is not completely clear; he generally allowed Curtius to make the case for the customs union, both in the cabinet and at the League of Nations, and when the plan ultimately failed, it was the foreign minister's head that rolled rather than the chancellor's. Brüning later suggested that he was ambivalent about the plan from the beginning, but at the time he may have seen it as a means to win back some of the nationalist votes that had defected to the Nazis in September 1930.[22]

When the German cabinet discussed the customs union on March 16, it became clear that this initiative, like the preferences for Southeastern European cereals, was intended to secure political rather than economic benefits. The cabinet did not welcome it, and Schiele argued that the accession of any additional countries to the union would be disastrous for German agriculture. The cabinet agreed to the plan two days later, after Curtius dropped a provision for arbitration of German-Austrian disputes by the World Court at The Hague and promised that the German tariff would almost invariably be adopted as the new common tariff.[23] After the proposal was announced, Austrian economic circles could not agree on its economic merits either; industrial and banking circles divided sharply on the issue of whether the union would be a blessing or a curse.[24]

Vienna and Berlin intended to unveil their new plan in a series of démarches in European capitals on March 23, but it leaked to the press about five days earlier. The reactions of other European capitals showed a great deal about attitudes toward German expansion in Southeastern Europe.

The Quai d'Orsay, led by Briand and Secretary General Philippe Berthelot, reacted sharply to both the form and content

[22] Köpke memorandum, Feb. 22, 1931, T-120/K49/K005116-21; Bennett, *Financial Crisis*, p. 46.

[23] Cabinets of Mar. 16, 18, T-120/3575/D675143-47, 167-70.

[24] German legation Vienna to AA, Apr. 22, 1931, T-120/4622/202831-36; British legation Vienna to Foreign Office (hereafter FO), Mar. 25, 1931, PRO, FO 371/15159, C2146/673/3.

of the new German initiative. On March 21 Briand angrily told
German Ambassador Leopold von Hoesch that Austria's treaty
obligations clearly prohibited this step. The German initiative
was a blow to Briand's domestic political standing and to his
chances in the forthcoming presidential election. Only three
weeks earlier Briand had publicly discounted the possibility of
Anschluss, and the Germans had not helped matters by portray-
ing the customs union as a first step toward Briand's Pan-
European union. Briand himself saw sinister implications in the
proposal: "The memorandum which had been communicated
by the German government," he told British Foreign Secretary
Arthur Henderson on March 28, "was similar in every respect to
a document prepared in 1917, dealing with the question of the
creation of a German bloc in Central Europe."[25] Briand's analogy with the Mitteleuropa scheme embodied in the 1917
Salzburg memorandum was, of course, entirely apt.

The spectre of Mitteleuropa also haunted Czech Foreign
Minister Eduard Beneš. Publicly, he opposed the Austro-
German customs union on legal grounds; privately, in talks with
Wilhelm Regedanz, a German international banker, he speculated that if Czechoslovakia were forced to join the customs
union, the country's 3,000,000 economic Germans would soon
control its entire economic life. The presence of 700,000 ethnic
Germans within Hungary would also compel that country to reject the union for the same reason. Beneš suggested that France
be invited to join the customs union as well; German influence
could only be balanced by the inclusion of another great industrial power. These talks, which Regedanz reported to Bülow,
confirmed the state secretary's view of the potential effects of the
customs union.[26]

British government reaction was mixed. Within the Foreign
Office, Owen O'Malley of the Central Department feared
neither the customs union nor the Anschluss to which it might
lead; as he minuted on March 24, he inclined toward "allowing
events to take now the course which they must inevitably tend to
take during the ensuing years." O'Malley continued to sym-
pathize with German expansion to the southeast throughout the

[25] German embassy Paris to AA, Mar. 21, 1931, T-120/4622/202595-98; Bennett, *Financial Crisis*, pp. 59-60.
[26] Regedanz reports, T-120/K1148/K005746-90; see also Johann Wolfgang
Brügel, *Tschechen und Deutsche, 1918-1938* (Munich, 1967), pp. 220-24.

1930s. But the foreign secretary in the Labour Government, Arthur Henderson, saw the matter in a different light; whatever the merits of the customs union, he realized it would undermine Briand's position and create the worst possible atmosphere for the forthcoming disarmament conference, of which Henderson was to be president. As he told the British cabinet on May 6, the proposed union had aroused such fears in Paris and Prague that it was capable "of endangering the whole policy of European cooperation and disarmament which it is the object of His Majesty's Government to promote." Henderson had already proposed submitting the question of the plan's legality to the League Council and, if necessary, to the World Court. The attorney general and the Board of Trade eventually concluded that the plan probably would violate the Geneva Protocol of 1922 by threatening Austria's economic independence, thereby reversing the original opinion of the Foreign Office Legal Adviser, but Henderson kept this opinion a secret, hoping to settle the question without alienating either Berlin or Paris.[27]

In Warsaw, Polish Foreign Minister Auguste Zaleski told the British minister that he feared that the union might threaten Polish coal and iron exports to Austria in the short run but that he would ultimately like to see the big powers waive their objections to Anschluss in return for German recognition of the German-Polish frontier as final.[28] After Hitler's accession to power in 1933, Zaleski's successor, Józef Beck, entertained similar hopes of satiating German appetites in the southeast as a means of protecting Poland. As we have seen, such hopes were no better founded in 1931 than they were under the Nazis; Bülow hoped that the customs union would lead to the revision of the German-Polish frontier.

The Italian government, which had its own ambitions in Southeastern Europe and had successfully curried favor in Vienna during the 1920s, was cool to the German initiative. Fearing isolation in the weeks after the customs union was announced, the Austrians, presumably under pressure from Rome, approached Berlin with a suggestion that Italy be in-

[27] O'Malley minute, FO 371/15158, C1942/673/3; cabinet of May 6, 1931, CAB 23/67; Bennett, *Financial Crisis*, pp. 63-67; attorney general's memorandum of Apr. 8, CAB 24/220, CP 86 (31); interdepartmental memorandum of Mar. 24, FO 371/15158, C1942/673/3.

[28] British legation Warsaw to FO, Apr. 21, 1931, FO 371/15160, C2620/673/3.

cluded in the union as well, but Bülow and Ritter would not agree.[29] Throughout the 1930s Berlin generally resisted Italian proposals for joint action in Southeastern Europe.

Since February, the French government had been working on proposals to flesh out Briand's Pan-European plan and relieve the Southeastern European cereals crisis; after the release of the German initiative, they transformed these proposals into a response to the customs union as well. The new French *Plan constructif*, which Paris disclosed at the League Council meeting in May after discussing it with the British, began by proposing that Germany, France, Czechoslovakia, Austria, Italy, and Switzerland import Southeastern European cereals at preferential tariff rates. This was the first time that Paris had expressed its intention to grant preferences, and the decision promptly aroused opposition among French agrarian interests. The French also proposed that Austria receive preferences for its industrial exports to compensate its industries for the loss of the prewar Austro-Hungarian market, that new, European-wide cartels coordinate industrial production and distribution to help Europe out of the depression, and that Central Europe receive new, long-term financial credits. In private, the French government made it clear that these credits could include a French loan to Germany if Berlin would give up the customs union. Lastly, the French plan proposed an International Agricultural Mortgage Credit Bank, financed by contributions from European governments, to help modernize Eastern European agriculture.[30]

The German government could have seized upon the French plan as an excuse for abandoning the Austro-German customs union, but Bülow and Curtius chose to make the project a point of pride and a symbol of German diplomatic freedom of action, and Brüning did not dissent. On May 11 the German cabinet found the French proposals broadly acceptable, but Curtius made it clear that he had no intention of giving up the customs union and that he believed Vienna would stand firm.[31]

[29] Bennett, *Financial Crisis*, pp. 74-78.

[30] British embassy Paris to FO, 23 Feb. 1931, FO 371/15694, W2210/7/98; on the plan itself see *DBFP*, 2, II, 31, 35, and LNP, *Minutes, 3rd Session, Commission of Enquiry for European Union* (1931.VII.7), pp. 52-60. On hostile French agrarian reaction see German embassy Paris to AA, June 6, 1931, T-120/L1508/446018-22.

[31] Cabinet of May 11, T-120/3575/D786459-66.

The British government also considered the French plan in preparation for the forthcoming meetings of the League Council and the Commission of Enquiry for a European Union. Interdepartmental and cabinet discussions of these and other proposals for the alleviation of European economic distress revealed a split between the Foreign Office, which generally favored the maintenance or extension of economic ties with Europe, and the Dominions Office and the Board of Trade, which leaned more toward cultivation of the empire market and protection of home industries. These crucial questions of British tariff and imperial policy were not to be decided until 1932, but discussions of the French proposals revealed battle lines already in place.

Interdepartmental meetings in late April and early May discussed several proposals: the French plan; a broader scheme under which participating nations might lower their tariffs by 25 percent toward all other nations willing to reciprocate, while Britain pledged to maintain free trade; and a similar scheme for inter-European preferences, which Jacques Rueff, a French Treasury expert, communicated to his British counterpart, Sir Frederick Leith-Ross, the Chief Economic Adviser to the Government. The Foreign Office supported Rueff's plan, combined with a British pledge to maintain free trade, but the Commercial Relations and Treaties Department of the Board of Trade argued that domestic political pressures would prevent Britain from making this commitment, and the Dominions Office argued that preferences for European agriculture would hurt Canada and Australia.[32] The cabinet denied Foreign Secretary Henderson authorization to commit the British government to any of these schemes on May 6, after several ministers insisted that Britain must not tie its hands before the Ottawa Imperial Conference of 1932.[33] The Dominions Office victory over the Foreign Office foreshadowed the extremely significant decisions that Britain would take in 1932.

[32] Memorandum by Philip Noel-Baker, Apr. 18, 1931, interdepartmental meeting of Apr. 23, and Leith-Ross's May 4 memorandum on talks with Rueff, FO 371/15160, C2701/C2790/C3201/673/3.

[33] Cabinet of May 6, CAB 23/67. The minutes of cabinet meetings frequently do not attribute remarks to specific ministers. Further controversy developed when Sir Orme Sargent of the Central Department, unaware of the cabinet decision, gave contradictory instructions to the British delegation in Geneva; see FO 371/15162, C3403/673/3.

When the Commission of Enquiry convened in Geneva on May 16 Curtius and Schober defended the customs union, and André François-Poncet, private secretary to French Premier Pierre Laval, presented the French *Plan constructif*. The commission appointed a subcommittee to consider these proposals and agreed to found the International Agricultural Mortgage Credit Company. It also asked the Austrian government to submit suggestions for the alleviation of its economic distress.[34] At the League Council on May 18, Henderson, supported by Briand and Italian Foreign Minister Dino Grandi, suggested that the issue of the legality of the customs union be referred to the International Court at The Hague. The council agreed, and Schober promised Henderson that he would not conclude a treaty with Germany until the court rendered its opinion.[35] Henderson had successfully put the issue of the customs union on ice for several months. By the time the court delivered its opinion in September, the Austrian financial crisis had put the issue in an entirely different perspective.

The collapse in May 1931 of the Creditanstalt, Austria's largest private bank and itself the holder of enormous industrial investments throughout Southeastern Europe, dramatically altered the diplomatic balance of power in relation to the Austro-German customs union proposal. Within a few weeks the Creditanstalt collapse called into question Austria's ability to pay its foreign debts, making the Austrian government a desperate supplicant for foreign capital and depriving it of its diplomatic freedom of action. In September France forced Vienna to abandon the projected customs union with Germany as the price of French financial assistance. The Creditanstalt crisis had other long-term effects as well. Financial panic spread quickly from Austria to Germany and eventually throughout Central Europe. The financial crisis led to the end of reparations, various partial and complete moratoriums on foreign debt payments, the imposition of exchange controls, and, ultimately, to new initiatives to relieve economic distress in Central and Southeastern Europe.

The crisis began with the Creditanstalt's announcement on

[34] LNP, 1931.VII.7, pp. 20-27, 62-63, 190-93.

[35] LN, *Official Journal*, XII, no. 7, pp. 1068-79; Bennett, *Financial Crisis*, pp. 110-111.

May 11, 1931, of enormous losses over the previous year. Because the announcement came at the height of the controversy
over the Austro-German customs union, and because it ultimately led to the abandonment of the project, many suspected
both then and subsequently that French financial interests acting
at the behest of the French government had purposely brought
about or exposed the bank's difficulties to weaken Austria's position.[36] All available archival material, however, including recently opened French documentation, tends to exonerate the
French government of this charge. It is clear, first of all, that
French deposits in the Creditanstalt were not large enough for
their withdrawal to cause such a dramatic crisis; the bank's chief
foreign creditors were British and American. Second, throughout the crisis Austrian, German, and French diplomatic sources
all absolved French financial interests of any blame for the sudden collapse. On May 13 German Minister to Austria Kurt Rieth
told the Wilhelmstrasse that no noteworthy French withdrawals
had taken place lately; he blamed the weakness of the bank on
the heavy losses of its industrial holdings throughout the former
Austro-Hungarian Empire and on the debts it had absorbed in
an earlier merger with another major Vienna bank, the
Boden-Creditanstalt. Newly available French archives show that
French Minister Bertrand Clauzel gave exactly the same expla-
nation for the collapse in his report of the original May 11 announcement, adding that the bank had postponed the revelation
of its position for two months. In succeeding weeks Clauzel reported that the crisis was worsened by Anglo-American withdrawals, not French ones. Both the French and German governments quickly tried to take advantage of Austria's financial
difficulties, but they appear to have been equally taken by surprise at the outset.[37]

The Creditanstalt's difficulties immediately rebounded upon

[36] Bennett, *Financial Crisis*, pp. 100-104, gives some support to this view.

[37] For figures on balances in the Creditanstalt see the *Economist*, July 4, 1931,
p. 16. At that time, despite substantial Anglo-American withdrawals, British
holdings totaled $27 million, American, $24 million, and French, just $6 million.
For Rieth's conversation at the Wilhelmstrasse see T-120/6075/E449679-80; see
also a July 1 AA summary of the crisis, ibid., E449980-81. See also Clauzel's telegrams of May 11 and 29 to the French Foreign Ministry (Ministère des Affaires
Etrangères; hereafter AE), Archives Nationales (hereafter AN), series F³⁰, Box
628 (hereafter cited series/box.) The F³⁰ series is available at the Ministry of Finance, not the Archives Nationales.

the Austro-German customs union; whoever rescued Austria from its growing financial distress could exert leverage on Austrian foreign policy. The German government, to which the Austrians disclosed their financial vulnerability in early April, quickly offered a credit of 20,000,000 Austrian schillings (£580,000), but after May 11, when the Austrian National Bank began planning the Creditanstalt's rescue, it became clear that Vienna would need help on a much larger scale. On May 31 the Austrian National Bank secured a credit of 100,000,000 schillings from the Geneva-based Bank for International Settlements, a newly formed institution, in which the Germans had little influence, designed to coordinate central banking. German attempts to form a consortium to which the German government would contribute about 30,000,000 schillings in secret German post office and state railways funds thus came to naught. After a new run on the Austrian National Bank began, the Austrians had to ask for another 100,000,000 schillings on June 8, and this time the Bank for International Settlements insisted that Vienna immediately negotiate a foreign loan of 150,000,000 schillings. The French government now held the whip; such a loan would have to come largely from the ample reserves of French banks, and Paris could tie financial assistance to abandonment of the customs union.[38] The Bank of France offered to take half of a 150,000,000-schilling loan in early June, while British and American interests took most of the other half.[39] However, the governor of the Bank of England, Montagu Norman, who was sympathetic to Germany and disturbed by the potential effects of the Austrian financial crisis, told Curtius on June 10 that he would try to help Austria and fight French efforts to tie political conditions to a loan.[40]

In the second week of June, while negotiations for a loan continued in Vienna, two heavily French-influenced Vienna banks made large foreign currency withdrawals from the Austrian Na-

---

[38] On German activity see Curtius to Hans Luther, Apr. 14, 1931, AA to German legation Vienna, Apr. 25, and Bülow's memorandum of May 18, T-120/6075/E449661-65, 66-67, 714-18. See also Stephen V. O. Clarke, *Central Bank Cooperation, 1924-1931* (New York, 1967), pp. 187-88, and minute by Georges Bizot, May 17, AN, F³⁰/629.

[39] Vansittart minute, June 3, 1931, FO 371/15150, C3835/61/3.

[40] Curtius to AA, June 10, 1931, T-120/6075/E449852-53. Norman gave this assurance during Brüning's and Curtius's visit to Chequers.

tional Bank, apparently in an effort to force the Austrians to come to terms. On June 15 the bank's directors agreed that they would have to declare a moratorium on the seventeenth, the day on which they had to release a balance statement, if they had not yet negotiated a new loan. On the night of June 15-16, Austrian negotiators agreed to French demands that the Austrian government guarantee the Creditanstalt's debts as a condition of the loan. On the morning of the sixteenth, however, the French cabinet met and decided to demand that Vienna also renounce the customs union and put its finances in the hands of the League Council before receiving the credit. The Austrian cabinet resigned rather than guarantee the Creditanstalt's obligations. Schober told Clauzel that no Austrian government could ever accept this condition.

Montagu Norman, acting independently to avert an Austrian moratorium, temporarily saved the Austrian government on June 16. Aware that the Austrian National Bank had to issue a balance statement on June 17, Norman on June 15 secured a letter from Philip Snowden, chancellor of the Exchequer, stating that although the Treasury could not exercise any control over international money markets, he recognized "the great importance in the public interest" of assistance for Austria. Snowden concluded: "I am sure you will take any steps that may be possible to secure the provision of such assistance." Norman advanced the 150 million schillings the next day. Although this step has been portrayed as a response to the French ultimatum of the same day, it is now clear that he advanced the money without having heard of the French demands upon Austria. Norman viewed the crisis as a financial rather than a political problem. He did not consult or inform the Foreign Office about what he was doing, and he extended his credit for just seven days in the expectation that negotiations for an international loan would be completed in the interval.[41]

In succeeding weeks it became clear that the bank's rescue of

---

[41] On this crisis see especially German legation Vienna to AA, June 24, 1931, T-120/6075/E449961-66, and Francis Rodd's June 20 memorandum, FO 371/ 15151, C4965/61/3. Rodd, a British banker who negotiated with the Austrians, reported the French withdrawals in early June. For Snowden's June 15 letter see ibid., C4543/61/3. British Minister Sir Eric Phipps confirmed from Vienna that Norman had advanced the loan without knowing of the ultimatum on June 17 (ibid., C4225/61/3).

Austria was only temporary and that Vienna would have to give up the customs union to secure necessary financial help from France. Prospects for the customs union worsened further when Germany's own financial position became critical during June. Withdrawals of foreign capital led to runs on German banks, and on June 20 American President Herbert Hoover proposed a one-year moratorium on reparations and war debts in an effort to halt the panic. By June 23 the British Foreign Office had concluded that Austria would have to appeal to the League for financial help and that Germany should drop the customs union in return for the moratorium. The Germans refused to discuss this gesture, but on July 9 Schober told the German and French ministers in Vienna that he intended to ask the League Council for a long-term 150-million-schilling credit in September. Schober suggested that this would give the French a chance to back out of their June 16 ultimatum; he might have added that it would also enable him to give up the customs union. As in May, Germany and Austria would have no allies in the League Council; the council would surely insist upon renunciation of the customs union—already widely viewed as a destabilizing element that had contributed to the financial crisis—as a condition of assistance. Schober informed the League secretary general on July 16 of his decision to ask for help and announced it publicly on August 11. By that time the Bank of England, increasingly preoccupied with problems of its own and weary of renewing its 150-million-schilling credit at one-week intervals, was also insisting that Austria arrange a long-term loan, even at the price of French conditions.[42]

When at the end of August Curtius went to Geneva for meetings of the Commission of Enquiry and the League Council, he knew that the customs union was doomed, whatever the opinion of the International Court. He tried to save the project by integrating it into a broader pan-European proposal, but even this expedient eluded him. At the Commission of Enquiry on September 3 Schober delivered a speech of renunciation drafted in

[42] Sargent and Vansittart minutes and FO to British embassy Paris, June 23, 1931, FO 371/15151, C4257/61/3; Curtius minute, July 1, T-120/K49/K005622-25; German legation Vienna to AA, July 7, T-120/6075/E450011-12; Bennett, *Financial Crisis*, p. 296; British legation Vienna to FO, Aug. 5, FO 371/15152, C5996/61/3; S. V. Waley to FO, Aug. 5, and British legation Vienna to FO, Aug. 9, ibid., C6112/6123/6124/61/3.

part by the French themselves. It had been clear from the outset, he stated, that the plan could succeed only if other states acceded to it. On September 5 the Hague Court ruled by a vote of eight to seven that the customs union was illegal under the Geneva Protocol of 1922.[43]

The failure of the customs union represented a major diplomatic defeat for the German government, and Curtius acknowledged his responsibility by resigning in late September. Brüning assumed the Foreign Ministry himself, a move that left State Secretary Bülow effectively in control of the Wilhelmstrasse. Bülow, together with the German Finance and Economic ministries, continued to seek influence in Austrian economic life. Never forgetting the Creditanstalt's extensive holdings throughout Southeastern Europe, the Germans tried to secure the appointment of a German national as the bank's new director. Two attempts failed when German bankers declined what they regarded as a hopeless position, and the Wilhelmstrasse finally retreated into the background.[44]

After two years of negotiations the Creditanstalt in 1933 reached an accommodation with its creditors, who agreed to absorb substantial losses in order to keep the bank afloat. More long and difficult negotiations led to agreement on a joint Franco-British government-guaranteed loan in late 1932. It was not until this loan was placed that the Austrian National Bank repaid the Bank of England's original one-week credit in full.[45] Thus, on the surface, the Austrian financial crisis had been settled by 1933, but the broader effects of the panic that had begun at the Creditanstalt lingered on for years.

The defeat of the Austro-German customs union did not change German policy in Southeastern Europe; the German government still sought to extend influence throughout the region by any available means. Thus, during the final stages of the customs union controversy Berlin began to seek international approval for its preference treaties with Rumania and Hungary.

[43] For Curtius's proposals see T-120/K49/K005684-86; see also Bennett, *Financial Crisis*, pp. 297-98.

[44] Regarding the attempts to place a German director, see T-120/6075/E450145-68.

[45] On this agreement see ibid., E450233-82, and the British Treasury memorandum of Apr. 28, 1932, FO 371/15922, C3572/58/62.

On June 27, 1931, the Cereals Committee of the Commission of Enquiry for a European Union approved preferences as "a temporary and limited exception" to the most-favored-nation rule, subject to the approval of all countries enjoying most-favored-nation rights. Several days later, German and Rumanian negotiators agreed to submit their treaty to the Commission of Enquiry and the League Council in September, and subsequently to those overseas countries enjoying most-favored-nation rights vis-à-vis Germany. They hoped to put the treaty in effect by October 15.[46]

In the meantime, other western powers negotiated various forms of preference treaties. The French government, which had endorsed preferences in the *Plan constructif* submitted in May, began negotiating preference treaties in the late summer of 1931. The Quai d'Orsay did not want to leave the Southeastern European field to the Germans, but in concluding preference treaties, French diplomats, like their German counterparts, had to overcome domestic protectionist pressure. The worldwide slump in agricultural prices had hit France in 1930, and by 1931 the peasantry was pushing hard for government assistance. Under pressure from the aggressive new minister of agriculture, André Tardieu, a conservative politician anxious to mobilize peasant support for the 1932 elections, the French government took decisions that restructured French foreign trade and severely curtailed trade with Eastern Europe for the rest of the decade.

In the second half of 1931 Tardieu introduced import quotas on virtually all agricultural products in order to restrict imports in spite of the fall in world prices. He made a special effort to protect the home market in wheat. Under the quota system, which remained in force for the rest of the decade, French commercial negotiators retained very little latitude in their dealings with foreign governments. Henceforth, they generally could only promise foreign nations a given *percentage* of total French imports of any particular good, rather than a specific *quantity*. The Ministry of Agriculture fixed total annual imports of specific agricultural products with an eye on protecting the home market at all costs. The quota system hit France's foreign

[46] LNP, 1931.VII.10, pp. 1-3; AA memorandum, June 27, 1931, T-120/5661/H010677.

trading partners particularly hard because French colonies—
already the beneficiaries of substantial tariff advantages—were
exempt from quotas. As a result, foreign producers' share of
France's total consumption of agricultural products dropped
from 14 percent in 1925-1929 to just 6 percent in 1935-1938; by
contrast, the colonial share rose in the same period from 8 to 15
percent.[47]

Within the limits of this framework, the French government
concluded preferential agreements with Hungary and Yugoslavia on September 25 and October 7, 1931. Both countries received a 30 percent tariff rebate on wheat exports to France, but
Paris could promise them only a 10 percent share of total French
wheat imports each, a quota estimated at 80,000 tons. In return,
the southeastern states reduced tariffs on various items of special interest to France, including wine, perfume, and silk. The
French government concluded a similar treaty with Rumania on
January 5, 1932, after French financial interests, whose loans to
Rumania were in jeopardy, had pressured the government to
increase imports from that country. The French Ministry of Agriculture opposed Rumanian demands for tariff preferences on
guaranteed import quotas for corn, but under the treaty
Rumania received a 30 percent tariff rebate on corn—subsequently extended to Hungary and Yugoslavia as well—and
a 10 percent corn import quota, expected to reach 80,000 tons.[48]

Unlike the German preferential treaties, these agreements
took effect in 1932, but their results were disappointing. Even
though total French wheat imports for 1932 exceeded the
800,000-ton estimate by about 80 percent, France imported only
15,000 tons from Yugoslavia and 13,000 tons from Hungary. In
1933 French wheat imports dipped sharply, and imports from
the southeastern states fell to negligible quantities, although
corn imports from Rumania remained above the projected level
in both 1932 and 1933, reaching 123,000 and 135,000 tons, respectively.[49] A 30 percent tariff rebate on wheat apparently did

[47] Gordon Wright, *Rural Revolution in France* (Stanford, 1964), pp. 42-44; Albert Sauvy, *Histoire économique de la France entre les deux guerres*, 4 vols. (Paris,
1965-1975), II, 385-86, 448-57; Olivier Long, *Le Contingentement en France. Ses Incidences économiques* (Paris, 1938), pp. 169-70.

[48] For the texts of the Franco-Hungarian, Franco-Yugoslav, and Franco-
Rumanian treaties see AN, F^{10}/2115, F^{30}/2081, and F^{10}/2139, respectively.

[49] Ministère des Finances, Direction Générale des Douanes, *Statistique mensuelle
du commerce extérieur de la France*, (Paris, various years) (hereafter *SMCF*), *1931*
no. 12, p. 61, *1933*, no. 12, pp. 32-33.

not enable the southeastern states to compete effectively with American and French North African suppliers. For the most part, further attempts to help these countries in the middle and late 1930s encountered similar difficulties.

The Italian government also made new agreements with Southeastern European states in the late summer of 1931. The Italians had consistently opposed preferences within the League and the Commission of Enquiry for a European Union for fear of retaliation from overseas trading partners, but Mussolini still coveted influence in Austria and Hungary and did not want Germany and France to outbid him. Rome turned to disguised forms of preference as a result. In late August 1931 the Italian government initialed the so-called Semmering agreements with Austria and Hungary, also known as Brocchi treaties after their chief architect. Although avoiding outright preferences, these treaties sought to encourage Italo-Austrian and Italo-Hungarian trade by forming government-supported export credit companies to finance such trade at advantageous terms. These treaties came into force in early 1932 and eventually led to the more far-reaching Rome Protocols of March 1934.[50]

In September 1931 the German government, with French support, began actively to seek international approval for its preferential agreements with Hungary and Rumania. The Commission of Enquiry for a European Union approved the agreements at its September meeting, adding that other states enjoying most-favored-nation rights need only extend "silent toleration" of the treaties rather than outright approval, and on October 5 the Wilhelmstrasse instructed all interested missions to seek the sanction of their host governments.[51]

Despite the treaties' numerous safeguards for the interests of third parties, Argentina, the Soviet Union, Czechoslovakia, and the government of India all protested the agreements in October and November.[52] The HPA concluded on November 17 that the treaties could not go into effect for some time, and the Ger-

[50] For a description of the Semmering agreements see Ministère des Affaires Etrangères, Documents diplomatiques français (1932-1939) (Paris, 1963-1977), Series 1, vol. IV, no. 53 (hereafter DDF, series, volume, number).

[51] LNP, 1931.VII.15, pp. 17-18; AA circular, Oct. 5, 1931, T-120/K2104/K573357-66.

[52] AA to German embassy Moscow, Oct. 21, 1931, German legation Prague to AA, Oct. 28, German legation Buenos Aires to AA, Nov. 9, German embassy London to AA, Nov. 25, Posse to AA, Dec. 30, T-120/K2104/K573462-69, 525, 598, 781, 873-76.

man government negotiated interim agreements with Rumania and Hungary in December.[53] The new German-Rumanian agreement put the treaty into effect, less the preferences and the Rumanian tariff concessions. The Germans also pledged to import 200,000 tons of Rumanian corn monthly beginning in January 1932; the Rumanians could denounce the agreement if this condition were not fulfilled. The new German-Hungarian arrangement was similar.[54] With French help, the Germans overcame Argentinian and Soviet objections to preferences in January and February, and Berlin decided to ignore the remaining objections. On March 12 the German government informed Bucharest and Budapest of its intention to put the preferences into effect soon, but on March 21 the United States, which had counted on other governments to block the preferences, suddenly registered its objections.[55]

Two weeks earlier, on March 5, André Tardieu, now the French premier, had circulated a new memorandum on economic help for Southeastern Europe. Paris persuaded the Rumanian government to delay the implementation of the German-Rumanian preference treaty until these new proposals had been discussed. As it turned out, the German telegram of March 12 represented the closest the preferences would ever come to going into effect.

The Tardieu plan for the economic reconstruction of the five Danubian states—Austria, Czechoslovakia, Hungary, Rumania, and Yugoslavia—dominated discussions of Southeastern European problems from March through May 1932. During late 1931 and early 1932 the depression led to serious financial difficulties in Austria, Hungary, Rumania, and Yugoslavia, and in many cases to the suspension of the service of foreign loans.

[53] T-120/7156/H152965.
[54] On the German-Rumanian talks see T-120/K2105/K575918-21, 925-27, and T-120/6120/E456246-52, 273-75; on the German-Hungarian talks, T-120/K2105/K573937-38, T-120/6145/E459895.
[55] German legation Buenos Aires to AA, Jan. 4, 1932, AA to German embassy Washington, D.C., Mar. 13, AA to German legations in Bucharest and Budapest, Mar. 12, German embassy Washington, D.C., to AA, Mar. 21, T-120/K2104/ K573891-92, K574064-66, 007-9, 082, 225-27. See also U.S. Department of State, *Foreign Relations of the United States* (Washington, D.C., various years), *1932*, II, 339-42.

Conceived to save French investments in Southeastern Europe, the Tardieu plan was modified to fit the needs of French diplomacy and domestic politics.

Financial distress spread from Austria to the other Danubian states during the latter half of 1931. Heavily burdened by foreign debt, Hungary's financial structure began to crumble under pressure from the financial crises in Austria and Germany. By the end of 1931, Hungary had suspended all foreign-exchange payments, despite the provision of an emergency £4-million loan in July. Rumania encountered serious difficulties in the fall of 1931; by the next spring, it had also partially suspended foreign-debt payments. Yugoslavia suffered enormously from the cessation of German reparations payments under the Hoover moratorium and had to secure help in the form of a 300-million-franc loan from France in October. Only Czechoslovakia retained financial stability.

In order to carry out a necessary minimum of foreign trade despite their lack of foreign currency, the afflicted countries established various forms of exchange control, including the rationing of available foreign exchange and the conclusion of bilateral clearing agreements designed to maintain trade without allowing currency to cross frontiers.[56] By early 1932 the southeastern states' situation was far worse than it had been when they first asked for help in the fall of 1930. The possibility of a total financial and economic collapse in Southeastern Europe was widely discussed.

Under pressure from French financial interests, French Finance Minister Pierre-Etienne Flandin wrote the Quai d'Orsay on December 5, 1931, asking what might be done to help Southeastern Europe. The Quai replied on January 18 that it had been working for a new Czechoslovak-Hungarian commercial agreement to which Austria, and perhaps eventually Rumania and Yugoslavia, might also adhere. Czech Foreign Minister Beneš had indeed approached both Vienna and Budapest in October and November with various schemes for customs unions, but the protectionist Czech Agrarian party remained a serious obstacle to any rapprochement with agrarian Hungary.[57]

[56] On the financial crisis and the imposition of exchange controls see Berend and Ránki, *Economic Development*, pp. 242-64.

[57] For Flandin's correspondence with the Quai see AN, F[30]/1396; on Beneš's negotiations see also T-120/K48/K004764-92.

The British Foreign Office also took note of the new crisis in Southeastern Europe, and in December 1931 Sir Orme Sargent of the Central Department cast about for a new scheme to replace the Austro-German customs union and the dormant French *Plan constructif*. After hearing of the various new proposals for unions among the five Danubian states, Sargent, after consulting the Treasury and the Board of Trade, suggested a customs union of the five states to Paris, Berlin, and Rome on January 14, 1932. The British preferred a customs union to a system of preferences because international law specifically exempted such unions from protests under the most-favored-nation clause. The British proposal immediately aroused opposition in Berlin and Vienna, which refused to consider any Central European union that would exclude Germany.[58]

European diplomats discussed the possibility of a Danubian customs federation at an unrelated series of meetings in Geneva in mid-February. On February 16 the Austrian government appealed to Germany, France, Italy, and Great Britain for economic help, expressing willingness to enter into discussions with all neighboring or interested states on an economic rapprochement.[59] Acting on instructions from Quai Secretary General Berthelot, René Massigli of the French delegation to the League of Nations suggested an economic rapprochement among Austria, Hungary, and Czechoslovakia to Beneš. The Czechoslovak foreign minister, wary of the Czech Agrarians, advocated a system of preferences for specified products rather than a full customs union and insisted that any new combination must include Rumania and Yugoslavia so as not to break up the Little Entente. Beneš tended to see the specter of a Hapsburg restoration, which the Little Entente was determined to prevent, behind any proposals for Austro-Hungarian-Czechoslovak rapprochement.[60] Informed of these discussions, Berthelot replied

[58] Sargent's interdepartmental correspondence with Sir Henry Fountain, Leith-Ross, and the Board of Trade, November 1931-January 1932, FO 371/ 15208, C8992/C9461/8992/62, FO 371/15918, C369/58/62; British proposal, Jan. 14, ibid. On reaction to the proposal see British legation Vienna to FO, Feb. 2, and British embassy Berlin to FO Feb. 2, ibid., C1051/C1152/58/62, and Bülow's Feb. 2 minute, T-120/4617/E195111-13.

[59] T-120/4617/E195118-19.

[60] AE to French mission Geneva, Feb. 16, 1932, French mission Geneva to AE, Feb. 17, AN, F³⁰/1396; British mission Geneva to FO, Feb. 13, FO 371/15918, C1364/58/62. On the Little Entente's opposition to a Hapsburg restoration see Reichert, *Kleine Entente*, pp. 79-86.

on February 22 that France would shortly have to respond to Austria's appeal for help and argued that any attempt to go beyond a tripartite combination would be far too complicated— and potentially dangerous as well. For thirteen years, he noted, France had sought to prevent Anschluss. "To attach Austria economically to the other members of the old Austro-Hungarian Empire," he wrote, "would crown this policy with success. To create a grouping of the five Danubian states to help her, however, would risk the most serious defeat for this policy. It would tend to create Mitteleuropa in order to prevent the Anschluss." Berthelot argued that such a five-state group could never absorb its own agricultural surplus; Germany would step in as a result. Massigli replied on February 27 that the British, Germans, and Italians were all discussing five-state schemes, and he added that to exclude Rumania and Yugoslavia would drive them into Germany's arms.[61]

In the midst of these discussions André Tardieu replaced Pierre Laval as premier and foreign minister on February 23. In less than two weeks Tardieu combined elements of various proposals into a plan bearing his name. A dynamic, aggressive, conservative-nationalist politician, Tardieu faced a difficult election in just two months. A dramatic foreign-policy success would help him in the coming electoral battle with the Radicals and Socialists. The plan that Tardieu presented to the British and Italian foreign ministers in Geneva on March 5 during sessions of the Disarmament Conference reflected his thinking in several ways. In foreign affairs, Tardieu was a disciple of Georges Clemenceau and thus anxious to exclude German influence from Eastern Europe; as agriculture minister during 1931 he had taken steps to protect French peasants from foreign competition. Thus the Tardieu plan, unlike the *Plan constructif* of 1931, made no mention of great-power preferences for Southeastern European cereals. Rejecting a customs union as too complicated, it called for an economic reorganization of the five Danubian states based on mutual preferences, adding vaguely that the new tariff arrangements would have to take account of "the legitimate interests of third countries." After such a reorganization, Tardieu suggested, the five states might receive new loans to help put them back on their feet.[62]

[61] AN, F³⁰/1396.

[62] For the text of the plan see T-120/4617/E195124-27, FO 371/15918, C1836/58/64, and AN, F³⁰/1396.

Any hopes Tardieu may have had for quick agreement to his new scheme were soon disappointed. The Italian government, fearing exclusion from Southeastern Europe, reacted by putting the 1931 Semmering agreements with Austria and Hungary into effect.[63] The Wilhelmstrasse also reacted negatively; Bülow read the French proposals as an attempt to exclude Germany from the Danubian states. The official German reply of March 15 rejected any combination excluding Germany. It argued that the five Danubian states could never absorb their agricultural surplus, cited the German preference agreements with Rumania and Hungary as attempts to deal with this problem, and called for more unilateral cereals preferences and preferences for Austria as proposed in the earlier French *Plan constructif*.[64]

The German reply led to a remarkable scene in Geneva on March 17 among Tardieu, Posse, and Viktor von Heeren of the Wilhelmstrasse. Stating that he wished to speak absolutely frankly, the French premier launched into a tirade, making it clear that he intended to put his plan into effect by any possible means. Only France, he argued, had the financial resources to put the Danubian states back on their feet; the German acceptance of the French preference plan of May 1931 was "alas, one year too late." "I think I understand the German mentality," he continued; "I cannot see, however, how in light of the circumstances—that a restoration in German interests must be effected and that it cannot be effected without French help—the German government can hesitate to join in my proposals. I do not understand what Germany hopes to gain from its opposition. We are right and will achieve our aim." Perhaps Tardieu's intemperate language reflected his eagerness to score a dramatic diplomatic success; even Berthelot confessed to German Ambassador von Hoesch on March 23 that Tardieu, in his opinion, was in far too much of a hurry.[65]

The five Danubian states, which had been virtually the last to hear of the new plan, had mixed reactions. Beneš, who had done as much as anyone to influence the final form of the plan, supported the new proposals while insisting that there be no five-

---

[63] Minute of Maurice Hankey, Mar. 12, 1932, FO 371/15919, C2053/58/62.

[64] T-120/4617/E195134-38.

[65] See German mission Geneva to AA, Mar. 17, 1932, T-120/4617/E195139-49, and Tardieu to AE, Mar. 17, AN, F³⁰/1037. See also German embassy Paris to AA, Mar. 23, T-120/4617/E195168-70.

power customs union and that no great power be allowed to participate on an equal footing. Rumanian and Yugoslav reaction was highly ambivalent; these countries needed both German markets for cereals and more French capital. After some deliberation the Rumanian government decided not to put the German-Rumanian preference agreement into effect. The Hungarian government argued that the plan was too complicated and proposed an Austro-Hungarian-Italian customs union instead. Despite their financial desperation, the Hungarians rejected any five-state unit that would confirm their existing frontiers. Austria continued to ask for help in any possible form.[66]

The Tardieu plan faced the British government with a difficult decision; having proposed a full customs union of the Danubian states, the British now had to take a position on the more ticklish question of preferences. In addition, since Tardieu's proposals made no distinction between agricultural and industrial goods, the new plan could give Czech or Austrian industrial products advantages over British goods. Foreign Office officials persuaded Sir John Simon, who had replaced Lord Reading as foreign secretary in the National Government, that Britain should make this relatively insignificant sacrifice for the Danubian states, but Board of Trade President Walter Runciman told Simon that he felt that Britain should receive some quid pro quo for any renunciation of its most-favored-nation rights in the Danubian states. During his tenure at the Board of Trade from 1931 through 1937 Runciman zealously guarded formal British trading rights in Eastern Europe while generally rejecting government intervention to increase trade with that region. When the cabinet discussed the question on March 16, Simon secured approval for preferences among the Danubian states over the objection of several ministers who wanted to maintain Britain's most-favored-nation rights. The cabinet insisted, however, that Britain share equally in any concessions to neighboring great powers—that is, Germany or Italy.[67]

[66] British mission Geneva to FO, Feb. 13, 1932, British legation Bucharest to FO, Mar. 29, British legation Budapest to FO, May 5, FO 371/15918-21, C1364/C2788/C3714/58/62; French mission Geneva to AE, Mar. 11, AN, F30/1396; French legation Belgrade to AE, Mar. 8, Apr. 3, AN, F30/1037.

[67] Sargent letter, Mar. 15, 1932, FO 371/15919, C2104/58/62; cabinet of Mar. 16, CAB 23/70; see also CP 98 (32), 101 (32), CAB 24/228.

In light of the disagreements among the great powers, the British government on March 22 suggesed a conference of the British, French, German, and Italian governments to discuss proposals for the Danubian states. All accepted, and the conference was scheduled to meet in London on April 6.[68] Before the conference met, the German and Italian governments on the one hand and the French and British on the other devised common strategies. In Rome in late March, Italian Foreign Minister Grandi and German Ambassador Schubert agreed to oppose the plan on the basis of their own countries' substantial trade with the Danubian states.[69] In London on April 4 the French and British delegations agreed to propose an all-around preferential 10 percent tariff reduction among the five Danubian states; the French suggested that neighboring great powers be invited to extend unilateral preferences to these states as well but agreed to limit such preferences to agricultural goods only when Runciman protested that preferences for industrial goods would discriminate against Britain.[70]

Distinguished delegations met in London on April 6. The British negotiators included Prime Minister Ramsay Mac-Donald, Simon, Runciman, and Chancellor of the Exchequer Neville Chamberlain, as well as numerous permanent officials; Bülow and Posse spoke for the Germans; Grandi came from Italy; and Flandin led the French delegation. Perhaps Tardieu did not attend because he foresaw the failure of the conference. On April 6 Neville Chamberlain, who did most of the talking for the British throughout, opened the discussion by proposing a 10 percent reduction of inter-Danubian tariffs; Flandin agreed, adding that the great powers might also extend unilateral preferences. Bülow, however, argued skillfully that a mere reduction of trade barriers within the Danubian area would not help the five states very much; in particular, the five Danubian states could never absorb their combined cereals surplus. Moreover, Germany, currently nearing the very lowest point of the depression itself, should not be asked to make sacrifices for the sake of Czechoslovakia, whose sufferings were not nearly as pronounced. Grandi also argued that the Danubian states' trade

[68] FO 371/15919, C2259/C2396/C2438/58/62.
[69] German embassy Rome to AA, Mar. 17, 25, Apr. 2, 1931, T-120/4617/195157-61, 162-65, 363-71.
[70] For minutes of these talks see FO 371/15920, C2328/C2693/58/62.

with other powers had to be taken into consideration. On April 7, in an effort to overcome Bülow's objection, Chamberlain suggested limiting the tariff reductions among the Danubian states to agricultural goods, but the German merely reserved his government's attitude. The delegates could not agree on any specific proposals at their last session on April 8. The conference had failed; the final communiqué was entirely noncommittal.[71] The French retreated from London in defeat; the Germans were content to have blocked a plan they regarded as a threat to their interests.

In retrospect, much of the conference's interest lies in the debate it provoked inside the British Foreign Office over the relative merits of French or German hegemony in Southeastern Europe. Sir Robert Vansittart, the permanent undersecretary of state, preferred the former; although hostile in principle to the French alliances in Eastern Europe, he suggested that French control in the region was "defensive," whereas German control, which he expected Berlin to pursue as soon as Germany recovered its strength, would be "aggressive and acquisitive." Sir Horace Rumbold, the British ambassador in Berlin, argued on the other hand that increased German political influence in the region would only represent "the political consequences of a logical economic development," whereas French hegemony could never be established on a sound economic basis and thus would always tend to produce instability. Owen O'Malley, later to head the Foreign Office department responsible for Southeastern Europe, minuted agreement with this view.[72] The debate continued throughout the 1930s. In general, it did not stem from differences over Eastern Europe itself; few British officials took any interest in the region. Instead, different attitudes toward French and German influence in Eastern Europe generally reflected different attitudes toward France and Germany. British officials were still split over this question when it became more acute in the latter part of the decade.

The financial crisis in Southeastern Europe continued in the wake of the London conference, but for several months the

[71] For stenographic records of all the sessions see T-120/4617/E195396 ff. or FO 371/15921, C2778/58/62. See also Bülow's Apr. 10 report, T-120/4617/E195591-98.
[72] Vansittart's Apr. 24 memorandum, FO 371/15922, C3025/58/62; Rumbold's Apr. 28 telegram and O'Malley's minute, ibid., C3518.

great powers took no concrete measures to alleviate it. In principle, the German government still sought to implement its preferential agreements with Rumania and Hungary. On April 13, 1932, however, the German cabinet concluded that a total financial and economic collapse of the Danubian states would not irreparably harm German interests.[73] In late April a committee of financial experts called by the London conference to meet in Geneva discussed the League Financial Committee's new recommendations for Austria and Hungary. French experts supported its proposals for new guaranteed loans to the Danubian states, but British experts refused to consider any loans unless these states abandoned the gold standard and abolished exchange control. The only loan the British favored was a new international credit to replace the Bank of England loan that Montagu Norman had granted to Austria the previous June.[74]

Several events revived interest in international action in Southeastern Europe by the time the Lausanne conference on reparations met in June 1932. First, on May 28 the United States government informed Berlin that although it could not acquiesce in the derogation of its most-favored-nation rights embodied in the German-Hungarian and German-Rumanian treaties, the American government would "give sympathetic consideration" to "a comprehensive general plan which has at its purpose improvement of economic and financial conditions throughout the whole of Europe."[75] German interest in a multilateral framework into which to integrate the two treaties revived. Second, in the French elections of May 1932 the Radical and Socialist *Cartel des Gauches* defeated Tardieu's conservatives. During the election campaign the left-wing parties had attacked French loans in Southeastern Europe as a wasteful means of extending political influence.[76] The accession of the Radical Edouard Herriot opened the door for revived Franco-German cooperation in the Danubian states.

---

[73] T-120/3598/D789811-16.

[74] British Treasury memorandum, Apr. 28, 1932, FO 371/15922, C3572/58/62.

[75] *Foreign Relations of the U.S., 1932*, II, 346-47; T-120/K2104/K574225-27. The United States government had not protested the French preference agreements because no Franco-American most-favored-nation treaty was then in force.

[76] Leith-Ross letter, June 6, 1932, FO 371/15889.

When the Lausanne conference met in June, Robert Coulondre of the Economic Section of the Quai d'Orsay told Karl Ritter, "The present French government does not intend to pursue the Tardieu plan. The Tardieu plan is dead." The two diplomats agreed to revive the idea of cereals preferences. Working within a committee of the conference, they drew up a common program that included cereals preferences, preferences for Austrian industrial goods, and a "common fund" drawn from international loans and supplemented by Danubian customs receipts to provide the Danubian states with new capital. The Final Act of the Lausanne conference approved this program and called for a conference of European agricultural and industrial states to discuss measures to reduce exchange control, revive trade, and restore cereals prices in Southeastern Europe. French Commerce Minister Georges Bonnet was named president of the conference, which was scheduled for the first week of September in Stresa, Italy.[77]

Despite high hopes for the Stresa meeting, by September 1932 protectionism had gained such ground in Germany, France, and Britain as to make real help for Southeastern Europe impossible. In Germany a new right-wing government led by Franz von Papen had replaced the Brüning coalition in June. German conservative publicists called for agricultural self-sufficiency to fight the domestic agricultural depression, and by late August the new agriculture minister, Magnus von Braun, was echoing these calls and asking the cabinet to regulate all agricultural imports with a quota system.[78] In France the quota system was becoming increasingly restrictive; in outlining French policy for the forthcoming Stresa conference, the French Finance Ministry noted the impossibility, given the internal French economic position, of increasing imports from the Danubian states to levels that would enable them to service their debts. France's problem, the ministry argued, was to balance "the interests of our investors, our industrialists, and our agriculturalists."[79] The British had revolutionized their commercial policy during the first half of 1932 by imposing a general 10 percent tariff on imports,

[77] Undated Ritter memorandum, T-120/L1709/L502056-62; Ritter memorandum, July 27, 1932, T-120/K1813/K457516-30; Final Act of the conference, July 9, ibid., K457457-86.
[78] Cabinets of July 21 and Aug. 27, 1932, T-120/3598/D791452-55, 596-97.
[79] Memorandum of Sept. 4, 1932, AN, F^{30}/1398.

exempting the Dominions from the tariff at the Ottawa Imperial Conference, and restricting imports of certain agricultural products through quotas.[80] By the time of the Stresa conference, domestic interests had deprived the great powers of any real freedom of action.

At the conference, French, German, and Italian negotiators quickly agreed to a combination of cereals preferences and loans to put the Danubian states back on their feet. The French successfully insisted on a common fund to provide agricultural credit and enable the Danubian states to abolish exchange control while maintaining the gold parities of their currencies. The French wanted to raise the fund through government-guaranteed loans but ultimately agreed to allow Germany and Italy to make their contribution in the form of cereals preferences. The British delegation, according to Bonnet, maintained a studied indifference to European problems in the wake of the Ottawa conference. They would support no guaranteed loans except a new loan for Austria. Thus the conference forwarded a recommendation for a common fund, noting British reservations, to the Commission of Enquiry for a European Union and again endorsed cereals preferences, preferences for Austrian industrial products, and the International Agricultural Mortgage Credit Company, which most European states had not yet ratified.[81] In practical terms, the Danubian states walked away virtually empty-handed, and in succeeding months the British blocked any progress toward a common fund or an International Agricultural Mortgage Credit Company.[82]

The Stresa conference had at least given the German government the international framework for the preferences that the United States had demanded as a condition of waiving its most-favored-nation rights, but the Wilhelmstrasse could not take advantage of it for domestic political reasons. In several September cabinet meetings the Papen government, which was dominated by right-wing interests and anxious to outbid the Nazis for the agrarian vote in the November Reichstag elections, decided to impose agricultural quotas over the objections of the new foreign minister, professional diplomat Constantin von

[80] See below, Chapter IV.

[81] For reports and comments on the conference see *DDF*, 1, I, 16, 17; AN, F^{30}/1398, F^{30}/1400; FO 371/15924; T-120/K1823/K457842 ff.

[82] See FO 371/15925, C8237/C8292/C8563/C9676/68/62; LNP, 1932.VII.13.

Neurath. The German government denounced or let lapse its trade treaties with Sweden, Holland, Yugoslavia, and France during the latter part of 1932. Both the government of Kurt von Schleicher, which replaced Papen's regime in December, and the Nazi-dominated coalition that took power on January 30, 1933, further increased agricultural protection. Despite frequent complaints from Bucharest and Budapest, the German Foreign Office could not put the preferences into effect against this background. On September 8 the Rumanian government protested that Germany had bought only 25,000 tons of Rumanian corn during the first eight months of 1932, despite its December 1931 promise to buy 200,000 tons monthly in January and February alone, and that Germany had imported no Rumanian cattle. The Wilhelmstrasse had to stall off such protests, although Ritter and Posse still held out hope of putting the preferences into effect.[83]

Though unable to offer any concessions on agricultural products, the Wilhelmstrasse made some progress on another front. On July 25, 1932, after the Lausanne conference had endorsed preferences for Austria, the Austrian government simultaneously proposed negotiations for preferences to the four other Danubian states, Bulgaria, Poland, Germany, and France. The German government replied favorably, and talks began in October. The Germans agreed to 50 percent tariff reductions on certain Austrian industrial products, including textiles and leather goods, but the Austrians also asked for larger import quotas, preferences on butter and eggs, and increased cattle and timber exports to Germany—all of which were rejected by the German negotiators. After talks broke off in December, Vienna negotiated preferences with France and Poland. The Austro-French treaty of December 30, 1932, provided for a preferential tariff on a specified quota of Austrian timber. In January 1933 Poland extended preferences on a wide variety of Austrian industrial products in return for increased Polish coal exports to Austria.[84]

[83] Cabinets of Dec. 14, 17, 19, 1932, T-120/3598/D790753 ff.; Rumanian note of Sept. 8, AA to German legation Bucharest, Nov. 23, Posse to Wiehl, Nov. 25, Ritter memorandum, Dec. 27, T-120/K2105/K575977, K2104/K574365 ff.

[84] Austrian note, July 25, 1932, German legation Vienna to AA, Aug. 3, Wiehl memorandum, Aug. 6, German legation Vienna to AA, Nov. 7, T-120/K1134/K293230-31, 234-35, T-120/K1136/K293370-71, 391-94, 400-410, T-120/6076/

Despite protests from local German chambers of commerce and the German leather and textile industries, the Wilhelm-strasse still hoped to conclude a preferential agreement with Austria in January 1933. On January 30 Neurath asked Chancellor von Schleicher to resolve the conflict between the Foreign Office and the Agriculture Ministry over butter and cheese concessions to Austria. Adolf Hitler replaced Schleicher on that very day, however, and the question was left unresolved. On April 11 the Austrian Foreign Ministry informed Ritter that Austria would drop its butter and cheese demands, but by this time the German-Austrian relationship was changing rapidly. All prospects of agreement vanished during the spring and summer of 1933.[85]

During 1931 and 1932 the Wilhelmstrasse tried to use German economic power to realize political goals in Eastern Europe, including the goal of revising Germany's eastern frontiers. A conservative-nationalist government would probably have continued to employ such strategies in its efforts to undermine the Treaty of Versailles. The dying Weimar government, however, was too weak to make its initiatives work. Domestic protectionism, stimulated by Germany's own agricultural crisis and falling demand for foodstuffs, prevented the Wilhelmstrasse from significantly increasing German purchases of grain and live animals from Southeastern Europe. In addition, the French government still staunchly defended many aspects of the post-war settlement in Eastern Europe, and during the crisis over the Austro-German customs union it used French financial strength to block Berlin's plans. A new era began on January 30, 1933, when Hitler took power. Under the Nazi regime, German trade with Eastern Europe expanded within the framework of a new, more radical foreign-policy strategy.

E450463-70. For the Austro-French and Austro-Polish treaties see T-120/K1136/K293505-6, 559-92.

[85] For the protests see T-120/K1136/K293479-620; Neurath's letter, T-120/8735/E510037-38; the Austrian communication, ibid., E610032-33.

III.

The Advent of Hitler and the German Trade Treaties of 1934-1935

Adolf Hitler came to power in 1933 possessed of a sweeping foreign policy program—a program in which Eastern Europe played a central role. His accession did not immediately transform German policy toward Eastern Europe, but from 1933 through 1939 his long-range goals increasingly determined German policy toward the successor states.

Recent research has shown that Hitler's ideas on foreign policy varied somewhat during the early 1920s but crystallized by the time he wrote *Mein Kampf* in 1925 and did not significantly alter for the rest of his life.[1] With regard to Eastern Europe, which of course played a vital role in Hitler's solution to the German problem, one can usefully identify three different, but interrelated, sources of his thinking: the Austro-German prejudices embodied in the propaganda of the Pan-German League; the German annexationist propaganda during the First World War; and vague geopolitical theories regarding the need for living space. It is necessary to examine the influence of each in some detail.

Hitler grew to political consciousness under the Hapsburg Empire, and even *Mein Kampf*, written seven years after that empire collapsed, overflows with the hostility of a resentful Austro-German toward his government's attempts to integrate its Slavic nationalities into the empire. In *Mein Kampf* he continually accused the Hapsburgs of pursuing a de-Germanization policy at the expense of the empire's worthiest subjects.[2] This complaint was not original; many Austro-Germans shared it,

[1] See Hugh Trevor-Roper, "Hitlers Kriegziele," *Vierteljahreshefte für Zeitgeschichte*, VIII, no. 2 (1960), 121-23; Axel Kuhn, *Hitlers aussenpolitisches Programm. Entstehung und Entwicklung 1919-1939* (Stuttgart, 1970).

[2] Adolf Hitler, *Mein Kampf*, trans. Ralph Manheim (Boston, 1943). Chapter 3 is devoted to this theme; similar references abound throughout the text.

and it underlay the slight pressure for Anschluss between German Austria and the new German Empire that persisted from
1871 through 1914. This was the position of the Austrian sections of the Pan-German League, whose members included Hitler's father and favorite history teacher. From these sources Hitler drew his emphasis on the need for Anschluss, as well as his
belief that Slavic nationalities, particularly the Czechs, must
make room for the Germans in Central Europe. It is true, as
Axel Kuhn has pointed out, that Hitler differed in some respects
from the Pan-Germans, who stressed Germany's need for colonies and advocated expansion along a north-south axis into
Switzerland and Scandinavia rather than to the east, but this
hardly means that they were without influence on his thinking.[3]

The second major source of Hitler's ideas on foreign policy
was undoubtedly the German annexationist propaganda of the
First World War. In a wartime letter Hitler discussed the need
for German annexations and the probable collapse of the
Hapsburg Empire, and his eventual program, as revealed in
Mein Kampf and in his second book (written in 1928 but never
published during his lifetime),[4] was essentially the program of
Ludendorff and the high command. Like Ludendorff, Hitler
downgraded the extension of German influence to the southeast—much less any multinational federation along the lines of
Naumann's Mitteleuropa—in favor of the creation of a new agricultural German empire in conquered territory in the east.[5]
Hitler's ideas were not identical to Ludendorff's; his ideas on resettlement and colonization were certainly more sweeping, and
as a good Austro-German he favored uniting the hereditary
Hapsburg lands with the Reich. Nevertheless, the similarity of
his program to the wartime colonization of the Baltic provinces,
Ludendorff's policies in Poland and the Ukraine, and the
Treaty of Brest-Litovsk is too striking to ignore. The possible extent of Ludendorff's *direct* influence on Hitler deserves further
attention. When Hitler wrote *Mein Kampf*, he was of course serving his sentence for leading the Beer Hall Putsch, in which
Ludendorff had been a close, albeit unpunished, collaborator. It
was also around the time of the putsch that Hitler definitively

---

[3] Meyer, *Mitteleuropa*, pp. 30-56; Kuhn, *Hitlers Programm*, pp. 115-21.

[4] Adolf Hitler, *Hitlers zweites Buch. Ein Dokument aus dem Jahr 1928*, ed.
Gerhard L. Weinberg (Stuttgart, 1961), pp. 80-85, 104-33.

[5] Kuhn, *Hitlers Programm*, pp. 27-28; Hitler, *Mein Kampf*, pp. 641-47.

opted for expansion to the east rather than colonies as the solution to Germany's space problems. It is easy to speculate about Ludendorff's influence on these aspects of Hitler's thinking, but, unless more research yields new discoveries, it is impossible to go beyond speculation.

The third influence on Hitler's thought, and probably the most difficult to trace precisely to its origins, relates to his emphasis on the need for *Lebensraum* to solve Germany's economic problems and make it secure as a world power in a new world of superstates. From various sources, Hitler developed a notion of the German economic problem that led him to see territorial expansion as essential to Germany's continued existence. His belief in the need for more territory became more and more apparent from *Mein Kampf* through his second book and some of his crucial private utterances as chancellor, including his August 1936 memorandum on the Four Year Plan and the Hossbach memorandum of November 1937.[6] In general, as Wolfgang Sauer has shown in his brilliant essay on Hitler's war aims, Hitler reduced Germany's economic needs to the feeding of the German population, a task for which he considered even Germany's pre-1914 boundaries to be grossly inadequate. He showed in the second book that he was well aware that Germany could attempt to pay for the foodstuffs it needed by exporting industrial goods, but he rejected this alternative—as he did in controversies with Hjalmar Schacht during the mid-1930s—because he felt that Germany could not in the long run compete with the British Empire and the United States, whose huge internal markets seemed to him to give them insuperable advantages.[7]

Hitler believed that Germany must have more territory in order to survive as a great power; ultimately, he chose the solu-

---

[6] Karl-Dietrich Bracher, *The German Dictatorship: The Origins, Structure, and Effects of National Socialism,* trans. Jean Steinberg (New York, 1970), p. 128, specifically cites the influence of the geopolitician Karl Haushofer. For the memorandum on the Four Year Plan see U.S. Department of State, *Documents on German Foreign Policy, 1918-1945, from the Archives of the German Foreign Ministry,* ed. Raymond Sontag et al., series C and D (Washington, D.C., 1949-1966), series C. vol. V, no. 490 (hereafter *DGFP,* series, volume, number); for the Hossbach memorandum see *DGFP,* D, I, 19.

[7] Wolfgang Sauer, "Hitlers Kriegsideen," in Karl-Dietrich Bracher, Wolfgang Sauer, and Gerhard Schulz, *Die nationalsozialistische Machtergreifung: Studien zur Errichtung des totalitären Herrschaftssystems in Deutschland 1933/34,* 2d ed. (Cologne and Berlin, 1960), pp. 744-65; Hitler, *Zweites Buch,* pp. 53-54, 59-60, 123-24.

tion of expansion to the east.[8] What did this mean for the successor states of Eastern Europe? One Hitler scholar has noted that *Mein Kampf*, while establishing Hitler's designs on the Soviet Union, says little about the new states lying between Germany and the Soviet Union,[9] but the second book and a 1932 speech reported by Hermann Rauschning in his book, *The Voice of Destruction* (1939), clarify this point. In the first place, Hitler proposed to carry out the annexations of territory to the east and northeast that had been proposed during the First World War, also adding the old hereditary Hapsburg lands, Austria and Bohemia-Moravia (the western part of Czechoslovakia). Germany would then continue to expand to the east, not by creating a multinational federation or by Germanizing Slavic peoples, but by subjugating the eastern nationalities to the German will and, when necessary, ruthlessly transferring populations in order to clear land for German colonization. Hitler cared little about Eastern Europe as a market for German exports. Instead, he sought a territorial and agricultural base that would make Germany a superstate equal in scope and power to the British Empire and the United States.

Hitler's 1932 speech to a small party meeting in Munich called by Walter Darré deserves to be quoted at some length. Darré, a Nazi theorist on agriculture and resettlement and a future minister of agriculture under Hitler, began the meeting by discussing the need to found a new German agrarian aristocracy in the east and stressing the need for depopulation to make room for German colonists. Hitler expressed general agreement with this plan and then referred to the need for a "nucleus of eighty to one hundred million colonizing Germans" to carry it out.

> Part of this nucleus is Austria. That goes without saying. But Bohemia and Moravia also belong to it, as well as the western regions of Poland as far as certain natural strategic frontiers. Moreover—and this you must not overlook—the Baltic states, too, are part of it—those states which for cen-

---

[8] Eberhard Jäckel, *Hitler's Weltanschauung: A Blueprint for World Power*, trans. Herbert Arnold (Middletown, 1972), pp. 32-33; Kuhn, *Hitlers Programm*, pp. 99-104. Kuhn argues that Hitler wavered during the early 1920s between colonial expansion in alliance with Russia and continental expansion in alliance with Britain.

[9] Eberhard Jäckel, "Hitler's Foreign Policy Aims," in Henry A. Turner, Jr., ed., *Nazism and the Third Reich* (New York, 1972), pp. 211-12.

turies have had a thin upper crust of Germanhood. Today in all these regions, alien races predominate. It will be our duty, if we wish to found our greater Reich for all time, to remove those races. . . .

The Bohemian-Moravian basin and the eastern districts bordering on Germany will be colonized with German peasants. The Czechs and the Bohemians we shall transplant to Siberia and the Volhynian regions. . . . The Czechs must get out of Central Europe. . . .

In the Baltic countries the case is completely different. We shall easily Germanize the population. They are peoples who are radically closely related to us and would have been German long since, had not the prejudices and social arrogance of the German Baltic barons artifically prevented it. . . .

Thus far there are no doubts. In the east and southeast, I do not follow General Ludendorff nor anyone else; I follow only the iron law of our historical development. When Germany has rearmed, all these small states will offer us their alliance of their own accord. But we have no intention of manufacturing a peaceful Pan-Europe in miniature, with the good Uncle Germany in the center, pleasantly shortening the time of his nephews' studies. We shall not breed our own usurpers. We must once and for all time create the politically and biologically eternally valid foundations of a German Europe.

My party comrades, I am not thinking in the first instance of economic matters. Certainly we need the wheat, the oil and the ores of these countries. But our true object is to set up our rule for all time, and to anchor it so firmly that it will stand firm for a thousand years. No political or economic agreements, such as Papen and Hugenberg dream of, will achieve this. These are liberal games, which end in the bankruptcy of a nation. Today we are faced with the iron necessity of creating a *new social order*.[10]

This is probably the most coherent summary of Hitler's plans for Eastern Europe available. It shows all the major influences on his thinking. The disclaimer of Ludendorff's influence is suspicious; it only emphasizes the similarity between his plans for Poland and the Baltic and Ludendorff's wartime schemes. This speech also shows the differences between Hitler's plans

---

[10] Rauschning, *The Voice of Destruction* (New York, 1940), pp. 32-39.

for Eastern Europe and the Wilhelmstrasse's projects for extending German influence in that region. While expressing some interest in the raw materials the area might provide, Hitler made it clear that he would not content himself with a traditional sphere of influence, much less with any multinational federation like Naumann's Mitteleuropa. Nor did he care especially about monopolizing Eastern European markets, as shown by his disparagement of "economic matters." He intended to extend German territory and the German population to the east, deporting the existing population when necessary. Such was Hitler's program—a program that he began to implement after war began.[11]

Obviously, such goals could not be achieved through the peaceful extension of economic influence in Eastern Europe; they would eventually require war. Thus, beginning in 1933, German economic policy in general, and German trade with Eastern Europe in particular, increasingly served the purpose of preparing Germany for a war of conquest. New economic and trade policies led to the conclusion of trade treaties with Hungary, Yugoslavia, and Rumania in 1934-1935 and to a vast expansion of German trade with Eastern Europe beginning in 1937.

This discussion of Hitler's foreign policy has inevitably raised the broader, highly controversial question of the continuity of German foreign policy from the Wilhelmine Empire through the Third Reich. With respect to Eastern Europe, it is true that virtually all the major aspects of Hitler's eastern policy— Anschluss with Austria, the conquest of *Lebensraum*, the establishment of a new German agrarian elite in the conquered eastern territories, and the subjugation, deportation, or elimination of the Slavic national groups in the east—had been discussed before the First World War. Many of them had been partially put into effect during that war. In short, much of Hitler's program was already common currency when he began his political career in the early 1920s. Furthermore, under Hitler the Wilhelmstrasse implemented its program of economic penetration in Eastern Europe. Evidence suggests, however, that when

[11] On the wartime implementation of Hitler's program see above all Norman Rich, *Hitler's War Aims: Ideology, the Nazi State, and the Course of Expansion*, 2 vols. (New York, 1973-1974).

Hitler came to power the German Foreign Office was not thinking in terms of future expansion on the scale of German policy
during the First World War. In addition, the behavior of traditional German foreign-policy and military elites in 1937 and
1938 suggests that a democratic or conservative-nationalist regime would not have committed itself so irrevocably to a war of
conquest. Significantly, as the decade wore on, leading representatives of the old elites who disputed Hitler's radical policies
continually lost power to Nazis—Hjalmar Schacht to Hermann
Göring in 1936, Werner von Blomberg to Hitler himself in
1938, and Neurath to Joachim von Ribbentrop in the same year.
This process accelerated after war began as the SS and other
Nazi agencies took over much of the administration of occupied
territories to implement Hitler's program. Lastly, Nazi wartime
occupation policies were far more radical than anything attempted during the First World War. Hitler employed new men
and new policies—policies that involved a qualitative break with
Germany's past.

Hitler came to power in January 1933 without any immediate
prospect of realizing his foreign-policy program. In the short
run, he pursued a generally defensive policy designed to
minimize risks during the critical period necessary to consolidate
the Nazi regime internally and to begin reconstructing Germany's military machine. During 1933 and 1934 he sought un-
derstandings with those foreign powers, like Britain and Italy,
whose alliance he hoped to secure to help realize his long-range
goals, and those that possessed both the motive and the opportunity to deal an immediate, mortal blow to the Nazi regime, including France, Poland, and Czechoslovakia. Hitler needed
breathing space, and in the short run he was willing to renounce
almost any of his goals for the sake of making a good impression. He had few immediate goals in Southeastern Europe; he
disliked France's Little Entente allies and sympathized with
Hungarian revisionism, but, in any case, German domestic
policies ruled out any immediate offers of commercial concessions in the southeast. In order to secure agrarian support, both
Alfred Hugenberg, the German Nationalist minister of agriculture from January through June 1933, and Walter Darré, the

Nazi ideologue who succeeded him, continued and strengthened the protectionist policies of the Papen and Schleicher governments.[12]

The one exception to Hitler's general caution and to his lack of interest in Southeastern Europe was Austria. Anschluss was probably Hitler's oldest dream, and he clearly hoped to achieve it simply by toppling Austrian Chancellor Engelbert Dollfuss and bringing a Nazi government to power in Vienna.[13] During the first few months of his rule, he undertook several unorthodox and undiplomatic steps designed to achieve the *Gleichschaltung*, or coordination, of Austria, much as he concurrently achieved the *Gleichschaltung* of the German state governments through local Nazi takeovers. These measures included large-scale Nazi party agitation in Austria, a prohibitive tax on visas for Austria in order to cut German tourist traffic, and demands for new Austrian elections—elections certain to increase Nazi representation in the Austrian parliament. He refused to conclude the pending German-Austrian preferential tariff agreement, even though Dollfuss offered to drop troublesome Austrian demands for butter and cheese preferences.[14] The Wilhelmstrasse opposed many aspects of Hitler's Austrian policy, but Hitler obviously felt that Austria was too important to leave to the diplomats. He ignored their protests while continuing to work through Nazi party channels.

Hitler's attempts to precipitate Anschluss led to several Italian, French, and British initiatives in Austria and the rest of Southeastern Europe designed to block it. These initiatives led in turn to a revival of late Weimar German commercial policy in Southeastern Europe. Paris and Rome renewed various earlier schemes for economic confederation and great-power prefer-

[12] On Hitler's foreign policy in the months after he took power see Gerhard L. Weinberg, *The Foreign Policy of Hitler's Germany: Diplomatic Revolution in Europe, 1933-1936* (Chicago, 1970), pp. 26-119. On Darré's efforts to curry favor with the peasantry see Martin Broszat, *Der Staat Hitlers. Grundlegung und Entwicklung seiner inneren Verfassung* (Munich, 1969), pp. 230-34.

[13] For fuller treatments of German-Austrian relations in 1933-1934, see Weinberg, *Foreign Policy*, pp. 87-107, Jürgen Gehl, *Austria, Germany, and the Anschluss, 1931-1938* (London, 1963), and Dieter Ross, *Hitler und Dollfuss. Die deutsche Österreich-Politik 1933-1934* (Hamburg, 1966). I have stressed only the aspects of the question having broader implications for Southeastern Europe.

[14] Weinberg, *Foreign Policy*, pp. 87-90; Gehl, *Austria*, pp. 52-58; Ritter memorandum, Apr. 11, 1933, T-120/8735/E610032-35; *DGFP*, C, I, 187.

ences, and Berlin responded by concluding disguised preferential treaties with Hungary and Yugoslavia in the winter and spring of 1934.

Benito Mussolini, who had dismissed his pro-western foreign minister, Dino Grandi, and assumed this office himself in July 1932, had already begun an Italian diplomatic offensive in Austria and Hungary when Hitler took power. Fulvio Suvich, the permanent secretary of state, hoped to build upon the Semmering agreements of 1931 to form an Austro-Hungarian-Italian political and economic bloc. Mussolini simultaneously began subsidizing the Austrian Fascist organization, the Heimwehr.[15] The Italian government also wanted to increase its economic influence in Southeastern Europe; evidently, however, it felt too weak to act alone. During 1932 and 1933 Rome therefore proposed joint economic ventures in the southeast to both Berlin and Paris. In December 1932 and January 1933 the Italian Foreign Ministry asked German Ambassador Ulrich von Hassell about the possibility of dividing up export markets in Southeastern Europe, both by territory and by product. Neurath, whom Hitler retained as foreign minister, was cool to this proposal, however, and Gerhard Köpke proposed that Germany instead use its own "economic trump cards" to break up the Little Entente, which had recently adopted a new, stronger statute of organization. Berlin did not pursue the Italian proposals.[16]

Mussolini moved quickly to consolidate his influence in both Austria and Hungary after Hitler began threatening Austrian independence in the late spring and early summer of 1933. In April Mussolini met with Austrian Chancellor Dollfuss and agreed to support Austrian independence in return for Dollfuss's promises to reform the Austrian constitution along Fascist lines and work for an Austro-Hungarian-Italian economic bloc. In July Hungarian Prime Minister Julius Gömbös agreed to join Mussolini in opposition to Anschluss. Gömbös, who had previously met with Hitler and generally encouraged both Germany and Italy to bid for his support, promised to cooperate with Mussolini's economic plans in exchange for Italian support of Hungary's territorial claims.[17]

[15] Gehl, *Austria*, pp. 45-49.
[16] *DGFP*, C, I, 14, 27, 35, 64. For the new Little Entente statute see Reichert, *Kleine Entente*, pp. 6-20.
[17] Gehl, *Austria*, pp. 50-51; *DGFP*, C, I, 382; *DDF*, 1, IV, 105.

Paris and London also reacted to Hitler's pressure upon Austria. They were still directly involved in Austrian financial questions; the new internationally guaranteed loan to Austria had been ratified by the French and British parliaments in late 1932 but had not yet been placed when Hitler came to power. Joseph Paul-Boncour, who had taken over the Quai d'Orsay in December 1932 and remained foreign minister until January 1934, believed strongly that encroachments by Nazi Germany must be resisted. Like Mussolini, he sought to aid Austria, but wanted to make such aid conditional upon Dollfuss's domestic and foreign policy. In the first half of 1933, however, two episodes showed that Mussolini had established preeminence in Vienna. First, when Austria was caught in early January reworking Italian machine guns and rifles in Hirtenberg in flagrant violation of the disarmament clauses of the Treaty of Saint-Germain, Mussolini apparently persuaded Dollfuss to reject an Anglo-French démarche of February 11 asking that Vienna publicly acknowledge this treaty violation and reexport or destroy the arms within two weeks. Despite heavy pressure from France's Little Entente allies, Paris and London had to accept an Austrian promise to reexport the arms within two months.[18] Then, after Dollfuss effectively suspended parliamentary government in Austria in mid-March, Paul-Boncour tried, but failed, to tie the Austrian loan to assurances that Dollfuss would respect the Austrian constitution. Austrian socialists pressured the French Socialist party, which formed part of the French government majority and of which Paul-Boncour had once been a member, to obtain these assurances as a condition of the loan, but Dollfuss steadfastly refused to promise to restore the constitution quickly or to consult the Austrian Socialist party on major decisions. In June Paul-Boncour agreed to let the loan go through anyway, accepting Dollfuss's contention that an alliance with the Austrian Socialists would strengthen the Austrian Nazis.[19]

Despite these setbacks, Paul-Boncour still tried to strengthen Austria economically and to erect a political and economic barrier to German expansion in Southeastern Europe. In July he tried to interest the Hungarian government in closer economic and political relations with Austria and the Little Entente, im-

---

[18] On the so-called Hirtenberg affair see Gehl, *Austria*, pp. 48-49; *DDF*, 1, II, 195-96, 210, 283, 331, 342, 347; FO 371/16631-35, C211/211/3 et seq.

[19] *DDF*, 1, III, 138, 158, 163, 183, 255, 281, 396.

plicitly offering Hungary equality of rights in armaments in return. Budapest, however, continued to insist on territorial revision in return for economic cooperation. On August 17 Paul-Boncour instructed French representatives in the Danubian states to urge their host governments to help Austria with preferences, higher import quotas, or general tariff reductions; he now hoped for Italian support in bringing the Hungarians around.[20] On August 23 an Italian Foreign Ministry official invited the French government to submit proposals regarding "the organization of the Danubian states." Paul-Boncour's reply two days later suggested preferential tariffs among the Danubian states, one-sided preferences granted by the great powers, improved communications, and cartels to supervise imports and exports—an obvious echo of the French plans of 1931 and 1932. It also proposed routing more trade through the Italian Adriatic ports of Trieste and Fiume. Although Mussolini replied on September 5 that Hungary, backed by Germany, would reject this proposal, Paul-Boncour submitted a formal aide-memoire embodying his plan on September 10. Together with French Finance Minister Georges Bonnet, the erstwhile president of the Stresa conference, he decided to push for action on the year-old Stresa recommendations at a meeting of the League Economic Committee in late September.[21]

At this meeting the Italian government presented its own proposals for the Danubian problem on September 30. They were clearly self-serving. Rejecting any new large-scale Danubian economic grouping—an obvious concession to the Hungarian position—they called for great-power cereals preferences and preferences for Austrian industrial goods. In return, each Danubian state would extend preferences to any great power with which it had a positive trade balance. Among the great powers, only Italy bought more than it sold in trade with the Danubian states. Although French and Little Entente representatives interpreted the plan as an attempt to tie Austria end Hungary to Italy and keep them out of any economic combination including the Little Entente, the French endorsed the broad objectives of the Italian proposal in order to maintain Franco-Italian cooperation.[22] The Italian government, however, did not

[20] DDF, 1, IV, 15, 23, 105, 118; British embassy Paris to FO, Sept. 8, 1933, FO 371/16679, C8247/76/62.

[21] DDF, 1, IV, 133, 143, 180, 193, 281.   [22] DDF, 1, IV, 281.

press for international adoption of these proposals, preferring to use them as a basis for its unilateral agreements with Austria and Hungary in February 1934.[23] The principal effect of the memorandum seems to have been to prevent the French, who were determined to maintain a common front with Italy on Austria and the southeast, from pressing ahead more resolutely on their own.

Although the British government took little part in these new discussions of multilateral help for the Danubian states, the Austrian government approached London directly in an effort to increase Austrian exports to the United Kingdom and counter Hitler's new boycott of Austrian trade. The Austrian approach triggered a debate within the British government that foreshadowed further efforts to interest London in economic help for Southeastern Europe later in the decade.

British civil servants and cabinet ministers intermittently discussed economic help for Austria from June 1933 through February 1934. Sir Robert Vansittart, the permanent undersecretary of state, emerged as the leading proponent of help for Austria. Vansittart was anxious to prevent Anschluss, and he argued as early as August 1933 that war with Nazi Germany was probably inevitable.[24] In August, after discussing with several Austrian officials a means of increasing Austro-British trade, he had the Central Department draw up a list of Austrian products for which Britain might give tariff preferences. The list included velour hats, wireless valves, and timber. At an interdepartmental meeting of civil servants on September 12, however, Board of Trade and Treasury representatives argued that Austrian hats and electrical equipment competed with British products and that timber concessions would provoke objections from Canada. Rather than extend British preferences, these representatives wanted to protest the Austro-Polish preferential agreement, which had increased Austrian imports of Polish coal at Britain's expense. In a letter to Vansittart of September 18, Sir Horace Hamilton of the Board of Trade attacked the principle of lowering tariffs for political reasons. The Board's opposition subse-

[23] See below, p. 76.
[24] See Vansittart's Aug. 28, 1933, memorandum for the cabinet, *DBFP*, 2, V, 254; Gehl, *Austria*, pp. 62-63; Ian Colvin, *Vansittart in Office* (London, 1965), pp. 27-29.

quently doomed an Austrian proposal for a barter arrangement involving British coal and Austrian timber.[25]

The British cabinet considered this issue in early 1934, after Vienna had again asked for preferences. In meetings on January 24 and 31 and February 2 the cabinet accepted the argument of its Board of Trade president, Runciman, that "our circumstances did not permit us to give direct assistance to Austria." Runciman was overruled on January 31 when he argued that Britain should not waive most-favored-nation rights even if other states gave tariff preferences to Austria, but on February 8 he told Austrian representatives that no British preferences would be given.[26]

In late 1933 the Austrian government received more bad news, this time from Paris, where French timber interests successfully blocked the application of preferential tariffs for Austrian timber, as embodied in the Franco-Austrian treaty of December 30, 1932. Minuting his disappointment on a report of this development, Vansittart noted, "we can't say much about it, as that is really the attitude of our own Board of Trade." British commercial interests and their allies at the Board of Trade and Treasury disliked mixing trade and politics; having fallen upon hard times, they were especially reluctant to make even small sacrifices in the name of foreign policy.[27] In the course of the decade, leading figures of the National Government, including Runciman, Sir John Simon, and Neville Chamberlain, would show that they shared these views. In neither London nor Paris could diplomats successfully assert the primacy of foreign policy over domestic economic interests—not, at least, where Eastern Europe was concerned. The German government undertook new initiatives in Eastern Europe because the Wilhelmstrasse successfully asserted the primacy of foreign policy and because German economic policy changed in ways that favored increased trade with Eastern Europe.

[25] Vansittart minutes of June 20, 24, 1933, FO 371/16647, C5609/5609/3, C5761/5761/3; FO memorandum, Aug. 30, interdepartmental meeting, Sept. 12, Hamilton's letter of Sept. 18, FO 371/16630, C7991/C8154/C7990/C8306/8/3. On the barter arrangement see ibid., C8509/8/3.

[26] Cabinets of Jan. 24, 31, Feb. 7, 1934, CAB 23/78; see also CP's 19, 35 & 39 (34), CAB 24/227.

[27] FO 371/16635, C8151/8/3.

Despite the failure of the various anti-German schemes for Southeastern Europe to make significant headway, the Wilhelmstrasse in late 1933 persuaded the rest of the German government that French, Italian, and Czechoslovak efforts to raise barriers against Germany in Southeastern Europe demanded some response. At the same time, the German government reorganized Germany's commercial relations with foreign countries in ways that allowed preferences to be given to the southeastern states without directly infringing upon others' most-favored-nation rights. Berlin concluded far-reaching commercial agreements with Hungary and Yugoslavia in February and May 1934, respectively, and with Rumania in March 1935. The Nazi government succeeded where Weimar had failed.

The German government, including Hitler personally, had to face the question of economic help for Southeastern Europe several times during the first half of 1933 but reacted slowly because of the priority of other issues and the effects of domestic economic policy. Hitler himself evaded both Hungarian and Rumanian requests for increased trade, arguing that German agricultural difficulties and, in the latter case, unfriendly Rumanian political attitudes stood in the way.[28] Hungary and Rumania retaliated with discriminatory measures against German trade; the Rumanians, whose financial difficulties had forced them to adopt strict import controls, began refusing import certificates for German goods, while the Hungarian government took similar measures and on May 13 denounced the German-Hungarian clearing agreement, which regulated all trade between the two countries. The HPA decided not to retaliate against Rumania in turn, but domestic agricultural policy restricted any attempts to come to terms.[29] In the short run, it seemed that German trade with these states might cease almost completely.

While the German bureaucracy stood by paralyzed, private interests worked out temporary *modi vivendi* to continue some trade. IG Farben, which had monopolized German dye and

[28] See Gömbös's Feb. 7 and Apr. 22 letters to Hitler and Hitler's reply, *DGFP*, C, I, 15, 179, 195; Rumanian Minister Nicolas Comnène's May 27 memorandum and conversation with Hitler, T-120/9580/E675060-63.

[29] *DGFP*, C, I, 247; Hungarian note of May 13, 1933, T-120/9583/E675105-7; German legation Bucharest to AA, Apr. 3, T-120/9711/E573157-59; AA circular, Apr. 20, ibid., E573179-80.

chemical production since its formation in the 1920s, was vitally interested in trade with Southeastern Europe, where international cartel arrangements in 1930-1931 had given it a commanding position. Karl Duisberg, its chairman of the board, had long advocated increased German trade with Southeastern Europe. The depression had sharply reduced the IG's exports to the Danubian states, and the huge company was seeking ways to continue trade despite exchange controls and German protectionism. Encouraged by Karl Ritter, who knew leading officials of the firm well, the IG began with Hungary, where it held large frozen credits. The firm decided to offer to purchase Hungarian cereals in exchange for new Hungarian purchases of its own exports and to evade domestic objections by reexporting these cereals to Holland, Britain, and Scandinavia.[30]

The responsible agencies of the German government quickly agreed to this procedure and helped to conclude a new arrangement along these lines on June 2 in Budapest. The German negotiators included representatives of the Budapest legation, the Economics Ministry, and the IG, and Werner Daitz of Alfred Rosenberg's Aussenpolitisches Amt (Foreign Policy Office; APA) of the Nazi party. The APA sought to encourage trade with Southeastern Europe—in which Daitz, the head of its Foreign Trade Office, believed firmly—in order to extend its own sphere of bureaucratic influence within the German government. We shall see that these attempts led to a direct clash with the Foreign Office in the fall of 1934 and to a defeat for the Nazi organization. Under the June 2 agreement, IG Farben promised to buy Hungarian cereals at the Hungarian market price, about 50 percent higher than the world price as a result of the Hungarian government's insistence on maintaining the Hungarian pengo at the official gold parity. IG Farben thus incurred a substantial loss in reexporting these cereals to the Netherlands, Britain, and Scandinavia, but the company partially made up for the loss by charging high prices for its own exports to Hungary.[31]

[30] Hans Radant, "Die IG Farbenindustrie AG und Südosteuropa bis 1938," *Jahrbuch für Wirtschaftsgeschichte*, 1966, pt. 3, pp. 150-61; Teichova, *Economic Background to Munich*, p. 285.

[31] Weinberg, *Foreign Policy*, pp. 112-13; Elek Karsai, "The Meeting of Gömbös and Hitler in 1933," *New Hungarian Quarterly*, III, no. 5 (1962), 172-78; Radant, "IG Farbenindustrie," pp. 155-56; agreement of June 2, 1934, T-120/9583/ E675124-30.

In August IG Farben negotiated a similar but more extensive compensation agreement with Rumania, promising to purchase several hundred thousand tons of Rumanian grain valued at 17.0 million RM in exchange for Rumanian purchases of 13.6-million-RM worth of German exports. Since IG Farben intended to reexport the cereals, the ultimate effect of the agreement on the German trade balance was favorable. The Reichsbank objected that the Rumanians had secured excessively favorable terms and that the agreement would not bring in enough foreign currency, but IG Farben persuaded the Wilhelmstrasse that the bargain was a good one in the context of Rumanian trade policy and would prevent France from supplanting Germany in Rumanian trade.[32]

The German government, however, did nothing to follow up on these private initiatives during the summer of 1933. Although Gömbös became the first foreign leader to visit Hitler on June 17-18, Hitler made no specific commitments in the economic sphere.[33] German and Hungarian officials discussed trade in Berlin during July and August without reaching agreement.[34] In late September, however, reports of Mussolini's efforts to create an Austro-Hungarian-Italian economic bloc stimulated German interest in an agreement with Hungary. On September 26 the German commercial attaché in Budapest reported that Gömbös had begun economic talks with Rome and Vienna in desperation but that he would prefer an economic rapprochement with Germany. Germany, he suggested, should give Hungary some form of preference or subsidy to make purchases of Hungarian goods possible despite the inflated Hungarian exchange rate.[35] Then, when on September 30 the Italian government presented its memorandum in Geneva, Karl Ritter eagerly seized upon it as a means of reviving the idea of German preferences for Southeastern Europe; clearly, he noted, it would make Germany's policy of the last few years easier to put into effect. He quickly issued a press communiqué praising this new

[32] Radant, "IG Farbenindustrie," pp. 186-95; *DGFP*, C, I, 414, 415; IG Farben to Neurath, Sept. 21, 1933, T-120/9698/E682907-13.

[33] Weinberg, *Foreign Policy*, 113-14.

[34] AA memorandum of July 14, 1933, HPA meeting of Aug. 18, T-120/9580/E675034-35, 5650/H003714.

[35] T-120/6145/E459904. See *DGFP*, C, I, 464, for another contemporary Hungarian approach.

Italian endorsement of long-held German views but opposing the provision under which the Danubian states would extend preferences in return to great powers having a passive trade balance with them. The German government was soon pleased to learn that Budapest also disliked this proposal.[36]

In the meantime, Hans Posse of the Economics Ministry successfully brought about a reorientation of German trade policy calculated to increase German trade with Eastern Europe. By the fall of 1933 German foreign trade had entered a crisis. Imports were increasing rapidly because of domestic economic recovery; exports were not keeping pace because of the rapid increase in domestic demand, the overvaluation of the reichsmark in relation to the devalued pound and dollar, and the imposition of trade barriers in Britain and France. Germany was already tightening exchange controls, and the problem of servicing German foreign debts was the subject of major commercial negotiations.[37] To meet this crisis, Posse suggested new, bilateral trading agreements designed to stabilize German foreign trade.

Despite the proliferation of exchange control in Central Europe, the German government in September 1933 remained committed to the free exchange of goods and to multilateral trade. For decades Germany had depended on triangular trade, whereby large imports of overseas foodstuffs and raw materials were paid for with exports to European neighbors. Although during 1932 Berlin had been forced to conclude clearing agreements with several Southeastern European states—themselves beset with financial difficulties—in order to continue trade, the German government regarded these pacts as emergency measures and disliked their tendency to balance imports and exports with the countries involved. As late as September 1933 the HPA agreed that Germany had to maintain an active trade balance with the maximum possible number of countries and should offer equal bilateral trade only in special circum-

---

[36] Ritter memorandum of Sept. 30, 1933, press communiqué, AA minute of Oct. 6, T-120/9160/E644364-74.

[37] For the most comprehensive, though far from definitive, discussion of the German trade crisis see Dörte Doering, "Deutsche Aussenwirtschaftspolitik 1933-35" (Ph.D. diss., Free University of Berlin, 1969). For negotiations on German foreign debt payments see the long but indispensable study by Bernd Jürgen Wendt, *Economic Appeasement: Handel und Finanzin der britischen Deutschland-Politik 1933-1939* (Düsseldorf, 1971), pp. 118-78.

stances.[38] In October, however, Berlin began to reverse this policy.

On October 4 Posse, now state secretary in the Economics Ministry, discussed German commercial policy at a cabinet meeting. Since regaining its freedom to impose tariffs in 1925, he began, Germany had pursued a commercial policy based on world trade and the most-favored-nation clause. In recent years, however, several nations had moved away from the most-favored-nation principle and toward bilateralism. Britain had adopted tariffs and imperial preferences, and the French quota system limited German exports to France. In light of these new circumstances, Posse asked the cabinet to approve an "active commercial policy based on reciprocity"—in other words, import only from countries willing to purchase equivalent quantities of German exports. Germany should concentrate on "markets ruled by German merchants, especially Southeastern Europe and the Northern European states." The new Italian plan, he noted, provided a partial framework for such a policy. The cabinet endorsed this policy after a very brief discussion. Hitler was not present, but Papen, acting as his representative, stated that the chancellor approved this new step, "particularly with regard to Hungary and the other countries of Southeastern Europe."[39]

Posse's proposals cleared the way for a revolution in German trade policy. Germany had depended on world trade since the industrial revolution; only the Allied blockade during the First World War had forced it to rely upon neighboring states for the maximum possible imports and exports. In effect, Posse was proposing a return to wartime policy in order to meet increased international competition for markets and trade. His attempt to balance Germany's trade with almost all its trading partners foreshadowed Schacht's New Plan of September 1934. The new policy accorded with Hitler's long-range goals insofar as it enabled Germany to draw some vital imports from strategically more secure sources and to control imports qualitatively to ensure that the needs of German rearmament were met. In the long run, however, such a policy could only emphasize the impossibility of fulfilling German economic needs solely within Eastern and Northern Europe; it would ultimately face Germany with a choice between economic collapse and a war of expansion.

[38] T-120/5650/H003733.   [39] T-120/3598/D793929-31.

Because the German bureaucracy had to negotiate a vital trade treaty with Holland first, Berlin did not approach Hungary for new talks until December. On January 17 Neurath, Finance Minister Count Schwerin von Krosigk and Economics Minister Kurt Schmitt specifically agreed to give some form of preferential treatment to Hungarian agricultural exports, largely in order to block Italian attempts "to bring about an Italo-Austro-Hungarian customs union." The preferences would somehow have to be concealed in order to evade German obligations to other countries under the most-favored-nation clause; at the same time, the ministers recognized that some other countries would have to be offered the same concessions given to Hungary, but they concluded that "Since we are willing . . . to change over to a completely new system of commercial policy," this problem was not insuperable.[40] Six days later, the HPA agreed upon the form that the new preferences for Hungarian goods would take. Hungarian exchange control had frozen large German credits in Hungary; Germany would contribute to Hungarian export subsidies out of these German balances, presumbably compensating German investors with some form of German government securities. These subsidies would overcome the disadvantage accruing to Hungarian exporters as a result of Budapest's insistence on maintaining the pengo at the official gold parity.[41]

The new German-Hungarian treaty, signed on February 21, 1934, after about one month of negotiations, served in many ways as a model for other German commercial agreements with Eastern European states. Published sections of the treaty included German promises to import 100,000 tons of Hungarian wheat (half to be reexported) and 75,000 tons total of corn and fodder barley annually. The Hungarians also received specified import quotas for butter and eggs, based on a formula embodied in the German-Dutch commercial treaty of December 1933, and limited facilities for cattle exports to Germany. The German Agriculture Ministry had evidently realized that Germany could not be self-sufficient in all areas of food production. In return, Hungary lowered tariffs on numerous items of special interest to Germany, including hats, shoes, plastics, glassware, steel, machine tools, and electrical goods. Because of

[40] *DGFP*, C, II, 189.
[41] HPA meeting of Jan. 23, 1934, T-120/5650/H003822-23.

Hungary's desperate foreign-exchange position, Berlin also undertook to sell Hungary specified quantities of certain products, including coffee, tea, and various metals, that could only be bought on the world market with hard currency.

The secret clauses of the treaty spelled out procedures for paying Hungarian export subsidies out of frozen German pengo accounts. The treaty also set up a new clearing system for payments between the two countries. Germany would make almost all payments for Hungarian goods in reichsmarks, depositing them in a special clearing account maintained by the Hungarian National Bank at the Reichsbank. The Hungarians would draw on this account to pay for their purchases from Germany; they could therefore buy German goods equal in value to their exports to Germany. No one seems to have suspected that they might have trouble finding enough goods on which to spend their money. Like the earlier German-Dutch commercial treaty, this treaty set up German and Hungarian government committees of civil servants to monitor the application of its provisions and, when necessary, to discuss changes. The treaty was scheduled to run for three years as a means of guaranteeing Hungary a stable export market.[42]

The Wilhelmstrasse expected substantial political benefits from the treaty; as Bülow suggested to the Chancellery, it was designed to strengthen Hungary's political independence vis-à-vis both Italy and the Little Entente. The Foreign Office was therefore somewhat taken aback when Gömbös, Dollfuss, and Mussolini concluded the so-called Rome Protocols, providing for closer economic and political relations among their three states, in Rome on March 17. Bülow, however, suggested that Italy had secured less than it had hoped for; Rome had wanted real steps toward a customs union but had to be content with a slight extension of the disguised export subsidies embodied in the 1931 Semmering agreements. In fact, the Rome Protocols had far less effect on Hungarian trade than the new German-Hungarian treaty.[43]

[42] For the text of the treaty and supplementary agreements see T-120/K6145/E459937-90. See also Berend and Ránki, *Economic Development*, pp. 268-71.

[43] *DGFP*, C, II, 322, 328. The Italian shares of Hungarian and Austrian trade never approached the German shares; see LNP, *International Trade Statistics* (Geneva, various years) (hereafter *ITS*), *1933*, pp. 32, 142, *1936*, pp. 32, 139, *1938*, pp. 93, 200.

The German government then moved to head off the second major danger to its interests in Southeastern Europe: the formation of a hostile economic bloc based upon the political alliance of the Little Entente. Berlin opened talks on a new trade treaty with Yugoslavia in March; Ritter noted that Germany "would have preferred to gain a firmer economic foothold in Rumania," but this seemed impossible as long as Nicolai Titulescu, who was known for his pro-French sympathies, remained Rumania's foreign minister.[44] Under the new German-Yugoslav commercial treaty of May 1, 1934, Germany promised to purchase 50,000 tons each of Yugoslav wheat and corn annually, the wheat to be reexported. The Germans also undertook to purchase substantial quantities of Yugoslav lard, oil seeds, fruits, and vegetables, effectively extending preferences on these products by promising to pay inflated prices for them. In return, Yugoslavia lowered its tariffs on rubber, textiles, glass, iron and steel products, machines, and electrical goods—all products of special interest to Germany. In a circular of June 21, 1934, the Foreign Office noted that the treaty was designed to give Germany "an economic foothold in Yugoslavia and thus also in the Little Entente from which it would be possible to prevent or at least render very difficult Yugoslavia's becoming economically bound up with other countries contrary to our wishes." The extent of German concessions to Yugoslavia, the circular added, coupled with the possibility of terminating the agreement at a crucial moment, "place us in the position of being able, if required, to exert adequate pressure on Yugoslavia."[45]

Berlin finally concluded a similar agreement with Rumania in March 1935. Although private interests, the Rumanian government, and the APA proposed several large-scale compensation agreements with Rumania during 1934, the German government did not decide to begin serious trade talks until December of that year. The reason was largely political; Neurath told the Rumanian minister to Berlin on May 28 that Germany, in Hitler's words, could not make sacrifices for nations that maintained an unfriendly political attitude. In addition, Hjalmar Schacht, who had returned as Reichsbank president in February 1933 and became economics minister in September 1934, op-

---

[44] *DGFP*, C, II, 318.
[45] For the text of the treaty see T-120/7684/E547721-846; for the circular, *DGFP*, C, III, 23.

posed German-Rumanian compensation agreements on economic grounds. Such agreements, he argued, generally sold German goods too cheaply and bought foreign products too dearly, and any new German-Rumanian agreement should allow Germany to buy Rumanian oil without spending foreign exchange.[46] The APA briefly secured agreement on a 10-million-RM German-Rumanian compensation agreement in October; the Nazi office hoped to channel some of the money to Octavian Goga, a right-wing Rumanian politician whom it subsidized for several years. When Neurath discussed this agreement with Hitler on November 2, however, Hitler denied the APA's claim that he had approved it, and he rejected "once and for all" the use of business dealings to influence the internal affairs of foreign countries.[47] This episode apparently finished the APA's efforts to control trade with Southeastern Europe; it never again played a major role in commercial negotiations during the 1930s.

The HPA finally authorized new negotiations on December 17, one month after the Rumanian government had denounced the existing German-Rumanian trade treaties.[48] Schacht then raised two new issues. The first grew out of Rumanian reparations claims on Germany arising out of the Treaty of Versailles. During the 1920s the Rumanians had converted German cash obligations due them as reparations into long-term orders for German goods, and the Germans had demanded payment for these goods as soon as reparations were canceled in 1932. The second issue involved Rumanian oil. Schacht, as we shall see,

[46] See the proposals by the Rumanian government and the German-Rumanian Chamber of Commerce, Feb. 9, 1934, T-120/9692/E681984-2004; Howard Ellis, *Exchange Control in Central Europe* (Cambridge, Mass. 1941), pp. 173, 217-21; Sarnow memorandum, Dec. 19, 1933, T-120/9692/E681978-90; *DGFP*, C, II, 468. The Germans and Rumanians concluded a 5-million-RM compensation agreement on June 5, 1934; see T-120/9692/E682075-76.

[47] On the APA's support of Goga see Jacobsen, *Aussenpolitik*, pp. 79-83. On this controversy see also: the AA memorandum of Aug. 23, 1934, T-120/9697/E682820-21; German legation Bucharest to AA, ibid., E682825-28; memorandum by Otto Sarnow, Sept. 24, 1934, ibid., E682818-19; Carl Clodius to Economics Ministry, Oct. 8, ibid., E682381; HPA meeting, Oct. 11, T-120/5650/H003954; *DGFP*, C, III, 295.

[48] German legation Bucharest to AA, Nov. 1, 1934, T-120/9711/E683204-8; Rumanian note of Nov. 16, T-120/9696/E682743; HPA meeting of Dec. 17, T-120/5650/H003981.

generally opposed paying generous prices for Southeastern European agricultural products, and in this case he wanted better access to Rumanian oil fields—in which Germany had been heavily interested before the First World War—in return for high prices for Rumanian cereals and cattle. Specifically, he proposed the formation of a new German-Rumanian oil company to exploit new deposits; the Germans would supply financing, men, and equipment, receiving repayment in the form of deliveries of Rumanian oil.[49]

Despite the Germans' eagerness to settle these two questions, the new commercial treaty they signed with Rumania on March 23 did not include agreements on either one. Bucharest was anxious to conclude a quick agreement, and Berlin contented itself with Rumanian promises to try to solve these questions in good faith. Instead, the Germans promised to buy specific quotas of Rumanian poultry, eggs, timber, and cattle, as well as unspecified quantities of cereals. They refused, however, to import Rumanian pigs. The treaty specified high prices for many Rumanian products; in return, Bucharest lowered its tariffs on many products of interest to Germany. Two months later, Helmut Wohlthat of the Reichstelle für Devisenbewirtschaftung, a new German agency charged with supervising German exchange control, negotiated details of a clearing agreement in Bucharest. Rumania would receive a 20 percent surplus of exports over imports to pay old debts and miscellaneous payments to Germany; the Germans would pay for about 30 percent of their oil imports from Rumania in foreign exchange or in goods that could only be purchased for foreign exchange on the world market.[50] He failed to reach agreement, however, either on reparations claims or on a German-Rumanian oil company.

Under the Nazi government, the Foreign Office and the Economics Ministry had successfully implemented the policies they had first conceived in 1931 by concluding new, far-reaching commercial agreements with the agricultural states of South-

[49] DGFP, C, IV, 6.

[50] On the talks see the AA memorandum of Feb. 16, 1935, T-120/9696/E682771-74, and DGFP, C, III, 551. For the text of the Mar. 23 treaty see T-120/7683/E547675-718. For the agreement of May 15, 1935, see T-120/9692/E682117-34.

eastern Europe. They dramatically increased German trade with Southeastern Europe in the years to come. Hitler himself had played only an indirect role in this development; the policy of increased trade with Southeastern Europe had preceded him, and he played virtually no part in negotiating the agreements of 1934-1935. In succeeding years, however, his influence on German trade with Eastern Europe increased. Although the Wilhelmstrasse retained most of the responsibility for commercial negotiations with the successor states, the course of German trade with Eastern Europe depended increasingly on National Socialist economic policy as a whole. This, in turn, tended to follow the dictates of Hitler's expansionist plans.

IV.

British Trade Policy and Eastern Europe, 1931-1935

While the German government tried to extend its economic and political influence in Eastern Europe during the 1930s, the British government avoided political commitments and neglected economic opportunities throughout the region, particularly in Northeastern Europe. British prestige remained high throughout Eastern Europe, and especially in the Baltic states, during most of the interwar period. The British government had helped to keep the Baltic littoral out of both German and Russian hands during the turbulent years following the First World War, and the new states of Estonia, Latvia, and Lithuania had never forgotten it.[1] During the 1920s, the new states had tailored their agriculture to Britain's needs, particularly encouraging the production of bacon, of which the United Kingdom was the world's only significant importer, and of butter and eggs, of which Britain also purchased substantial quantities.[2] By 1929 Britain was the leading importer of Latvian and Estonian products, with Germany a close second. In Lithuania the situation was reversed, principally because of the heavy trade between Germany and the formerly German territory of Memel. Britain's exports to the Baltic states, however, lagged far behind its imports and far behind German exports to the same countries. In effect, the Baltic states paid for their German trade deficit with their British trade surplus. Poland enjoyed a similar situation.[3] Although British trade with Southeastern Europe during the 1920s was much less significant, Britain's policy of free trade in grain made it at least a potential customer of the Danubian

[1] Edgar Anderson, "The British Policy toward the Baltic States 1918-20," *Journal of Central European Affairs*, XIX, no. 3 (1959), 276-89.

[2] See above, Chapter II.

[3] For figures on the trade of Northeastern Europe in the late 1920s see LN, *ITS 1930*, pp. 109-12, 172-81.

states. During the 1930s, however, Britain neglected Eastern Europe because of conscious decisions to stimulate domestic and empire production at the expense of commerce with foreign nations. In 1932-1933 London imposed a general tariff, instituted imperial tariff preferences, and established quotas to protect home agriculture. These restrictions especially affected British trade with Eastern Europe, reducing commerce and making it virtually impossible for the British government to respond to the numerous calls for help addressed to it by the Eastern Europeans during the rest of the decade.

This trade policy reflected the general policy of the National Government, which ruled Britain from 1931 through 1940 under Prime Ministers J. Ramsay MacDonald, Stanley Baldwin, and Neville Chamberlain. Called into being by the economic crisis of 1931, the National Government placed its highest priority upon the restoration of the British economy. In foreign policy, it emphasized the defense of the British Empire and tried to keep European involvement within tight, well-defined limits. The British Foreign Office, which had traditionally favored free trade and emphasized Britain's European role, recognized the consequences of the new trade policy and argued against it. But within the National Government the Foreign Office enjoyed little prestige, often failing to secure even the support of its own secretary of state. Its advice was ignored in the course of the key decisions of 1931-1932, and it was unable to reverse those decisions during the rest of the decade.

The National Government came into office in August 1931, after Ramsay MacDonald's Labour Government had split on the issue of reducing unemployment insurance to halt a run on the pound. Sterling owed its long-term weakness to the 1925 decision to restore the pound to its prewar gold value. The National Government promptly went off the gold standard and in October 1931 won a landslide victory over those Labourites who had broken with it, including former Foreign Secretary Arthur Henderson.[4] Although MacDonald continued as prime minister, the Conservative party supplied most of the National Gov-

---

[4] A.J.P. Taylor, *English History, 1914-1945*, Pelican edition (London, 1970), pp. 357-73; Robert Skidelsky, *Politicians and the Slump: The Labour Government of 1929-1931* (London, 1967).

ernment's key ministers and effectively controlled the new cabinet. Lord President of the Council Stanley Baldwin and Chancellor of the Exchequer Neville Chamberlain quickly emerged as its most important members. The return of the Tories to effective power and Britain's continuing balance of payments problems combined to raise the question of a general tariff. Baldwin's earlier attempt to impose a tariff under the Conservative Government of 1923 had led to a Tory defeat in the 1924 general election, but under the impact of the depression the idea that Britain should abandon free trade for the sake of its home industries was gaining ground.[5] The National Government had discussed the possibility of going to the country on a protectionist platform before the October general election, but because of the opposition of its Liberal ministers, led by Home Secretary Sir Herbert Samuel, it had contented itself with a vague formula referring to a need for steps to improve the state of British industry. After the election, however, the cabinet created a committee on the balance of trade, with Neville Chamberlain as chairman, to discuss measures to improve that balance.[6]

Chamberlain quickly took charge. In theory, the committee was supposed to devise ways to improve the trade balance; in fact, Chamberlain wanted to use this pretext to impose a general tariff on manufactured goods as a means of stimulating home industry. Chamberlain proposed a general 10 percent ad valorem tariff on all imports, with provision for higher duties on industrial products especially competitive with British home production. In response to Liberal President of the Board of Trade Walter Runciman's objections, he agreed to exempt wheat, meat, and bacon from the general tariff. The Balance of Trade Committee reported to the cabinet on January 19, 1932, arguing that the tariff would immediately improve the balance of trade by reducing imports and that it would provide the government with a bargaining counter enabling Britain to secure reductions in foreign tariffs in future commercial negotiations. The tariff would also allow the government to offer the British Dominions tariff preferences or free entry for their goods in exchange for Dominion tariff concessions on British goods at the

[5] Taylor, *English History*, pp. 266-69, 408-12.
[6] Cabinets of Oct. 2, 6, and Dec. 11, 1931, CAB 23/68-69.

forthcoming Ottawa Imperial Conference. The cabinet approved a balance of trade bill based on the committee's report on January 29.[7]

Simultaneously, another cabinet committee was preparing for the Ottawa conference scheduled for July 1932. The committee originally included only Chamberlain, Runciman, Dominions Secretary J. H. Thomas, and Agriculture and Fisheries Minister Walter Elliott. It was subsequently enlarged to include the foreign and colonial secretaries, but, despite the clear foreign-policy implications of the committee's work, Foreign Secretary Simon never attended its meetings. In effect, the committee members asked what concessions the government could offer the Dominions in exchange for reduction of the Dominions' high tariffs on British goods. They immediately agreed to offer the Dominions a wheat quota in excess of their existing share of British wheat imports and discussed the possibility of preferential tariffs for the Dominions on butter and eggs. Perhaps because Liberal ministers still objected to duties on foodstuffs, the full cabinet reserved its decision on preferential tariffs on agricultural goods while embracing the principle of imperial preference in general in December 1931.[8]

In the midst of these deliberations, the Foreign Office made one desperate attempt to prevent new trade policies from reducing British influence in Europe. On December 2, 1931, Sir John Simon circulated to his cabinet colleagues a Foreign Office memorandum on the European situation and the potential consequences of tariffs and imperial preference. The first part of the memorandum drew heavily upon a September 27 minute by Sir Orme Sargent, which stressed the close connection between the European problems of disarmament, security, reparations and war debts, and trade barriers and the need for them to be attacked simultaneously rather than individually. The memorandum then discussed the potential effects of new British tariffs, especially if duties were subsequently frozen under im-

[7] January 1932 memorandum on the Balance of Trade Committee and its deliberations, Neville Chamberlain papers, University of Birmingham Library, Birmingham, England, NC 8/18/1; report of the Balance of Trade Committee, Jan. 19, 1932, CAB 24/227, CP 25 (32); cabinet of Jan. 29, CAB 23/70.

[8] Cabinets of Nov. 13, 18, 1931, CAB 23/69; Ottawa Preparatory Committee meetings of Nov. 16, 23, and Dec. 14, CAB 27/473; cabinets of Dec. 2, 16, CAB 23/69.

perial preference agreements. British tariffs, it noted, could serve as a lever to reduce foreign tariffs or as a wall around the British Empire—but not both. Whitehall argued that British tariffs should be used as a bargaining counter in a comprehensive effort to reach a general settlement of European problems. Well aware that others might regard tariffs and imperial preference as outside the Foreign Office's terms of reference, the authors of the memorandum stated their case somewhat defensively, but unequivocally:

> It is not within the competence of the Foreign Office to advise as to the relative advantages of the Dominions markets and of other foreign (and especially European) markets for British exports. It is, however, our duty to emphasize the great importance of the British market in foreign countries, and to draw attention to the evident anxiety with which they regard any tariff proposals in Great Britain.
>
> . . . we must expect retaliation, and we must be prepared to bear the consequences. A high protective tariff, combined with Empire preference, implies a measure of dissociation from Europe, a corresponding diminution of our influence over European affairs, and possibly a growth of economic antagonism. . . .
>
> *To our foreign policy, therefore, this tariff question is all important.* We urge that it should not be decided purely on grounds of domestic or Empire convenience; but that, especially in view of the present crisis, its efficacy as an instrument of foreign policy should be given the fullest consideration.[9]

In retrospect, this is a powerful memorandum; many of its predictions were accurate. Within the cabinet, however, there was no one to fight for it; it was never discussed at any length or even submitted to the cabinet committees on tariffs and imperial preference. Sir John Simon, who must have been prevailed upon by his subordinates to submit the paper, foresook the advocate's role. "The considerations in the Memorandum," he told his cabinet colleagues on December 2, "deserved the most careful attention, but he had not yet formulated his own conclusions

[9] CAB 24/225. CP 301 (31) (italics in original). For Sargent's original minute see FO 371/15197, C7932/172/62. This is evidently the "Sargent chain" memorandum discussed in Martin Gilbert, *The Roots of Appeasement* (London, 1966), pp. 130-31.

on them."[10] Simon, like most of his colleagues, put more stock in the protection of British industry than in European policy considerations.

When the government introduced the general 10 percent tariff in February, it exempted the Dominions and India from it in preparation for the forthcoming imperial conference. Further meetings of the British government preparatory committee also decided to establish a low tariff on imported wheat—once again exempting the Dominions—after British grain traders complained that the quota scheme would be too complicated. Cabinet discussions on the terms Britain was prepared to offer were kept to a minimum in the weeks before the conference, probably because Liberal ministers opposed tariffs on foodstuffs.[11]

The British delegation to the Ottawa Imperial Conference of July and August 1932 included Baldwin, Chamberlain, and Runciman. It faced a difficult task. After the conference the delegates claimed to have achieved the vague but emotionally satisfying goal of tightening the bonds of empire. In reality, they were merely entering into commercial negotiations with several effectively independent countries, including Canada, South Africa, Australia, New Zealand, and, in many respects, India. Britain could give these trading partners concessions only at the expense of other, technically, "foreign" countries whose trade was often of equal or greater importance to the United Kingdom, including the Scandinavian countries, the United States, and Argentina. Nevertheless, the British Foreign Office had almost no representation at the Ottawa conference. Relations with the Dominions and India were the province of the Dominions and India offices. The senior Foreign Office official present at the conference was H. O. Chalkley, commercial counselor at the British embassy in Washington. Frank Ashton-Gwatkin of the Foreign Office attended the conference as an observer and reported on the proceedings to Whitehall, but the Foreign Office was clearly not expected to react to the proceedings on a day-

[10] CAB 23/69.

[11] Cabinet of Feb. 3, 1932, CAB 23/70; Ottawa Preparatory Committee meetings of May 3, 24, 1932, CAB 27/473; cabinets of July 12 and Aug. 4, 1932, CAB 23/71.

to-day basis. Ashton-Gwatkin's reports traveled to London by ship, arriving ten days to two weeks after they were written.[12]

Despite the absence of Foreign Office leaders, the conference turned on a major issue of British foreign policy: the imposition of tariffs and quotas on foreign foodstuffs. The Dominions asked for preferential treatment for their agricultural produce in return for lowering their own tariffs, and the British delegation ultimately gave in to their requests.[13] Britain agreed to maintain the 10 percent ad valorem tariff and new duties on foreign eggs, butter, cheese, and wheat for five years, thus precluding any reduction of these duties in negotiations with foreign countries. Although London had never before regulated imports quantitatively, the government agreed to meat and bacon quotas designed to reduce foreign imports by 20 to 30 percent. The immediate effects of these measures on foreign countries were obvious. The meat quota hit Argentina especially hard, while the new bacon quotas and the tariffs on butter and eggs severely affected the Scandinavian countries, the Baltic states, and Poland. The situation of foreign bacon exporters was particularly critical because Britain was the world's only significant bacon importer. The Board of Trade immediately began planning commercial negotiations with these countries in order to stabilize trade under the new conditions. Although the Board recognized that it could offer little more than promises not to introduce additional restrictions, it nonetheless intended to ask for effective measures to increase British exports in return. It was especially anxious to increase exports to the Scandinavian and Baltic countries, with which Britain had large negative trade balances.[14]

When the Ottawa agreements came before the British cabinet, they quickly led to the resignation of Liberal Home Secretary Sir Herbert Samuel and Labour Lord Chancellor Lord Snowden. Baldwin and Chamberlain admitted that in the short run Britain had perhaps given more than it had received, but they argued

[12] See Sir Henry Fountain's July 15, 1932, memorandum, Ashton-Gwatkin's reports, and a summary memorandum by Chalkley, FO 433/1, Vol. I.

[13] See Ashton-Gwatkin's reports, FO 433/1, Vol. I, nos. 16, 20, 24, 26.

[14] Unsigned FO memorandum on the effects of the Ottawa agreements, FO 433/1, Vol. I, no. 34; Board of Trade memorandum, Oct. 6, 1932, CAB 24/233, CP 336 (32).

that the agreements had been necessary for the very survival of the "bonds of empire." Samuel remained unconvinced. On September 28 he announced his resignation, arguing that the disadvantages of the agreements far outweighed any concessions Britain might have secured. The agreement to fix British tariffs for five years, he claimed, inevitably prejudiced the results of the World Economic Conference, scheduled to meet in the summer of 1933, by precluding any British tariff reductions. Britain had consistently led efforts to reduce restrictions on trade; now the government had ruled out mutual tariff reductions with foreign countries. The small Liberal party split into independent and National Liberal factions.[15]

Before the end of 1932, and before commercial negotiations with foreign countries could begin, the government dealt another blow to foreign trade by adopting a radically new policy for British agriculture. British farmers had labored without government protection ever since the repeal of the Corn Laws in 1846, and their number had gradually diminished until by 1931 agriculture occupied just 5.7 percent of the working population.[16] Falling prices in home agriculture, however, coupled with the movement toward protection, aroused new interest in official measures to reorganize and increase home production and help the British farmer. The National Government had created a cabinet committee on agricultural policy in December 1931. The committee's report, presented on January 18, 1932, argued that depressed conditions in agriculture rendered "exceptional measures, whether permanent or temporary, involving a departure from our basic economic policy" as appropriate for agriculture as for industry. The report cited the domestic pig industry as a possible area for expansion, and the government appointed the Lane-Fox Committee to consider proposals for the encouragement of the British pig industry.[17]

The committee's report, delivered to the cabinet in October 1932, recommended an immediate and significant reduction of total bacon and ham imports and a steady expansion of British production. These measures would increase the home share of

[15] Cabinets of Aug. 27 and Sept. 28, 1932, CAB 23/72.
[16] Board of Trade, *Statistical Abstract of the United Kingdom* (London, various years) (hereafter *SAUK*), *1913, 1922-35*, p. 113.
[17] Cabinet of Dec. 10, 1931, CAB 23/69; report of Jan. 18, CAB 24/227, CP 21 (32).

the market from one-sixth to one-third within three years. Board of Trade President Runciman immediately objected, arguing that these proposals, combined with existing obligations to *increase* imports from Canada, would result in an immediate reduction of foreign imports of about one-third. Such a step would be devastating to the Scandinavian countries, particularly Denmark, and would make the British position in forthcoming trade talks with the Scandinavians extremely difficult. Nevertheless, a compromise submitted by Runciman and Agriculture Minister Elliott on December 12 differed little from the original Lane-Fox report. It envisioned reducing total British bacon imports to 75 percent of the 1931 level by 1933 and to 67 percent by 1935. The cabinet approved this plan two days later, and it was put into effect the following June. In the meantime, however, a crisis in domestic bacon prices had already forced the government's hand. On November 8, 1932, foreign governments were informed of Britain's intention to reduce bacon imports immediately by about 15 percent. Thus, proportional reductions in foreign imports began before the imposition of more severe restrictions in July. Not surprisingly, the decision to regulate bacon imports was quickly followed by demands to protect other branches of home agriculture in the same manner. In March 1933 the cabinet agreed to an agricultural marketing bill empowering the Board of Trade to restrict imports of any agricultural commodity for which the government undertook to regulate domestic production and distribution.[18]

The decision to protect home agriculture, like the imposition of the tariff and the extension of imperial preference, had enormous foreign policy implications, but it too was made without effective Foreign Office participation. The new measures were designed to stimulate home agriculture and, perhaps, as Agriculture Minister Elliott hinted during one cabinet meeting, to secure the farm vote for the National Government.[19] Within

[18] Lane-Fox report and Runciman's dissent, Oct, 20, 21, 1932, CAB 24/233, CP 353 (32) and 356 (32); cabinet of Oct. 26, CAB 23/72; Dec. 12 memorandum, CAB 24/235, CP 429 (32); cabinet of Dec. 14, CAB 23/73; FO circular, Nov. 8, FO 371/16294, N6438/5805/63; Ashton-Gwatkin's Feb. 23, 1933, memorandum, FO 433/1, Vol. II, no. 5; Ashton-Gwatkin's Feb. 6 memorandum, FO 371/17212, N812/1/63; cabinet of Mar. 1, CAB 23/75.

[19] Elliott referred to the "political aspects of the matter" while discussing meat quotas in the cabinet of Mar. 15, 1933, CAB 23/75.

that government, the Foreign Office was generally excluded from decisions thought to be of a primarily economic or commercial character. The new agricultural policy provoked strong objections from Whitehall, exemplified by the reaction of Laurence Collier, head of the Northern Department and thereby responsible for relations with the Scandinavian and Baltic states. "For my own part," Collier wrote in March 1933, "I feel strongly that, for a nation with a population 80% urban and depending for its livelihood on export trade it is folly to jeopardize any export market for the sake of home agriculture. The example of Germany (where conditions are much less unfavorable for a policy of 'agriculture first') should be sufficient warning of the effects of such a policy."[20]

In retrospect, the reorientation of British commercial policy in the early 1930s does not appear to have brought Britain any great economic benefit. The new tariff was supposedly designed to improve the balance of trade, but during the general revival of foreign trade from 1932 to 1937 Britain's import surplus, expressed as a percentage of exports, declined only very slightly. The Ottawa agreements diverted British trade to the empire, but in a manner quite unfavorable to the mother country. British imports from the Dominions and colonies increased dramatically, rising from 27.0 percent of total imports in 1931 to 38.3 percent in 1937. British exports to the empire, however, rose much more slowly, increasing from a share of 43.7 percent of total exports in 1931 to only 48.3 percent in 1937.[21]

The Baltic states and, to a lesser extent, Poland immediately recognized the significance of British bacon import quotas, imperial preference, and tariffs on butter, eggs, and timber. As soon as the terms of the Ottawa agreements became known, they approached the British government with proposals for commercial negotiations in an attempt to preserve what was left of their markets. The Foreign Office, led by Northern Department chief Collier, was anxious to respond to these overtures. Inside the British government, however, in contrast to the German government, commercial negotiations were the exclusive province of the Commercial Relations and Treaties Department of the Board of Trade; the Foreign Office rarely even participated in

[20] Minute on Ashton-Gwatkin's Feb. 6, 1933, memorandum, FO 371/17212.
[21] These percentages are based on figures in *SAUK, 1913, 1922-35*, pp. 358-68, *1935-46*, p. 179. Figures for imports represent retained imports.

such talks. In this instance Whitehall had to content itself with asking the Board when talks with the Baltic states might begin. The Board responded on November 14, 1932, that those talks would have to await completion of negotiations with the Scandinavian countries, Argentina, Germany, and Italy. The British government would have little to offer the Baltic states in any event; in the wake of the Lane-Fox report, they would have to be asked to reduce their exports to Britain but increase their imports to further equalize their trade balances with the United Kingdom.[22]

The Foreign Office, led by Collier and Sir Hugh Knatchbull-Hugessen, the British minister to all three Baltic states favored official encouragement of trade with Poland and the Baltic States but had to contend with apathy among British traders, the Board of Trade, and the Department of Overseas Trade (DOT), a joint department of the Foreign Office and the Board of Trade designed to encourage British exports. During 1933 Knatchbull-Hugessen complained that British traders frequently ignored valuable opportunities in the Baltic states—and in some cases seemed unaware of their very existence—even though chaos in Germany and German agricultural protection presently offered the British a golden opportunity. Moreover, the Baltic states themselves wanted to increase trade with Britain and avoid excessive dependence on Germany. Collier forwarded some of these reports to the DOT, arguing that the government should try to force traders to take advantage of these opportunities. Almost alone among high British civil servants, Collier believed that the unsettled conditions in international trade and the special problems of Eastern European markets required government action to increase trade. He admitted that his proposal would be regarded as "unprecedented Government interference" but added, "I cannot see that in these days any degree of Government interference can be regarded as 'unprecedented,' and in this case the interference would be merely negative and not positive." On the other hand, the DOT and the Board of Trade argued that "the Baltic States . . . in our view, do not appear to be capable of much sound development for some time to come."[23] They rejected any major British role in the

[22] For the various approaches see FO 371/16385-86, N5805/5805/63 et seq., and Board of Trade to FO, Nov. 14, 30, 1932, ibid., N6562/N7012/5805/63.

[23] See Knatchbull-Hugessen's Jan. 23, 1933, letter, Collier's minute, and the

commercial development of the Baltic states. The Northern Department of the Foreign Office fought them unsuccessfully throughout the decade.

In late 1932 Poland also expressed interest in increased trade with Britain, partly, perhaps, because of the German government's continuing refusal to settle the longstanding German-Polish tariff war, but the Board of Trade was cool to Polish overtures as well. The Board was principally preoccupied with Poland's role as a competitor with British exports of coal. In 1926 the Poles had taken advantage of the British general strike and the overvaluation of the pound to make substantial inroads into the coal market in Scandinavia and the Baltic. The devaluation of sterling in 1931 had improved the British position somewhat, but competition continued. In December 1932 Sir Henry Fountain of the Treasury told Collier that he would put off talks with Poland until he could determine whether he could force the Poles out of the Scandinavian coal market altogether in talks with Denmark, Sweden, Norway, and Finland. Failing that, he would try to squeeze concessions from the Poles in exchange for conceding that percentage of the coal market he had failed to secure in talks with the importers. When Collier argued that the Poles merited more consideration, Fountain replied that "he attached little importance to the Polish market."[24]

During the first half of 1933 the Board of Trade negotiated new commercial agreements with the Scandinavian countries, Argentina, and Germany. The British promised the Baltic states that negotiations with them would begin as soon as preparations for the World Economic Conference had been completed, but in July they attempted to put off the talks further, preferring to deal with France next. The Foreign Office promptly protested on July 4, succinctly presenting the case for an active British policy:

> Both for geographical and historical reasons the pull of Moscow and of Berlin is likely to become very strong as soon as these great centers emerge from their present disorders. Then, especially in these days of "regional agreements," the

DOT's comments, FO 371/16387, N591/591/59. For additional reports on Estonia and Latvia see ibid., N3520/N3920/591/59. See also Knatchbull-Hugessen to FO, Oct. 16, FO 371/17186, N7689/6839/59.

[24] Collier memorandum, Dec. 12, 1932, FO 371/16387, N7005/5805/63.

little states of the Baltic are in danger of being swallowed up. British influence in the Baltic should be strengthened as much as possible during the present opportunity. . . .

Poland is very important politically, and in spite of the coal competition is friendly disposed. It is a great future market, having already a population of thirty millions.

The Board of Trade agreed to begin talks by the end of the year, but by the time commercial negotiations between Britain and the Baltic states finally began in late 1933, strict limits on British concessions had been established. The British government had defined its policy on imports of bacon, butter, and eggs, the commodities in which the Balts were most interested, while negotiating new commercial treaties with the Scandinavian countries. Denmark and Sweden, the principal foreign suppliers of these products, had been guaranteed percentage quotas of the total British imports of these goods, based on their market shares before quotas were instituted. However, the British government had not promised to import specific annual quantities of these goods, and it reserved the right to reduce total imports of these products at any time.[25] The Baltic states had to be offered the same terms, that is, a specific percentage of total British imports of these products based on their exports to Britain in previous years. Latvia, Lithuania, and Estonia all entered the negotiations hoping to increase their agricultural exports to Britain; in the end, each had to be content with quotas 35 to 50 percent lower than it had hoped.

The new commercial treaties that Britain signed with the three Baltic states during the first half of 1934 were all similar. In each case the British government promised equal treatment for Baltic products in the event of any further reduction of agricultural imports. In return, Britain received some tariff concessions and concluded secret purchase agreements with all three governments providing for Baltic imports of British coal, iron, steel, textiles, and salt. The purchase agreements were kept

[25] FO memorandum, July 4, 1933, FO 371/17213, N5064/1/63; Ashton-Gwatkin memorandum, July 11, FO 271/17319, W8174/285/50. The talks were nearly delayed still further in September, when Vansittart, fearing an imminent United States trade offensive in Latin America, asked whether British commercial negotiations with Latin America might begin at once. Collier successfully insisted on simultaneous approaches to Latin America and the Baltic states; see Vansittart's letter of Sept. 11, FO 371/17186, N6838/6838/59.

secret to disguise their obvious violation of the most-favored-nation principle. The Baltic states also recognized their responsibility to try to equalize their trade balances with Britain.[26]

After completing negotiations with the Baltic states, the British began talks with Poland in June 1934. These talks, which lasted until February 1935, proved perhaps the most difficult of all the negotiations Britain entered into in the wake of the Ottawa agreements. The Poles were always tough bargainers during the interwar period; in this instance they were anxious to conclude a wide-ranging treaty that would serve as a model in talks with other foreign countries and to improve trade relations with Britain while protecting their own nascent industries. The talks broke down several times over Polish demands for higher British import quotas on agricultural products. The ultimate agreement of February 27, 1935, met few of the Poles' wishes but provided for Polish tariff reductions on many British goods, including herrings, textiles, machinery, and electrical goods. The length and difficulty of the talks left a bad taste in the mouths of the British negotiators.[27]

The new agreements, which were hamstrung by British agricultural policy, kept British imports from the Baltic within strict limits. Total British imports from the Baltic states in 1935 did not reach the level of 1928. In addition, despite the British government's attempts to improve its trade balance with the Baltic states through government purchases, British exports to the region continued to lag behind imports.[28] The United Kingdom failed to take advantage of Germany's temporary commercial paralysis in the Baltic; in 1935 Germany was still the leading exporter to the Baltic region, trailing Britain only in Lithuania, against which the Germans were pursuing a tariff war over the Memel question.[29] Britain's continuing negative trade balance reflected the lack of any combined public and private export offensive.

[26] For negotiations with all three Baltic states see FO 371/17212-14 (for 1933), 18212-21 (for 1934). For the Anglo-Latvian commercial agreement of Mar. 29, 1934, see FO 371/18216; for the Anglo-Lithuanian commercial agreement of July 6, 1934, FO 371/18219; for the Anglo-Estonian commercial agreement of July 11, ibid.

[27] For the 1934-1935 Anglo-Polish negotiations see FO 371/17775-82, 18885-86; for the text of the commercial agreement of Feb. 27, 1935, see FO 371/18886, C3651/46/55.

[28] *SAUK, 1913, 1922-35*, pp. 358-65.

[29] LN, *ITS, 1936*, pp. 106, 171, 176.

The British government's response to the growth of exchange control in Eastern Europe also limited prospects for expanded British trade with the region during the 1930s. It is axiomatic that the structure of international commerce underwent a major change from multilateral exchanges of goods to bilateral trade and state intervention during this decade, and Great Britain was clearly not immune to these trends. The new tariffs, the Ottawa agreements, the regulation of agricultural imports, and the attempt to structure British trade around bilateral agreements clearly represented abandonment of the century-old British tradition of free and unregulated trade. However, British reaction to the growth of exchange control, and particularly to the appearance of clearing agreements, reflected the continuing strength of orthodox economic thinking at the Bank of England, the Treasury, and the Board of Trade and did little to improve prospects for British trade in Eastern Europe.

Questions of exchange control first became an issue in the British government in mid-1932, when British traders began to report serious difficulties in securing payment for their exports to various Eastern European countries, particularly Hungary. The Hungarian government had assumed control of all foreign-exchange receipts, and, perhaps because Britain had an active balance of trade with Hungary and because the Hungarian government desperately needed sterling to service foreign loans, British traders were not receiving payments for their exports in hard currency. In June 1932 the Board of Trade drew up a memorandum on clearings, which private traders were demanding as a means of forcing the payment of their debts. Under a clearing, all British sterling payments for Hungarian exports would go into a Hungarian account at the Bank of England, thence to be paid out to Hungary's British creditors. Even though other European nations were already resorting to clearings, the Board distrusted state intervention in international trade and rejected clearings for two major reasons. First, the Board cited the problem of exchange rates. The Hungarian National Bank was still trying to maintain the Hungarian pengo at its artificially high official gold value, and private traders would undoubtedly try to circumvent any clearing that respected the official rate in order to get more favorable terms. Second, British exporters and bondholders possessing old Hungarian debts would inevitably demand priority for the service of their obligations, and payments for current trade would have to wait. The

Board rejected pleas that the British government at least be given the authority to impose clearings. In Parliament Runciman replied negatively to numerous questions calling for clearings to relieve the problems of British traders.[30]

Private interests continued to protest through the latter half of 1932. In early 1933 the government formed a committee of civil servants and private interests to discuss the issue of clearings further. Chaired by S. V. Waley of the Treasury, the committee included representatives of the Federation of British Industries, the Association of British Chambers of Commerce, and bankers accustomed to dealing in foreign exchange. Although uncollected debts to British traders owed in Southeastern Europe totaled £1,500,000, Waley still opposed clearings designed to collect them. Under his influence, the committee ultimately rejected clearings on the grounds that they would inevitably lead to the elimination of Britain's favorable trade balance with several of the Southeastern European countries and because, in the view of the civil servants, clearings already established by other nations had worked poorly. Waley clearly felt that Britain's relatively insignificant trade with Southeastern Europe did not justify potentially far-reaching state intervention in the mechanics of international trade.[31]

The British government finally decided to assume the power to impose clearings in June 1934 because of developments in Anglo-German trade relations, but it did so reluctantly and hedged its powers about with significant restrictions. Pressure to impose a clearing upon trade with Germany had arisen in June 1933, when Reichsbank President Schacht declared a moratorium on foreign-exchange payments to holders of the Dawes and Young loans. British bondholders wanted a clearing to force the Germans to pay them in sterling.[32] London and Berlin reached a new agreement on servicing these loans in January 1934, but the Foreign Office also asked for clearing powers both to deter Germany from future moratoriums and to use as a lever in commercial negotiations. The Bank of England and the Treasury still opposed clearings for fear that they would disrupt

[30] Board of Trade memorandum of June 14, 1932, FO 371/15926, C4982/185/62; parliamentary questions, ibid.

[31] For the committee's deliberations and its Mar. 16, 1933, report see FO 371/16681, C265/265/62 et seq.

[32] Wendt, *Economic Appeasement*, pp. 68-72, 129-41.

longstanding patterns of international trade involving the discounting and acceptance of bills of exchange at London financial institutions. These institutions might be ruined by the imposition of a clearing. The Board of Trade, except for T. St. Quinton Hill, whose jurisdiction included Germany and Hungary, still opposed clearings too, but the government formed an interdepartmental committee, chaired by Leith-Ross, to discuss the issue.[33]

Leith-Ross wrote to Runciman on May 15 suggesting that the government be empowered to impose clearings both "as a reprisal against restriction of payments" and, as desired by the Foreign Office, as a means "to secure a better balance of trade with certain foreign countries." With Runciman's support, however, the Board of Trade and Treasury successfully stripped from the proposal the clause granting power to impose clearings to improve trade balances—a power they feared would provoke numerous requests from private traders to impose clearings merely to increase their own sales. Once again, the Foreign Office had been outmaneuvered and excluded from a decision that carried major foreign-policy implications. In the cabinet on June 18 Neville Chamberlain made clear his hope that he would not have to use these new powers;[34] in fact, even after Germany imposed the New Plan for the control of foreign trade in September, the British ultimately accepted Schacht's promises to set aside enough of Germany's sterling receipts to pay commercial debts and interest on the Dawes and Young loans.[35] As we shall see, the government used its clearing powers sparingly throughout the 1930s.

Despite the proliferation of exchange control, clearings, discriminatory quotas, and barter agreements all over Europe, the British government generally attempted to maintain normal

[33] On the system of bills of exchange see Charles P. Kindelberger, *International Economics*, 3d ed. (Homewood, 1963), pp. 46-54. See also Wendt, *Economic Appeasement*, pp. 133, 167-70; FO letter, Mar. 29, 1934, and Board of Trade comments, PRO, BT 11/274.

[34] Leith-Ross's letter, T-188/88; minutes of a Board of Trade meeting, May 25, ibid.; Board of Trade minute of a June 5 meeting, BT 11/274; St. Quintin Hill minute, interdepartmental meeting of June 16, T-188/88; joint memorandum, chancellor of the Exchequer and president of the Board of Trade, June 18, CAB 24/228, CP 163 (34); cabinets of June 13, 16, 1934, CAB 23/79.

[35] Cabinets of Sept. 21 and Oct. 3, 24, 30, 1934 CAB 23/79-80; Wendt, *Economic Appeasement*, pp. 260-87.

methods and procedures in international trade. The government's attitude was not completely consistent—its conclusion of secret purchase agreements with the Scandinavian and Baltic countries, for example, represented an obvious infringement upon the most-favored-nation principle, which the government claimed to wish to maintain—but officially it continued to proclaim orthodoxy. Private interests continued to protest. In early 1934, for example, the various departments of the Foreign Office discussed a suggestion by the Manchester Chamber of Commerce that Britain drop the most-favored-nation clause from its commercial treaties. The chamber argued that in numerous important markets quota restrictions and exchange control had effectively deprived the clause of any meaning; Britain would be better off bargaining for preferential access to specific export markets in return for concessions on imports. E. H. Carr of the newly created Southern Department, which took over responsibility for the states of the former Hapsburg Empire in January 1934, commented that within his area of responsibility restrictions were indeed depriving the clause of much of its meaning. Collier was far more definite, arguing that Britain could do without the most-favored-nation principle, not only within his own jurisdiction but also throughout the world. Since Britain bought more than it sold from nearly every country in the world, the government could easily drive advantageous bargains without it.[36] But the Board of Trade remained wedded to the principle, and the chamber's proposal was dropped. The world was changing; the British government seemed to have difficulty changing with it. Its failure to adopt more flexible trading methods seriously limited prospects for trade with Eastern Europe.

The British government's decisions of 1931-1934 set the pattern for British commercial policy toward Eastern Europe for the rest of the decade. The new agreements with the Baltic states and Poland reduced trade from predepression levels; imperial preference virtually ruled out extensive cereals purchases from Southeastern Europe; and the British aversion to clearings became a serious obstacle to increasing trade with Eastern Europe as a whole. With few exceptions, the responsible members of the British government attached little importance to the economic

[36] For the minutes on this proposal see FO 371/18468, W1562/18/50.

possibilities of Eastern Europe; in addition, they generally rejected the kind of government intervention that might have increased trade with the successor states. These attitudes prevailed for the rest of the decade, even when the Eastern Europeans renewed their calls for help and when assistance to them became a political question as well as an economic one.

The career of Laurence Collier, who ran the Northern Department of the Foreign Office from 1932 through the remainder of the 1930s, illustrates the character of British foreign policy during the 1930s. Only forty-two in 1932, Collier had risen rapidly to become a department head. Brilliant and opinionated, he agitated ceaselessly for a stronger British presence in Eastern Europe, for resistance to German expansion under Hitler, and, above all, for a more active, aggressive style in British commercial and foreign policy. Never could he overcome the inertia of his colleagues, who seemed to lack his faith in Britain's *capacity* to affect events. A shortage of British officials who, like Collier, had some sense of what Britain must do to compete in the world of the 1930s led to catastrophe late in the decade. The question of why Britain produced so few such men during the interwar period is beyond the scope of this study.[37] The example of Collier, who never rose to a position commensurate with his abilities, suggests that many of his colleagues simply could not come to terms with the world they lived in.

[37] For a brilliant and provocative discussion of the outlook of the British governing class during the interwar period and its effect on foreign policy, see Correlli Barnett, *The Collapse of British Power* (London, 1972). Such a social-psychological approach is certainly necessary to understand British policy during these years.

V.

Political Diplomacy in Eastern Europe, 1931-1935

While Germany extended its economic influence in Eastern Europe during the first half of the 1930s, a parallel shift took place in the political balance among the great powers. Paris, which had built an extensive alliance system in Eastern Europe during the 1920s, had given much cause by 1932 to doubt its devotion to the Franco-Polish alliance. This in turn enabled Hitler dramatically to improve German-Polish relations and ultimately to conclude a nonaggression agreement with Poland in January 1934. Led by Foreign Minister Louis Barthou, the French then tried to restore their position. They failed to break up the new entente between Warsaw and Berlin but eventually concluded the Franco-Soviet Pact in 1935. Great-power political diplomacy in Eastern Europe from 1931 to 1935 revealed significant disagreements in Paris and London over the proper response to Nazi Germany. These controversies during the early 1930s foreshadowed the great crisis of 1938, which ultimately established German domination of Eastern Europe.[1]

For the French government, relations with Poland in the late 1920s and early 1930s presented a problem of conflicting objectives. How could France maintain its alliances with Poland and Czechoslovakia and its agreements with the other Little Entente countries while simultaneously pursuing good relations with Britain and, if possible, a reconciliation with Germany? Briand, foreign minister from 1924 through early 1932, emphasized relations with Britain and Germany at the expense of France's eastern allies. Like most enlightened European statesmen,

---

[1] The issue of the German-Polish frontier, the German-Polish Non-Agression Declaration, and the negotiations leading to the Franco-Soviet Pact have all been treated extensively in secondary works. The best accounts are: Hans Roos, *Polen und Europa. Studien zur polnischen Aussenpolitik, 1931-39* (Tübingen, 1957); Weinberg, *Foreign Policy of Hitler's Germany*; William Evans Scott, *Alliance against Hitler: The Origins of the Franco-Soviet Pact* (Durham, 1962); and Marian Wojciechowski, *Die polnisch-deutschen Beziehungen 1933-1938* (Leiden, 1971).

Briand dreamed of a real and lasting reconciliation of Germany and France. After the settlement of reparations under the Young Plan in 1929 and the evacuation of the Rhineland in 1930, two major German demands remained outstanding: equality of rights in armaments and revision of Germany's eastern frontier. Disarmament would be taken up at the Disarmament Conference of 1932; Poland and the Franco-Polish alliance loomed as the other great obstacle to a final Franco-German reconciliation and an enduring European settlement.

By early 1931, Briand seems to have been increasingly preoccupied with the problem of the German-Polish frontier. In March Leopold von Hoesch, the German ambassador in Paris, reported rumors that Briand had urged Warsaw to come to terms with Germany. In January the British Foreign Office discussed similar rumors; the Central Department analyzed the question of the German-Polish frontier on the assumption that the issue was of interest to the British government because it threatened peace. The department queried British missions in Berlin, Paris, and Warsaw on the possibility of settling the question by returning the Corridor to Germany. In exchange, Poland would receive guaranteed access to the sea and new assurances for the security of the revised frontiers. Neither the Warsaw legation nor the Berlin embassy held out any hope of a solution along these lines. Warsaw stated that Poland would never peacefully give up the Corridor, which, under the pressure of government policy, had become heavily Polish. Berlin replied that if negotiation could not bring the German government satisfaction regarding the Corridor, the problem would have to be settled by war or threat of war. From Paris, British Ambassador William (Lord) Tyrrell confirmed that the Quai d'Orsay was anxious for a new solution but that "in this matter they cannot make the Poles see reason." "Sooner or later," commented Sir Orme Sargent, the head of the Central Department, "it will be necessary in some form or other to *force* a settlement on Poland."[2]

[2] German embassy Paris to AA, Mar. 6, 1931, T-120/K396/K240611-26. Briand was quoted as telling the Poles, "Mais arrangez-vous avec les allemands!" See also Philip Nichols memorandum, Jan. 9, British legation Warsaw to London, Jan. 19, British embassy Berlin to FO, Jan. 21, Sargent's minute, British embassy Paris to FO, Feb. 17, and British embassy Berlin to FO, Feb. 23, FO 371/19221, C173/C560/C561/C1099/C1360/173/1.

During the rest of 1931 the Austro-German customs union proposal and the financial crisis in Central Europe diverted attention from the problem of the German-Polish frontier. Questions of European security arose once again at the Disarmament Conference, which convened in early 1932. The early stages of the conference found France in firm accord with its eastern allies. The issue of armaments—particularly the extension of equality of rights in armaments to Germany and the other disarmed powers, Austria, Hungary, and Bulgaria—was of vital interest to France, but even more important to Poland and the Little Entente. As long as Germany was limited to a 100,000-man army and denied tanks and military aircraft, the Polish frontier was essentially safe; Poland could defend itself against Germany as long as it avoided a simultaneous conflict with the Soviet Union. Similarly, the disarmament of Hungary protected the Little Entente from the threat of Hungarian alliances with larger powers. Thus, at the outset of the conference France and its allies all insisted that equality of rights in armaments could not be granted until a new, stronger system of security could be developed. The original French plan, supported by France's allies, called for an international police force and mandatory guarantees against aggression. By the summer of 1932 the conflict between these demands and the German insistence on immediate equality threatened to deadlock the conference.[3]

Changes in the French and German governments in June opened up new possibilities of Franco-German reconciliation—perhaps at Poland's expense. At the beginning of June the Brüning government yielded to a conservative-nationalist cabinet led by Chancellor Franz von Papen and Defense Minister Kurt von Schleicher. Papen wanted a long-term agreement with France; Schleicher was known to favor a German-Soviet alliance against Poland. At the same time, the conservative French Tardieu government was replaced by a center-left coalition led by the Radical Edouard Herriot. In Lausanne, on June 16, Papen proposed to Herriot a far-reaching Franco-German settlement, including a consultative pact, contacts between the two general staffs, a customs union, and German equality of rights in arma-

[3] John Wheeler-Bennett, *The Pipe Dream of Peace: The Story of the Collapse of Disarmament* (New York, 1935), pp. 14-15. Edward W. Bennett, *German Rearmament and the West, 1932-1933* (Princeton, 1979), appeared too late to be used.

ments. Although it is not clear whether Papen specifically mentioned the German-Polish frontier, and although his proposals got nowhere in any case, the possibility of Franco-German accommodation led Marshal Piłsudski, the dictator of Poland, to alter the emphasis of his foreign policy. On November 2, 1932, he replaced his pro-French foreign minister, Auguste Zaleski, with Józef Beck. According to Beck, Piłsudski warned that the decade-old structure of European politics embodied in the peace treaties would soon collapse. Poland would have to base its security, first, on its own forces, *second*, on good relations with its powerful neighbors, and, only third, on alliances. Beck ratified the pending Polish-Soviet Non-Aggression Pact almost immediately. This step violated an earlier Polish pledge not to ratify until Poland's ally Rumania had reached a similar accord with Moscow.[4] It exemplified the new policy of valuing good relations with Poland's neighbors more highly than its existing alliances.[5]

In the meantime, continuing failure to reach agreement within the Disarmament Conference had led to talks among French, German, British, Italian, and United States representatives in Geneva in early December. On December 11 the five powers issued a joint declaration endorsing "the grant to Germany, and to other powers disarmed by treaty, of equality of rights in a system which would provide security for all nations." At one stroke, the great powers had effectively abrogated a major provision of the Paris peace treaties. France's allies reacted sharply. The Poles objected, having previously stated they would not be bound by any five-power decision. On February 16, 1933, the Little Entente, whose enemy Hungary had explicitly received equality of rights as well, adopted a new statute of organization calling for a common foreign policy in an effort to avoid being left out of further significant decisions.[6]

---

[4] On the Soviet-Rumanian nonagression negotiations see *DDF*, 1, I, 50, 56, 66, 84, 90, 94, 134, 207, 238, 251, 314. The key issue was the Rumanian seizure of Bessarabia in 1918. The Soviets would not recognize the seizure, and the Rumanians would not admit that a conflict existed between the two states.

[5] Scott, *Alliance against Hitler*, pp. 49-61; Roos, *Polen und Europa*, pp. 45-47, 54-56.

[6] Wheeler-Bennett, *Pipe Dream of Peace*, pp. 82-84. On Polish reaction see Roos, *Polen und Europa*, p. 58, and the Polish minister's Dec. 3, 1932, declaration in London, FO 371/16469, W13398/1466/98. On the Little Entente see Reichert, *Kleine Entente*, pp. 6-14, 55-56, and *DDF*, 1, II, 98, 120, 187, 209, 254, 302, 334. The new statute represented a compromise between Yugoslavia, which wanted

During December and January of 1932-1933, European foreign ministries buzzed with talk of a new solution to the German-Polish frontier question. Now that Germany had received equality of rights in armaments, Berlin might join in new security guarantees in exchange for revision of the eastern frontier. On January 2 Hans Dieckhoff of the German Foreign Office told British Ambassador Sir Horace Rumbold that the Corridor question might shortly be raised in connection with new security guarantees, and an unidentified Wilhelmstrasse official suggested the return of the Corridor, accompanied by an exchange of populations, to French Ambassador André François-Poncet on January 7. Simultaneously, leading French and German industrialists discussed the problem, apparently with official encouragement. On January 30, 1933—the day that Hitler took power—the industrialists sent recommendations to the Wilhelmstrasse. They proposed the return of the Corridor and Danzig to Germany, minor rectifications of the Upper Silesian frontier, compensation for Poland in the Memel region, a large German indemnity to Poland for the port of Gdynia, and guaranteed Polish access to the sea. In return, France, Germany, Belgium, and Poland would conclude a security pact providing for general-staff contacts as part of a disarmament agreement. Before submitting these proposals to the Quai d'Orsay, the industrialists asked whether the new German government would accept them. Bülow and Neurath, however, decided not to exploit these private contacts; the time was not yet ripe, they felt, for the solution of the Polish frontier question, and in some respects the proposals did not go far enough for their tastes.[7]

The Polish government feared that further disarmament and security negotiations would lead to new decisions at Poland's expense. In early February the Polish delegation at Geneva suddenly withdrew its support for the comprehensive French plan

---

the Little Entente converted to an alliance against any aggressor, owing to difficulties in Yugoslav-Italian relations, and Rumania and Czechoslovakia, which wanted to limit their commitments to the existing alliance against Hungary. In subsequent years these positions were reversed.

[7] British embassy Berlin to FO, Jan. 2, 1933, FO 371/16714, C316/316/18; French embassy Berlin to AE, Jan. 7, *DDF*, 1, II, 175; memorandum of the French and German industrialists' proposals, *DGFP*, C, I, 2; undated Neurath memorandum and Bülow memorandum, Feb. 10, T-120/4624/E203075-81, 086-87.

for disarmament and security. Beck explained to French Ambassador Jules Laroche that Warsaw resented the lack of Franco-Polish consultation on disarmament and feared that negotiations would lead to further great-power revision of the peace treaties.[8]

Hitler's accession to power on January 30 led quickly to a new crisis in German-Polish relations. Piłsudski's well-known military measures in early March—the reinforcement of the Polish army garrison at the Westerplatte, the entrance to Danzig harbor, and the movement of several Polish divisions to the environs of Danzig—may have been designed merely to guard against a possible Nazi coup in Danzig. They may also have been designed to intimidate the Germans by threatening a preventive war. Whether Piłsudski, as numerous rumors would have it, actually discussed a preventive war with the French remains highly questionable. No evidence for such discussions has emerged from Polish or French archives.[9] We shall see that Piłsudski apparently frightened Hitler into an accommodation with Poland, and this may have been his aim all along. The Four Power Pact, which Mussolini proposed in early March 1933, threatened Polish security more immediately than the accession of the Nazis.

The idea of the Four Power Pact—a great-power directorate of France, Germany, Britain, and Italy that would begin the revision of the peace treaties in the interests of peace—first became generally known after Ramsay MacDonald and Sir John Simon visited Rome on March 18. Mussolini, however, had first suggested it to the French ambassador to Italy, Henry de Jouvenel, on March 4. Mussolini planned to solve the problem of Nazi Germany by a series of territorial adjustments and new guarantees in Eastern Europe. Specifically, he wanted to protect his own interests in Austria, satiate German appetites at Poland's expense, and realize the revisionist ambitions of his Hungarian ally. Thus he suggested to Jouvenel that France, Britain, and Italy jointly propose a new solution to the Corridor question, in-

---

[8] French mission Geneva to AE, Feb. 6, 1933, and French embassy Warsaw to AE, Feb. 9, *DDF*, 1, II, 266, 279.

[9] Weinberg, *Foreign Policy*, pp. 59-60; Roos, *Polen und Europa*, pp. 62-65. For summaries of the literature on the preventive war question see Weinberg, p. 57n, and Wojciechowski, *Polnisch-deutschen Beziehungen*, p. 16n. Wojciechowski, pp. 15-20, argues cogently against the preventive war thesis.

volving a new corridor across it, that they maintain joint opposition to Anschluss, and that they encourage a revision of Hungarian frontiers along ethnic lines.[10]

Jouvenel enthusiastically informed Paris of the plan, but it received a cold response. French Foreign Minister Joseph Paul-Boncour believed firmly in the covenant of the League of Nations and in the maintenance of France's existing alliances, both of which the new proposal would contravene. He immediately instructed Jouvenel to make it clear that his government did not consent to Mussolini's proposals and to convey "the most specific reservations with respect to the question of the Corridor and of the Hungarian frontiers." He informed neither his allies nor the British prime minister and foreign secretary, whom he met in Geneva just before their trip to Rome, of the details of Mussolini's proposals.[11]

Mussolini gave MacDonald and Simon a draft of his Four Power Pact on March 17 in Rome. The key provision, Article 2, provided for joint action by the four powers to implement revision within the framework of the League of Nations. Mussolini again made clear that the Polish and Hungarian frontiers were intended to be immediate subjects of revision. Both the British ministers and the British Foreign Office received the project enthusiastically. On March 22 MacDonald praised the proposals before the cabinet, implying that French intransigence blocked their adoption. On their way home, he and Simon had stopped in Paris and told the French ministers that "the present position could not be held forever. . . . The greatest service we could render France at the moment was to get her to realize what was going on in Europe outside her own country." MacDonald later embraced the principle of revision before the House of Commons.[12]

---

[10] French embassy Rome to AE, Mar. 4, 1933, *DDF*, 1, II, 368.

[11] AE to French embassy Rome, Mar. 10, ibid., no. 391. For the Geneva conversations of Mar. 14, 16, and 17 see ibid., nos. 412, 418, 420. The French ministers indicated that Mussolini would want to discuss treaty revision.

[12] For the text of the original proposal see *DGFP*, C, I, 83; for the Rome conversations, *DBFP*, 2, V, 44, 45. For Foreign Office reaction see Sargent's and Vansittart's minutes of Mar. 15, 21, 24, FO 371/16683, C2680/C2720/2607/62. Sargent argued that existing League Convenant procedures for revision clearly did not work and that Mussolini's proposals seemed an excellent alternative. Vansittart characterized the proposals as "the last chance for good relations with Italy, perhaps even the last chance for peace." For the cabinet meeting see CAB

Britain's enthusiasm for the pact faced the French government with its recurring dilemma. Outright rejection of the proposal would alienate Britain and Italy; its acceptance would virtually repudiate France's eastern alliances. Paul-Boncour and Alexis Saint-Léger Léger, who had just replaced Philippe Berthelot as secretary general in the Foreign Ministry, decided that the pact in its present form, with its emphasis on revision, could not be reconciled with the maintenance of the French alliance system. To avoid antagonizing the British, however, the French set about amending the pact rather than rejecting it outright. After long negotiations, they generally prevailed: the pact initialed in Rome on June 7, 1933, specified that revision must follow the procedures of the League Covenant and explicitly cited Article 19, under which revision required the consent of all involved parties. Paris successfully assuaged the fears of the Little Entente, which had originally protested this implied attempt to coerce smaller powers as a relic of a bygone era; in an exchange of letters on the occasion of the initialing of the pact France pledged to respect existing treaties and observe Article 19.[13]

Polish Foreign Minister Beck refused to be satisfied with any such assurances, however, and bitterly protested French agreement to the pact in any form. During the pact negotiations he threatened that Poland would leave the League if the pact were adopted, and he warned French Ambassador Laroche in an April 21 memorandum that, "With regard to Franco-Polish relations, the pact could in the course of its application put the French government in a difficult situation relative to Polish interests." When the pact was initialed, the Polish government stated its implementation would "produce a crisis in the domain of the organization of the League of Nations. The Polish government will express its attitude on this subject at the appropriate time."[14]

In fact, although the pact was signed on July 15, it was never

---

23/75. MacDonald also referred to "the extraordinary regeneration of Italy under the Facist regime."

[13] See Léger's Mar. 18, 1933, memorandum and the AE circular of Mar. 24, *DDF*, 1, III, 7, 35, and the documents listed in the table of contents, ibid., under the heading, "Le pacte à quatre." See also Konrad H. Jarausch, *The Four Power Pact, 1933* (Madison, 1965). On the French negotiations with the Little Entente see *DDF*, 1, III, 84, 321, 331, 377.

[14] Roos, *Polen und Europa*, pp. 72-77; *DDF*, 1, III, 84, 156, 378.

ratified or put into force. It nonetheless revived old Polish fears that France would one day renounce the Franco-Polish alliance for the sake of a settlement with Germany. Given the stiffening of Paul-Boncour's attitude under the impact of Hitler's rise to power, it is ironic that Beck's fears should have peaked at the time of the Four Power Pact; he seems to have had more to worry about from other directions in late 1932 and early 1933. From Beck's standpoint, in any case, his first eight months in office had only confirmed the wisdom of Piłsudski's instructions to rely more on good relations with Poland's great neighbors than on the League or on alliances. Within months, he willingly responded to a new German initiative.

Adolf Hitler's 1933 decision to improve relations with Poland and his early 1934 agreement with Warsaw on a mutual pledge not to resort to force in settling disputes represented his most dramatic break with Weimar foreign policy. In January 1934 Hitler seemingly renounced the most publicized objective of Weimar foreign policy—the revision of Germany's eastern frontier—for ten years. Weimar policy, restated by Neurath before the German cabinet on April 7, 1933, had rejected any accommodation with Poland, preferring to keep international tension over the question of the German-Polish border at a high level. By making the tension unbearable, Germany would secure satisfaction with respect to the Corridor and Upper Silesia. German efforts to maintain tension—and a foothold in the lost territories—included extensive propaganda activities and the subsidy of German businesses in Polish Upper Silesia.[15] During 1933 and 1934 Hitler reversed this policy. In an attempt to gain time for more far-reaching plans, he reached a modus vivendi with Poland that no Weimar government could possibly have considered.

Hitler's overtures to Poland represented only one of his several attempts to come to terms with potential enemies. Perhaps he pressed hardest for agreement with Poland because it was from Poland that he had the most to fear. Whether or not Piłsudski really intended a preventive war against Germany in the spring of 1934, he indisputably convinced the German govern-

---

[15] For Neurath's briefing see *DGFP*, C, 1, 142; see also the Foreign Office memorandum of Apr. 26, 1933, cited in Weinberg, *Foreign Policy*, pp. 62-63. On previous German efforts to maintain tension see Riekhoff, *German-Polish Relations*, pp. 226-94.

ment that he was at least considering one. It has been argued that Piłsudski, disillusioned with the Franco-Polish alliance, was in fact attempting to frighten Hitler into an accommodation with Poland. If so, he succeeded.[16]

The movement toward Polish-German rapprochement began in mid-April 1933, when Beck, fearing a Nazi coup in Danzig, told Alfred Wysocki, the Polish minister in Berlin, to ask Hitler for a declaration affirming Polish rights in the Free City and to warn him of "difficulties" if one could not be given. Over the objections of the Wilhelmstrasse, Hitler met Wysocki on May 2 and agreed to a communiqué promising that Germany would not transgress the limits of existing treaties. In late May Hitler instructed Danzig Nazis to maintain calm in preparation for the Danzig Senate elections on May 28. After the Nazis had won a majority and ascended to power without serious incident, Hitler told Hermann Rauschning, the new president of the Danzig Senate, that in the short run he was resolved both "to get on with Poland" and "to make any treaty that would ease the position of Germany." In September the HPA decided to begin negotiations to end the German-Polish tariff war.[17]

Hitler's decision to leave the League and the Disarmament Conference in October 1933 precipitated the further movement in German-Polish relations that led to the agreement on January 26, 1934. This sequence of events was typical of German-Polish relations between the wars. Each capital usually tried to take advantage of any new uncertainty or insecurity in the international position of the other by seeking a new accommodation on favorable terms.[18] Hitler indicated his interest in an agreement with Poland to Neurath and Rauschning within a week of announcing Germany's departure from the League on October 14, and on October 17 Neurath discussed the need to settle all outstanding questions with Józef Lipski, the new Polish minister in Berlin. In early November Piłsudski instructed Lipski to ask Hitler

[16] See Weinberg, *Foreign Policy*, pp. 109-10, 170-72, for Hitler's approaches to Czechoslovakia and France. On Piłsudski's attitude see Wojciechowski, *Polnisch-deutschen Beziehungen*, pp. 15-20.

[17] Wojciechowski, *Polnisch-deutschen Beziehungen*, pp. 20-43; Weinberg, *Foreign Policy*, pp. 63-69; Rauschning, *Voice of Destruction*, pp. 85-87; HPA meeting, Sept. 21, 1933, T-120/5650/H003732-33.

[18] In the most dramatic of these episodes, the Polish government proposed to settle the frontier question definitively at the height of the Munich crisis in 1938; see below, Chapter X.

to compensate Poland for the loss in Polish security resulting from Germany's exit from the League; Warsaw would seriously consider a nonaggression pact. When Lipski carried out his instructions on November 15, Hitler agreed at once to a communiqué expressing both powers' intention to solve questions of mutual interest by negotiation rather than force, and he suggested that this declaration might be embodied in a written agreement. He affirmed Poland's need for access to the sea but suggested that the Corridor should have been created further to the east. Hinting at a potential solution of this problem at Lithuanian or Soviet expense, he stated that "perhaps sometime in the future certain problems can be settled with Poland in a friendly atmosphere, for example, by compensation." In a meeting of ministers the next day, Hitler secured agreement to the principle of a nonaggression treaty with Poland. The same meeting also produced agreement to offer to import a quota of Polish Silesian coal, a long-refused concession, should this prove necessary to settle the longstanding tariff war.[19]

Complicated negotiations on the text of a nonaggression agreement, or "declaration" as it was ultimately called, began on November 27 and lasted for two months. Neurath and Lipski signed the ten-year declaration pledging to settle disputes peacefully on January 26, 1934. On month later, on February 28, negotiators in Warsaw concluded an agreement ending the German-Polish tariff war.[20]

Not content with paper agreements, the German government quickly showed that it meant seriously to improve German-Polish relations. The two countries curtailed propaganda against each other, and Berlin diminished its support for German-speaking minority organizations within Poland to an extent that frightened older leaders of the German minority.[21] Eventually

---

[19] Weinberg, *Foreign Policy*, pp. 70-71; Józef Lipski, *Diplomat in Berlin, 1933-1939: Papers and Memoirs of Józef Lipski, Ambassador of Poland*, ed. Wacław Jędrezejewicz (New York, 1968), pp. 96-100; Wojciechowski, *Polnisch-deutschen Beziehungen*, pp. 71-72.

[20] For details of the negotiations see Wojciechowski, *Polnisch-deutschen Beziehungen*, pp. 91-100, and Lipski, *Diplomat in Berlin*, pp. 108-11. For the text of the political agreement see *DGFP*, C, II, 219; for the economic agreement, ibid., III, 73.

[21] On propoganda and the minorities question see Wojciechowski, *Polnisch-deutschen Beziehungen*, pp. 112-14, 237-42, and Jacobsen, *Aussenpolitik*, pp. 212-13, 593-94.

the German government even yielded before a long Polish campaign against German-owned businesses in Polish Upper Silesia; in February 1935 a German cabinet-level meeting decided to let the Poles seize some of these businesses on grounds of bankruptcy rather than continue the subsidies that Weimar governments had begun. We shall see that German-Polish trade relations continued to improve.[22] In short, Hitler reversed Weimar policy in virtually every area of German-Polish relations.

How the new agreement fit into Hitler's long-range goals would only become clear in succeeding years. Piłsudski and Beck clearly hoped that the agreement represented the tendency of the Austrian Hitler to turn from the east to the southeast, and they seized eagerly upon real or imagined indications that Hitler was decreasing Prussian, anti-Polish influence within the German government.[23] Ironically, the French government, which would have welcomed such an agreement at any time before 1933, now reacted sharply. The German-Polish agreement led directly to French proposals for an "Eastern Locarno," to restore and extend the Franco-Polish alliance, and eventually to the conclusion of the Franco-Soviet Pact.

The negotiations during 1934 and 1935 for a new collective security agreement including Germany, Poland, Czechoslovakia, the Baltic states, and the Soviet Union, and guaranteed by France—an Eastern Locarno—and the eventual signing of the Franco-Soviet Pact in May 1935 illustrate the fundamental duality of French and British policy toward Nazi Germany and Eastern Europe from 1933 through 1939. On the one hand, given

[22] For documents relating to the difficulties of German enterprises, principally IG Kattowitz, in Polish Upper Silesia see *DGFP*, C, II, 41, 340, 352, 373, III, 401, 496, 498. See also the German cabinet meeting of Apr. 22, 1933, T-120/3598/D792407-16, and T-120/9093, entire.

[23] Thus, as Beck remarked to British Minister William Erskine on Dec. 12, 1933: "The agitation against the Corridor had come largely from Prussia, which had hitherto dominated German aspirations and policy. He attached great importance to the fact that Herr Hitler by his policy of unification was eliminating the predominance of Prussia and increasing the influence of South Germany" (FO 371/16716, C10861/316/18). In fact, many of Hitler's institutional reforms *increased* the power of the Prussian bureaucracy; see Broszat, *Der Staat Hitlers*, p. 156. We have seen that Beck's predecessor, Zaleski, also hoped that German expansion could be channeled to the southeast; see above, Chapter II.

Hitler's withdrawal from the League and the Disarmament Conference and the beginning of large-scale German rearmament, the French and British governments might immediately have concluded that Hitler must eventually threaten their vital interests and that they must begin their own rearmament and organize the broadest possible coalition against him. On the other hand, they could draw back before the costs of such a policy and seek a comprehensive settlement with Germany that would concede some German demands. Louis Barthou, the French foreign minister who first proposed the Eastern Locarno, favored the first policy; Barthou's successor, Pierre Laval, and the British National Government tended toward the second. What is striking about the 1934-1935 negotiations is how Barthou, Laval, and the British all successfully adapted the Eastern Locarno and the Franco-Soviet Pact to their own purposes. To Barthou, these agreements offered important new guarantees of French security; to Laval and the British, they were means of persuading Hitler to reach a general settlement with France and Britain. French and British policy toward Hitler showed this ambivalence throughout the decade; Paris and London never definitively chose either to resist him or to accommodate him during the 1933-1939 period, especially with regard to Eastern Europe.

Three events in early 1934 combined to encourage an active new French policy toward Eastern Europe: the breakdown of disarmament negotiations, the rapid reemergence of the Soviet Union as a factor in European politics, and the German-Polish Non-Aggression Declaration of January 26, 1934. Disarmament talks among the great powers had continued even after the German government had left the Disarmament Conference in October 1933. In late January 1934 the British government proposed to legalize a limited degree of German rearmament as part of a general disarmament agreement. Hitler showed some interest in such an arrangement, but the French government was displeased by the British refusal to offer any remedy but consultation in the event that a power transgressed the limits of the projected agreement. On March 19, 1934, the center-right government of Gaston Doumergue, a so-called national government that had taken office after the Paris riots of February 6, 1934, rejected any legalization of German rearmament not accompanied by new international security guarantees. When the

German government announced large increases in military expenditures in late March, the French argued in a note of April
17 that Berlin, by pursuing rearmament unilaterally, had destroyed the basis for further negotiations. France, the note
stated, had no alternative but to "place in the forefront of her
preoccupations the conditions of her own security."[24]

It fell to Louis Barthou, the aging but vigorous foreign minister of the Doumergue government, to look for new means to
achieve French security. In March Barthou had opposed outright rejection of the British disarmament plan because he believed good relations with Britain to be essential to French security, but he was still determined to build a new coalition against
Nazi Germany. Barthou, as is often noted, had read *Mein Kampf*,
in which Hitler had cited France as the principal obstacle to the
realization of his goals, and he clearly felt that France would
have to face the possibility of armed conflict with Nazi Germany.
Immediately upon taking office in February 1934, he decided to
create an expanded and revitalized French alliance system based
on stronger ties to Eastern European states. He specifically
likened his policy to the Third Republic's alliance policy before
the First World War.[25]

Coincidentally, the Soviet Union was trying to improve relations with France and increase its influence in Europe. Fearing
the Japanese presence on their eastern border following the occupation of Manchuria in 1931, the Soviets had begun improving relations with their western neighbors. During 1932 Maxim
Litvinov, the peoples' commissar for foreign affairs, concluded
nonaggression pacts with Poland, Latvia, Estonia, and France.
In September 1933 the Soviets began sounding out the French
about new security arrangements, but Paris did not immediately
respond.[26] The German withdrawal from the League and the
Disarmament Conference, however, apparently moved French
Foreign Minister Paul-Boncour to receive these overtures more
favorably.

[24] Wheeler-Bennett, *Pipe Dream of Peace*, pp. 200-225.

[25] Scott, *Alliance against Hitler*, pp. 160-62. For the analogy with policy before
the First World War see Maurice Gamelin, *Servir*, 3 vols. (Paris, 1946-1947), II,
125-26.

[26] Adam Ulam, *Expansion and Coexistence: The History of Soviet Foreign Policy,
1917-67* (New York, 1968), pp. 209-11; Scott, *Alliance against Hitler*, pp. 30-33,
56-73, 67-130. On Soviet overtures to Paris in August 1933 see *DDF*, 1, IV, 249,
251, 252, 266.

The lack of any mention of a Franco-Soviet alliance in the published French documents until late October 1933 confirms Paul-Boncour's postwar assertion that the German withdrawal from the League on October 14 led him to pursue the possibility. After discussing the idea with his permanent officials, Paul-Boncour raised the question with Litvinov in Paris on October 31. He insisted that no alliance was possible unless the Soviet Union joined the League of Nations; under the Locarno Treaty, France could not make war upon Germany except in pursuance of a decision by the League Council. Furthermore, France could only promise to assist the Soviets in *European* conflicts, and any Franco-Soviet agreement would have to be coordinated with the existing Franco-Polish alliance. Litvinov expressed interest, and in subsequent weeks Valerian Dovgalevsky, the Soviet ambassador in Paris, confirmed Moscow's interest in mutual-assistance pacts with France, Poland, and the Little Entente. Soviet refusal to join the League, however, held up progress until after Barthou became foreign minister in February.[27]

With the signing of the German-Polish nonaggression agreement of January 26, 1934, the Quai d'Orsay suddenly became anxious to repair Franco-Polish relations. The Franco-Polish alliance, which had been a mixed blessing as long as Franco-German reconciliation remained a goal of French policy, again become a useful instrument of French security under the impact of German rearmament. "The adhesion to the principle of a mutual assistance accord," a March 30, 1934, memorandum by the Political Section of the Quai d'Orsay began, "is seemingly the form in which Poland could most opportunely manifest her attachment to the policy of international solidarity and remove the suspicion of ambiguity that her position has acquired in European politics since the pact with Germany." After reports that the Soviets were ready to join the League had opened the door to such a pact, a memorandum of April 28 noted that German adherence would have to be sought "if one remains attached to

[27] *DDF* contains no record of the Litvinov–Paul-Boncour meeting, although a departmental note of Oct. 30, 1933, *DDF*, 1, IV, 375, states that the two ministers would meet the next day. Scott, *Alliance against Hitler*, pp. 135-36, has pieced together a detailed account of the meeting from memoirs and postwar testimony; see also Joseph Paul-Boncour, *Entre deux guerres. Souvenirs sur la troisième république*, 3 vols. (Paris, 1945-1946), II, 364-65. For subsequent discussions in December and January see *DDF*, 1, V, 88, 193.

the idea of mutual assurances and wishes to avoid falling into the old system of so-called defensive alliances." The memorandum envisioned a pact including Germany, the Soviet Union, Poland, the Baltic states, and Czechoslovakia, under which all contracting parties would undertake to assist any neighboring contracting party attacked by another signatory to the pact.[28]

Although Barthou wanted to revitalize the Franco-Polish alliance, he was more interested in an alliance with the Soviet Union. He recognized, as French Chief of Staff Maurice Gamelin later wrote, that only the Soviets "could in fact play the role of the oriental counterpoise that we needed against Germany." Here Barthou differed from his senior permanent officials, who, as we shall see, never enthusiastically supported a Franco-Soviet pact during the 1934-1935 negotiations. Barthou met with Litvinov at a session of the rump Disarmament Conference in Geneva in late May and early June and secured agreement on two new pacts: an Eastern Pact of mutual assistance, to include the Soviet Union, Germany, the Baltic states, Poland, and Czechoslovakia, and a separate Franco-Soviet agreement, under which France pledged to assist the Soviets against aggression by any Eastern Pack signatory and the Soviets assumed the obligations of a signatory of the Locarno Treaty toward France. Barthou agreed to go ahead with the treaties without Germany if Berlin refused to join. The French cabinet approved these proposals on June 5, with Pierre Laval the only vocal dissenter.[29]

Barthou decided to inform London before approaching the other projected signatories to the Eastern Pact. Certainly he never imagined that the British might join the pact, but he was anxious to do nothing to alienate the British while searching for new eastern allies. Barthou's proposals confronted the British with the larger question of how to deal with Nazi Germany. In the eighteen months since Hitler had taken power, the British cabinet had recognized the drastic change that had come over the international situation but had drawn no clear conclusions. Though worried by Hitler, they were far from ready to abandon hope of an accommodation with him and feared provocative steps that might alienate Germany from the western powers.

[28] *DDF*, 1, VI, 54, 154.
[29] Gamelin, *Servir*, II, 132; *DDF*, 1, VI, 221; Scott, *Alliance against Hitler*, pp. 171-72.

The British cabinet had begun discussing its policy toward Germany in October 1933, after Hitler had left the League and the Disarmament Conference. Fearing the financial consequences of a new arms race and preoccupied with its far-flung, worldwide defense commitments, the National Government continued to hope for a new disarmament agreement and flatly rejected any new European commitments. The cabinet, in fact, was relieved to learn in early November, after consulting the Law Officers of the Crown, that Britain could not even be forced to make war against Germany against its will under the Locarno Treaty. Sir John Simon's October 20 memorandum on British policy after the breakdown of the Disarmament Conference showed that he did not share Vansittart's view, as stated in the permanent undersecretary's August 20 memorandum on Austria, that Germany would probably have to be contained by force. "Our overriding purpose," Simon wrote, "is to promote peace in Europe; to improve relations between France and Germany, upon which the prospect of continued peace mainly depends; to allay the ruffled feelings of Germany towards ourselves, and to bring her back into the circle, and to prevent, by every possible means, a new race in armaments."[30]

Even after the breakdown of further disarmament discussions in March 1934, Simon refused to recognize any acute German threat to Britain. "He himself," he told the cabinet on March 19, "inclined to the view that a German menace, if it developed, was more likely to be to the east and south rather than the west. Austria, Danzig and Memel appeared to be particularly menaced." He gave no indication that such a menace would con-

---

[30] During 1933 the British had steadfastly refused to consider any new European commitments even as part of a new disarmament agreement. As Simon told the cabinet on Sept. 20, if a permanent disarmament commission detected a violation of a new agreement, "then the other signatories would be discharged from their obligations. That would be all. There could be no further commitment on our part and [Simon] could not agree to give any other answer" (CAB 23/77). For discussions of Britain's Locarno obligations see the cabinets of Oct. 18 and Nov. 2, 6, 1933, ibid. In a memorandum of Jan. 9, 1934, Foreign Office legal adviser Sir William Malkin concluded that Britain would be compelled to help France to resist a German reoccupation of the Rhineland demilitarized zone only if the German action were taken "with the clear intention of making war," a judgment that the British government might reserve for itself (FO 371/17746, C247/247/18). For Simon's memorandum see CAB 24/243, CP 240 (33); the cabinet approved it on Oct. 23, stressing the need to seek new agreements (CAB 23/77).

cern Britain. On March 22 the cabinet decided to try again to reach agreement with Germany while rejecting an alliance with France. "Given the conditions in France today," the minutes of this meeting read, "to ally ourselves with France was a terrible responsibility." Furthermore, the French would insist upon a larger British army, and London preferred to spend money on other forms of defense. Although the cabinet discussed a possible new commitment to Belgian independence, it refused even to link a new commitment to France with a new disarmament agreement.[31]

When the French first informed the British officially of the projected Eastern Pact and Franco-Soviet agreement on June 27, 1934, Foreign Office reaction was cool. Sargent minuted skeptically that the pact was not fully reciprocal; although France received a guarantee from the Soviets, Germany did not, and the Soviet Union was the only eastern nation to receive a French guarantee. Even though Sir William Malkin's legal opinion found the project generally acceptable under the League Covenant, Simon's first reaction was extremely negative. "I strongly suspect," he minuted, "that M. Barthou would exploit any approval which we showed into something like Anglo-French cooperation against Germany." Would not British approval of the project and Soviet admission to the League make a German return to Geneva "more unlikely to be achieved than ever? In other words, is not French policy in this matter really part of the general scheme of turning the League of Nations into an anti-German organization?"[32]

Simon's personal relations with Barthou were strained; on May 29, in Geneva, the French foreign minister had publicly attacked British views on security in general and Simon's attempts to reach agreement with Germany in particular. Nonetheless, it is not altogether surprising that Simon agreed to support the proposed Eastern Pact after talks with Barthou and permanent officials of the two foreign ministries in London on July 9-10. For although the British rejected Barthou's emphasis on the

---

[31] Cabinets of Mar. 19, 22, and July 11, 1934, CAB 23/78-79.

[32] For Sargent's and Simon's reactions see FO 371/17747, C4098/277/18. Sargent's objection was not very logical, since France already had mutual-assistance treaties with Poland and Czechoslovakia; Lithuania was the only German neighbor that would remain uncovered by the pact. Perhaps even Barthou shrank from guaranteeing Memel. See also DDF, 1, VI, 398.

containment of Germany and still sought an agreement with Hitler, the instrument of containment that Barthou proposed was relatively unobjectionable from their point of view. The reason was simple: the Eastern Pact did not require any new British commitments. Mere endorsement of the pact was far easier to grant than French requests for military staff conversations or British military contributions to a new security system would have been. Thus the British agreed to recommend the project to the other parties involved, provided that French and Soviet guarantees were accorded to Germany as well as to each other and that the Eastern pact was linked to the conclusion of a new disarmament agreement. Barthou quickly agreed to offer the Germans new guarantees but warned that he might conclude a Franco-Soviet alliance should the Eastern Pact fail. He refused to discuss the legalization of German rearmament, however, until *after* the new pact was signed. Ultimately, the two governments agreed that the pact would be "a starting point for the resumption of negotiations for the conclusion of a convention providing for a reasonable interpretation of German equality of rights in relation to armaments in a regime of security for all nations."[33]

The French, with British help, now began seeking the approval of other signatories to the pact. The Czech government was enthusiastic; Beneš also wanted to bring the Soviet Union into European politics. He endorsed the pact, tried to improve relations between the Soviets and his Little Entente partners, and told Litvinov in July that he would sign a bilateral Czech-Soviet pact if the Eastern Pact failed. The Baltic states reacted cautiously, but all three eventually expressed willingness to sign the pact if Poland and Germany did so.[34] The keys to the situation clearly lay in Berlin and Warsaw.

[33] Scott, *Alliance against Hitler*, p. 170. For minutes of the Franco-German talks see *DBFP*, 2, VI, 487-89, and *DDF*, 1, VI, 457. Interestingly enough, in the cabinet of July 11 Simon explained Britain's decision to support the Eastern Pact but also announced his decision to drop the proposed new declaration in support of Belgian independence. This, he stated, might lead to an unwanted Franco-British-Belgian alliance; he preferred to let Barthou press on with his own plans (CAB 23/79).

[34] On Beneš's attitude see Reichert, *Kleine Entente*, pp. 111-13. On June 9, 1934, Prague and Bucharest opened diplomatic relations with Moscow, but the fanatically anti-Bolshevik Yugoslav government refused to do so. Barthou had

It is doubtful that Barthou ever expected the Germans to accept the pact; he did not even communicate its text to them officially until August 20, six weeks after his talks with the British. When British Ambassador Sir Eric Phipps discussed the pact with Neurath on July 13, Neurath stated that Germany would have to receive equality of rights in armaments before entering into any such arrangement, and he even denied that Germany needed anything like the Eastern Pact. The pact could not have appealed to Hitler, who always insisted on dealing bilaterally with other nations and avoided long-term commitments that would tie his hands. On July 16 the Wilhelmstrasse informed German diplomatic missions abroad that Germany would reject the pact, but Berlin delayed a formal reply to avoid blame for the project's failure.[35]

In Warsaw, Beck too seems to have decided almost at once to reject the pact, but he avoided a direct, immediate reply so as not to appear too negative. In talks with French and British diplomats in early July, he raised a series of technical objections to the proposal: it would be difficult for Poland to assume new obligations toward Lithuania, with which Warsaw did not even maintain normal diplomatic relations because of the Vilnius dispute, or Czechoslovakia, whose inclusion would involve Poland in "Danubian questions." Beck had committed himself to maintaining good relations with Germany, and he told the Germans during the summer of 1934 that he would do nothing to disturb their new relationship. The Polish government was not very interested in mutual-assistance pacts with Germany or Russia; diplomatic reports suggested that in the event of war with one of its two great neighbors, the Polish government hoped the other would remain neutral rather than offer assistance. Beck specifically told Neurath on September 6 that he would not accept the Eastern Pact in its present form, and the German government officially rejected it four days later. Warsaw followed suit on

---

discussed the Eastern Pact on visits to Bucharest and Belgrade in late June, but he had never intended Rumania or Yugoslavia to be signatories; see Scott, *Alliance against Hitler*, pp. 174-75. On the Baltic states' attitudes see Wojciechowski, *Polnisch-deutschen Beziehungen*, pp. 140-41, Scott, pp. 186-87, and *DDF*, 1, VI, 452. Scott notes that Finland, which Litvinov had hoped would join the pact, refused to be considered.

[35] Weinberg, *Foreign Policy*, pp. 184-85; *DBFP*, 2, VI, 499; *DGFP*, C, III, 92.

September 27, insisting that Poland would not join unless Germany did so.[36]

The Eastern Pact was clearly dead in its original from. How Barthou would have proceeded had he lived longer will never be known. Judging from his previous statements, he would probably have moved rapidly to an independent arrangement with the Soviets. Since the assassination of Austrian Chancellor Dollfuss by Austrian Nazis on July 25, 1934, Barthou had become increasingly preoccupied with Austrian security and Franco-Italian relations. He now wanted to reach a new agreement with Mussolini to safeguard Austrian independence, thus blocking Hitler in the southeast in the same way that the Eastern Pact would have blocked him in the east. At Geneva, in late September, Barthou arranged a Franco-British-Italian communiqué of September 27 reaffirming the necessity of Austrian independence, and he promised to visit Rome in November. While working with Mussolini, however, Barthou had to take account of the susceptibilities of the Little Entente and particularly of Yugoslavia, whose relations with Italy were strained. On October 9, Barthou and King Alexander of Yugoslavia, who had arrived in Marseilles to discuss Franco-Yugoslav-Italian relations, were assassinated by Croatian terrorists during a parade. Barthou's death led to a radical change in the spirit of French foreign policy.[37]

The choice of Pierre Laval to replace Barthou at the Quai d'Orsay illustrates the fundamental anarchy of French cabinet politics during the 1930s.[38] Both Laval and Barthou were iden-

[36] On Beck's initial response see: Wojciechowski, *Polnisch-deutschen Beziehungen*, pp. 127-30; Central Department memorandum, July 30, 1934, FO 371/17749, C5258/247/18; *DDF*, 1, VI, 431; *DBFP*, 2, VI, 492. The seizure of Vilnius had occurred in 1920, and Lithuania still refused to enter into normal diplomatic relations with Poland as a result. Polish-Czechoslovakian tension stemmed from disputes over the province of Teschen (Těšín), which the Czechs acquired over Polish objections after the First World War, and from Czech behavior during the Soviet-Polish war in 1920-1921. Beck, who always maintained good relations with Hungary, did not want to defend Czechoslovakia against Hungarian revisionism or to stand in the way of German expansion to the southeast. On Poland's decision to reject the pact see *DGFP*, C, III, 194, 226, and Wojciechowski, pp. 145-47.

[37] *DBFP*, 2, XII, 127; Scott, *Alliance against Hitler*, pp. 201-4; J. B. Hoptner, *Yugoslavia in Crisis, 1934-41* (New York, 1962), pp. 22-28.

[38] On Laval see Geoffrey Warner, *Pierre Laval and the Eclipse of France* (London, 1968), and Scott, *Alliance against Hitler*, pp. 206-8. Neither sheds much light

tified as men of the right, but their views on foreign policy turned out to be radically different. Barthou had viewed Hitler as an inevitable threat to French security; Laval, a former pacifist, sought a real reconciliation with Germany despite the rise of Hitler. Although on the surface Laval continued his predecessor's policies, he transformed their objectives completely. Barthou had wanted the Eastern Pact, the new pact with Mussolini, and the possible Franco-Soviet alliance in order to contain Hitler. Laval pursued all these initiatives, but for him they had a different purpose: to encourage a lasting Franco-German settlement. Ultimately, in May 1935, public opinion and the rest of the French cabinet forced Laval to sign the Franco-Soviet alliance, but his goal remained a general settlement with Germany. Laval's emphasis on accommodation with Germany pleased the British, who gladly renewed their support of a modified Eastern Pact as part of a disarmament and security agreement with Berlin. By subsuming the project under a general settlement with Germany, the French and British provided Hitler with almost endless opportunities for diplomatic delay while continuing to put off effective action of their own.

Rather than move quickly to a bilateral agreement with the Soviet Union, Laval decided to pursue the Eastern Pact and seek German adherence. He immediately told the Soviets that his ultimate goal was a settlement with Germany; new Franco-Soviet agreements were principally a means to this end. Quai d'Orsay permanent officials supported this policy; both Léger and Political Director Henri Bargeton told British diplomats that they wanted to avoid a bilateral agreement with the Soviet Union. Paris tried to meet Polish objections to the Eastern Pact, offering on November 30 to exempt Poland from any obligations toward Lithuania or Czechoslovakia and insisting that France too wanted to include Germany in the pact. The Poles delayed a reply to Paris but told Berlin that they still opposed the pact. Laval's maneuvers disturbed the Soviets. In Geneva, in late November, Litvinov asked Laval to promise not to carry out sepa-

---

on the reasons for the choice of Laval to replace Barthou. It was not immediately obvious that his selection would mean a change in policy; British Minister Ronald Campbell wrote London on Oct. 30 that he expected Laval to hold to Barthou's "nationalist" course (*BDFP*, 2, XII, 156). Hoesch, the German ambassador to London, correctly suggested that Laval represented an improvement from the German point of view (*DGFP*, C, III, 254).

rate negotiations for an Eastern Pact. On December 5 Laval and Litvinov signed a protocol pledging support for the Eastern Pact, promising to keep each other fully informed of any negotiations relating to it, and agreeing to consult should negotiations fail. Laval did not, however, let these written promises stand in his way in succeeding weeks.[39]

Laval moved more actively to improve relations with Italy and block Germany in Southeastern Europe. He told British Minister Ronald Campbell on October 30 that he intended to carry out Barthou's projected visit to Rome at an appropriate time and to seek an agreement among Italy, Yugoslavia, and Czechoslovakia on specific action to be taken if Austrian independence were threatened. On December 13 Laval told Sir George Clerk, the British ambassador to France, that he was thinking of a broader agreement on Austrian independence and integrity, one that would include the Little Entente, Hungary, Italy, Germany, France, and Britain.[40]

In the meantime, the Eastern Pact had received an unexpected boost from the British, who decided to include it in a new disarmament and security package. By late 1934 the British government felt increasing anxiety about German rearmament. As Simon suggested in a memorandum for a new cabinet Committee on German Rearmament on November 29, "the best course would be to recognize that Germany's rearmament in breach of the Treaty is a fact which cannot be altered and to reach the conclusion that this had better be recognized without delay in the hope that we can still get, in return for legalization, some valuable terms from Germany." Recognizing that France would demand new security guarantees in return for legalization, Simon suggested that Britain make a further, albeit dubious, effort to persuade Germany to agree to the Eastern Pact. His colleagues authorized him to make these proposals to Laval and Flandin, who had replaced Doumergue as premier in November.[41]

In talks with Simon in Paris on December 22, Laval explicitly reversed Barthou's policy and agreed to work for the Eastern

---

[39] Warner, *Laval*, p. 74, quotes Soviet sources describing Laval's Oct. 19 conversation with a Soviet diplomat. See also *DBFP*, 2, XII, 188, 243, *DGFP*, C, III, 379, and Scott, *Alliance against Hitler*, pp. 210-12.

[40] *DBFP*, 2, XII, 155, 288.

[41] Ibid., no. 235; Simon memorandum, Nov. 29, 1934, CAB 27/572; cabinet of Dec. 19, CAB 23/80.

Pact and a new disarmament agreement at the same time; the pact "should be taken in combination with, and not before, discussion with Germany of agreement about armaments." First, however, he intended to go to Rome and secure Mussolini's agreement to a multilateral guarantee of Austrian independence.[42]

Unfortunately, as Laval admitted to the British, his negotiations with Rome were not going well. Although Mussolini wanted to protect Austria, he did not want to alienate Hungary by making an agreement with Yugoslavia and Czechoslovakia; nor did he want to pledge to respect the integrity of Yugoslavia. Under the circumstances, Léger advised against an immediate trip to Rome, but Laval, perhaps looking for a dramatic success to bolster his personal prestige, instead made new concessions to make the visit a success. Dropping the proposal that Austria's neighbors commit themselves to defend its independence by force of arms, the French now agreed to a weaker proposal under which Austria and its neighbors, including Germany, would join in a pledge not to intervene in one another's internal affairs. The Austrian pact was rapidly being transformed into a document that Germany could accept, rather than one that would contain Hitler effectively. On December 27 diplomats in Rome reached agreement on this basis, and Laval arrived for a five-day visit on January 4, 1935. He confirmed the projected new Austrian agreement, settled outstanding Franco-Italian colonial questions, and gave controversial assurances to Mussolini regarding Ethiopia, the exact nature of which remains a matter of debate.[43]

Laval then tried once more to gain Polish and German approval of the Eastern Pact, but neither country would budge. On January 30 the Wilhelmstrasse also refused to commit the German government to the Austrian Pact, or Danubian Pact as it was sometimes called, in a memorandum for the French and Italian governments. Nonetheless, in talks in London on February 1-3, French and British ministers agreed to make another attempt to secure general assent to the Eastern and Danubian pacts. The communiqué issued at the close of these conversa-

[42] DBFP, 2, XII, 311.

[43] Scott, Alliance against Hitler, pp. 215-17. Laval's negotiations with Rome can also be followed in FO 371/17750, R7146/R7148/R7186/R7280/R7283/R7407/R7415/R7827/5311/67.

tions called for a general settlement of disarmament and security questions. When the German government suggested that a British official come to Berlin to discuss these questions, Simon agreed to meet with Hitler in the first week in March.[44]

Inevitably, the French and British began to modify the Eastern Pact to suit German tastes. Both Whitehall and the Quai d'Orsay developed proposals in February designed to take advantage of Hitler's oft-repeated willingness to conclude nonaggression pacts with his neighbors. Sargent designed a scheme under which France, Germany, and the Soviet Union would guarantee the existing nonaggression pacts between Germany and Poland, the Soviet Union and Poland, and the Soviet Union and Lithuania, as well as new nonaggression pacts between Germany and Czechoslovakia and Germany and Lithuania. On February 20, Quai Political Director Bargeton gave Clerk an even weaker proposal: a general, multilateral pact of nonaggression and consultation, with provision for optional bilateral mutual-assistance agreements between members. Laval broke his promises to Litvinov in an effort to reach agreement with Germany; he admitted to Simon in late February that he had discussed Bargeton's proposals with German Ambassador Roland Köster, but only *unofficially*, to avoid violating his December pledge to Litvinov. Both Laval and Léger told Clerk they still hoped to avoid a Franco-Soviet alliance; Léger said on February 26 that he had fought for two years against the general staff, public opinion, and Foreign Ministers Paul-Boncour and Barthou to prevent one.[45]

Events in early March overtook Laval's policy of putting Berlin before Moscow. On March 5 Hitler postponed Simon's visit to Berlin, letting it be known that a British white paper acknowledging that British rearmament was partly related to developments in Germany had displeased him. Then, on March 16, he announced the existence of the German air force and the reintroduction of conscription in Germany, justifying the latter step on the grounds that France had increased compulsory military

[44] Wojciechowski, *Polnisch-deutschen Beziehungen*, p. 158. On the German attitude see *DGFP*, C, III, 440, and *DBFP*, 2, XII, 362. On the Danubian Pact see *DGFP*, C, III, 453, 460, 466. For the Franco-British talks and the German invitation to London see *DBFP*, 2, XII, 397, 398, 400, 437, 441, 446, 463, 477, 479, 487, 490.

[45] *DBFP*, 2, XII, 468, 482, 509, 517.

service from one year to two. The British, increasingly desperate for agreement with Germany, docilely postponed Simon's visit, but the French cabinet reacted sharply. On March 20 Flandin and Herriot, prevailing over Laval, insisted that France bring Hitler's violations of the Treaty of Versailles before the League Council. Laval countered by offering to accept Litvinov's invitation to discuss Franco-Soviet relations in Moscow. On March 23 Laval told Lord Privy Seal Anthony Eden that other cabinet members were pressuring him to pursue a less conciliatory policy toward Germany, and he added that mutual assistance must be included in any Eastern Pact.[46]

On March 25-26 Simon and Eden discussed disarmament and the Eastern and Danubian pacts with Hitler, Neurath, and Disarmament Commissioner Joachim von Ribbentrop in Berlin. Hitler refused to sign even a multilateral nonaggression pact with optional bilateral mutual-assistance clauses. Such a pact, he claimed, would extend German approval to a Franco-Soviet Pact. Neurath instead gave the British an outline of a ten-year multilateral pact of nonaggression, arbitration, and consultation. Regarding the Danubian Pact, Hitler denied any desire to annex Austria and expressed willingness to conclude a nonaggression agreement with Vienna, but he argued that a general definition of noninterference would be impossible to achieve.[47]

At Mussolini's invitation, the French, British, and Italian governments prepared to discuss disarmament and security at Stresa beginning on April 11. In the meantime, Laval, prodded by Herriot, began negotiating the details of a Franco-Soviet Pact in late March and early April. On April 9 the French cabinet decided to sign a mutual-assistance pact with the Soviets regardless of the results of the Stresa conference. Members of the British Foreign Office still opposed a Franco-Soviet Pact, and Sargent even suggested that Hitler should perhaps be allowed to move due east, where he would not threaten Italian interests on the Danube or Franco-British interests on the Rhine.[48]

[46] Weinberg, *Foreign Policy*, pp. 204-5; Scott, *Alliance against Hitler*, pp. 235-36; *DBFP*, 2, XII, 524, 641, 642.

[47] For the record of the conversations and Neurath's draft see *DBFP*, 2, XII, 651, or *DGFP*, C, III, 555. These meetings provide an excellent example of Hitler's diplomatic technique.

[48] Scott, *Alliance against Hitler*, pp. 238-40; *DBFP*, 2, XII, 621, 634. For Sargent's comments see FO 371/18834, C2656/C2922/55/18.

At Stresa, on April 11, Laval asked Simon whether the Germans would accept a multilateral nonaggression pact with provision for optional mutual assistance between members and, when the foreign secretary could not give him an affirmative answer, indicated that he might soon conclude a mutual-assistance treaty with the Soviets. Trying to keep the possibility of agreement with Germany open, Simon telegraphed Phipps, instructing him to ask Neurath whether such an arrangement would doom the multilateral nonaggression pact. Neurath, with Hitler's approval, told Phipps that Germany could not object if other powers made separate agreements, provided they were not referred to in the nonaggression pact. The Germans apparently feared being too negative while the three other western powers were meeting to discuss Germany. When Simon passed this declaration on to Laval, the French minister merely noted that France "now had the latitude to make with Russia a bilateral pact of mutual assistance without hindering the negotiation and conclusion of a multilateral pact of non-aggression."[49]

The conference also discussed the proposed Danubian or Central European Pact but could not resolve the various questions that had arisen since Laval and Mussolini first proposed it in January. When the Little Entente foreign ministers had discussed the plan, Beneš had endorsed it, but Bogolyub Jevtich of Yugoslavia and Titulescu of Rumania had held back. Both feared a Hapsburg restoration in Vienna more than the Anschluss, and both were determined not to rule out armed intervention to block such a restoration by pledging non-interference in Austria's "internal affairs." Hungary, on the other hand, insisted on recognition of its equality of rights in armaments as a condition of accession and would do nothing to reaffirm its existing frontiers. At Stresa, Mussolini noted the difficulty of finding acceptable definitions of nonintervention and noninterference, and, in an attempt to please the Hungarians, he suggested that the conference immediately approve Austrian, Hungarian, and Bulgarian equality of rights in arms. At Laval's insistence, the conference merely recommended that this question be discussed together with the proposed Central European Pact. Attempts to organize a conference to discuss the

---

[49] For the Stresa conversations see *DBFP*, 2, XII, 722; for the Simon-Phipps correspondence, ibid., 715, 717; for the Newton-Neurath conversation, *DGFP*, C, IV, 24.

pact dragged on during the spring and summer but were over-shadowed by the dispute between Italy and Ethiopia.[50]

After Stresa, Laval negotiated the details of a Franco-Soviet Pact with Litvinov in Geneva and Soviet Ambassador Vladimir Potemkin in Paris. He and Potemkin signed the pact on May 2, 1935. To ensure that France, in coming to the assistance of the Soviets after a German attack, would not force Britain to assist Germany in accordance with the Locarno Treaty, the final text tied French action to a decision of the League Council, adding that France would render assistance if the council could not agree. The pact included a statement calling for a broader agreement along the lines of the original Eastern Pact. Two weeks later, on May 16, Beneš signed an almost identical mutual-assistance treaty with the Soviet Union. This treaty included the significant provision that it was to operate only if France came to the assistance of the country attacked.[51]

The Franco-Soviet Pact could have begun a new era in European diplomacy. It did not because its signature did not change Laval's essential goal: a lasting settlement with Germany. On his way to Moscow to celebrate the new pact, Laval stopped in Berlin and Warsaw on May 10 and 11. He told both French Ambassador François-Poncet and Beck that he still hoped to conclude a multilateral nonaggression pact that would include Germany, and he even suggested to Beck that such a pact might *supplant* the new Franco-Soviet Pact![52] The Germans, however, had other ideas. On May 27 the German government circulated a memorandum to the other Locarno signatories arguing that the provisions of the Franco-Soviet Pact—specifically, the undertak-

[50] On the attitudes of the Little Entente and Hungary see Reichert, *Kleine Entente*, pp. 86-88, and British legation Budapest to FO, Jan, 25, 1935, FO 371/19497, R655/1/37. See also the Stresa conversation of Apr. 13, 1935, *DBFP*, 2, XII, 722. During May and June the French and Italian governments agreed on military cooperation against German aggression against Austria or France; see Scott, *Alliance against Hitler*, p. 241. British Ambassador Sir Eric Drummond reported on July 23 that Mussolini subsequently seemed to lose interest in the Danubian Pact (FO 371/19499, R4649/1/67).

[51] For the negotiations and the final text see Scott, *Alliance against Hitler*, pp. 242-50, 272-75. The British were satisfied with these safeguards; see Malkin's minute of May 4, 1935, affirming the compatibility of the pact with Locarno (FO 371/18838, C3612/55/18).

[52] British embassy Berlin and British legation Warsaw to FO, May 10, 11, 1935, FO 371/18839, C3834/C3844/55/18; Warner, *Laval*, p. 81.

ing to assist each other even if the League Council failed to reach a decision—contravened the Locarno Treaty. In June, Neurath refused to discuss proposals for a multilateral nonaggression pact until the western powers had satisfactorily answered this argument.[53] Hitler ultimately used the Franco-Soviet Pact as his pretext for the remilitarization of the Rhineland in March 1936 in violation of Locarno.

Laval continued to hope for a Franco-German settlement; on July 27, 1935, he told German Ambassador Köster that his real goal remained agreement with Germany. If Germany signed a multilateral nonaggression pact, he implied, he would abandon the Franco-Soviet alliance.[54] The Germans, however, refused to bite. The Ethiopian question was already assuming center stage; the real object of Laval's policy remained frustrated. Relations with Germany stayed in the background until the reoccupation of the Rhineland.

France lost ground in Eastern Europe during the first half of the 1930s because successive French governments had not consistently supported the status quo. In 1925, at Locarno, Briand had implicitly accepted a distinction between Germany's western and eastern frontiers; in 1930 he had evacuated the Rhineland without giving Poland any additional security guarantees. We have seen that by 1931 he apparently contemplated further treaty revision at Poland's expense. By 1932 Marshal Piłsudski had concluded that Poland could no longer rely upon the French alliance. Piłsudski and Beck responded to Hitler's overtures in 1933 after the Four Power Pact had further shaken their confidence. When in 1934 Barthou attempted to draw them back into the French orbit, they decided to rely upon their entente with Gemany.

[53] *DGFP*, C, IV, 106, 107; British embassy Berlin to FO, June 24, 1935, FO 371/18847, C4956/55/18.

[54] For Köster's account of the conversation see *DGFP*, C, IV, 231. Bülow gave Phipps an account of this conversation on July 30; see FO 371/18849, C5730/55/18. When Clerk raised the matter with an unidentified Quai official on Aug. 1, the official replied that he was "totally unable to respond." Clerk suggested that Laval often spoke freely with the German ambassador and probably kept his subordinates in the dark (ibid., C5771/55/18). On Aug. 7 Laval essentially confirmed his conversation with Köster but added that the German had promised not to report it (ibid., C5860/55/18).

Barthou's views, in any event, hardly represented the consensus of opinion in either Paris or London. Like Piłsudski and Beck, most British and French politicians and civil servants still hoped to solve many of their major foreign-policy problems by reaching a new settlement with Germany. Members of the British National Government, desperate to avoid either a European war or an arms race, remained willing to pay for such a settlement with substantial concessions. Already some politicians and civil servants had suggested that some German expansion eastward should be tolerated, if only to ease German threats to more immediate French and British interests. The assumption upon which this policy rested—that Hitler would be satisfied with relatively small gains in the east—was totally false. Shortly after the signing of the German-Polish Non-Aggression Declaration in 1934, Hitler told Hermann Rauschning that he would never be content with German-dominated customs unions in Eastern Europe or with a Central European federation modeled after the British Empire. Germany must conquer its own living space in the east and reduce the remaining states of the region to complete subservience.[55] Paradoxically, however, the advent of Hitler had only made the British more desperate to reach a settlement with Germany, and Pierre Laval also sought an accommodation with Hitler. Only after the French and British governments had abandoned hope of peace with Hitler would they be willing to defend the status quo in Eastern Europe. Unfortunately, key officials retained such hopes right up until September 3, 1939.

[55] Rauschning, *Voice of Destruction*, pp. 116-27.

VI.

German Trade with Eastern Europe, 1934-1937

Nazi Germany's trade with Eastern Europe, and especially with Southeastern Europe has been the subject of numerous studies. Many of them, written during the 1930s, are polemical and only partially accurate, and most subsequent treatments have not progressed very far beyond the contemporary analyses.[1] In general, the secondary literature fails correctly to place German trade policy toward Eastern Europe within the context of Nazi economic policy as a whole. For although the original impetus behind German trade agreements with Southeastern European countries in 1934-1935 was largely political, trade under the Nazi regime increasingly had to serve pressing economic needs generated by Hitler's rearmament policies. The Wilhelmstrasse encouraged trade with Eastern Europe as a means of increasing German political influence. Under Hitler, such trade helped to prepare Germany for a war of conquest.

German trade policy toward Eastern Europe under the Nazis falls into two periods. The first, from 1934 to 1936, coincides with the economic dictatorship of Hjalmar Schacht, the New

---

[1] The best contemporary discussions are Antonín Basch, *The Danube Basin and the German Economic Sphere* (New York, 1943), and Ellis, *Exchange Control in Central Europe*, pp. 257-70. More polemical are Gerhard Schacher, *Germany Pushes Southeast* (London, 1937), Norbert Mühlen, *Der Zauberer. Leben und Anleihen des Dr. Hjalmar Horace Greeley Schacht* (Zurich, 1938), and Arnold Toynbee et al., *Survey of International Affairs, 1936* (London, 1937), pp. 526-33. More recent discussions include two articles by Hans-Jürgen Schröder, "Deutsche Südosteuropapolitik 1929-36," pp. 5-32, and "Südosteuropa als 'Informal Empire' Deutschlands 1933-39. Das Beispiel Jugoslawien," *Jahrbücher für Geschichte Osteuropas*, XXIII (1975), 70-96; Doering, "Deutsche Aussenwirtschaftspolitik," pp. 108-16; Hans-Erich Volkmann, "Aussenhandel und Aufrüstung in Deutschland 1933 bis 1939," in Friedrich Forstmeier and Hans-Erich Volkmann, eds., *Wirtschaft und Rüstung am Vorabend des Zweiten Weltkrieges* (Düsseldorf, 1975), pp. 103-10; William Carr, *Arms, Autarky and Aggression: A Study in German Foreign Policy, 1933-39* (London, 1972); and Berend and Ránki, *Economic Development*, pp. 265-84.

Plan in foreign trade, and the achievement of maximum German agricultural self-sufficiency. Although trade with Eastern Europe expanded significantly during this period, prevailing economic and agricultural policies kept total trade within fairly severe limits, and, in general, German trade with the east did not reach the predepression levels of 1928. Furthermore, lagging German exports led to the accumulation of large reichsmark balances in German clearings with Eastern European states, and this development—which was *not* regarded as a beneficial one by responsible German authorities—impeded the development of a smooth pattern of trade. For the purposes of this study, the second period in German trade policy toward Eastern Europe extends from 1937 through 1939, although it actually continued through the Second World War. It began with Hermann Göring's assumption of full power over German foreign trade under the Four Year Plan of 1936 and witnessed an expansion of German trade with Eastern Europe as a result of new import and export policies. On the one hand, the failure of German agriculture to provide for domestic needs led to an enormous increase in imports of foodstuffs; on the other, the problem of German exports was substantially alleviated by the encouragement of large-scale, long-term exports of arms.

Political considerations, of course, played a major role in determining trade policies, as did the initiatives of private concerns. The Foreign Office remained interested in such trade for political reasons, and IG Farben and other German firms looked after their own interests. On the whole, however, German rearmament and its impact on the German economy had the greatest influence on German trade with Eastern Europe. What began as a traditional attempt to extend influence gradually became a temporary and imperfect solution to some of Germany's major economic and trade problems. Because normal trade with Eastern Europe could never meet all of Germany's needs, however, and because Hitler was determined to solve Germany's economic problems through a war of conquest whatever the risks, this solution could never be more than temporary and imperfect.

International trade was not a major preoccupation of the Nazi regime during its first year in power; in the economic sphere, unemployment and agricultural questions took up most of the government's time.[2] By early 1934, however, the government had to deal with a worsening trade balance. As we have seen, the rapid expansion of domestic demand engendered by new government spending on public works had begun to affect German foreign trade by late 1933. Domestic revival led to rapid increases in imports of raw materials, while overvaluation of the reichsmark, increases in domestic orders, and some foreign boycotts of German goods tended to prevent corresponding increases in exports. The crisis in the fall of 1933 led to Hans Posse's first suggestions for the reordering of German trade along bilateral lines.[3] The situation worsened during 1934. The import surplus became so great in the first half of the year that there were widespread rumors of an imminent German devaluation. Ultimately, Germany showed an import surplus of 284 million RM, or 7 percent, compared with an *export* surplus of 667 million RM, or 16 percent, for 1933.[4] As a result, the government adopted the New Plan for foreign trade in September 1934. Under the New Plan, a new series of *Überwächungsstelle*, or supervisory agencies, tightly controlled imports by authorizing the issuance of foreign exchange or payments into clearings for them. The New Plan sought to equalize German imports and exports with individual trading partners, buying only from countries willing to buy German goods in return.[5]

The chief architect of the New Plan was Hjalmar Schacht. Coincident with the promulgation of the New Plan, Schacht consolidated his position as economic chief of the Third Reich by assuming the Ministry of Economics while remaining president of the Reichsbank. Schacht was a conservative nationalist, and his career exemplifies the relationship of traditional conservative elites to Hitler and the Nazi regime. In March 1932, when Hitler's accession to power had become a real possibility, Schacht prepared for that contingency by forming a committee designed to formulate economic policy, make contact with the Nazis, and

[2] Doering, "Deutsche Aussenwirtschaftspolitik," pp. 215-16.
[3] See above, Chapter III.
[4] Volkmann, "Aussenhandel," p. 85.
[5] Doering, "Deutsche Aussenwirtschaftspolitik," pp. 202-61; Volkmann, "Aussenhandel, pp. 81-90; Reichsbank circular on German exports, July 12, 1934, T-120/9272/E657695-706; Reichsstelle für Devisenbewirtschaftung circular on the New Plan, Sept. 1, 1934, T-120/9037/E633344-49.

attempt to influence their economic thought. Having established personal contact with Hitler in 1932, he was reappointed Reichsbank president in March 1933 (he had held the position during the 1920s until his resignation in protest against the Young Plan). He did not, however, join the Nazi party.[6]

By devising new methods to finance German rearmament, Schacht probably did more than any other individual to help Hitler fulfill his foreign-policy goals. In many respects, however, he maintained a relatively orthodox line in economic policy, and his basically traditional orientation in economic thought led to his gradual eclipse in 1936 and 1937. Although he instigated the New Plan—an obvious departure from traditional principles of normal trade—he apparently regarded it as a temporary emergency measure, to be discarded when Germany was offered the opportunity to reenter the world economy on suitably favorable terms. He clearly rejected the autarky theories of Nazi and other conservative ideologues, recognizing that German dependence on overseas raw materials would always require substantial German participation in world trade, but he was not above *threatening* foreign powers with German autarky in order to secure concessions. With regard to Eastern Europe, Schacht's views were also traditional. As a good German nationalist he resented the loss of German territory to Poland, and he favored the extension of German influence in the area generally. A member of the Arbeitsausschuss für Mitteleuropa during the First World War, he admitted to a Nuremberg interrogator in 1945 that he had hoped for a revival of the Mitteleuropa scheme during the 1930s.[7] Although he also sought to increase German participation in the development of raw materials in Southeastern Europe, he certainly did not view increased trade with this region as a solution to Germany's economic problems. These, he felt, could only be solved on a world scale. The return to world trade that he desired would have reduced trade with

[6] Doering, "Deutsche Aussenwirtschaftspolitik," pp. 246-47; Weinberg, *Foreign Policy*, p. 31. Hjalmar Schacht, *76 Jahre meines Lebens* (Bad Wörishofen, 1953), p. 375, states that Hitler told him he would not have to join the Nazi party.

[7] Doering, "Deutsche Aussenwirtschaftspolitik," pp. 38-39; Dieter Petzina, *Autarkiepolitik im Dritten Reich. Der nationalsozialistische Vierjahresplan* (Stuttgart, 1968), pp. 24-25; International Military Tribunal, *Trial of the Major War Criminals before the International Military Tribunal, Nuremburg, 14 November 1945-1 October 1946*, 42 vols. (Nuremburg, 1947-1949), XXXIII, 5. This portrait of Schacht also draws on episodes treated later in the text.

Eastern Europe, and we shall see that he was by no means as enthusiastic about such trade as has been supposed. In his eyes, the
goal of foreign trade was to secure the maximum essential imports at the lowest possible price.

Equally important to the development of Nazi trade with
Eastern Europe was Nazi agricultural policy, directed from
mid-1933 onward by the Nazi theorist and minister of agriculture Walter Darré. Like his predecessors Schiele, Braun, and
Hugenberg, Darré sought maximum domestic production in
agriculture, with the ultimate goal of complete agricultural
self-sufficiency. In public, these policies were embodied in the
Erzeugungschlacht, or battle of production, first declared in
1934.[8] Schacht supported this policy, hoping to keep German
agricultural imports to a minimum as a means of saving foreign
exchange. Schacht, in fact, protested Darré's attempts to establish an emergency reserve of foreign grain in 1934 and fought
his requests to make up shortages of feed grains with imports in
1935. This policy led to shortages of butter, meat, and pork in
1935-1936, and ultimately to the crisis that precipitated
Schacht's downfall.

On the whole, German trade and agricultural policy had contradictory effects on trade with Eastern Europe from 1934
through 1936. On the one hand, restrictions on German cereals
imports kept German imports of Southeastern European cereals
well below the levels specified in the agreements of 1934-1935.
On the other hand, increasing German domestic consumption,
combined with domestic fodder shortages, led to increased imports of meat, meat products, and butter during the same period, benefiting the region as a whole. Various parts of Eastern
Europe also benefited from increased German demand for certain industrial raw materials.

The entire course of German trade with Eastern Europe from
1933 through 1939 is shown in Table A.1. Table VI.1 shows the
course of trade with the agricultural countries from 1933
through 1936. German trade with Austria and Czechoslovakia,
which consisted mostly of industrial products, need not be discussed in detail. As shown in Table A.1, the shares of these
countries in German trade remained stable between 1933 and

[8] Robert Lorenz, "The Essential Features of Germany's Agricultural Policy
from 1870 to 1937" (Ph.D. diss., Columbia University, 1941), pp. 99, 111-18.

TABLE VI.1
Value of German Imports and Exports from Eastern Europe,
1933-1936
(In Millions of Reichsmarks)

	1933	1934	1935	1936
Hungary				
Imports from	34.2	63.9	77.9	93.4
Exports to	38.1	39.6	62.9	83.0
Rumania				
Imports from	46.1	59.0	79.9	92.3
Exports to	46.0	50.9	63.8	103.6
Yugoslavia				
Imports from	33.5	36.3	61.4	75.2
Exports to	33.8	31.5	36.9	77.2
Poland*				
Imports from	77.1	78.1	75.5	74.0
Exports to	82.4	55.1	63.3	73.9
Estonia				
Imports from	8.4	8.2	13.1	13.8
Exports to	7.1	7.3	11.4	17.6
Latvia				
Imports from	17.5	21.1	31.1	33.2
Exports to	17.2	18.8	27.9	31.2
Lithuania				
Imports from	22.1	15.1	2.6	9.1
Exports to	19.7	14.7	6.7	7.3

SOURCES: *SJB, 1936*, pp. 253-54, *1938*, pp. 280-82.
* Includes Danzig.

1937. Hitler's attempts to boycott Austrian products notwithstanding, on the whole these countries were much less affected by government policy than the more agrarian states.[9]

The substantial increases in German imports from Hungary and Yugoslavia relative to 1928 and the partial recovery of imports from Rumania took place even though the grain imports anticipated by the 1934-1935 agreements failed to materialize. German trade figures show no retained German imports of

[9] On the composition of German trade with Austria and Czechoslovakia see *SJB, 1936*, pp. 256-57, *1938*, pp. 284-85.

Hungarian wheat, corn, or fodder barley during this period. Rumania exported about 200,000 tons of cereals to Germany in 1934, and Rumania and Yugoslavia sold 50,000 and 90,000 tons, respectively, in 1935, but cereals imports from both countries virtually disappeared in 1936 because of Schacht's import restrictions. IG Farben may have bought some cereals from these countries for reexport, but only small quantities found their way onto the German market.[10]

The southeastern states—and the northeastern states as well—benefited far more from increases in German imports of meat and meat byproducts, which approximately doubled from 1934 through 1936. Hungarian meat exports to Germany doubled during these years, Yugoslav meat exports increased fivefold, and Rumania, Poland, and the Baltic states also increased their meat exports to Germany. German cattle imports from Eastern Europe began in 1935 and increased sharply in 1936 to meet domestic shortages; all the eastern states benefited to varying degrees. German pig imports also increased, from 11,000 tons in 1935 to 54,000 tons in 1936; Poland and the Baltic states supplied 40 percent of the new total, and Hungary benefited as well.[11] The high prices of some of these Eastern European products reflected the political impetus behind the purchases. Hungarian meat and cattle, for example, sold for 20 to 40 percent more than the same Danish products.[12]

The recovery in German trade with the Baltic states and Poland owed much to the steady increases in German imports of butter, eggs, and timber from 1934 through 1936. During the depression prohibitive protective measures against imports of these commodities had crippled German trade with the Baltic littoral; by 1933 the four countries' combined butter exports to Germany amounted to just 47 percent of their 1928 total, egg exports had fallen to virtually nothing, and timber exports were just 26 percent of their 1928 level.[13] In December 1933 the Nazi

[10] It is virtually impossible to trace German purchases for reexport in official statistics, especially since they sometimes did not even cross German frontiers. For these figures see *SJB, 1936*, pp. 260-71, *1937*, pp. 274-84.

[11] *SJB, 1936*, pp. 270-71, *1937*, pp. 274-84.

[12] *SJB, 1936*, pp. 232-24. This price comparison is rough, since it is based on total figures for the cost and quantity of German meat and cattle imports from Denmark and Hungary. The differential is sufficiently large, however, to indicate a significant difference in cost.

[13] *SJB, 1930*, pp. 243-51, *1934*, pp. 236-41.

regime tried to stabilize total butter and egg imports at less than half of the 1928 levels, and Estonia, Latvia, and Poland received percentage quotas for 1934 based on this figure. These quotas quickly proved insufficient, however, and Poland and the Baltic states steadily increased their butter and egg exports to Germany. As early as March 1934, Estonia received a 40 percent tariff rebate on butter and eggs to encourage exports of these commodities to Germany. German timber imports increased 48 percent from 1933 through 1936, and timber imports from Poland and the Baltic states increased 26 percent.[14]

In contrast to the general trend, German-Lithuanian trade fell drastically in 1934-1935. The Lithuanian government, fearing the growth of National Socialism among Memelland Germans, dismissed suspect German officials, outlawed the Nazi party during 1934, and put Nazi leaders on trial in December. Berlin retaliated by restricting trade. With the help of the western powers, however, the Germans ultimately secured the restoration of the Memellanders' internationally guaranteed political rights, and German-Lithuanian trade revived after Berlin and Kovno concluded a new commercial agreement on August 5, 1936.[15]

German rearmament dramatically increased German imports of many key raw materials between 1933 and 1936, but the Eastern European states benefited relatively little from these increases because they had few vital raw materials to sell. Hungary and Yugoslavia supplied slightly more than half of Germany's bauxite imports, which rose from virtually nothing in 1933 to 981,000 tons in 1936. Yugoslav copper exports to Germany also increased steadily.[16] Rumania benefited disproportionately from a 50 percent increase in German petroleum imports from

[14] HPA meeting, Dec. 18, 1933, T-120/5650/H003798-801; German-Polish agreement of Mar. 7, 1934, T-120/9195/E646727-83; German-Estonian agreement of Mar. 29, Politisches Archiv, Bonn (hereafter PA), Sonderreferat Wirtschaft, Handel 13, Estland; *SJB, 1934*, pp. 210-16, *1936*, pp. 227-28, *1937*, pp. 240-45. The Scandinavian countries remained Germany's largest timber suppliers.

[15] *DGFP*, C, IV, 42: Weinberg, *Foreign Policy*, p. 301; Ritter memoranda, Nov. 29, 1935, Jan. 21, 1936, T-120/5696/E435621-22, 611-14; Department II memorandum, Jan. 13, *DGFP*, C, IV, 495; Neurath to Schacht, Feb. 7, 1936, T-120/5926/E435609-10; meeting of Feb. 18, ibid., E435596-601; *SJB, 1936*, p. 254, *1939-40*, p. 294.

[16] *SJB, 1936*, pp. 260-71, *1937*, pp. 274-84.

1933 through 1936; its share grew from 7 to 20 percent, and the 41.7-million-RM increase in the value of Rumanian oil exports to Germany accounted for virtually the entire increase in the value of Rumanian export trade with the Germans during this period.[17] IG Farben also tried to lessen German dependence on overseas sources of oil seeds, especially soybeans, by founding soybean-growing companies in Rumania and Bulgaria. Although this attempt to tailor Eastern European production to German needs received wide publicity, its effects were slight; the Rumanian share of German oil-seed imports had reached just 3 percent by 1939.[18]

Despite the increase in German imports, various economic factors combined to wipe out the predepression German active trade balance with Eastern Europe and to keep German exports generally below imports. As a result, large reichsmark balances accumulated in the Eastern European states' clearing accounts, leading to extensive discussions between Germany and its Eastern European trading partners.

The tendency of Eastern European countries to accumulate large reichsmark balances in their clearings with Germany attracted widespread attention during the 1930s. Several anti-Nazi authors sought the source of this problem in Machiavellian German schemes, arguing that the German government purposely bought more from its eastern trading partners than could possibly be absorbed in return, thereby promoting the growth of clearing balances as a means of increasing political leverage. Some later authors have made similar arguments.[19] In fact, however, as we have seen, the scale of German imports from Eastern Europe from 1934 through 1935 was by no means unprecedented, and there was no serious reason to suppose that Germany would not continue to run an active balance with Eastern Europe, as it had done before and during the depression. IG Farben's practice of buying Eastern European products through clearings and selling them on the world market may have had

---

[17] *SJB, 1934*, pp. 210-16, *1935*, pp. 246-47, *1936*, p. 267, *1937*, pp. 277-78.

[18] On the founding of the soybean company see the HPA meetings of Sept. 15, Oct. 18, and Nov. 2, 8, 1934, T-120/5650/H003936, 952, 968, 971. For statistics see *SJB, 1935*, pp. 212-15, *1936*, pp. 234-37, *1937*, pp. 251-52, *1938*, pp. 266-69, *1939-40*, pp. 279-81. Germany imported oil seeds primarily from Manchuria and the tropics, and sometimes from the Soviet Union. IG Farben also tried, but failed, to start a soybean company in Yugoslavia.

[19] See note 1 above, especially works by Schacher, Mühlen, Doering, and Carr.

some effect on German trade balances with Eastern Europe but would hardly account for the problem. The problem lay not in any clever German manipulation of trade, but in economic trends affecting German exports as a whole. First, the domestic economic boom and the overvaluation of the reichsmark had hurt Germany's competitive position in exports and diverted German firms to production for the home market. Second, because the German government desperately needed foreign exchange to pay for vital raw materials, it was forced to subsidize German exports in ways that tended to divert them to hard-currency countries rather than to countries with which Germany maintained a clearing.

The overall pattern of German foreign trade during the first few years of the Nazi regime followed generally accepted macroeconomic models of the effects of domestic expansion on imports and exports. On the one hand, rising domestic demand led to rapid increases in imports; on the other, it occupied domestic industry with production for the home market and kept prices high, thus restricting exports. Nazi public works programs and rearmament kept domestic demand high. Because the general domestic recovery was brought about almost exclusively by increased government expenditures and domestic consumption, the share of exports in the German GNP fell steadily, from 22.5 percent in 1923 to 16.2 percent in 1937 and only 13.1 percent for the first half of 1938. Furthermore, the refusal of the Nazi government to devalue the reichsmark in response to the devaluations of the pound and dollar—a refusal motivated chiefly by political and psychological prejudices—kept German prices high relative to world prices and hurt the competitive position of German exports. The Germans, in fact, were extremely fortunate that the prices of raw materials, which made up most of their imports, generally remained low during the 1930s relative to the prices of the finished goods that dominated their exports. Only this development enabled Germany to maintain anything like an equal trade balance.[20]

The problem of lagging German exports continually engaged

[20] Volkmann, "Aussenhandel," p. 91; Doering, "Deutsche Aussenwirtschaftspolitik," pp. 219-21; Ellis, *Exchange Control,* pp. 193-94, 232-42; René Erbe, *Die nationalsozialistische Wirtschaftspolitik 1933-1939 im Lichte der modernen Theorie* (Zurich, 1958), pp. 68-83. Ellis concludes that by the late 1930s a devaluation of at least 33 to 43% would have been necessary to bring the reichsmark into line with other major currencies.

the attention of various branches of the German government in the 1933-1936 period. Ultimately, Schacht's insistence that more resources be devoted to export industries rather than to rearmament contributed to his loss of control over German trade in 1936. The various government authorities who addressed the problem of exports, including the Foreign Office, the Economics Ministry, the Reichsbank, and occasionally even Hitler himself, generally blamed it on high German prices, foreign boycotts, and, above all, diversion of production to domestic orders.[21] Although it refused to devalue, the government nevertheless adopted two successive export subsidy schemes that had the effect of partial devaluation.

The first scheme, introduced in 1933, was known as the *Zusatzausfuhrförderung* (Promotion of Additional Exports), or ZAV. Its aim was to enable German exporters to offer their goods at lower prices by giving them domestic subsidies for "additional" exports and *not* for "normal" exports, which could presumably continue without subsidies. Under the two types of ZAV in effect from 1933 through 1935, exporters used part of their foreign-exchange receipts to purchase German bonds or scrip held overseas. Because of the partial transfer moratoriums in effect in Germany, these bonds generally traded at substantial discounts in overseas markets. The exporter then resold the bonds to special financial institutions in Germany for their full value. The success of these schemes in encouraging exports to hard-currency countries was limited; their effect on exports to Eastern Europe was nil. Exports paid for through clearings were *not* subsidized, since they produced no foreign exchange that could be used to purchase scrip or bonds.[22] If anything, this procedure diverted exports away from Eastern Europe.

A new system of export subsidy introduced in 1936 was hardly more favorable to exports to Eastern Europe. This system is still known only in general outline, but its broad features are clear. The German government imposed a general levy of 2 to 3 per-

---

[21] A Mar. 22, 1935, circular signed by Hitler stated: "The extraordinary increases in production for domestic use—directly and indirectly stimulated by public expenditure—have reduced the exporting zeal of German business" (T-120/9238/E649251-54). See also the Economics Ministry circular of June 9, 1934, ibid., E649195, and a Reichsbank memorandum, of July 12, 1934, and an AA circular of Nov. 27, T-120/9792/E657695-706, 741-43.

[22] Doering, "Deutsche Aussenwirtschaftspolitik," pp. 196-202.

cent on commerce, industry, banking, and agriculture, the proceeds of which were to be spent on export subsidies. Although existing evidence suggests that most exports were subsidized regardless of their destination, subsidies seem to have been higher for exports to hard-currency countries. Thus this system, too, encouraged exporters to peddle their wares in Western Europe and overseas, rather than in Eastern Europe.[23]

Changes in the economies of the Eastern European states also reduced German exports. During the 1930s both the German government and western observers often stressed the "complementary" relationship of the German and Eastern European economies; in fact, however, the extent of such complementarity diminished as the decade wore on. Industrialization in the agrarian states of Eastern Europe changed the structure of their import needs. The share of industry in the economies of the agrarian states increased during the 1930s, and the Eastern Europeans imported fewer of the finished goods they had bought from Germany during the 1930s and more of the raw materials that could only be purchased overseas.[24] Hardest hit were German textile manufacturers, who had been the leading German exporters to every Eastern European country in 1928. The value of German exports of textile products to the seven agricultural countries of Eastern Europe totaled 182.7 million RM in 1928, but only 26.6 million RM in 1936. This decline resulted partly from increased British competition in the Baltic, but the development of home production in Rumania, Hungary, and especially Poland was far more significant.[25] More and more, the agricultural countries of Eastern Europe wanted not

[23] This system seems to have gone into effect on May 15, 1936, after a long series of meetings attended by Schacht, Göring, and numerous civil servants and industry representatives; see T-77/35/748261-300. See also Ellis, *Exchange Control*, pp. 239-41, and Arthur Schweitzer, *Big Business in the Third Reich* (Bloomington, 1964), pp. 476-85.

[24] On the structural changes in the Eastern European national economies see Berend and Ránki,*Economic Development*, pp. 285-318. The Polish case is particularly striking in this respect: in 1928 Polish imports totaled 16.2% foodstuffs, 34.9% raw materials, and 40.4% manufactures; in 1934 the figures were 10.0% foodstuffs, 52.0% raw materials, and 31.7% manufactures (LN, *ITS, 1929*, p. 283, *1935*, p. 231.

[25] *SJB, 1930*, pp. 243-57, *1937*, pp. 274-84. For figures on raw cotton consumption and synthetic fiber production in Eastern Europe see B. R. Mitchell, *European Historical Statistics* (New York, 1975), pp. 430-31, 455.

to exchange their agricultural produce for manufactured goods but to sell it for foreign exchange with which to purchase raw materials available only overseas. Thus, as we shall see, their governments frequently adopted measures to stimulate exports to hard-currency countries rather than to Germany. Many of their problems were not complementary to those of Germany, but similar.

The chronic German import surplus relative to Eastern Europe and the steadily accumulating reichsmark balances within clearings led to long and difficult negotiations with all the Eastern European agricultural states except Hungary in the 1934-1936 period.[26] Without following these negotiations in detail, it is useful to examine individual cases to see how the Germans attempted to deal with these problems.

Within six months of the conclusion of the German-Yugoslav trade treaty in May 1934, Belgrade complained about its escalating reichsmark clearing balance in Berlin. By March 1936 the balance had reached 26 million RM, or more than 40 percent of Germany's imports from Yugoslavia in 1935. Led by its foreign trade expert, Milivoje Pilja, Belgrade took two steps to deal with the problem. First, in January 1936 the Yugoslav National Bank began selling its reichsmark balance to domestic importers in the form of "clearing checks." It pegged these checks at an average price of 13.6 dinars to the reichsmark—an effective devaluation of 25 percent from the official rate of 17.6 dinars. The Germans protested bitterly.[27] At a meeting of the German and Yugoslav government committees in March 1936, Pilja agreed to a solution more to Berlin's liking. In return for German promises to purchase more Yugoslav pigs and cattle, he promised to import more German coal and textiles.[28] In April he introduced import licenses to divert purchases of these goods toward the Germans, mostly at Britain's expense.[29] The new import licenses helped to

[26] Even in the case of Hungary, the two countries had to take new measures to increase German exports; see the Apr. 16, 1935, meeting of the German and Hungarian government committees, T-120/9841/E692160-99.

[27] See Sarnow's correspondence with the German legation in Belgrade, Nov. 2, 1934, and Jan. 11, 16, 1935, Clodius's Mar. 6 minute of the government committees' meeting, the agreement of Mar. 1, German legation Belgrade to AA, Apr. 26, May 7, and June 4, Reichsgruppe Industrie circular of Jan. 24, 1936, T-120/5655/H006738-913. See also Ellis, *Exchange Control*, pp. 263-64.

[28] Protocol, Apr. 1, 1936, T-120/9841/E692070-103.

[29] German legation Belgrade to AA, Apr. 8, 1936, T-120/5655/H006972-75.

raise imports from Germany from 36.9-million-RM worth in 1935 to 77.2-million-RM worth in 1936 and reduced the clearing balance somewhat.[30]

The Yugoslavs were particularly vulnerable to German courtship in early 1936. They had lost their best customer, Italy, as a result of their participation in League of Nations sanctions designed to stop Mussolini's war on Ethiopia, and France and Britain had done little to compensate them for their losses.[31] In September 1936, however, in the midst of a general revival in the world market for raw materials, Belgrade began demanding hard currency for Yugoslav lead, zinc, wool, and other raw materials. To Germany, these commodities were essential; copper and zinc shortages were currently holding rearmament in check. At a further meeting of the two government committees in October, the Germans secured the withdrawal of some of these restrictions in return for higher import quotas on Yugoslav agricultural produce. Nevertheless, clearing checks continued to trade below the official rate, and the Yugoslav clearing balance did not disappear.[32] The course of German-Yugoslav trade was hardly smooth, but as of 1936 the increased German demand for foodstuffs—combined with British and French inaction—still kept it flowing faster and faster.

Trouble in German-Rumanian trade arose within a few months of the conclusion of the commercial treaty of March 1935. Much of the difficulty stemmed from differences within the Rumanian government and from the Rumanian tendency—reported many years later by Sir Frederick Leith-Ross—to accept almost any terms in order to reach an agreement without reference to their willingness to live up to them. Pro-German elements within the Rumanian government wanted to expand trade with Germany, while Foreign Minister Nicolai Titulescu

[30] Ellis, *Exchange Control*, p. 264; *SJB, 1936*, p. 254, *1939-40*, p. 294.

[31] See below, Chapter VII. The rapid accumulation of the German clearing balance during the sanctions period suggests that private German interests may have been buying Yugoslav goods through the clearing and reselling them to Italy.

[32] On the effects of copper and zinc shortages in Germany see the Economic and Armaments Office reports of July 28 and Aug. 3, 1936, T-77/35/748226-32. See also German legation Belgrade to AA, July 7, 1936, Reichstelle für Devisenbewirtschaftung letter, Sept. 6, PA, Ha Pol IV a, Fin 16 (1) Jugoslawien, Bd. 1; protocol, Oct. 20, T-120/7275/E533806-20. The Yugoslavs agreed to supply zinc through the clearing, but not chrome and silicon.

and the Rumanian National Bank, which was heavily influenced by French advisers, sought to restrict German economic influence. Thus, for example, Titulescu and the National Bank successfully blocked the establishment of Schacht's projected German-Rumanian oil company in the spring of 1935, only months after the conclusion of the new commercial treaty.[33]

Two major issues dominated German-Rumanian trade relations during 1935-1936: the Rumanians introduced several trade and currency control measures designed to increase exports to hard-currency countries and reduce sales to Germany, and the two governments frequently quarreled over the proper means of payment for Rumanian oil exports to Germany. In June 1935 the Rumanian government imposed varying percentage levies on all imports while subsidizing exports to hard-currency countries. The new scheme taxed German imports at 44 percent to make up for the overvaluation of the reichsmark but paid no subsidy at all for exports to Germany.[34] Enraged, the Germans imposed a retaliatory levy of 44 percent on imports from Rumania, but the HPA decided on July 3 to refund the levy to importers of key commodities—oil, oil-bearing plants, and timber.[35] In September the Rumanians promised to end their discrimination against Germany in exchange for German promises to purchase 20,000 pigs, but the Rumanians ignored the agreement, refusing to subsidize exports to Germany, and Berlin canceled its pig imports in return.[36] In November 1935 the Rumanian government abolished its levy-subsidy system for imports and exports, but the Rumanian National Bank began purchasing hard currency at a premium—thus encouraging exports to hard-currency countries—while allowing the reichs-

[33] Sir Frederick Leith-Ross, *Money Talks: Fifty Years of International Finance* (London, 1968), p. 192. See German legation Bucharest to AA, May 29, 1935, T-120/9692/E682145-48; Clodius to German legation Bucharest, May 29, 30, T-120/5662/H010745-48, 749-51. Titulescu told German Minister Wilhelm von Pochhammer on June 21 that the oil company agreement "contains unheard of conditions" and "should never have been concluded" (T-120/9711/E683260-66).

[34] German legation Bucharest to AA, June 11, 1935, T-120/6711/E683211-12.

[35] AA to German legation Bucharest, June 15, 1935, ibid., E683218-22; HPA sittings, June 14, July 3, T-120/5650/H004022-27.

[36] Agreement of Sept. 7, 1935, T-120/6646/E504636-50. See also *DBFP*, C, IV, 297; Reichsgruppe Industrie circular, Sept. 13, T-120/9692/E682213-16; German legation Bucharest to AA, Oct. 14, 22, 28, 1935, ibid., E682253, 239, 244-48; *SJB, 1936*, p. 267, *1937*, p. 280.

mark to trade freely.[37] With regard to oil, Bucharest asked during 1936 that Germany either pay for a higher percentage of its oil imports in foreign exchange or pay for 15 percent of its growing oil imports with "colonial goods"—a contemporary term for tropical raw materials—imported into Rumania through Germany.[38]

After nine months of negotiations, the German and Rumanian government committees drew up a new clearing agreement in September 1936. Perhaps because of the growing importance of Rumanian oil to the Gemany economy, Helmut Wohlthat, director of the Reichstelle für Devisensbewirtschaftung, the agency in charge of distributing foreign exchange for imports, became chairman of the German government committee for German-Rumanian trade in June 1936. Wohlthat remained a key figure in German-Rumanian trade for the rest of the decade. Under the new agreement, the Germans again promised to limit oil purchases through the clearing to 25 percent of their total clearing purchases; they would pay for additional oil with long-term German investments or deliveries of German arms. In the latter respect, the agreement foreshadowed the future course of German trade with Eastern Europe. Although the agreement proved a satisfactory basis for continued trade, the longstanding difficulties between the two countries, combined with Titulescu's pro-French orientation, led Schacht to omit Bucharest from a tour of southeastern capitals during 1936.[39]

During 1933-1936 large reichsmark balances also accumulated in German trade with Estonia and Latvia, both of which introduced special incentives to divert trade to hard-currency countries. The Estonians introduced a free market in reichsmarks, which began trading at about 8 percent below the official rate; the Latvians began paying premiums for exports to hard-currency countries. Two factors, however, hampered their at-

---

[37] German legation Bucharest to AA, Nov. 26, 1935, Jan. 9, 1936, T-120/9692/E682266-69, 313-16.

[38] Undated Rumanian memorandum, late 1935, and AA comments, T-120/5662/H010730-40, T-120/9692/E682300-304.

[39] Clodius to German legation Bucharest, May 5, 1936, T-120/9692/E682371-72. Wohlthat's negotiations can be followed under T-120/9692/E682309-72, T-120/5662/H010769-850, and T-120/5650/H004087. For a description of the Sept. 24 agreement see T-120/6669/E506102-3; its text is under T-120/6646.

tempts to divert trade from German markets: the steadily increasing German purchases of butter and live animals, and the
failure of the British to combat more aggressively the German
resurgence in the Baltic.[40]

German trade relations with Poland presented unique, but
equally difficult, problems. The German-Polish trade agreement
of March 7, 1934, ended the tariff war between the two countries and theoretically normalized trade between them, but because Poland maintained a rigidly orthodox financial and trade
policy and eschewed exchange control, the two countries did not
establish a clearing, and Germany had to pay for Polish goods in
Polish zĺotys or foreign exchange. The German-Polish compensation agreement of October 11, 1934, was designed to increase
trade on an equal basis, but German imports from Poland, including large timber imports, ran far in excess of corresponding
exports. On Janaury 23, 1935, Hans-Adolf von Moltke, the
German minister in Warsaw, estimated Germany's negative balance of trade with Poland at 58 million RM for 1934—clearly an
anomaly in the era of the New Plan.[41]

After intermittent negotiations, Berlin and Warsaw signed a
new trade agreement on November 4, 1935. The talks, which
had begun in the spring, were interrupted by a currency crisis in
Danzig in the summer. The Wilhelmstrasse, led by Bülow,
pressed for agreement, citing the "important" political relations
between the two countries; Schacht opposed extensive concessions to the Poles, particularly regarding the prices of Polish agricultural products. Through the agreement, the Poles tried to
ensure that Germany would not run up a debt with Poland similar to those it had with other Eastern European countries; the
agreement created a clearing, but the Poles insisted on *monthly*
meetings between the German and Polish government committees, which would determine quotas on the basis of the previous
month's trade. As Ritter noted, the state of German agriculture
had enabled the Germans to extend substantial concessions, particularly regarding pigs and meat.[42]

---

[40] See the Dec. 5, 1935, account of German-Estonian talks, PA, Sonderreferat
Wirtschaft, Handel 13 Estland, and the Dec. 7, 1936, account, PA, Ha Pol Vb,
Handel 13a Estland, Bd. 1. On Latvia see the correspondence of July-September
1936, PA, Ha Pol Vb, Handel 13a Lettland, Bd. 1.

[41] T-120/5643/H000830-49; *DGFP*, C, III, 487.

[42] On these talks see: *DGFP*, C, IV, 53, 192, 204, 217, 271, 301; German lega-

A more difficult issue—the question of German foreign-exchange payments for railway traffic across the Polish Corridor—preoccupied the two governments from early 1935 until December 1936. A German-Polish agreement of April 21, 1921, obligated the Germans to pay the charges for this traffic in Polish złotys or foreign exchange, but by early 1935 Schacht was refusing to continue foreign-exchange payments.[43] Schacht's anti-Polish feelings typified his conservative nationalism; at one point during this dispute he suggested publicly that Polish Upper Silesia should return to Germany, and he argued in an internal memorandum that the question had arisen "only because of the nonsensical rearrangement of Europe by the Versailles *Diktat*."[44] He succeeded in blocking any concessions during 1935, even though the Poles complained repeatedly that the mounting German foreign-exchange debt, which reached 20 million RM by November 1935, had become acutely embarassing to Foreign Minister Beck.[45]

The Germans finally compromised in principle under the pressure of the Rhineland crisis of March 1936. Although Berlin had carefully warned Beck about the coming denunciation of Locarno and reoccupation of the Rhineland, and although he did not protest this step when it occurred on March 7, he implicitly linked his tolerant stance to the Corridor payments question. This question, he told Moltke five days after the reoccupation, was provoking "great agitation"; the Germans "could scarcely imagine how difficult his position was becoming, particularly in view of impending political decisions."[46] Berlin took

tion Warsaw to AA, May 7, 1935, T-120/9213/E647890-91; HPA meetings, July 18, Aug. 22, T-120/5650/H004031, 036-40; German legation Warsaw to AA, Oct. 23, and Sarnow's and Ritter's memoranda of Oct. 24, 28, T-120/5643/H000735-36, 731-32, 730; text of the Nov. 4 agreement, T-120/9202/E647270-336; Ritter to German legation Warsaw, Nov. 9, T-120/5643/H000709-12; Reichsgruppe Industrie circular, Nov. 12, T-120/9391/E665368-75. On the Danzig currency crisis see Weinberg, *Foreign Policy*, pp. 189-201.

[43] LN, *Treaty Series*, XII, 63-175; *DGFP*, C, III, 419.

[44] Weinberg, *Foreign Policy*, p. 248; Schacht memorandum, Oct. 19, 1936, T-120/9172/E645473-75.

[45] *DGFP*, C, III, 419; HPA meeting, Mar. 22, 1935, T-120/5650/H004006-07; *DGFP*, C, IV, 392; German legation Warsaw to AA, T-120/9172/E645175-77; Lipski, *Diplomat in Berlin*, pp. 225-27, 232-33, 246; *DDF*, 2, I, 118.

[46] *DGFP*, C, V, 82. "Impending political decisions" probably referred to the stand Poland would take at the upcoming League Council meeting on the Rhine-

the hint. Hitler entrusted Göring with the settlement of the Corridor question, and the two countries concluded a draft agreement on April 7 despite Schacht's objections. The Germans promised to pay 1.5-million-RM worth of hard currency per month for Corridor traffic, paying the rest in goods and perhaps though the liquidation of German capital claims in Poland.[47] When ṭhe crisis cooled, however, the Germans backed out of some of these commitments; as Göring noted in late May, "it is no longer so necessary as it seemed to be a few weeks ago, on account of considerations of foreign policy, to meet the Polish desires to so great an extent."[48] The Germans consented to pay 1.5 million RM in foreign currency monthly for three months in a provisional agreement signed on August 31, 1936, but Schacht successfully reduced this figure to 7.5 million RM in hard currency *annually* in a new, long-term agreement signed on December 22, 1936.[49] The agreement treated the Germans so favorably that it embarrassed the Polish negotiators; Berlin had intimidated them by threatening to divert a large portion of the Corridor traffic to sea transport.[50]

The dispute over Corridor traffic presents two special points of interest. First, although, as we have seen, Germany's trade with Eastern Europe reflected its broad political goals within the region, this controversy represents virtually the only occasion during the decade on which the Germans made economic concessions for specific political reasons. Warsaw had given Berlin vital assistance during the Eastern Pact discussions, and the Wilhelmstrasse felt that the new German-Polish relationship was

land question. On Polish behavior during the crisis see also Wojciechowski, *Polnisch-deutschen Beziehungen*, pp. 263-64, Lipski, *Diplomat in Berlin*, pp. 249-50, and George Sakwa, "The Franco-Polish Alliance and the Remilitarization of the Rhineland," *Historical Journal*, XVI, no. 1 (1973), 125-46.

[47] For the agreement and Schacht's Apr. 9 letter, which protested "most emphatically" that the draft had been accepted over his objections, see T-120/9172/E645379, 382-83.

[48] *DGFP*, C, V, 356; see also T-120/9172/E6453689 ff., T-120/5643/H000524 ff.

[49] Aug. 31 agreement, T-120/5643/H000477-500. For accounts of further talks and the Dec. 22 agreement see T-120/2040/445065-68.

[50] Schacht memorandum, Oct. 19, 1936, and Ritter memorandum, Nov. 2, T-120/9172/E645473-75, 484-85. Ritter admitted that the threat was largely an idle one, since East Prussian port facilities could not accommodate much more traffic. On the agreement and Polish reaction see German embassy Warsaw to AA, Jan 12, 19, 1937, T-120/9172/E645497-500.

worth some sacrifices to preserve. Second, the Corridor dispute foreshadowed the crisis of 1938-1939 that led to the outbreak of the Second World War. In the context of the continuing German foreign-exchange crisis, the outlay of *any* hard currency for rail traffic with East Prussia was an increasingly onerous burden, and as early as May 1935 Moltke had suggested to Beck that an autobahn might be constructed across the Corridor to East Prussia.[51] It was the German request for an extraterritorial passageway across the Corridor on which to build an autobahn and railway, together with the request that Danzig be returned to the Reich, that led to the crisis of 1938-1939.

German-Polish trade stayed within sharply defined limits. Almost alone among Eastern European states, the Polish government resisted the accumulation of any substantial reichsmark balance in its clearing with Germany. Total German imports from Poland during 1936 were only 74 million RM, compared with the projected level of 83 million RM. German exports to Poland lagged only slightly behind; the continual monitoring of the course of trade by the two government committees ensured a roughly equal balance.[52]

Although the revival of German imports from Eastern Europe between 1933 and 1936 was impressive, it by no means represented a dramatic new pattern of trade or an unprecedented reliance on that area. Relative to 1928, Germany bought a somewhat higher percentage of its imports of oil, meat products, pigs, and cattle from Eastern Europe, but in no case did the majority of its purchases of these goods come from that region.[53] In 1936 the nine successor states of Eastern Europe—Austria, Czechoslovakia, Hungary, Rumania, Yugoslavia, Poland, and the three Baltic states—still supplied only 13.8 percent of German imports. Although the corresponding share for 1928 was only 5.9 percent, the increase reflects the drop in Germany's trade with the rest of the world rather than any drastic expansion in trade with Eastern Europe. At constant prices, total German imports in 1936 were still only 41 percent of their 1928 level.[54]

---

[51] German embassy Warsaw to AA, Oct. 22, 1937, *DGFP*, D, V, 14. Rauschning, *Voice of Destruction*, pp. 204-5, states that Hitler wanted such an autobahn as early as 1934.
[52] *SJB, 1938*, p. 282.   [53] *SJB, 1936*, p. 254, *1939-40*, p. 294.
[54] *SJB, 1929*, p. 234, *1937*, pp. 266, 296.

Beginning in 1937, however, German trade with Eastern Europe increased much more rapidly, owing to fundamental changes in German economic policy. Until then, as we have seen, some aspects of German agricultural and trade policy— especially the drive toward German agricultural self-sufficiency—had severely limited trade in certain vital commodities, especially cereals. Schacht, who exercised responsibility for German foreign trade until mid-1936, did what he could to hold down agricultural imports; in addition, he specifically opposed buying Eastern European products at inflated prices. By early 1936 these policies had created severe food shortages within Germany, and Berlin soon faced a severe foreign-exchange crisis whose resolution involved fundamental issues of Nazi domestic and foreign policy. As a result, Schacht lost much of his power over the German economy to Hermann Göring in the summer of 1936. Göring, guided partly by Hitler's memorandum on the Four Year Plan, restructured foreign trade, immediately increasing cereals imports and dramatically expanding trade with Eastern Europe. In addition, he eventually solved much of the problem of the German import surplus from Eastern Europe by encouraging long-term, large-scale exports of German arms.

We have seen that Schacht supported Agricultural Minister Darré's efforts to achieve maximum German self-sufficiency. The two quarreled in the fall and winter of 1934-1935, however, when Darré pressed for higher imports of feed grains and oil seeds; Schacht successfully cut 1935 imports of feed grains to about half of the 1934 levels.[55] Then, in September 1935, Schacht attacked the practice of guaranteeing Eastern European countries high prices for agricultural produce in commercial agreements. He specifically mentioned many Hungarian and Yugoslav products, Estonian butter and eggs, and a new German commitment on Rumanian cattle. It made no difference, he argued, that Germany paid these prices in reichsmarks through clearings; those reichsmarks should be used to subsidize German exports.[56] The Wilhelmstrasse, while agreeing to end tariff rebates on Estonian and Finnish butter, successfully argued that

[55] *SJB, 1935*, p. 210-12, *1936*, pp. 232-34.
[56] Memorandum of Sept. 19, T-120/9249/E653885-94; see also *DGFP*, C, IV, 209.

political considerations required the maintenance of existing arrangements with the southeastern states. Carl Clodius of the Economic Department noted on October 5 that backing out of agreed arrangements for Rumanian cattle would seriously disturb German-Rumanian trade. He elaborated his view with reference to Hungary and Yugoslavia:

> The well-known political considerations that led to the conclusion of the relevant treaties in February and May of 1934 continue in all respects today. The remark that political and economic considerations go together with all countries is incorrect, failing as it does to take into account the well-known special political conditions in the Danubian area and Germany's aims there.[57]

On October 8 the HPA decided to retain the existing arrangements regarding Hungarian and Yugoslav cereals.

By late 1935, Schacht's food import controls had led to serious domestic difficulties. German home agricultural production had peaked by 1934, but the demand for foodstuffs, stimulated by the rapid increase in employment, rose steadily. The index of domestic agricultural production rose from 110 for the agricultural year 1933-1934 to 115 for 1934-1935, but fell back to 110 for 1935-1936 and rose only to 113 for 1936-1937. Declining grain harvests in 1935 and 1936, combined with Schacht's restrictions on imports of feed grains, led to widespread slaughter of pigs and cattle during 1935-1936 for want of fodder. At the same time, domestic consumption of meat and butter increased.[58] The effects of these trends emerged in late 1935.

One enduring Nazi legacy is the now-famous metaphor of guns and butter. What has generally been forgotten is that when Joseph Goebbels first used the phrase on Janaury 17, 1936, there was nothing metaphorical about it. "We can well do without butter," Goebbels declared publicly, "but we must have guns, because butter could not help us if we were to be attacked one day." In fact, the German people *had* been intermittently doing without butter—as well as pork, bacon, beef, and lard—at least since the previous September.[59] Goebbels was merely trying to

---

[57] T-120/9249/E653916-22.

[58] Petzina, *Autarkiepolitik*, pp. 30-44; Lorenz, "German Agricultural Policy," pp. 116-17.

[59] Goebbels is quoted in the *Economist*, Jan. 25, 1936, pp. 175-76. For reports

provide a rationale for the German government's failure to import enough foreign butter—and, he might have added, foreign fodder for German dairy cattle—to head off these shortages. By March 1936, Schacht had to give in to some of Darré's new demands for increased food imports. On January 14 Darré, blaming Schacht's policies for current shortages, had requested foreign exchange to purchase 850,000 tons of feed grains during 1936, or double the total for 1935. Schacht argued that the same foreign exchange was needed to prevent "shortages in industrial raw materials and thus increased unemployment." A meeting with Hitler on February 5 failed to produce a decision, but in March Schacht granted about half of Darré's requests for the second quarter of 1936. Schacht complained that the failure of German agriculture to produce up to capacity was the real problem; Darré claimed that Schacht's decisions would lead to further consumer shortages.[60]

By the spring of 1936 the food crisis was only one aspect of a general crisis involving shortages of vital imports and foreign exchange. Shortages of imported copper, lead, and rubber were creating bottlenecks in arms production, and in April Schacht even suggested slowing the tempo of rearmament. Hitler steadfastly rejected this alternative, instead entrusting Göring on April 6 with authority to take "all requisite measures" to improve the raw materials and foreign-exchange situation. Ironically, Schacht himself favored this delegation of authority to Göring, evidently counting on the Prussian minister-president's prestige to overcome recalcitrance in party agencies.[61]

Faced with the need to increase imports further in order to keep up the tempo of rearmament, Göring first took the radical step of mobilizing the foreign assets of German private interests. This, however, was only a temporary solution. By August the German economy was clearly at a crossroads. Responsible agencies of the German government predicted catastrophic short-

---

of food shortages see ibid., Sept. 7, 1935, p. 467, Sept. 14, pp. 514-15, Oct. 5, pp. 565-67, Oct. 26, p. 804, Nov. 2, p. 852, Nov. 16, p. 958, Jan. 1, 1936, p. 173.

[60] Schacht's minute on the Oct. 8 meeting, Darré's Jan. 14 letter, Schacht to Lammers, Jan. 18, meeting of Feb. 5, Darré's and Schacht's letters of Mar. 12, 16, 1936, T-120/9238/E649331-37, 353-61, 370-71, 373-75, 387-90, 393-95, 407-16. See also Petzina, *Autarkiepolitik*, pp. 30-33.

[61] *DGFP*, C, V, 260; Petzina, *Autarkiepolitik*, pp. 30-40; Berenice Carroll, *Design for Total War: Arms and Economics in the Third Reich* (The Hague, 1968), p. 125.

ages of foreign exchange over the next year; apparently, only the sudden increase in the demand for German exports as a result of worldwide economic recovery prevented an immediate collapse. Schacht and Carl Goerdeler, who had formerly held the position of price commissar, argued for a return to more orthodox policies, including slower rearmament, free trade, and perhaps devaluation of the reichsmark. Even the Economic and Armaments Office at the War Ministry, led by Colonel Georg Thomas, suggested slowing rearmament and increasing exports; civilian industries would suffer unemployment unless some raw materials could be diverted from the arms industry. Hitler, however, had other ideas. Anxious above all to continue armaments production at the highest possible rate of speed, he composed his memorandum on the Four Year Plan in August, entrusting Göring with the future direction of the German economy.[62] The adoption of the plan and the eclipse of Schacht's authority resulted in new economic policies, new trade policies, and greatly expanded German trade with Eastern Europe.

Hitler's memorandum on the Four Year Plan, written sometime in August 1936, is an important document in many respects.[63] Although, like most of Hitler's writings, it is somewhat confused and rambling, it confirms the essential continuity of his foreign-policy goals and his thinking on economics and politics. Hitler argued that foreign trade could not solve Germany's economic and political problems. Their ultimate solution lay only in the conquest of *Lebensraum*; in the interim it would be necessary, as far as possible, to produce domestic substitutes for scarce imported raw materials. The memorandum closes with injunctions to make the German army and the German economy ready for war within four years. The memorandum also includes some slightly more specific comments on the food situation—comments that apparently influenced Göring to increase vastly Germany's imports from Eastern Europe.

Hitler opened his discussion of Germany's economic position

---

[62] Carroll, *Design for Total War*, pp. 122-29; Petzina, *Autarkiepolitik*, pp. 40-48. See also the extremely pessimistic *Wirtschaftsbilanz* drafted by the Economic and Armaments Office of the War Ministry in August 1936, dealing with shortages of skilled labor, raw materials, and foreign exchange and their effects (T-77/35/ 748119-56).

[63] For the memorandum see *DGFP*, C, V, 490.

with some remarks on the food situation. He noted, quite accurately, that the present "run on the foodstuffs market" stemmed from increased employment and the recovery of purchasing power under the Nazi regime. Germany, in fact, could no longer feed itself from its own resources; "the yield of our agricultural production can undergo no further substantial increase." But this problem could not be solved by curtailing consumption. Only after a new program had made Germany less dependent on foreign raw materials would it be "possible for the first time to demand sacrifices from the German people in the economic sphere and the sphere of foodstuffs." In fact, Hitler remained preoccupied with the provision of adequate foodstuffs and consumer goods well into the Second World War, and the fear that shortages would lead to domestic discontent often restrained him from more drastic mobilization measures.[64] Hitler, then, explicitly recognized the need for further imports of foodstuffs as well as of certain raw materials: "all means must be employed to make these imports possible." But he quickly added a key caveat: "It is, however, impossible to use foreign exchange allocated for raw materials to import foodstuffs without inflicting a heavy and perhaps even fatal blow on the rest of the German economy. *But above all it is utterly impossible to do this at the expense of national rearmament*" (italics in original).

Characteristically, Hitler allowed this thought to trail off into an unrelated discussion of raw-material stocks, never explaining precisely how imported food was to be secured without foreign exchange. Nevertheless, he made it clear that imports would have to be increased to ease shortages, and the solution Göring adopted during the next few months in fact required relatively little foreign exchange. Although agreeing immediately to import much larger quantities of foodstuffs, particularly cereals, he attempted to secure as much as possible from countries with which Germany maintained clearings, especially Argentina and the agricultural countries of Southeastern Europe.

---

[64] Albert Speer, *Inside the Third Reich* (New York, 1970), p. 281, argues that Hitler's fear of popular discontent, and especially of a repetition of the 1918 revolution, kept Germany from adopting mobilization measures and restrictions on production and consumption of consumer goods on the scale of those in the western democracies. The Nazi regime's fear of domestic discontent and its consequent restraint is also a major theme of Timothy W. Mason's study, *Arbeiterklasse und Volksgemeinschaft. Dokumente und Materialien zur deutschen Arbeiterpolitik 1936-39* (Opladen, 1975).

As director of the Four Year Plan, Göring was given ultimate authority over both the Economics and Agriculture Ministries and thus the power to resolve the longstanding controversy between Schacht and Darré over agricultural imports. When Göring took over in the fall of 1936, long-term German needs for imported cereals were immense; the Agriculture Ministry would shortly project those needs at 1.16 millon tons of bread grains and 1.20 million tons of feed grains for 1937, and even these totals eventually proved inadequate.[65] Göring reversed Schacht's policy, and German imports of cereals increased by more than an order of magnitude from 1936 to 1937. Furthermore, as Tables VI.2 and VI.3 show, Eastern European countries supplied a substantial portion of these new imports, which greatly increased Eastern Europe's total trade with Germany over 1934-1936 levels.

Göring personally supervised new grain purchases from Eastern Europe. He had always taken a lively political interest in the area; in 1934-1935 he had visited Poland, Yugoslavia, and Hungary, and he had designated Franz Neuhasen as his personal representative in Belgrade.[66] With his prodding, the German government approached the Eastern Europeans regarding grain purchases. As the tables show, Berlin was generally successful, but the talks did not go smoothly. Having failed to import promised quantities of cereals from 1934 through 1936, the Germans sought to revive and expand their purchases in the context of a revitalized world cereals market. The Eastern Europeans, no longer desperate for buyers, wanted to sell as much as possible for free exchange. Often Germany only secured its objective at the price of substantial concessions. In addition, Schacht continued to object to large purchases that could not immediately be paid for with German exports and to the accumulation of new clearing balances. Ultimately, Göring was fairly successful in expanding German imports of cereals in exchange for long-term exports of arms.

At Göring's direction, the Germans approached Hungary in September 1936 regarding new Geman purchases of grain. The initial response was disappointing; having accumulated a substantial reichsmark balance, Budapest at first refused to sell any

[65] Memorandum of Dec. 16, 1936, T-120/9238/E649417-27.
[66] Weinberg, *Foreign Policy*, pp. 227-29.

TABLE VI.2
German Cereals Imports, 1936-1939
(In Thousands of Tons)

	1936	1937	1938	1939
Wheat				
Total	74	1,129	1,268	956
Overseas sources[1]	41	834	720	101
Hungary	—	—	114	236
Rumania	—	40	210	177
Yugoslavia	—	173	53	188
Corn				
Total	172	2,159	1,895	586
Overseas sources[2]	164	1,590	1,726	262
Hungary	—	82	51	46
Rumania	—	373	15	127
Yugoslavia	—	106	69	30
Rye				
Total	24	181	85	134
Hungary	—	—	15	—
Poland	18	18	41	88
Rumania	—	60	—	1
Barley				
Total	48	46	456	397
Rumania	—	34	142	132

SOURCES: *SJB*, *1937*, p. 251, *1938*, p. 267, *1939-40*, pp. 278-79, *1941-42*, pp. 295-96.
[1] Includes Argentina, Australia, Canada, India, and the United States.
[2] Argentina, South Africa, United States.

wheat through the clearing. Despite repeated German requests for cereals, along with threats to divert purchases of meat to Argentina, the Germans could pry only about 40,000 tons of corn and 5,000 tons of wheat flour out of Hungary during the first six months of 1937. When the Germans argued that the 1934 treaty entitled them to 125,000 tons of Hungarian grain annually, Budapest replied that Hungary had already sold the bulk of its harvest to Switzerland, Holland, and Belgium. When negotiations to renew the original treaty opened in June 1937, the Hungarians at first threatened not to sell any more cereals through the clearing but ultimately agreed to provide 100,000 tons of corn and 50,000 tons of wheat—less than 10 percent of

TABLE VI.3

Value of German Imports from Eastern European Cereals-Growing
States, 1936-1939
(In Millions of Reichsmarks)

	1936	*1937*	*1938**	*1939*
Hungary				
Total imports	93.4	114.1	110.0	222.5
Cereals imports	—	8.5	22.8	38.6
Poland				
Total imports	74.0	80.8	109. 4	97.8
Cereals imports	—	4.5	7.5	10.0
Rumania				
Total imports	92.3	179.5	140.4	209.5
Cereals imports	—	58.4	50.8	51.8
Yugoslavia				
Total imports	75.2	132.2	107.9	131.5
Cereals imports	—	36.4	12.4	22.9

Sources: *SJB, 1937*, pp. 277-83, *1938*, pp. 282-309, *1939-40*, pp. 307-11, *1941-42*, pp. 325-44.
* Does not include Austria.

their annual surplus and half of what the Germans wanted—
during the next year. In return, the Germans promised to supply Hungary with chrome and manganese, which the Hungarians could not afford on the world market.[67]

Göring and the Wilhelmstrasse encountered similar difficulties when they approached Yugoslavia. From November 1936
through March 1937, Belgrade refused to sell the Germans
150-200,000 tons of cereals through the clearing, citing the rising Yugoslav clearing balance. Clodius protested that since 1934
Germany had been buying Yugoslav products of dubious necessity in order to develop German-Yugoslav trade and that Belgrade should be more forthcoming. In an exchange of notes on

[67] Clodius memorandum, Oct. 9, 1936, T-120/7417/E539338-39; protocol,
German and Hungarian government committees meeting, Nov. 19, T-
120/7870/E570235-64; AA memorandum, Nov. 24, and protocol of Nov. 27,
T-120/5571/E344339-44, 451-54; Göring correspondence with Kálmán Darányi,
Dec. 18, 31, T-120/7417/E539359-61, 71-73; agreement of Mar. 9, 1937,
T-120/7870/E570265-70; Ritter memorandum, June 21, and German legation
Budapest to AA, June 25, PA, Ha Pol IVa, Handel 13a Ungarn, Bd. II; agree-
ment of July 9, T-120/7870/E570271-361.

March 24, 1937, the Yugoslavs finally agreed to sell 150,000 tons of corn and wheat through the clearing. In return, Berlin had to guarantee the existing exchange rate for the Yugoslav clearing balance and agree to limit German exports of consumer goods to Yugoslavia in favor of the capital goods Belgrade wanted. At a meeting of the German and Yugoslav government committees in September 1937 the Yugoslavs again refused to promise more than 150,000 tons of cereals for the forthcoming year, despite German promises to buy more Yugoslav pigs. In fact, they proved more generous than their bargaining position indicated; grain sales to Germany during 1937 totaled 173,000 tons of wheat and 105,000 tons of corn, perhaps because other markets did not come up to expectations.[68]

As the tables show, the Germans fared best with Rumania during 1937. They purchased 400,000 tons of feed grains, but the Rumanians made difficulties regarding exports of wheat. They insisted on payment in foreign exchange and "foreign-exchange-worthy goods," including raw materials, tractors, capital goods, or arms. During the first half of 1937 the Germans concluded a few small compensation agreements on this basis. In December 1937, after long negotiations, Helmut Wohlthat of the Reichstelle für Devisenbewirtschaftung, the chairman of the German government committee for trade with Rumania, finally secured promises of 150,000 tons of Rumanian wheat and 500,000 tons of feed grains during the coming year. In return, the Germans had to stabilize their purchases of Rumanian oil at the 1937 level, pay high prices for Rumanian cattle and pigs, accept an exchange rate that pegged the reichsmark at an average of 38.5 lei rather than the official parity of 40.0 lei, and limit exports of consumer goods to 50 percent of their total exports during the next nine months. Like the Yugoslavs, the Rumanians wanted to import more capital goods and fewer consumer

[68] Agriculture Ministry memorandum, Nov. 3, 1936, PA, Ha Pol IVa, Fin 16, Bd. 1 Jugoslawien, Bd. 1; Ritter memorandum, Dec. 29, 1936, and memorandum of Jan. 15, 1937, T-120/7270/E533605-6, 614-15; Göring to Schacht, Jan. 20, and German legation Belgrade to AA, Feb. 27, T-120/7270/E533610-12, 624; Clodius memorandum, Mar. 4, T-120/5655/H007012-13; Belgrade legation to AA, Clodius's Mar. 6 reply, T-120/7270/E533631-39; agreement of Mar. 24, T-120/5655/H007033-36, T-120/7271/E533697-98; protocol of Sept. 29, T-120/7275/E533831-43; Sarnow memorandum, Oct. 4, T-120/7272/E533760-63; *SJB, 1938*, pp. 293-94.

goods. The new agreement anticipated annual German-Rumanian trade at the level of 200.0 million RM, compared with German imports of 179.5-million-RM worth of goods for 1937.[69]

Wohlthat hoped that this agreement would usher in a new era in German-Rumanian relations, especially as Titulescu, the pro-western foreign minister, had fallen from power in August 1936. After Wohlthat concluded the December agreement, Rumanian ministers gave him the outline of a new economic program designed to tighten relations with Germany by modernizing agriculture, introducing new crops, and jointly exploiting mineral resources. Political turmoil in Rumania, however, blocked the implementation of these proposals. In late December 1937 the existing center-right government yielded to an extreme right-wing, anti-Semitic regime led by Octavian Goga, whom Rosenberg's APA had subsidized for years. Goga's immediate anti-Semitic measures led to economic chaos and British and French protests. King Carol dismissed him after only a few weeks in power. A new, pro-western government introduced a new system of export premiums in April to divert exports to hard-currency countries, and the German legation in Bucharest cautioned Berlin not to expect any progress in economic relations with Rumania, at least until the new harvest put pressure on Bucharest to increase grain exports. Ultimately, total German imports from Rumania for 1938 lagged 22 percent behind 1937 levels, despite the Anschluss and the incorporation of the Sudetenland into the Reich.[70]

In early 1937 the German government also turned to Poland to meet its bread grains needs. At one time, the Germans hoped to import as much as 200,000 tons of Polish rye, but Warsaw's continuing precautions against accumulating a clearing balance with Germany kept actual imports at much lower levels. The Germans also bought small quantities of cereals from the Baltic

[69] German legation Bucharest to AA, Dec. 31, 1936, T-120/7423/E539600; AA memorandum, Jan. 12, 1937, and exchange of notes of Feb. 16, T-120/5662/H010907-8, 919-20; Bucharest legation to AA, Mar. 24, May 5, 20, July 16, and AA to German legation Bucharest, Sept. 11, T-120/5662/H010958, 994, 1004, 1020-22, 1036; Wohlthat memorandum, Nov. 18, T-120/6669/E506112-21; Wohlthat to Göring, Dec. 13, *DGFP*, D, V, 154; agreement of Dec. 9, T-120/6646/E504581-617; *SJB*, *1938*, p. 267, *1939-40*, p. 294.

[70] *DGFP*, D, V, 154, 155, 179; Seton-Watson, *Eastern Europe*, pp. 208-9; German legation Bucharest to AA, Apr. 21, 1938, T-120/7421/E539500-502.

states, even though these countries rarely had extra grain to spare.[71] Poland and the Baltic states also benefited from continued growth in German imports of pigs, cattle, meat, and timber. Total German purchases from these four countries rose from 120.0 million RM in 1936 to 167.5 million RM in 1937 and 236.5 million RM in 1938. In addition, as part of Germany's attempt to secure more fuel from nearby sources, IG Farben, a leader in the development of synthetic fuel within Germany, began the exploitation of Estonian shale oil deposits in 1937.[72]

Total German imports from the agricultural states of Eastern Europe rose from 364.5 million RM in 1936 to 555.8 million RM in 1937, representing an increase in their share of total German imports from 9.3 to 10.8 percent. German purchases in Eastern Europe involved substantial sacrifices. German imports of Yugoslav wheat cost 151 RM per ton in 1937, compared with 125 RM/ton for Canadian wheat; Rumanian corn cost 106.9 RM/ton compared with 75 RM/ton for Argentinian corn.[73] However, with the exception of Argentina, the largest overseas cereals growers sold their crops only for hard currency. After buying as much as they could from Argentina, the Germans turned to their eastern neighbors.

During 1937 Schacht, who still hoped for an early German return to normal world trade, fought the trend toward large new purchases from Eastern Europe through clearings, but he could no longer do anything to prevent them. After his loss of effective power in August 1936, Schacht tried to restore his position by arranging a settlement with France and Britain. He proposed to trade a new disarmament agreement and an end to German exchange control and export subsidies for the return of German colonies in talks with French Premier Léon Blum in August 1936 and Sir Frederick Leith-Ross in February 1937.[74] In the

[71] Agriculture Ministry memorandum, Feb. 6, 1937, T-120/4026/E059539-62; *SJB, 1938*, p. 282, *1939-40*, p. 286; German-Latvian agreement, Oct. 31, 1937, T-120/5920/E435240-42; German-Estonian agreement, Oct. 24, PA, Ha Pol Vb, Handel 13 Estland, Bd 1.

[72] IG Farben memorandum, Sept. 26, 1937, PA, Ha Pol Vb, Rohstoffe, Estland, Petroleum. See also Table A.1.

[73] *SJB, 1938*, p. 267.

[74] C. A. MacDonald, "Economic Appeasement and the German Moderates, 1937-39: An Introductory Essay," *Past and Present*, no. 56 (August 1972), 106-7; Leith-Ross, *Money Talks*, pp. 237-39. On Hitler's changing attitude toward colonies see Klaus Hildebrand, *Vom Reich zum Weltreich: Hitler, NSDAP und koloniale Frage 1919-1945* (Munich, 1969), pp. 441-607.

meantime, he fought measures that he felt would increase German clearing balances in Eastern Europe and thus hamper a return to normal trade. On January 20, 1937, he protested that a proposed clearing purchase of 200,000 tons of Yugoslav grain would inevitably disrupt trade; Germany could not possibly pay for it in normal exports, and it would reinflate the clearing balance, thereby helping the British, French, and Czechs to draw Yugoslavia away from Germany.[75] Then, on July 16, 1937, the Reichsbank, of which Schacht was still president, wrote to the Foreign Office. The letter called attention to the escalating balances in Germany's clearings with Rumania, Yugoslavia, and Hungary—as well as with Greece, Turkey, and Bulgaria—and protested the tendency to purchase cereals through the clearings without arranging any corresponding exports. As a result, the reichsmark was currently trading at a 31 percent discount in Rumania and a 28 percent discount in Yugoslavia. Emil Wiehl, director of the Economic Department, merely replied on July 27 that the matter fell within the responsibility of the Economics and Agriculture ministries. A further Reichsbank protest on July 31 brought the response that nothing could be done once the Economics and Agriculture ministries had decided on imports of foodstuffs.[76] Göring was the ultimate authority making such decisions.

These clashes over clearings reflected the continuing problem of lagging German exports, but here a new solution was emerging. The German government had found one way of reconciling the need for more exports with the demands of rearmament. The solution, a clever blend of economic and political strategy, took advantage of the political instability within Europe that the Germans themselves had introduced. It turned on the large-scale, long-term export of arms.

Although German arms exports in the late 1930s ultimately had political effects, their roots were economic. They represented a response to the dilemma of any heavily armed nation in peacetime: how to maintain a sufficiently steady demand for

[75] T-120/7270/E533610-12. On Feb. 8, 1937, Finance Minister Count Schwerin von Krosigk wrote to Schacht: "I am aware that your organization feels it to be particularly important" for Southeastern European states to have fairly high clearing balances in Germany, in order to force them to buy from Germany (T-120/7270/E533618-20). All other evidence, however, indicates that this was *not* Schacht's policy.

[76] PA, Ha Pol IVa Südeuropa, Fin 16, Bd. 1.

armaments to keep production at or near peak levels of efficiency.[77] The Treaty of Versailles and the German law on war
material of June 27, 1927, had prohibited German arms exports
throughout the Weimar period. After Hitler's accession to
power, German military authorities first raised the question of
renewing arms exports in June 1935. On June 24 War Minister
General Werner von Blomberg wrote Neurath that "The promotion and facilitation of German exports of war materials and
of the trade in arms and ammunition with other countries is
highly desirable for economic and defense reasons. . . . The
manufacture of arms for exports is, in the long run, the most
important, indeed the only way of keeping our armaments firms
productive and financially independent."[78]

Pressure from the War Ministry led to the drafting of a new
law on war material and the formation of the Ausfuhr-
gemeinschaft für Kriegsgerät (Arms Export Company; AGK) in
August 1935. Representatives of the War Ministry, led by Colonel Thomas, continued to insist upon the economic importance
of arms exports, adding that the unusual modernity of German
arms—a consequence of the recent nature of German
rearmament—would give Germany a considerable advantage in
seeking foreign orders. A Foreign Office circular on arms exports, dated November 19, 1935, established the primacy of
economic considerations: "Overseas sales should be handled
from the standpoint of commercial policy, while taking account
of the political relations with the purchasing country from time
to time." Ultimately, the Wilhelmstrasse confirmed the essentially economic character of these transactions by shifting responsibility for the monitoring and encouragement of arms exports from the Political to the Economic Department in May
1937.[79]

Arms exports played a vital role in keeping the German economy afloat in the years before the outbreak of war. From November 1935 through July 1940 they totaled 1.25 billion RM, or
about 5 percent of total German exports in this period.[80] In es-

[77] Volkmann, "Aussenhandel," pp. 92-110, discusses the importance of German arms exports in general.

[78] *DGFP*, C, IV, 22.

[79] Ibid. (editor's note); Thomas memorandum, July 11, 1935, T-120/5560/
E396332-36, AA circular, Sept. 7, 1936, T-120/4795/E236518-21; interdepartmental correspondence, May 10, 15, 1937, T-120/6781/E512909-12.

[80] Volkmann, "Aussenhandel," pp. 84, 95.

sence, Germany drew economic advantage from the political uncertainty that it inspired itself. Hitler's denunciation of the disarmament clauses of the Treaty of Versailles in March 1935 and of Locarno in March 1936 were especially significant in Eastern Europe, where Hungarian and Bulgarian revisionism had never died out and the peace settlement was generally felt to be most fragile. Because the Germans sought arms exports most aggressively, they benefited more than any other power from the increased international uncertainty and the fear of a new war.

In seeking customers for arms exports, the AGK first turned to Germany's First World War allies, Hungary and Bulgaria, and to China, with which the German General Staff had long maintained close relations. Evidently, the Hungarians did not wait for international sanction before upgrading their military forces. During 1936 Budapest contracted for 36.8-million-RM worth of German arms, ultimately importing 5.3-million-RM worth in 1936 and 33.8-million-RM worth in 1937. The latter figure represented 30 percent of German exports to Hungary in 1937.[81]

The Germans also secured substantial orders in Greece and, to a lesser extent, in Yugoslavia and Rumania. Although these antirevisionist states had been aligned against Germany politically, several factors combined to turn them toward the German arms market. Their principal inducement to purchase arms from Germany was, of course, the accumulation of large amounts of reichsmarks in their clearings. At last the Germans were offering valuable, high-quality exports that were increasingly in demand because of the uncertain political situation. Both Belgrade and Bucharest investigated the possibility of arms purchases from Germany during 1936-1937. Although both capitals preferred to rely on their Little Entente ally, Czechoslovakia, or on Britain and France for arms, their reichsmark balances and the difficulty of placing orders in Britain and France gave the Germans room to maneuver. Total German sales in these markets during 1936-1937 were relatively small—11.0 million RM to Rumania and 8.1 million RM to Yugoslavia—but they established a significant precedent. The

[81] AGK annual report for 1937, PA, Ha Pol, Handel mit Kriegsgerät, Allgemeines, Bd. 3; AGK report, Oct. 31, 1936, T-120/4795/E236509-40; meeting of May 2, 1938, T-120/7054/E524036-68.

AGK summarized the situation accurately in its annual report of October 31, 1936:

> It would appear that these small and principally French-influenced countries are placing significant arms orders in Germany as part of a rearmament directed against Germany. The political weakness of France over the last year, the confidence in German quality, and not least of all the consequences of the clearing agreements between Germany and these countries have brought about these active commercial connections.[82]

Originally, the German government, led by Göring, had hoped to use arms exports to secure free exchange and vital raw materials, but gradually the role of these sales in reducing clearing balances with Eastern European states became equally important. When officials of the Four Year Plan asked in early 1937 that more foreign exchange be demanded for arms, the Reichsgruppe Industrie replied that Germany, because of its long exclusion from the arms trade, had originally been forced to seek markets in the areas of least political and economic resistance, that is, in Southeastern Europe, rather than insist upon free exchange. As a result of German imports from Southeastern Europe, clearing balances had arisen "which threatened to block trade, and which could only be covered by German weapons deliveries. These balances were partially freed by weapons deliveries. In this way markets for arms as goods were created which, because of the need for further deliveries of the same caliber and type, promise to provide long-term markets." The Germans had originally asked for 15 percent payment in foreign exchange, supposedly to cover the cost of foreign raw materials used in arms production; in fact, this amount accounted for only 4-5 percent of the total cost, and the demand

---

[82] T-120/4795/E236509-40. On Rumanian approaches, see the AGK meeting of Jan. 15, 1936, T-120/5662/E396943-44; German legation Bucharest to AA, July 22, 1936, T-120/7421/E539472-90; German legation Bucharest to AA, Jan. 6, 1937, and minute by Ernst von Weizsäcker, Jan. 15, T-120/5555/E395045, 048. On Yugoslav approaches see the Belgrade legation's correspondence with the AA, Mar. 11, 13, 1936, T-120/5562/E397123,125-26; German legation Belgrade to AA, July 1, 1937, and OKW comment, T-120/5570/E398734, 36. For 1937 figures see the AGK annual report for 1937, PA, Ha Pol, Handel mit Kriegsgerät, Allgemeines, Bd. 3.

sometimes had been dropped to ensure that orders would be secured.[83]

Further protests from Göring that arms exports were not bringing in enough foreign exchange led to the adoption of a new policy in the summer of 1937. Henceforth, Germany would refuse to sell arms through clearings and would require 100 percent payment in foreign exchange *or* goods that could only be purchased for foreign exchange. With respect to Eastern Europe, these goods turned out to be precisely those that the Eastern Europeans were refusing to sell to Germany through clearings. Under guidelines developed in early 1938 for arms transactions, Hungary was to be asked for 25 percent payment in foreign exchange and 75 percent in cereals, Rumania, 100 percent payment in petroleum or cereals, Yugoslavia, 100 percent payment in cereals, Lithuania and Latvia, 100 percent payment in timber, flax, hides, cereals, or foreign exchange, and Estonia, 15 percent foreign exchange, 35 percent shale oil, and 50 percent other exports.[84]

Ultimately, Germany secured large arms orders and expanded trade with all these countries on this basis in 1938-1940, when the pattern of exchanges of German arms for Eastern European foodstuffs and certain vital raw materials began to dominate trade. Of all the agricultural countries of Eastern Europe, only Poland refused to be drawn into such a pattern, steadfastly curtailing its exports to Germany and refusing to buy German arms for the sake of its political independence. The absorption of Austria, the Sudetenland, and Bohemia-Moravia into the Germany economy in 1938-1939 accelerated the development of this pattern.

As Tables A.4 and A.7 show, the Eastern European share of German trade increased steadily, as did the German share of the trade of the Eastern European countries. The Eastern European share of German imports rose from 9.9 percent in 1933 to 13.8 percent in 1936, 16.1 percent in 1938, and 17.7 percent in 1939. The Eastern European share of German exports rose steadily from 10.7 percent in 1933 to 17.7 percent in 1939. However, increased trade with Eastern Europe could not solve Germany's

[83] Reichsgruppe Industrie letter, Feb. 10, 1937, T-120/6781/E512849-54.
[84] T-120/6781/E512968-73, 78-79; AA circular to missions, Aug. 18, 1937, ibid., E513004-5; guidelines of Jan. and Apr. 9, 1938, PA, Ha Pol, Handel mit Kriegsgerät, Allgemeines, Bd. 3.

long-term economic problems. Hitler himself reaffirmed his commitment to a different solution at a high-level conference on November 5, 1937—the meeting often referred to as the Hossbach conference, after the colonel who took notes.

Although this conference originally met to resolve a dispute between Göring and War Minister Blomberg over the allocations of armaments expenditures, Hitler seized the occasion to restate the essence of his beliefs on foreign policy and to reveal his long-range plans.[85] His lengthy exposition, which he asked to be regarded as his last will and testament, confirms the essential continuity of his thinking as revealed in *Mein Kampf*, his second book, and the memorandum on the Four Year Plan, but it also shows how circumstances had led him to change his plans for realizing his goals.

As usual, Hitler began by noting the need to solve the problem of Germany's inadequate living space. But before discussing how territory might be conquered, he surveyed two alternative solutions: autarky and increased participation in the world economy. Autarky, he noted, had achieved only limited success; some important raw materials could be produced synthetically, but many could not. Autarky was clearly impossible in the vital area of food; here Hitler referred implicitly to the tenfold increases in agricultural imports during 1937. Food consumption was continuing to increase, "and it was therefore certain that even with the maximum increase in production, participation in world trade was unavoidable." Germany's continuing dependence upon imports intensified the risk of a catastrophic food shortage year by year. Even in years of good German harvests, "not inconsiderable" quantities of foreign exchange went to pay for food imports; bad harvests would raise these amounts to "catastrophic proportions." Hitler's reference to foreign exchange implicitly recognized that Germany could not satisfy its needs through clearings alone. The continual growth of Germany's population increased the risk of a disaster every year. Later, while arguing that the living-space problem must be solved at the latest by 1943-1945, he emphasized the danger to

[85] On the genesis of the conference see Harold C. Deutsch, *Hitler and His Generals* (Minneapolis, 1974), pp. 59-61. Present were Hitler, Blomberg, Army Commander Werner von Fritsch, Navy Commander Erich Raeder, Göring, Neurath, and Hitler's adjutant, Friedrich Hossbach. All quotations from the conference are from Hossbach's minutes, *DGFP*, D, I, 19.

the Nazi regime itself: "If we did not act by 1943-45, any year could, in consequence of a lack of reserves, produce the food crisis, to cope with which the necessary foreign exchange was not available, and this must be regarded as a 'waning point of the regime.' "[86]

Hitler then rejected increased participation in the world economy on practical and ideological grounds. Market fluctuations, the inability to enforce commercial treaties, and the increasing industrialization of agrarian states all militated against dependence on world trade. The trend of the age was toward new colonization and large economic empires, as reflected in the policies of Italy and Japan as well as Germany. "The boom in world economy caused by the economic effects of rearmament could never form the basis of a sound economy over a long period," he continued, ironically echoing British Prime Minister Neville Chamberlain, "and the latter was obstructed above all also by the economic disturbances resulting from Bolshevism." Dependence on foreign food supplies carried with it a "pronounced military weakness," since Britain's command of the seas would cut off these supplies in wartime. "The only remedy, and one which might appear to us as visionary, lay in the acquisition of greater living space—a quest which has at all times been the origin of the formation of states and the migration of peoples."

Hitler's sense in late 1937 of an increasingly urgent need to conquer living space was not accidental; his own economic policies had created a long-term crisis within the German economy from which there was no easy way out. By ending unemployment and increasing domestic demand, he had brought about the food crisis; by giving rearmament priority over exports, refusing to devalue the reichsmark, and increasing imports of raw materials for rearmament, he had created a chronic balance of payments problem. By late 1937 recession in the United States had checked the boom in world trade—the boom that had been so crucial to seeing Germany through the foreign-exchange crisis of 1936. German economic authorities were desperately seeking to increase exports while continuing rearmament. Economic expansion had outstripped the capacities of the German labor supply, and manpower shortages

---

[86] The actual German phrase—"Schwächungsmoment des Regimes"—might also be translated "weak point for the regime."

were crippling German agriculture and beginning to hurt German industry. The government continued to finance rearmament with huge loans; as early as December 1936, Göring had speculated that the government would have to pay off its state debt through conquest.[87] Hitler's economic policies were rapidly turning his warnings against dependence on foreign trade into self-fulfilling prophecies; the longer Germany continued to rearm, the worse its trade position inevitably became.

Hitler thus proposed to begin solving the German living-space problem by conquering Austria and Czechoslovakia—if possible during the coming year, by 1943-1945 at the latest. The annexation of these territories, he argued, "would mean an acquisition of foodstuffs for 5 to 6 million people, on the assumption that the compulsory emigration of 2 million people from Czechoslovakia and 1 million people from Austria was practicable." His analysis was not completely accurate; Austria and Czechoslovakia, like Germany itself, were densely populated and industrialized, and, as we shall see, their annexation hardly solved Germany's economic problems.[88] Successful action against Austria and Czechoslovakia would depend upon the nonintervention of Britain and France; Hitler speculated that either civil war in France or a Mediterranean war pitting France and Britain against Italy might enable Germany to proceed during 1938. Neurath, Blomberg, and Army Commander Werner von Fritsch all questioned the feasibility of these schemes; their dissent helped lead to their removal three months later.[89]

Hitler's exposition, concluding with his reaffirmation of the need for a war of conquest, helps to put German trade with Eastern Europe during the 1930s into proper perspective. Before Hitler, the region had played a relatively minor role in Geman trade; it could not compete successfully with overseas suppliers of German imports and absorbed a relatively small quantity of German exports. After 1933, the Wilhelmstrasse and

[87] For a brief survey of the German economic crisis see Timothy W. Mason, "Innere Krise und Angriffskrieg 1938/39," in Forstmeier and Volkmann, eds., *Wirtschaft und Rüstung*, pp. 161-65. See also the October 1937 economic report of the Economic and Armaments Office of the War Ministry, T-77/140/872907-19.

[88] Ludwig Beck, the Army Chief of Staff, raised this point in a Nov. 12 memorandum after seeing Hossbach's notes; see Deutsch, *Hitler and His Generals*, p. 73.

[89] Ibid., pp. 69-74.

the Economics Ministry helped to increase the Eastern European share of German trade, but Hitler himself never hoped to solve Germany's economic problems merely by diverting German trade from overseas to the east. Throughout his political career, he consistently rejected any long-term solution to the German problem based on a Central European economic bloc or informal empire. We have seen that, in the short run, his policies helped to increase trade with Eastern Europe: the husbanding of foreign exchange to pay for vital raw materials and the worsening food shortage combined to increase purchases through clearings, while growing political tension created markets for German arms. In the long run, however, such trade could be only a temporary expedient, useful in keeping the German economy afloat until Germany was ready for a war of conquest. Ultimately, trade with Eastern Europe proved inadequate even for this role. We shall see that in the summer of 1939 the prospect of war with France and Britain forced Hitler to look beyond Eastern Europe for help.

VII.

Britain and Eastern Europe, 1935-1937

The expansion of German trade with Eastern Europe during the mid-1930s posed important questions for the British government. Should London allow Berlin freely to draw upon Eastern European resources for its own purposes, or should the British respond with a counteroffensive? More fundamentally, in the midst of a generally deteriorating world situation and with war threatening on several fronts, should Britain take a stand against German economic, political, and perhaps even military domination of Eastern Europe? Because no decisive crises arose during these years, the British government did not yet have to give a final answer to the latter question, but government opinion generally rejected any action to contest German influence in Eastern Europe. The government did not regard the region as an area of significant economic interest; tariff and quota policies instituted in 1932-33 had already cut British trade with Northeastern Europe and virtually ruled out increases in trade with the region as a whole. In addition, most British ministers and diplomats still hoped eventually to reach an overall political settlement with Germany, and many officials regarded Eastern Europe as an area in which concessions to Germany could usefully be made.

German trade expansion in Southeastern Europe provoked relatively little debate within the British government. British diplomatic missions routinely reported the German trade treaties with Hungary, Yugoslavia, and Rumania in 1934-1935, and serious discussion of German moves in Southeastern Europe, including expanded trade and the threatened Anschluss, began by the spring of 1935. From the beginning, the Foreign Office generally discounted the possibility of British resistance to German expansion. On March 30, E. H. Carr of the Southern Department—an offshoot of the Central Department,

created in January 1934, with responsibility for the agricultural
Danubian states—argued that Britain should avoid any declaration on behalf of Austrian independence; "public opinion"
would not agree to British involvement in a war to prevent
Anschluss, even in alliance with France and Italy. In June, after
the British legation in Budapest had reported German plans for
a "peaceful penetration" of Southeastern Europe, Owen O'Malley, the head of the Southern Department, discounted any German intention to annex territory inhabited by non-Germans and
praised Germany's role in the Danubian states. "Unquestionably
Germany regards it as her mission to become the predominant
Power in the Danubian basin," he wrote, "and to reorganize the
economic life of the countries there which are at present slip-
ping back into barbarism ["Come, come," wrote Vansittart in the
margin, "are they? And if so, more than Germany herself?"] and
even if she did not events could almost inevitably force this role
upon her, since nature abhors a vacuum which is what the de-
mise of the Austrian Empire created." Vansittart continued to
stress the ultimate dangers of German expansion eastward, but
his subordinates generally rejected his views. In November 1935
Frank Ashton-Gwatkin of the Economic Section minuted that a
"German preferential area" was forming under the clearing system and that "nothing can be done to stop it so long as Germany
continues to buy from the countries concerned."[1]

The British thoroughly reexamined their attitude toward
German expansion eastward in early 1936. In February the new
Foreign Secretary, Anthony Eden, began a full-scale review of
the chances of a lasting settlement with Germany. Although
Eden favored rapid British rearmament and a strong League of
Nations, he also wanted to explore the possibilities of a peaceful
settlement with Berlin. He regretted the failure to reach such a
settlement in the spring of 1934, when Hitler had expressed willingness to accept a 300,000-man limit on the Germany army, but
Paris had refused agreement along these lines. As Eden argued
in the cabinet on February 5, 1936, "the policy of reconditioning
the Defense Services must be accompanied by some attempt at

---

[1] For reports of the German-Hungarian, German-Yugoslav, and German-
Rumanian treaties, see FO 371/18409, R117/117/21 et seq., FO 371/18455,
R1599/371/92 et seq., and FO 371/19570, R761/761/37 et seq. For the Carr and
O'Malley minutes see FO 371/19498, R2201/R3811/1/67; see also Vansittart's
minute, ibid., and further comments in June 1935, FO 371/19499, R4208/
R4209/1/67. For Ashton-Gwatkin's minute see FO 371/19570, R6921/761/37.

an arrangement in the political sphere with Germany, although
he [Eden] could not at the moment specify when and in what
circumstances."[2]

In preparation for a further presentation to the cabinet, Eden
queried British Ambassador to Germany Sir Eric Phipps and
various Foreign Office officials regarding German aims, and
Vansittart ultimately wrote a memorandum for the cabinet tem-
pering his subordinates' contributions with his own views.
Phipps reported on January 22, basing his analysis largely on
conversations with Göring. The Germans wanted "full cultural
autonomy" for the ethnic Germans in Czechoslovakia, a refer-
endum on Anschluss in Austria analogous to the earlier vote
that had returned the Saar to Germany, "greater economic possibilities" in Southeastern Europe, and the return of former
German colonies. Phipps stressed that any settlement would
have to meet German economic needs. Carr endorsed these demands with respect to Austria, Czechoslovakia, and Southeastern Europe; no one, he argued, believed that German expansion could be blocked everywhere, and it would be best to permit
it in the southeast. Laurence Collier of the Northern Department dissented. Germany could and should be blocked; it owed
its economic problems solely to the overvaluation of the reichsmark. William Strang of the Central Department also supported
the German demands regarding Czechoslovakia and economic
concessions in the southeast, and he suggested that Britain stop
declaring its interest in Austrian independence and agree to
abandon the demilitarization of the Rhineland.[3]

Ashton-Gwatkin and his colleague in the Economic Section,
Gladwyn Jebb, made more specific recommendations in a January 31 memorandum. To them, the heart of the German problem lay in the extreme concentration and "rationalization" of
German industry and the resulting German need for exports.
However, since a devaluation of the reichsmark would increase
German competition in world markets at Britain's expense, they
suggested that Britain renounce its most-favored-nation rights
in Southeastern Europe in return for limitations on German

---

[2] CAB 23/85. On Eden's attitude see also the meeting of the cabinet Committee on Germany, Feb. 17, 1936 (CAB 27/599), and Harold Nicolson's diary entry
of Feb. 13 confirming Eden's desire to reach a settlement (Harold Nicolson,
Diaries and Letters, 1930-39, ed. Nigel Nicolson [London, 1966], p. 243).

[3] For Phipps's report and minutes see FO 371/19984, C585/4/18.

competition in Scandinavia and "the Baltic area." Remarkably, they believed that the backward markets of Southeastern Europe could compensate Germany for exclusion from richer areas. They also suggested the possible return of the German colonies or the extension of greater trade facilities to Germany within the British Empire.[4]

Vansittart's summary memorandum, which Eden submitted to the cabinet on February 11, embodied the basis of British policy toward Germany for the next twenty-one months, until the Halifax mission of November 1937. With remarkable accuracy, the permanent undersecretary forecast Hitler's ultimate aims in Eastern Europe: annexation of Austria, parts of Czechoslovakia, Memel, Danzig, and parts of western Poland; conquest of the Ukraine; and assumption of political control of the Baltic states. Although rejecting a blind defense of the status quo, he refused to go as far as the Central or Southern departments to meet German demands. He ruled out British acquiescence in German "spoilation of Lithuania, Czechoslovakia, or Austria"; German expansion within Europe would involve "both robbery and murder." Instead, he recommended abandoning the Rhineland demilitarized zone, returning the German colonies, and possibly establishing, under appropriate conditions, a German economic "special area" in Central Europe, "such as clearings, in his view, were already tending to create."[5]

Prompted by Eden, the government created a cabinet committee to discuss possible bases for a settlement with Germany. The committee included the most powerful members of the National Government: Prime Minister Baldwin, Lord President of the Council MacDonald, Chancellor of the Exchequer Neville Chamberlain, Home Secretary Simon, Board of Trade President Runciman, Lord Privy Seal Lord Halifax, and Dominions Secretary J. H. Thomas. The committee turned almost immediately to the question of concessions to Germany in Eastern Europe. O'Malley submitted a further memorandum on concessions in Southeastern Europe on February 26; significantly, a contemporary memorandum by Collier advocating resistance to German demands on the Baltic states did not go before the committee. Going as far as he could without actually violating Vansittart's strictures against German territorial expansion,

---

[4] Ibid., C807/4/18.   [5] CAB 24/260, CP 42 (36).

O'Malley suggested an undefined compromise for the Austrian question, advocated leaving Czechoslovakia to German political and economic domination, and proposed that Germany be allowed to expand throughout Southeastern Europe politically and economically, "consistent with the principles of the [League] Covenant." O'Malley cited Central and Southeastern Europe as the regions in which British political and economic interests would be least directly threatened by German expansion. "The economic regeneration of Central and South-Eastern Europe by Germany promises incalculable material advantages to Germany and to the Danubian countries," he wrote. Britain could not arrest this process despite its political risks and should ensure that it would not work to the detriment of British trade.[6]

The cabinet committee did not oppose concessions to Germany in Eastern Europe in principle. At its first meeting, on February 17, Neville Chamberlain noted that Germany needed "an opening in Central Europe" more than it needed colonies or access to raw materials. Runciman, however, quickly rejected the idea of special German trade privileges in Southeastern Europe as a dangerous precedent. To recognize a German special area, he argued in a February 26 memorandum, "would destroy the grounds for resisting the formation of similar tariff groups throughout the world, in America under the hegemony of the United States, in the Far East under that of Japan, and in the Near East under that of Russia or Germany." The consequences for Britain would be disastrous, and German gains within its special area would be offset by losses elsewhere. Runciman somewhat hypocritically neglected to mention that Britain had created its own special area at the Ottawa conference, but his estimate of the limited importance of Southeastern European markets to Germany was correct. In any case, the cabinet committee apparently accepted his point of view; it abandoned the idea of a special trading area and subsequently concentrated on proposals for the return of German colonies.[7]

Although the British government decided not to encourage German trade expansion to the southeast officially, its attitude

[6] FO 371/20385, R1167/1167/67.

[7] Meeting of Feb. 17, CAB 27/599. See also the further meetings of the Committee on Germany; after July 1936 it was absorbed into the Foreign Policy Committee, whose meetings are under CAB 27/603. For Runciman's Feb. 26 memorandum see ibid.

toward such expansion remained benevolent during 1936 and 1937. Officials continued to argue that expanded German trade with the area was, if anything, beneficial and that Britain could do nothing to affect it in any case. Eden conceded during a foreign-policy debate in Parliament in June 1937 that "in trade and economic matters other nations have a closer interest than we in the Danubian Basin."[8] Attitudes toward Britain's own trade with Southeastern Europe reflected the general disinterest in the region.

British trade with Southeastern Europe remained insignificant throughout the 1930s. British imports from the five Danu‹ bian states never exceeded 2.3 percent of total British imports; the corresponding figure for British exports never exceeded 1.4 percent. British trade was only slightly more important from the standpoint of the Danubian states; the British shares of their imports and exports varied from 5 to 10 percent.[9] In theory, British imports from Southeastern Europe could have been expanded greatly; Britain remained the world's largest importer of the Danubian states' leading export, cereals. As Table VII.1 shows, however, the British bought only very small percentages of their enormous annual purchases of wheat, barley, and corn from Eastern Europe during the 1930s. The reason was simple: Southeastern European prices were higher than world prices, and imperial preference diverted British purchases to the Dominions and the empire. Two major factors kept British exports to the Danubian states below British imports: the agricultural states used much of their meager sterling resources to service foreign debts or buy raw materials on the world market, and the British, unlike the Germans, declined to take advantage of the booming arms market in Southeastern Europe.

British commercial relations with Hungary and Rumania during the mid-1930s revolved largely around the problem of outstanding long-term and commercial debts. Both states, as we

[8] For further comments see the June 1936 minutes by O'Malley, Ralph Wigram, Ashton-Gwatkin, and Vansittart, FO 371/20385, R3919/1167/67, and the FO memorandum of Aug. 17, ibid., R4969/1167/67. For Eden's statement see Great Britain, *Parliamentary Debates* (hereafter *PD*) House of Commons, 5th ser., CCCXXV, 1602-4.

[9] See Tables A.5 and A.7.

TABLE VII.1
Selected British Imports, 1934-1939

	1934	1935	1936	1937	1938	1939
Wheat						
(in thousands of metric tons)						
Total	2,262	2,232	2,222	2,135	2,240	2,338
British countries	1,224	1,206	1,860	1,396	1,416	1,072
(% share)	(54)	(54)	(84)	(65)	(63)	(48)
Eastern European countries	47	83	164	78	81	176
(% share)	(2)	(4)	(7)	(4)	(4)	(8)
Barley						
(in thousands of metric tons)						
Total	341	377	403	401	438	303
British countries	51	66	58	95	164	98
(% share)	(15)	(18)	(14)	(24)	(37)	(32)
Eastern European countries	48	6	113	14	6	11
(% share)	(14)	(2)	(28)	(4)	(1)	(4)
Corn						
(in thousands of metric tons)						
Total	1,353	1,310	1,616	390	1,269	1,023
British countries	37	92	48	116	162	163
(% share)	(3)	(7)	(3)	(30)	(13)	(16)
Eastern European countries	44	21	41	26	102	58
(% share)	(3)	(2)	(3)	(7)	(8)	(6)
Refined Petroleum Products						
(in millions of gallons)						
Total	2,269	2,305	2,404	2,548	2,516	2,457
Rumania	194	173	209	153	109	87
(% share)	(9)	(8)	(9)	(6)	(4)	(4)

SOURCES: *TUK, 1935*, II, 1-2, 83, 115, 316, *1939*, II, 1-2, 80, 108, 288-89.

have seen, had frozen many foreign claims during the depression, and British traders and bondholders continued to have difficulty securing payment of their claims in the mid-1930s. Eventually, the government reluctantly concluded clearing and payments agreements with Rumania in 1935 and with Hungary in 1936 to collect these claims. The agreements required the two states to set aside specified portions of the sterling they earned from exports to pay British claims. Unlike German clearings, these agreements did not increase trade; if anything, they tended to limit it. By assigning the highest priority to the payment of old debts, they sometimes caused British exporters to miss out on favorable opportunities. In addition, they did not oblige the Hungarians and Rumanians to use whatever sterling they had left over after debt service to buy British goods. The Eastern Europeans spent many of their surplus pounds on "colonial goods," including raw materials for their expanding industries. Rumanian officials sometimes noted the political importance of increasing Anglo-Rumanian trade, but the Board of Trade, which usually handled negotiations for clearing and payments agreements, disliked mixing trade with politics.[10] Thus, even though Britain annually imported huge quantities of refined petroleum products, the Rumanian share of these imports, as shown in Table VII.1 generally stayed at about 10 percent.

British trade with Yugoslavia received more attention in the 1935-1937 period. The Yugoslavs bombarded London with requests for tariff concessions and increased trade; they succeeded in getting their foot into the door in late 1935, when Britain agreed to help compensate them for losses incurred through their participation in League of Nations sanctions against Italy. They also tried to buy substantial quantities of British arms. Because of this relatively high level of activity, British-Yugoslav trade relations provide the best barometer of British government interest in the Danubian states.

When the League of Nations imposed financial and economic sanctions against Italy in November 1935 in response to Mussolini's attack on Ethiopia, Yugoslavia stood to lose as much as any power involved. Italy generally bought about 25 percent of Yugoslavia's exports, and most of this trade would be lost under the sanctions. Nonetheless, Belgrade decided to observe the sanctions for political reasons; Mussolini was Yugoslavia's most dangerous enemy, and sanctions might either topple him or deter him from further adventures. While agreeing to apply sanctions, Belgrade attempted to capitalize on a November 18 League resolution asking that League members try to compen-

---

[10] On the agreements with Hungary and Rumania see FO 371/20394, R9/9/21 et seq., and FO 371/21185, R1852/48/37. For more discussion of British-Rumanian trade relations see British legation Bucharest to FO, Dec. 28, 1936, Anglo-Rumanian conversations of Apr. 28-30, 1937, agreement of May 27, and British legation Bucharest to FO, May 15, FO 371/21184-85, R183/R3871/ R3982/R3388/48/37.

sate those member states especially affected by sanctions. Yugoslav foreign trade expert Milivoje Pilja, who also handled German-Yugoslav commercial relations, visited London in November 1935 to ask for larger British import quotas and lower duties on Yugoslav bacon, eggs, and poultry. The Foreign Office was sympathetic, but the Board of Trade and the Ministry of Agriculture opposed concessions. Runciman argued that Britain could buy more Yugoslav poultry only at the expense of Hungary, which had refused to participate in sanctions but needed sterling to pay its debts to Britain, and that it seemed unfair to compensate foreigners while refusing to help British nationals suffering sanctions-related losses. However, in a cabinet meeting on December 4 the Foreign Office secured approval for some higher quotas and duty reductions for Belgrade, partly on the understanding that only small amounts of goods would be involved.[11]

The Yugoslav government was delighted, particularly since Paris had refused to provide effective assistance. Belgrade decided to try to use these temporary British concessions as a basis for a long-term expansion of Anglo-Yugoslav trade. In the spring of 1936 the Yugoslavs imposed a new system of import control. We have seen that this step was designed partly to equalize trade with Germany, and it initially reduced certain imports from Britain, including coal, to Germany's advantage. Nevertheless, Pilja told British Minister Ronald Campbell on June 18 that he hoped to force London to increase Anglo-Yugoslav trade, thus reducing Belgrade's dependence on Germany. He expressed interest in coming to London for talks but was disappointed when the British wanted to discuss only the discriminatory and unfavorable effects of the Yugoslav import control system and not increased bilateral trade. He postponed his visit after the Board of Trade indicated that any discussion of preferential tariff concessions would be fruitless.[12]

[11] On Yugoslavia and sanctions see Hoptner, *Yugoslavia in Crisis*, pp. 37-38, 98-100. On Pilja's visit and the British government decision see his conversations of Nov. 18, 19, 1935, FO 371/19579, R6973/6938/3306/92; Secretary of State for War Leslie Hoare-Belisha to Runciman, Nov. 15, ibid., R7303; two memoranda of Nov. 29, R7335/7336/3306/92; cabinet of Dec. 4, CAB 23/82.

[12] On the French failure to provide help see British legation Belgrade to FO, Feb. 21, 1936, FO 371/20432, R1079/11/92. See also British legation Belgrade to FO, June 6, 18, Aug. 7, Sept. 1, 30, 1936, FO 371/20432-33, R3683/R4478/R5187/R5823/11/92.

Pilja ultimately came to London in mid-November, but the Board of Trade still refused to offer anything more than an "equitable" share of British import quotas in exchange for the issuance of "adequate import licenses for British goods." Under the quota system the British had first instituted in 1932, the percentage shares of individual countries depended on their shares of British imports of the commodity in question during a specified base period. Throughout the 1930s London refused to deviate from this rule; in some cases, to have done so would have violated the Ottawa agreements of 1932. Pilja had to be content with an agreement tying the issuance of import licenses to the level of Yugoslav exports to Britain. The Board of Trade refused either to set up a joint committee to oversee Anglo-Yugoslav trade—an obvious parallel to the German government committees—or to send a British trade mission to Yugoslavia, despite the endorsement of the Southern Department of the Foreign Office.[13]

On December 2, 1936, the Yugoslav minister in London asked Eden for a long-term, £1.3-million credit to purchase arms and military clothing in Great Britain. This sum represented 130 percent of the total British exports to Yugoslavia in 1936. The Treasury immediately stated that Yugoslavia's credit position probably ruled out such a loan. The only conceivable solution was a loan guaranteed by the Export Credits Guarantee Department (ECGD), but this, as the Treasury quickly pointed out, presented legal difficulties.[14]

London's attitude toward export credits for arms illustrates the widely differing views on rearmament and arms exports prevailing in the British and German governments. The German military authorities had recognized the importance of arms exports in keeping production at a high level almost from the beginning of German rearmament, and economic authorities had seized upon these exports as a means of improving the German trade balance. In Britain, however, not only was rearmament proceeding much more slowly,[15] but prevailing at-

[13] St. Quintin Hill minutes, Nov. 5, 6, 1936, agreement of Nov. 28, Welch (BT) to Ashton-Gwatkin, December 1936, Southern Department and Board of Trade comments on a commercial mission, Dec. 17, FO 371/20433, R6593/R6594/R7265/R7309/R7599/11/92.

[14] Eden minute, Dec. 2, 1936, FO 371/20435, R7304/102/92; Treasury letter, Jan. 9, 1937, FO 371/21194, R212/21/92.

[15] For statistical comparisons of German and British rearmament see T. W.

titudes toward arms exports were also highly ambivalent. The issue of export credits for arms sales had surfaced in 1933, when the 1921 Export Credit Guarantee Act had come up for renewal. Under the act, the ECGD insured long-term credits for British exports. Because of public opposition to the arms trade, the act had outlawed guarantees for "munitions of war." In 1933 the Principal Supply Officers Committee of the Committee of Imperial Defence, echoing their German counterparts, had asked that this prohibition be repealed on the grounds that the British arms industry needed export markets to maintain its health. A cabinet committee had endorsed the committee's request, but in December 1933 the full cabinet decided against export credits for arms on political grounds. The government did not want to seem to encourage the international arms trade. The prohibition of credits for "munitions of war" remained in effect in 1937, and it was generally interpreted to include any items destined for military use—including clothing.[16]

Thus, in January 1937 the Treasury quickly ruled out export credit guarantees for arms exports to Yugoslavia. O'Malley minuted agreement with the Treasury position on January 12, arguing that Britain should not follow the French precedent of arms loans, but Vansittart and Sargent disagreed. Italy's conquest of Ethiopia and intervention in Spain had made Mediterranean defense a more serious problem, and the two senior officials wanted to thwart Italian efforts to draw Belgrade into the Fascist camp. Vansittart asked Eden to discuss the matter with Chancellor of the Exchequer Neville Chamberlain, adding, "I attach a great deal of importance to being helpful in this case."[17]

By early 1937, Chamberlain was probably the most powerful member of the National Government. His elevation to prime minister was only months away; already, as chancellor of the Exchequer, he had decisively influenced the course of British rearmament. Fearing the effects of rearmament on the British economy and the domestic capital market, he had tried to keep the diversion of productive capacity to military needs at the level

Mason, "Some Origins of the Second World War," *Past and Present*, no. 29 (December 1964), 78-94.

[16] Memorandum of Apr. 8, 1933, CAB 24/239, CP 99 (33); report of the Committee on the Private Armaments Industry, June 23, 1933, CAB 24/245, CP 289 (33); cabinet of Dec. 13, 1933, CAB 23/77.

[17] Minutes, Jan. 12, 1937, FO 271/21194, R212/21/92.

that he regarded as the essential minimum.[18] Wishing to limit rather than stimulate arms production, he opposed export credit guarantees for arms; in February he informed the Foreign Office that Yugoslavia could not receive a credit guarantee. When British Minister Campbell called for more concessions to head off an imminent Italo-Yugoslav pact of friendship, Eden wrote to Chamberlain on March 13 asking for a reconsideration. Runciman also wrote the chancellor on March 23, stating that "at the Board of Trade we are also anxious for purely commercial reasons to assist Yugoslavia in getting away from German influence." Moreover, he noted that the ECGD had recently made an exception to the interpretation regarding military clothing for a credit to the Soviet Union. Chamberlain refused to modify his stand in his reply of April 2.[19]

On March 17 and May 5 the British cabinet discussed amending export credit regulations to permit arms export credit guarantees. Chamberlain was absent on March 17, owing to the death of his half-brother Austen Chamberlain, and cabinet opinion seemed to favor a change in the law; members referred to the loss of a recent order for Yugoslavia. Chamberlain was present on May 5, however, and the cabinet decided not to modify the law. On June 18 Campbell informed Yugoslav Prime Minister Milan Stoyadinovich that no credit could be given.[20]

The Yugoslavs instead began private negotiations for the purchase of twelve Bristol Blenheim bomber aircraft. They reached agreement with Bristol but ran up against slow British production and unfavorable British strategic priorities. When informed of the proposed transaction, the Air Ministry refused to release more than one plane for immediate sale. Prodded by Campbell, who stressed the danger to Britain should Belgrade turn to other sources of supply, the Foreign Office asked for a reconsideration, but the Air Ministry would only increase the allocation from one plane to two. The two planes arrived in November

[18] On Chamberlain's attitude see below, Chapter IX.

[19] Sargent and Eden minutes of Feb. 11, 25, 1937, FO 371/21194, R1064/21/92; British legation Belgrade to FO, Feb. 15, FO 371/21197, R1147/224/92; Eden to Chamberlain, Mar. 13, Runciman to Chamberlain, Mar. 23, Chamberlain to Runciman, Apr. 2, FO 371/21194-95, R1494/R2082/R2389/21/92. On the Italo-Yugoslav agreement see FO 371/21197 and Hoptner, *Yugoslavia in Crisis*, pp. 61-93.

[20] CAB 23/87; Campbell to Stoyadinovich, June 18, 1937, FO 371/21195, R4357/21/92.

1937 and immediately became the pride of the Yugoslav air
force, but the experience did not encourage Belgrade to rely
upon the British arms market.[21]

The British failure to supply more aircraft reflected British
defense priorities, as enumerated by the Chiefs of Staff in a
memorandum for the cabinet in early 1937: defense of the
United Kingdom, France, and the Low Countries; defense of
British possessions in the Far East; defense of the eastern
Mediterranean; and defense of India against potential Soviet
threats. An arms priority list drawn up within the Foreign Office
in May 1937 to help allocate arms exports reflected this order of
priorities; it particularly stressed defense of the Mediterranean
and the Suez Canal. The first twenty countries on the list, in order, were Egypt, Afghanistan, Belgium, Portugal, Turkey,
Saudi Arabia, Yugoslavia, Greece, Argentina, the Netherlands,
Finland, Estonia, Latvia, Lithuania, Poland, Rumania, China,
Iran, Yemen, Brazil, and Chile. The list omitted the United
States, France, Germany, Italy, Japan, and Czechoslovakia on
grounds either of unfriendliness or self-sufficiency; the Soviet
Union ranked thirty-seventh and last. Given the relatively small
quantities of arms available for export, particularly up-to-date
arms, it was unlikely that significant quantities would be available to more than the first five or ten countries on the list. Thus,
Yugoslavia could not receive ten Blenheim bombers because of a
previous allocation of planes to Turkey. Eastern European states
without an Adriatic coastline had much less chance of purchasing late-model British arms.[22]

British military authorities recognized the contrast between
British and German attitudes toward arms exports, and they put
the issue before the cabinet in May 1938. Minister for the Coordination of Defence Sir Thomas Inskip circulated a Committee of Imperial Defence paper analyzing German rearmament.
It perceptively noted how the Germans had combined large-
scale production and clearing agreements to boost arms exports,
obtain vital raw materials, and keep production at optimal levels

[21] British legation Belgrade to FO, May 17, 20, 1937, Air Ministry to FO, July
26, British legation Belgrade to FO, Nov. 22, FO 371/21195, R3859/R3455/
R5206/R8180/21/92.
[22] Chiefs of Staff memorandum, Feb. 22, 1937, CAB 24/268, CP 73 (37); on
the compilation of the list see FO 371/21228, W4487/W8034/W9498/902/50, and
Air Ministry to FO, July 26, FO 371/21195, R5206/21/92.

of efficiency. Lord Halifax, the foreign secretary, was impressed; he had already written Inskip on April 17 suggesting that Britain might have to remodel its "system of rearmament" along German lines. When the cabinet discussed the paper on May 18, Secretary of State for War Leslie Hoare-Belisha noted that Germany had acquired an interest in "keeping the world in a state of trouble." While Germany used arms exports to bring other countries into its political orbit, Britain could not even supply the Dominions and other allies. Prime Minister Chamberlain argued on the other hand that it would be impossible to reach German levels of arms production without copying the entire German apparatus of economic controls, including abolition of hours limitations, institution of compulsory training and movement of workers, and control of raw materials and finance. "He doubted whether the nation would be prepared to go as far as that at the present time." Chamberlain refused to introduce anything smacking of a wartime measure in peacetime, and Britain's conservative arms export policies remained an obstacle to successful competition with Germany in Eastern Europe for the rest of the decade.[23]

The British government's lack of interest in the Danubian states was not surprising. The area had never been important to British trade, and the Board of Trade and Treasury generally opposed government intervention to increase commerce with Southeastern Europe. Although British investors had put substantial capital into Southeastern European private enterprises, they exerted no pressure on the government to become more involved on their behalf.[24] Until the Anschluss, London avoided economic initiatives in the Danubian states. Attempts to reverse this trend after the Anschluss were haphazard, controversial, and mostly ineffective.

On the other hand, the British government had already established a significant position in the trade of Northeastern Europe.

[23] Memorandum of May 13, 1938, and Halifax's Apr. 17 letter, CAB 24/276; cabinet of May 18, CAB 23/93.

[24] On British capital investment see Bernd Jürgen Wendt, "England und der deutsche 'Drang nach Südosten.' Kapitalbeziehungen und Warenverkehr in Südeuropa zwischen den Weltkriegen," in Immanuel Geiss and Wendt, eds., *Deutschland in der Weltpolitik des 19. und 20. Jahrhunderts* (Düsseldorf, 1973), pp. 483-512, and Alice Teichova, "Die deutsch-britischen Wirtschaftsinteressen in Mittelost- und Südosteuropa am Vorabend des Zweiten Weltkrieges," in Forstmeier and Volkmann, eds., *Wirtschaft und Rüstung*, pp. 279-95.

Even though the 1934-1935 trade agreements with the Baltic states and Poland had kept Britain's total imports from these countries within tight limits, the pacts represented a commitment to a strong British position in the Baltic market. Furthermore, although the Northeastern European share of British trade only slightly exceeded that of the Danubian states, the British government was well aware of being the northeastern states' largest customer for exports and at least their second-largest supplier of imports. The personal beliefs of Foreign Office officials had much to do with London's somewhat greater interest in Baltic markets. Whereas the Southern Department lauded German trade expansion within its area of responsibility and discounted British interests there, the Northern Department, led by Sir Laurence Collier, fought German influence while advocating a more active British commercial policy.

Beginning in 1934, the revival of German trade with Northeastern Europe challenged Britain's preeminence in the region's trade. In Poland, the Anglo-German rivalry continued as before; until 1938 Britain maintained a slight lead as an importer from Poland, while Germany maintained a similar margin in exports. In the Baltic states, however, the revival of German imports of timber and agricultural products after 1934 enabled the Germans almost to equal the British as purchasers of Baltic products while they widened their lead in sales to the region. By 1937 the Germans were running roughly equal balances of trade with the Baltic states, while Britain's balances were heavily negative.[25]

London's reaction to the German challenge showed how difficult it was to get the British government to take any initiatives in commercial policy, even in defense of recognized interests. Led by Collier, the Northern Department of the Foreign Office quickly pointed out the German resurgence in the Baltic and recommended steps to counteract it, but three obstacles prevented any government action. First, the Treasury and the Board of Trade refused to impose clearings merely to improve negative trade balances, even though clearings could easily force the Baltic states to buy nearly as much from Britain as they sold there. Second, the restrictive quota policies limiting British agricultural imports could not be loosened; at one time, even

[25] See Tables A.1, A.2, and A.7.

stricter measures were contemplated. Lastly, German competition in the Baltic was only one aspect of worldwide German export competition, and most British government officials wanted to deal with this problem through cartel agreements with German producers rather than engage in aggressive competition. As a result, London was hardly more active in defending its position in Northeastern Europe than in pursuing opportunities in the Danubian states.

Collier feared the German resurgence in the Baltic from the beginning. He suggested in February 1936 that the Germans aimed at the return of Memel, and eventually at "a protectorate, probably political and certainly commercial, over all three [Baltic] states." In December 1935 and again in July 1936 he asked for British government action, including the power to impose clearings to improve trade balances, to fight German competition. The Board of Trade replied in February 1936 that the general policy of clearings was "not one which has so far commended itself" to the British government. In July, Collier successfully persuaded Ashton-Gwatkin, who had initially opposed clearings, that the power to impose a clearing to improve Britain's trade balance might at least be a useful tool in commercial negotiations. The Foreign Office raised this question with the Board of Trade, but before the Board responded, its president, Runciman, publicly denounced any increased use of clearings before the House of Commons on July 15. Discussing Britain's general foreign trade position, he noted that the government had occasionally imposed clearings to collect debts but opposed establishing them merely to increase British exports:

> Upon certain countries and for a certain period we could, no doubt, force a greater quantity of United Kingdom goods, but we do not believe a policy of force in this region would prosper for long. It would lead to the impoverishment of our customers and of third parties in whose prosperity we are interested, and, eventually to a fall in our own trade.

The Board of Trade generally argued that clearings would reduce multilateral trade, upon which Britain depended. Collier replied that multilateral trade was disappearing because of exchange control and that Britain should rely on its position as an importer to increase exports. In succeeding months the Board maintained its opposition to new clearings despite further pressure from the Foreign Office and private interests, and Britain's trade balances in Northeastern Europe remained heavily negative.[26]

Britain's trade agreements with the Baltic states, Poland, the Scandinavian countries, and Finland came up for renegotiation in 1936, and substantial pressure emerged within the British government for reducing imports from these countries still further. In the spring of 1936, when the cabinet created a Trade and Agriculture Committee to consider this question, the government intended to replace the existing quota system for bacon, eggs, and dairy products with levies on imports and subsidies for home producers. Runciman noted in June that these changes would inevitably reduce imports from foreign countries; the object of renegotiation would therefore be "to reduce the benefits enjoyed by foreign countries" under existing arrangements. Eden protested in July that this step would concede important political influence to Germany. In the event, existing arrangements with the Scandinavian and Baltic countries were allowed to continue in force because the government could not agree on its new domestic agricultural policy. The Trade and Agriculture Committee's initial approval of Runciman's proposals, however, emphasized the continuing primacy of domestic policy within the British government.[27]

[26] For reports of increased German trade with the Baltic states see British legation Riga to FO, Feb. 14, Oct. 15, 1935, and British embassy Berlin to FO, Nov. 29, FO 371/19398, N862/N5378/459/59, FO 371/19396, N6248/153/59. For Collier's memorandum of Feb. 13, 1936, see FO 371/19398, N855/427/59. For his Dec. 17, 1935, proposal and the Board of Trade's Feb. 19, 1936, reply see FO 371/19396, N6248/153/59, FO 371/20309, N990/523/59. For Collier's July 8 minute, Ashton-Gwatkin's Aug. 6 comments, and their proposal to the Board of Trade see FO 371/20306, N3996/32/39, FO 371/20460, W5149/299/50. For Runciman's remarks see *PD*, Commons, 5th ser., CCCXIV, 2079-81; by "region" he did not mean any particular territorial region. For further discussion of this issue see Collier to BT, July 16, 1936, Hill's reply, conversation of July 23 with London Chamber of Commerce representatives, Riga legation to FO, Dec. 16, FO 371/20331-32, N3666/N3695/N3839/N6280/40/63. For figures see Table A.2.

[27] On the expiration of the agreements and the formation of the cabinet committee see the interdepartmental meeting of Dec. 18, 1935, FO 371/20331, N40/40/63; memorandum of Apr. 3, 1936, CAB 24/261, CP 104 (36); cabinet of Apr. 8, CAB 23/83. For Runciman's June memorandum, the committee's approval of his proposals, and Eden's protest, see FO 371/20460, W5887/299/50, TAC 53 (36), and W6851/299/50. Documents noting agreement to maintain existing arrangements in force are listed in the FO 371 index but were not re-

The problem of meeting German competition in Northeastern Europe was only one aspect of the broader problem of competing with German exports worldwide. By 1935, German export subsidies, barter agreements, and clearings had emerged as
effective weapons against British competition, and British private interests began bombarding their government with requests
for help. In June 1936 the Department of Overseas Trade circulated a memorandum on German export competition, and an
interdepartmental meeting of civil servants discussed this issue
on October 30. Gladwyn Jebb of the Economic Section, who
generally sympathized with German trade expansion, represented the Foreign Office. The meeting concluded that unless
the British government introduced export subsidies or more
clearings of its own—steps that did not commend themselves to
the Board of Trade—it would generally remain helpless against
German competition. The best solution to the problem, therefore, lay in officially encouraged discussions between British and
German industrialists, with a view to a division of export markets. Sir Frederick Leith-Ross raised the question of such cartels
with a group of German industrialists in late October, and on
November 18 Runciman authorized the Federation of British
Industries to contact German producers. In December, Leith-
Ross recommended cartel agreements with German industry in
a memorandum for the cabinet on the British balance of trade.[28]

Gladwyn Jebb's apparent failure to circulate the results of this
meeting throughout the Foreign Office led to a minor explosion
in late December. On December 23 an amazed Laurence Collier
learned from Cecil Farrar of the Department of Overseas Trade
that the Foreign Office had approved the principle of Anglo-
German industrial cartels. Vansittart immediately expressed as-
tonishment, asking who had given Foreign Office assent to this

---

tained in the files. For further discussion of domestic agricultural policy and the
eventual failure to adopt the levy-subsidy system see W. S. Morison to Oliver
Stanley, June 9, 1937, BT 11/735, memorandum of Nov. 5, CAB 24/272, CP
268 (37), and cabinets of Nov. 18, 24, CAB 23/90.

[28] For a detailed discussion of Nazi competition in various markets and the
protests of British private interests see Wendt, *Economic Appeasement*, pp. 274-
416. See also Department of Overseas Trade memorandum, June 13, 1936, BT
59/22/540; Board of Trade memorandum for Runciman, Nov. 22, BT 59/540a;
Leith-Ross's Nov. 3 minute of his talks with German industrialists, ibid.; Arthur
Mullins's undated memorandum, FO 371/20731, C87/87/18; Leith-Ross's Dec. 7
memorandum for the cabinet, CAB 24/265, CP 339 (36).

proposal and agreeing with Collier that both the Foreign Office
and the service departments should have been fully consulted.
Jebb replied on January 6, 1937, that in responding favorably to
the proposal for cartels, "I trusted that my remarks . . . were in
accordance with the views of the Central Department, which
alone among the political departments the question seemed to
concern." In his view, the whole question was really "the province of the Department of Overseas Trade and the Board of
Trade." He added that Sargent, whose responsibility included
the Central Department, agreed with him. Collier complained
that the Board of Trade, having concluded valuable purchase
agreements with the Baltic states, was now encouraging cartels
that would prevent these agreements from being carried out.
But Ashton-Gwatkin supported the principle of cartels, and Sir
Alexander Cadogan of the Western Department agreed with
Jebb that the issue was primarily the concern of the trade departments. Vansittart surrendered with a "very well" on January
13, and the Foreign Office instructed John Magowan, the British commercial counselor in Berlin, to encourage discussions between British and German industrialists.[29]

Such conversations made little progress during 1937. Magowan opposed them, arguing correctly that Germany used its exports solely to finance rearmament; moreover, a boom in world
trade eased the export situation generally during the first half of
the year. Nonetheless, this episode revealed London's general
response to German competition: the trade departments wanted
to avoid any further government intervention in international
commerce, and even the Economic Section of the Foreign Office
wanted to resolve the problem through accommodation, not retaliation. In advocating an aggressive British response, Collier
emerged as a minority of one. We shall see that the British revived cartel negotiations in 1938, after a world recession had put
renewed pressure on British exports. By that time the government had committed itself even more firmly to an accommodation with Germany.[30]

With regard to German territorial expansion in Eastern
Europe, Vansittart's memorandum of February 11, 1936, re-

[29] For all these minutes and Magowan's instructions see FO 371/20731, C87/
87/18.
[30] For Magowan's reaction see ibid., C1454/87/18.

mained the basis of British government policy until late 1937. Vansittart had argued that the British government could not officially countenance German territorial expansion or openly disinterest itself in Eastern Europe; he insisted that Britain had a strategic interest in that region, arguing that it would be impossible to defend France and the Low Countries if the rest of Europe were overrun.[31] Thus, during negotiations for a new security treaty in the wake of Hitler's remilitarization of the Rhineland in March 1936, London opposed German efforts to distinguish between Germany's western frontiers, for which Berlin proposed new multilateral guarantees, and its eastern frontiers, with which the Germans refused to deal until a new western pact had been concluded. The British also supported French demands that a new western pact not prohibit France from coming to the aid of its eastern allies.[32] On the other hand, the British government refused to commit itself specifically to defend the status quo in Eastern Europe. O'Malley and Sargent protested bitterly in February 1936 upon hearing that Beneš had claimed that Britain would stand by Czechoslovakia if it were attacked by Germany, and in July 1936, when war threatened because of the German-Polish Danzig currency crisis, the cabinet agreed that Britain could not possibly afford to become involved in such a war at the present time.[33] Furthermore, during 1936 the Foreign Office and the cabinet also discussed amending Article 16 of the League Covenant so as to reduce Britain's chances of involvement in an unnecessary war. The experience of the Italo-Ethiopian conflict had convinced London that the application of economic sanctions under Article 16 was too risky. These discussions revealed widespread fear of British involvement in a war arising out of German aggression in Eastern Europe.[34] We

[31] CAB 24/260, CP 42 (36). See also Vansittart's May 1937 minutes on Lord Lothian's account of talks with Hitler, FO 371/20735, C3621/270/18.

[32] On these negotiations see CAB 24/261, CP's 100 and 123 (36); cabinets of Apr. 3, May 4, 6, CAB 23/84, CAB 24/264-65, CP's 278, 307, 308 (36); Foreign Policy Committee meeting of Aug. 25, 1936, CAB 27/622; cabinet of Nov. 13, 1936, CAB 23/86.

[33] FO 371/20376, R999/999/12; cabinet of July 6, 1936, CAB 23/85.

[34] On the amendment of Article 16 see Strang's June 3, 1936, memorandum and minutes, FO 371/20474, W6374/79/78; Foreign Policy Committee meetings of Apr. 30, July 21, Aug. 25, 1936, CAB 27/622, and related memoranda, CAB 27/626. Strang, Ralph Wigram of the Western Department, and Gladwyn Jebb all felt that Britain should not be committed to sanctions against German aggression in Eastern Europe. Collier dissented, arguing that Britain should instead

shall see that in early 1937 London helped to block a French attempt to conclude a defensive alliance with the Little Entente, largely on the grounds that it would increase the chances of French and British involvement in an unnecessary war.[35]

In public, Foreign Secretary Anthony Eden avoided a direct answer to the question of what Britain would do in response to German aggression in Eastern Europe. Twice—at his Leamington constituency on November 20, 1936, and in the House of Commons on June 25, 1937—he affirmed that Britain would use its new armaments to defend the United Kingdom, the British Empire, and, if necessary, France and the Low Countries. "In addition," he added, "our armaments may be used in bringing help to a victim of aggression in any case where, in our judgement, it would be proper under the provisions of the Covenant to do so." Although noting on the latter occasion that Britain could not disinterest itself in Central Europe, he added that the word *may* "reflected the lack of any League obligation to take armed action against aggression."[36]

This statement embodied the policy of "cunctation"—procrastination and ambiguity—rather than a renunciation of interest in Eastern Europe or a declaration of willingness to defend the status quo. Eden's subordinates did not support this policy unanimously. Vansittart continued to argue that Britain should oppose German hegemony in Central Europe, but Strang commented that statements like Eden's "have in them a fair admixture of bluff." He found it "difficult to conceive" that the government would take "the incalculable risk to our existence" of a war to defend the status quo in Central Europe. Instead, he advocated attempting to deter Germany while pursu-

---

propose that League members' obligations under Article 16 be strengthened to include military action at the direction of the League Council; should this proposal be rejected, Britain should leave the League. He recognized that an enormous gulf existed between his views and those of his colleagues and of the cabinet but concluded: "I have put them down on paper, however, since you have asked me to say something and since I am vain enough to hope that they may be preserved in order that I can point to them when, as I am convinced, they are justified by the events which I foresee in the next few years" (minute on W6374, ibid.).

[35] See below, Chapter VIII.

[36] Anthony Eden, Earl of Avon, *Facing the Dictators* (London, 1962), pp. 477-78; *PD*, Commons, 5th ser., CCCXXV, 1602-4.

ing "a parallel policy, the object of which would be to ensure, if possible, that if changes in the peace settlements take place at all, they should take place in peaceful and orderly conditions, rather than by violence." Sir Alexander Cadogan supported this suggestion.[37]

In fact, despite Eden's statement, the accession of Neville Chamberlain as prime minister in May 1937 had already ensured the adoption of Strang's policy. Chamberlain rapidly took control of British foreign policy and resolved the ongoing debate within the British government in favor of toleration of German expansion in Eastern Europe, provided that it took place peacefully. By encouraging peaceful change, he hoped to promote a general European settlement. Within seven months of Chamberlain's accession, London had gone on record in favor of peaceful change in Eastern Europe and against war to preserve the status quo.

By the time he became prime minister, Chamberlain had developed strong views on foreign policy. In the wake of the Italo-Ethiopian war, he believed that collective security as a deterrent to aggression had failed. Although he initially supported sanctions against Italy, Mussolini's successful defiance of them turned him against sanctions and led him to abandon hope in the League of Nations as an effective instrument for world peace. More important, by mid-1937 Chamberlain believed that Britain could afford neither a major war nor a protracted arms race. He had already shown his concern for Britain's financial and economic health as chancellor of the Exchequer; as prime minister, his sensitivity to economic and financial questions emerged as perhaps the most important determinant of his foreign policy.[38]

As chancellor of the Exchequer throughout most of the depression-plagued 1930s, Chamberlain had emphasized confidence in Britain's economic future as the key to recovery and

[37] In late July 1937 Sargent attributed the characterization "cunctation" to J. M. Keynes (minute on FO 371/20736, C5316/270/18). For Strang's and Cadogan's minutes see FO 371/20711, C4757/3/18.

[38] This portrait of Chamberlain is based on Keith Feiling, *The Life of Neville Chamberlain* (London, 1946), Keith Middlemas, *Diplomacy of Illusion: The British Government and Germany, 1937-1939* (London, 1972), pp. 44-58, Wendt, *Economic Appeasement*, pp. 418-27, and on episodes to be dealt with in the text. On Chamberlain's attitude toward the League and the Italo-Ethiopian war see Feiling, pp. 295-96, and Middlemas, pp. 51-52.

prosperity; the threat of war or disproportionate expenditures on armaments could destroy such confidence. Few others, he felt, grasped the magnitude of this problem. As he wrote in late 1935, "I know no one that I would trust to hold the balance between rigid orthodoxy and a fatal disregard of sound principles and the rights of posterity." To follow Winston Churchill's advice and "sacrifice our commerce to the manufacture of arms," he wrote in November 1936, would "inflict a certain injury on our trade from which it would take generations to recover," would "destroy the confidence which now exists," and would "cripple the revenue." As chancellor of the Exchequer he had kept rearmament within well-defined limits, cutting appropriations for the army to the point where it would be unable to play an effective Continental role. He still believed, however, that even existing appropriations for rearmament might prove an intolerable burden on the British economy, and the recession of 1937-1938 exacerbated his fears. Throughout the 1937-1939 period he continually voiced the hope that the settlement of pending diplomatic disputes would lead quickly to the end of the arms race.[39]

Chamberlain's policy of appeasement followed naturally from these principles: since Britain must if possible avoid war and halt the arms race, and since collective security had failed, London must help to secure peace by removing existing sources of conflict. In this respect, it is essential to understand the sense in which Chamberlain used the word *appeasement*. The word has since acquired an association with the word *appetite*; many refer to Chamberlain's attempts to "appease" Hitler, using this verb as a synonymn for *satiate*. In fact, the word stems from the French *apaisement*, and thus originally from *paix*, or *peace*. Chamberlain himself referred not to the appeasement of Hitler or of Germany, but to the appeasement of Europe—the pacification of Europe, in other words—by removing existing sources of fric-

[39] For these quotations see Feiling, *Neville Chamberlain*, pp. 275, 314. Middlemas, *Diplomacy of Illusion*, pp. 32-37, 55-58, 116-28, covers Chamberlain's role in rearmament at length. Chamberlain was much influenced by Liddell Hart's advocacy of a small, mobile British army that could be sent anywhere within the empire on short notice; see Williamson Murray, "The Change in the European Balance of Power, 1938-39" (Ph.D diss., Yale University, 1974), pp. 42-43.

tion. Until 1939, he refused to believe that Hitler would inevitably begin a war; he preferred to think that the Geman dictator would content himself with the bulk of what he wanted rather than risk general war for the sake of complete satisfaction.[40]

Specifically, Chamberlain was willing to make concessions to Germany in Eastern Europe in order to avoid a European war, and in the fall of 1937 he redefined official British policy in this sense. In October he seized upon an invitation to Lord Halifax, the Lord Privy Seal, to attend a hunting exhibition in Berlin as a means of approaching Hitler directly. Chamberlain and Halifax decided to accept without consulting Eden or the Foreign Office. When in late October Eden spoke to Halifax in response to pressure from Vansittart, he received assurances that Halifax would "confine himself to warning comments on Austria and Czechoslovakia" rather than encourage German designs. Halifax, however, prepared notes for his conversation with Hitler that took a different line, officially endorsing possible territorial changes in Eastern Europe for the first time. The notes apparently referred to Danzig, Austria, and Czechoslovakia as "questions which fall into the category of possible alterations in the European order which might be destined to come about with the passage of time." Britain's interest was "to see that any alterations should come through the course of peaceful evolution and that methods should be avoided which might cause far-reaching disturbances." After discussing these notes, Vansittart, Sargent, and Strang implicitly criticized this passage in a joint memorandum:

> It is not only forcible action which may produce a European situation of great difficulty. Any substantial change that may take place, even without war, may disturb the balance and produce readjustments in the situation of far greater moment

[40] Chamberlain long refused to believe that the Nazi regime was inevitably expansionist and would have to be resisted by force. After reading Stephen Roberts's *The House that Hitler Built*, a grim but accurate account of the Nazi regime and its purposes, he was briefly shaken; he even told Eden that Britain might have to attempt the "encirclement" of Germany after all (Eden, *Facing the Dictators*, pp. 570-71). He wrote privately, however, that he rejected Roberts's view that war was inevitable; see Feiling, *Neville Chamberlain*, p. 328. See also *The Diplomatic Diaries of Oliver Harvey, 1937-40*, ed. John Harvey (London, 1970), pp. 80-81.

than the character of the change itself. This is not necessarily an objection to such changes; but it is a material consideration when changes are contemplated.

The comments then referred specifically to Austria, Czechoslovakia, and Danzig, warning in each case against any specific encouragement of German initiatives. Halifax, however, stuck to his plan and made the declaration quoted above to Hitler at Berchtesgaden on November 19, 1937.[41]

Evidence suggests that Chamberlain inspired this wording. He virtually duplicated it three days later in a private letter: "I don't see why we shouldn't say to Germany 'give us satisfactory assurances that you won't use force to deal with the Austrians and Czechoslovakians, and we will give you similar assurances that we won't use force to prevent the changes you want, if you can get them by peaceful means.' " In the same letter he showed that he underestimated German goals: "Of course they want to dominate Eastern Europe," he noted, "they want as close a union with Austria as they can get, without incorporating her into the Reich, and they want much the same thing for the Sudeten Deutsch as we did for the Uitlanders in the Transvaal."[42] In succeeding months, however, Chamberlain willingly conceded the Germans much more in order to prevent war.

When French Premier Camille Chautemps and Foreign Minister Yvan Delbos came to London after the Halifax visit,

[41] See Eden minute, Oct. 26, 1937, FO 371/20751, C7423/7423/18; Eden, *Facing the Dictators*, pp. 508-13; Middlemas, *Diplomacy of Illusion*, pp. 133-34. For the Foreign Office comments see FO 371/20751, C7886/7324/18. The Foreign Office archives do not contain a copy of Halifax's notes; the quotation is from the minutes of his conversation with Hitler in *DGFP*, D, I, 19. The text of the Foreign Office comments on his notes leaves no doubt that they included a similar declaration.

[42] Quoted in Middlemas, *Diplomacy of Illusion*, pp. 137-38. The letter was written to one of his two sisters, to whom he recounted the most intimate details of government policy each week.

Chamberlain's analogy between the Sudeten Germans and the British Uitlanders in the Transvaal in the late 1890s has fascinating implications. Just as Hitler used the Sudeten German question to provoke a conflict with Czechoslovakia, so the British government used the Uitlander grievances to provoke the Boer War in 1899. Most striking of all, the Uitlanders' chief advocate within the British government was none other than Chamberlain's father, Joseph Chamberlain.

Chamberlain further elaborated his policy toward Eastern
Europe. The talks began on November 29 with Delbos stating
that France remained faithful to its obligation toward Czechoslovakia. Chamberlain, apparently without consulting Eden and
certainly without consulting the cabinet, said that "he wished to
say something about British public opinion which would not be
new to his French friends."

> There was a strong feeling that we ought not to be entan-
> gled in war on account of Czechoslovakia, which was a long
> way off and with which we had not a great deal in common.
> But the public would welcome anything that could be done to
> bring about a settlement in Central and Eastern Europe. He
> therefore thought it well to say that he did not think it would
> be possible to mobilize opinion in England in supprt of forci-
> ble intervention against Germany on behalf of Czechoslova-
> kia.

This declaration clearly represented a step backward from
Eden's June 25 House of Commons statement, which had left
unanswered the question of British assistance to future victims
of aggression. Repeating his analogy with the Uitlanders in the
Transvaal, Chamberlain suggested that Czechoslovakia would
have to improve the position of its German minority. He refused, however, to promise to support Czechoslovakia, even if
Prague made specified concessions.[43]

Having redefined British policy toward Eastern Europe,
Chamberlain quickly removed two crucial subordinates who did
not share his faith in a settlement with Germany. In December,
Sir Alexander Cadogan replaced Vansittart as permanent
undersecretary of state at the Foreign Office, and in February,
Eden resigned as foreign secretary, giving way to Halifax.
Cadogan soon emerged as a loyal supporter of Chamberlain's
policies, sometimes consenting to unpopular decisions on behalf
of the Foreign Office without consulting his subordinates; Vansittart assumed the new post of Chief Diplomatic Adviser to the
Government, a position theoretically closer to the prime minister but actually removed from the decision-making process in
the Foreign Office. In Halifax, Chamberlain acquired a foreign

---

[43] For this conversation see FO 371/20737, C8234/270/18.

secretary willing to follow his lead, and one whose presence in the House of Lords gave the prime minister primary responsibility for discussing foreign policy in the Commons.[44]

With regard to Eastern Europe, one can argue that Chamberlain's accession did not lead to a dramatic departure in British policy. Burdened with worldwide commitments and preoccupied with Britain's limited resources, most British officials, as we have seen, shied away from an aggressive defense of the status quo in Eastern Europe and viewed German expansion eastward as a benign or even favorable development. In the economic sphere, the Board of Trade's and the Treasury's longstanding prejudices against government intervention in international commerce virtually ruled out any steps to increase trade. Many Foreign Office officials also held to this tradition, which dated back at least a century, and the National Government, itself composed largely of businessmen, shared this view as well.[45] Most British ministers and high civil servants favored conciliating Germany rather than competing with it, especially in areas where they recognized few interests of their own. Chamberlain, however, took office determined to put his own stamp on foreign policy, and this he indisputably did. Britain might have accepted German hegemony in Eastern Europe without him, but it is doubtful that another prime minister would have played such an active role in bringing it about.

[44] On Vansittart's dismissal see Middlemas, *Diplomacy of Illusion*, pp. 77-78, and Colvin, *Vansittart in Office*, pp. 169-73. On Eden's resignation see Eden, *Facing the Dictators*, pp. 547-68, and Middlemas, pp. 143-53. Eden resigned on the issue of opening immediate conversations for an Anglo-Italian agreement; earlier, he had split with Chamberlain over President Roosevelt's secret proposal for a conference of world leaders.

[45] On the longstanding Foreign Office tradition of noninterference in international commerce see D.C.M. Platt, *Finance, Trade and Politics in British Foreign Policy, 1815-1914* (London, 1968), pp. 81-150.

VIII.

France and Eastern Europe, 1935-1937

We have seen that French influence in Eastern Europe declined during the early 1930s. Paris's doubtful devotion to the Franco-Polish alliance, as reflected in French policy at the Disarmament Conference and the French government's acceptance of a modified Four Power Pact, helped to prepare the way for the German-Polish Non-Aggression Declaration of January 1934; Louis Barthou's attempts to repair the damage by concluding an Eastern Pact failed. Although Pierre Laval signed the Franco-Soviet Pact in the spring of 1935, he continued to concentrate on reaching a settlement with Germany rather than building up a solid anti-German front in Eastern Europe. In the years 1935-1937, the German government challenged French influence among the successor states in two new ways: by expanding trade with Eastern Europe and by remilitarizing the Rhineland in March 1936. Although successive French governments took some steps to counter these new threats, they did not respond effectively to either one. Civil servants and ministers who proposed new initiatives in Eastern Europe, such as René Massigli, the political director of the Foreign Ministry, and Yvan Delbos, foreign minister from mid-1936 until early 1938, could not overcome the obstacles to a stronger French policy in Eastern Europe.

The French diplomats who reported the conclusion of the new German trade treaties with Hungary and Yugoslavia in 1934 immediately recognized their potential political significance. In June, Louis Mathieu de Vienne, the French minister in Budapest, wrote that these agreements "could lead to economic tutelage, and hence to political tutelage"; he hoped that the present state of the German economy would prevent Berlin from keeping its promises. In Belgrade, French Minister Emile

Naggiar commented that the new German-Yugoslav arrangements "are such as to put the problem of the economic reconstruction of Central Europe on a new basis—a most favorable one for German influence." King Alexander of Yugoslavia explicitly linked the new treaty with Germany to French indifference. "Given the current economic situation," he told Naggiar on May 8, "and given that we find practically no outlets for our products in friendly countries—notably in France, which accords us derisory quotas—who could criticize us?" Yugoslav pleas and protests were without effect, however. During 1934 the French Finance Ministry refused to permit a new government-guaranteed loan or export credit guarantee to Yugoslavia to finance new arms purchases, despite pressure from the Foreign and War ministries.[1]

The French government took no new economic initiatives in Eastern Europe until February 2, 1936, when it concluded a new agreement with Rumania to increase trade between the two countries. Virtually no French documentation on this pact is now available, but the agreement seems, like the subsequent Rambouillet credit to Poland, to have served both political and financial interests. It provided for the formation of a new French company that would annually dispose of 750,000 tons of Rumanian oil exports, paying the royalties on these exports to the Rumanian government in free exchange. Bucharest would spend this free exchange on French arms and on the service of French loans. To help make the agreement work, Paris pledged to buy 20,000 tons of crude oil annually. The agreement was less than a complete success. The French market for Rumanian oil was limited throughout the 1930s for one reason: whereas Rumania exported virtually all its petroleum in the form of refined products, France imported a large and growing portion of its petroleum in the form of crude oil. Despite this agreement, France never imported significant amounts of Rumanian crude during the 1930s; in addition, lack of productive capacity prevented the French from supplying promised arms.[2]

[1] *DDF*, 1, VI, 184, 275, 295. On the issue of new credits for Yugoslavia see ibid., 55, 266; Léger to Finance Ministry, Apr. 20, 1934, Finance Ministry to Léger, Nov. 20, AN, F[30]/2081. The Finance Ministry argued that Yugoslavia was not credit-worthy.

[2] For the text of the agreement see *Journal officiel de la République Francaise, décrets & lois*, May 23, 1936, pp. 5370-72. For figures on French oil imports see *SMCF, 1935*, XII, 106-7; *1937*, XII, 106-7.

On July 9, 1936, in the wake of further diplomatic reports of German trade gains in Eastern Europe, René Massigli, the assistant director for political affairs at the Quai d'Orsay, analyzed the German danger in a perceptive memorandum for Foreign Minister Delbos. A diplomat of strong views and broad perspective, Massigli had been involved in many of the most important diplomatic episodes of the interwar period, including the Paris Peace Conference in 1919, the Washington Conference in 1921-1922, and the Geneva disarmament talks. During the 1930s he consistently showed an awareness of what had to be done to resist Nazi Germany. Significantly, Massigli rose to a higher position than his Whitehall counterpart, Laurence Collier, but lost his job at the Quai after the Munich crisis of 1938. Throughout the interwar period Massigli tried to maintain French influence in Eastern Europe; in 1925 he was instrumental in ensuring that the Locarno Treaty did not invalidate France's eastern alliances. In his 1936 memorandum, he noted the various ways in which Germany was benefiting from its trade with Eastern Europe:

> Already partially dependent on the Reich economically, Central and Eastern Europe is now menaced by its military influence. Having begun its intensive rearmament, Germany can offer arms in payment of its commercial debts. By doing so she can also keep her arms factories running and improve her own materiel. She is also interested in assuring her supplies of raw materials from the neighboring countries, which are not separated from her by the sea—which she does not command—and which are in fact her commercial creditors.

Massigli noted that Germany had concluded arms deals with Greece, Turkey, and Bulgaria and had designs on the Little Entente market and on Poland. To meet these dangers, he suggested that a new international economic plan be implemented in order to restore free trade and reduce Eastern European dependence on Germany and that France offer economic concessions to its allies. Despite France's own economic difficulties, he wrote, "the moment has come to furnish our allies with tangible proof that we intend to put our economic relations in harmony with our political ones, and practice our alliances." The Little Entente countries should receive tariff preferences, special quotas, and, in general, "all import facilities compatible with the safeguarding of our metropolitan and colonial economy." Above all, they must receive needed shipments of arms.[3]

Massigli's memorandum had some effect. It may have helped to persuade the French government to grant the Rambouillet credit to Poland two months later. In addition, on December 5, 1936, Paris signed an agreement with the Yugoslav government promising to buy 200,000 tons of Yugoslav wheat during 1937, and the Yugoslavs received a substantial tariff rebate to facilitate this purchase. The two parties successfully carried out this agreement, but the French Ministry of Agriculture resented the concessions it included and later tried to prevent it from becoming a precedent. Once again, financial considerations played a role: the purchase helped the Yugoslavs to service their French loans.[4] These, however, were isolated instances; Massigli did not secure the large-scale application of the principles of his memorandum.

Significantly, Massigli proposed the exact strategy that Berlin successfully implemented in 1937-1938, namely, the exchange of Eastern European agricultural products for armaments. France failed to follow this strategy for two reasons. First, French tariff and quota policies continued to favor the French Empire over foreign markets. As a result, even though France imported between 1.0 and 1.5 million tons of cereals, principally feed grains, annually from 1933 through 1938 and hundreds of millions of francs worth of timber, French trade with Eastern Europe lagged far behind that of both Germany and Britain throughout the decade. It remained insignificant both as a percentage of total French trade and as a percentage of the trade of the Eastern European countries.[5] Second, the slow pace of French rearmament, which did not begin in earnest until 1936

[3] *DDF*, 2, II, 404. On Massigli's role at the time of Locarno see Vincent J. Pitts, "France and the German Problem: Politics and Economics in the Locarno Period, 1924-29" (Ph.D. diss., Harvard University, 1975), pp. 87-89. For diplomatic reports on German activity in the first half of 1936 see *DDF*, 2, I, 40, II, 317.

[4] On this agreement, see the AE memoranda of Oct. 29 and Nov. 9, 1936, and Robert de Dampierre's Dec. 5 report, AN, F^{30}/2081; see also the Agriculture Ministry's memorandum of May 29, 1938, AN, F^{10}/2163. Curiously, although these documents state unequivocally that France purchased 100,000 tons of wheat from Yugoslavia under this agreement, the statistics in *SMCF* do not reflect such purchases. The wheat may have been reexported.

[5] See Tables A.6 and A.7.

and took at least two years to get into high gear, kept France from making inroads into the Eastern European arms market. France's failure to make good on many promised deliveries of arms to Eastern Europe left the field relatively clear for German enterprise.

Although the strengthening of ties between France and its empire during the interwar period was probably more significant than the corresponding changes in Britain's relations with its empire, it has been discussed by historians only in the most general terms. France and its empire became increasingly unified during the 1920s and 1930s. This process had begun in 1884, when Algeria was brought into a customs union with France; it moved forward in 1892 with the creation of the status of "assimilated colonies" sharing French tariffs. Tunisia entered into almost complete customs union with France in 1928, and other colonies, including the sugar islands and Indochina, gradually came into partial tariff union with the mother country as well. Perhaps most important, French colonies were excluded from the French import quota system imposed in 1931. These measures greatly increased the empire's share of France's trade. From 1933 through 1936, the French failure to devalue the franc caused French trade with the rest of the world to shrink and increased the colonial share still further.[6] As Table VIII.1 shows, French colonies, particularly those in North Africa and Indochina, made great strides as cereals exporters to France. Their gains left little room for significantly larger purchases from Eastern Europe.

At the same time, France failed to supply its eastern allies with significant quantities of arms during the 1930s because its own rearmament proceeded so slowly. Although most available information on French rearmament during the 1930s comes from postwar testimony rather than contemporary documentation, one can at least outline the problems that France faced.[7] France

[6] For a very general discussion of French policy toward the empire see D. W. Brogan, *France under the Republic* (New York, 1940), pp. 623-50. On economic relations with the French colonies see Fouchet, *Politique commericale en France*, pp. 156-63, and Long, *Contingentement en France*, pp. 169-70.

[7] Robert Jacomet, *L'Armement de la France, 1936-39* (Paris, 1945), is the only comprehensive account of French rearmament. Jacomet was the controller-general of the War Ministry during this period; he was tried by the Vichy government for alleged failure to arm France adequately. For other testimony on this subject see *Les Evénements survenus en France de 1933 à 1945. Témoignages et*

TABLE VIII.1
Selected French Imports, 1928, 1935-1939

	1928	1935	1936	1937	1938	1939
Wheat						
(in thousands of metric tons)						
Total	1,413	701	526	463	471	343
French colonies	367	468	360	243	270	234
(% share)	(26)	(67)	(68)	(52)	(57)	(68)
Eastern European countries	—	—	—	—	—	1
(% share)						(0)
Barley						
(in thousands of metric tons)						
Total	85	169	341	126	44	90
French colonies	65	151	295	82	14	74
(% share)	(76)	(89)	(87)	(65)	(32)	(82)
Eastern European countries	1	14	38	31	17	9
(% share)	(1)	(8)	(11)	(25)	(38)	(10)
Corn						
(in thousands of metric tons)						
Total	736	725	712	749	707	529
French colonies	119	505	537	597	681	497
(% share)	(16)	(70)	(75)	(80)	(96)	(94)
Eastern European countries	14	8	90	66	4	21
(% share)	(2)	(1)	(13)	(9)	(1)	(4)
Gasolines						
(in millions of hectoliters)						
Total	20.7	9.0	8.0	8.4	7.4	5.7
Rumania	1.6	3.8	3.5	4.4	2.4	1.4
(% share)	(8)	(42)	(44)	(52)	(32)	(24)
Other Refined Petroleum Products						
(in thousands of metric tons)						
Total	*	517	689	953	587	592
Rumania	—	100	49	136	14	4
(% share)	(8)	(19)	(7)	(14)	(2)	(1)

SOURCES: *SMCF, 1928*, XII, 54, 57-58, *1935*, XII, 63-68, *1936*, XII, 106-7, *1937*, XII, 63-68, *1938*, XII, 63-65, 106-7, *1939-40*, I, 67-68, 106-7.
* Not available in metric tons.

had remained the most heavily armed nation in Europe during the 1920s, but economic and political factors fundamentally weakened its position during the 1930s, especially during the crucial period 1933-1936. When Germany began large-scale rearmament in 1933, it benefited from its late start inasmuch as the new German armed forces could be equipped with a new generation of weapons. Largely because of budgetary pressures, France did not immediately respond and fell two to three years behind Germany in the production of new weapons, especially artillery, tanks, and aircraft. French production of new types of weapons did not reach significant levels until 1938 or 1939; by then, Germany had secured large arms contracts all over Eastern Europe.

After the Second World War, various French politicians, generals, and bureaucrats cited two crucial reasons for the slow development of new weaponry during the early 1930s: the failure of military authorities to specify what new weapons they wanted and the budget cuts dictated by prevailing economic policy. The first factor became the center of a bitter postwar debate;[8] the second cannot be doubted. Largely because of the depression, which struck France several years later than Britain, Germany, and the United States, French governments from 1933 through 1936 struggled with the problem of balancing the budget despite declining revenues. Four governments fell over this question from December 1932 through January 1934. In retrospect, it is clear that France's economic slowdown and the decline in government revenue that went with it stemmed principally from the increasing overvaluation of the franc relative to the pound and dollar, but until 1936, successive governments tried to deal with the problem through deflation, not devaluation. Public spending fell from 55.7 billion francs in fiscal 1931-1932 to about 50.0 billion in 1935; expenditures for national defense bore a disproportionate share of the burden, falling from 15.3 billion francs to 10.4 billion. In addition, because military per-

---

documents recueillis par la Commission d'enquête parlementaire. Rapport de M. Charles Serre, député au nom de la Commission d'enquête parlementaire, 9 vols. (Paris, 1947-1950). See especially the testimony of General Weygrand (I, 231 ff.), Guy La Chambre (II, 295 ff.), Edouard Daladier (III, 16 ff.), L. Germain-Martin (III, 697 ff.), General Dassault (V, 1459 ff.), General de Sablet (VI, 1579 ff.).

[8] See Jacomet, Armement, and the testimony of the various generals in Les Evénements survenus en France.

sonnel had to be paid and fortifications maintained despite these
cuts, most of the reductions came out of appropriations for new
weaponry. In 1934, for example, credits for armaments bore the
full weight of a 20 percent cut in the entire military budget.[9]

French rearmament finally began in earnest in June 1936,
when Léon Blum's Popular Front government introduced a
comprehensive four-year program for the construction of new
weapons. The government also nationalized major components
of the arms industry and began much-needed modernization.
Unfortunately, the early stages of the program encountered
such bottlenecks within the industrial plant that it proved impossible even to spend the amounts allotted for weapons construction. The government had to carry over 30 percent of the 1936
credits for new arms to the next year, 12 percent of the 1937
credits, and 10 percent of the 1938 appropriation. Nor was the
new program immune to financial pressure. After the Blum
government fell on financial questions in June 1937, Georges
Bonnet, the finance minister in the new Chautemps government, cut the military budget to help restore financial stability.[10]

For all these reasons, full production of many new French
weapons did not begin until 1938—in the crucial area of aircraft,
not until 1939. France's own forces lacked new weapons; almost
none could be spared for export to Eastern Europe. We shall
see that the Rambouillet credit to Poland went unspent, and
Rumania continually complained that France had not made
good on promised arms deliveries. Total French arms exports to
Poland, Yugoslavia, and Rumania were negligible from 1935
through 1937.[11] Paris never made up for lost time.

Unwilling or unable to extend many tariff concessions or provide needed arms to Eastern Europe, the French government

[9] Sauvy, Histoire économique, II, 77-110, 151-64, 577; Jacomet, Armement, pp.
105-6.

[10] Jacomet, Armement, pp. 54, 121-28. Interestingly enough, Jacomet suggests
that the introduction of the 40-hour week was not a major cause of production
delays. See also Jacomet, pp. 137, 274-83; Daladier testimony, in Les Evénements
survenus en France, III, 16-20, 140-43. Georges Bonnet, Défence de la paix, Vol. I,
De Washington au Quai d'Orsay (Geneva, 1946), p. 54, claims that he made cuts
only when productive capacity was insufficient to absorb projected expenditure.

[11] La Chambre testimony, in Les Evénements survenus en France, II, 295-307;
Bonnet, De Washington au Quai d'Orsay, p. 91; LN, Statistical Yearbook of the Trade
in Arms, 1938 (Geneva, 1939), p. 99.

did not follow Massigli's other recommendation—to propose a
new plan for the financial reconstruction of the area—until late
1937. The idea of a multilateral scheme to increase trade and
prosperity in the Danubian basin, which had faded from view
after 1933, was first revived in early 1937 by Czechoslovakian
Prime Minister Milan Hodža. As Hodža explained in an inter-
governmental memorandum of May 6, 1937, he hoped to rec-
oncile Austria and Hungary with the Little Entente through a
system of tariff preferences. Although he promised to safeguard
both German and Italian interests, Berlin responded coolly; in
late May, Wohlthat made clear to Ashton-Gwatkin that he preferred the existing situation. Hodža's plan never seems to have
approached fruition.[12] In the fall of 1937, however, Paris seized
upon a new plan for the financial reconstruction of Central
Europe. Designed by Richard Schüller, the foreign-trade spe-
cialist of the Austrian Foreign Ministry, the plan provided for
the immediate abolition of exchange control in the Danubian
states. The central banks of Britain, France, and perhaps the
United States would guarantee new exchange rates for the
Danubian currencies and, if necessary, extend new loans. The
plan would free trade, reintegrate the Danubian states into the
world economy, and reduce German economic influence in Central Europe.[13]

The French legation in Vienna communicated the plan to the
Quai d'Orsay on November 2, and Foreign Minister Delbos
quickly passed it on to Foreign Secretary Eden. British Foreign
Office officials showed some interest in the plan, but the Treasury, led by Leith-Ross and Chancellor of the Exchequer Sir John
Simon, quickly quashed it on political grounds. In mid-
November, Simon expressed his views in a letter to Prime Minister Neville Chamberlain. He discussed not only Delbos's proposal but also the forthcoming report on international trade and
exchange control being prepared for the League by Paul van
Zeeland, the Belgian prime minister. Simon argued that Britain
must not endorse any plan for freeing Central European exchanges that could be interpreted as anti-German, for fear of

---

[12] On the Hodža plan see Hodža's May 6 memorandum and Ashton-Gwatkin's
May 28 minute of his conversation with Wohlthat, FO 371/21139, R3270/
R3901/770/68, and Milan Hodža, *Federation in Central Europe* (London, 1942).

[13] *DDF*, 2, VII, 181.

compromising Chamberlain's search for an Anglo-German settlement. He referred specifically to Halifax's forthcoming visit to
Germany to see Hitler:

> we must examine such a plan with *great* care to see whether it
> might not be regarded and represented as assisting the policy
> of "encirclement" of Germany. It is significant that M. Delbos
> commended such a plan to the Foreign Secretary *on these
> grounds*. That cuts right across the Halifax visit.[14]

On November 25 Chamberlain replied that although an operation to free the trade of the Danubian states might work, it
"would certainly be regarded by Germany as inspired by political motives and would consequently be liable to wreck the prospects of a general settlement." Simon emphasized to Eden on
December 13 that Britain would not guarantee Danubian exchange rates and that both Germany and Italy would regard this
plan as "one more move in the French game of encirclement." It
would therefore become a new obstacle to a European settlement. The Foreign Office decided to wait for the van Zeeland
report before taking a stand.[15]

In an effort to anticipate the van Zeeland report, the French
government gave the British a memorandum on the Schüller
plan on January 24, 1938. Noting that the Danubian states held
about 100 million RM in clearing balances, it suggested that
France, Britain, and other hard-currency countries offer credits
equal to this amount as a means of diverting Danubian trade to
free-exchange countries. "The present economic and above all
political dependence of the States of Central and Southeastern
Europe on Germany would thus be sharply attenuated." On
February 9, after the van Zeeland report had been issued,
Ashton-Gwatkin commented: "The last thing we wish to see is
the distortion of the van Zeeland Plan from its very outset into
an anti-German Danubian policy." Leith-Ross suggested that if
the French really wanted to do something, they could liberalize
their import quotas. The British put off new French suggestions
during February and early March, including a proposal that
Britain purchase a specified portion of Danubian cereals. Events

---

[14] Minutes on FO 371/21141, R7372/770/67; Simon's letter, PRO, T 160/727,
F12659/03/3 (Treasury papers).
[15] Chamberlain's letter, T 160/727, F12659/03/3; Simon's letter and minutes,
FO 371/21141, R8395/770/67.

finally overtook the Schüller plan; as a junior Foreign Office official minuted on March 25, the Anschluss had "knocked all these plans endwise."[16]

Despite Massigli's efforts, and despite its political pretensions in Eastern Europe, France during the 1930s played an even lesser economic role in that region than did Britain. French and British economic influence in Eastern Europe suffered for many of the same reasons: emphasis on protecting domestic agriculture; preference, embodied in commercial policies, for imperial products over foreign ones; and general prejudice in both governments against state intervention in trade or the economy. Although the Quai d'Orsay maintained a much greater interest in Eastern Europe than the British Foreign Office, it was hardly more successful in bending the rest of the government to its will. One reason may have been the failure of the French cabinet to provide an effective forum for making decisions and resolving disputes; perhaps because the cabinet kept no official, written records, its meetings seldom seem to have resolved policy disputes among departments. Individual ministries frequently vetoed new policies. We shall see that even in 1938-1939, when the German peril had become much more acute, the Agriculture Ministry blocked trade concessions to the Danubian states. The structure of the Third Republic had dismayed advocates of a stronger foreign policy since the inception of the regime; during the 1930s it hindered French attempts to strengthen France's alliances in Eastern Europe.

The German reoccupation of the Rhineland on March 7, 1936, dealt a further blow to French prestige in Eastern Europe. In the Eastern European capitals, the French failure to act cast new doubts on the dependability of France's commitments. In retrospect, it is clear that the crisis showed that Paris no longer had plans to make these commitments effective. The French military had no plans for immediate military intervention in the Rhineland; one must conclude that they would have been just as helpless had Germany moved east instead of west—as indeed they were in 1939. General Gamelin maintained throughout the

[16] French memorandum and minutes, Leith-Ross letter, Feb. 24, 1938, French memorandum, Feb. 28, minute by Sir Andrew Noble, Mar. 25, FO 371/22341, R897/R1846/R2628/R2765/94/67.

crisis that France could only move into the Rhineland after a general mobilization and that without the support of France's allies, including Britain and Italy, he could not guarantee ultimate victory over Germany. Heeding these views, the government of Albert Sarraut (in which Flandin served as foreign minister) quickly decided against military action; ultimately, it decided to trade implied consent to this violation of Locarno for new, firmer British military commitments to France itself.[17]

Nevertheless, the Rhineland crisis hardly ended French interest in Eastern Europe. The remilitarization of the Rhineland obviously reduced France's utility to its eastern allies, but the growth of German power made those allies more important to France itself. During the second half of 1936 the Popular Front government undertook two new initiatives to strengthen French ties to the east. It did *not* try to put new teeth into the Franco-Soviet Pact. Sensitive to accusations of communist influence, the Popular Front government shied away from closer contacts with Moscow, especially after Soviet intervention in the Spanish Civil war, and it generally evaded Soviet requests to supplement the pact with a military convention.[18] The government did, however, extend a major new loan to Poland and offered to conclude a full defensive alliance with the Little Entente.

In the wake of the Rhineland crisis, Paris made yet another attempt to repair the Franco-Polish alliance. Polish Foreign Minister Beck's equivocal behavior during the crisis had not been helpful to France. In February he had evaded a request from Flandin to join in a warning to the Germans against reoccupying the Rhineland, even though Göring had already warned him that Berlin might use the ratification of the Franco-Soviet Pact as an excuse to denounce the Locarno Treaty. Beck soon decided privately that a German move into the Rhineland would *not* bring the Franco-Polish alliance into play.[19] On March 7, in a conversation with French Ambassador Léon Noël, he expressed a wish "to have the exchange of views foreseen by our alliance." "We must remain in close contact, in

[17] On the Rhineland crisis see Anthony Adamthwaite, *France and the Coming of the Second World War* (London, 1976), pp. 38-42. For Gamelin's Mar. 8 statement on French military prospects see *DDF,* 2, I, 334.

[18] See Adamthwaite, *France*, pp. 45-50, for an excellent discussion of this point.

[19] Wojciechowski, *Polnisch-deutschen Beziehungen*, pp. 268-71; Sakwa, "Franco-Polish Alliance," pp. 129-37.

the spirit of our alliance, and in taking account of its aim."[20] Beck avoided resolving the inherent ambiguity of this statement—and, specifically, the question of whether Poland would join France in a war to restore the status quo—because Paris never asked him to do so.

As the crisis cooled, both Warsaw and Paris sought to reconfirm their alliance. The French still regarded Poland as a vital ally in the event of war; Beck still needed the French alliance as insurance against Germany, and he wanted to conciliate pro-French elements within the Polish army.[21] Financial problems—specifically difficulties in the service of old French loans to Poland—helped to determine the form that the regenerated Franco-Polish alliance would take. Like the French, the Poles had stuck to the gold standard throughout the 1930s; their trade had consequently shrunk until they could no longer service their French loans. In May 1936 Warsaw denounced the existing Franco-Polish commercial agreement in an effort to secure a larger active trade balance. A new agreement of July 18, 1936, was only partially satisfactory; the French Agriculture and Public Works ministries rejected larger imports of Polish timber and coal, which would compete with home production, and the Ministry of Commerce refused to cut French exports to Poland by more than 10 percent.[22]

In August 1936 General Gamelin visited Poland in an effort to demonstrate Franco-Polish friendship and secure a Polish commitment to assist Czechoslovakia against Germany. As a military man, Gamelin could sidestep Beck and deal directly with Marshal Edward Śmigły-Rydz, who had become inspector general of the Polish army and de facto head of government upon Piłsudski's death in 1935. The Polish military authorities told Gamelin that they would willingly cooperate with Czechoslovakia should war occur, but they refused to make any specific new commitments. They also asked for a new, forty-year, 2.5-billion-franc loan, which would enable them to purchase French arms and help them to service existing loans from France.[23]

After the Second World War, French Ambassador Léon Noël

[20] *DDF*, 2, I, 303.

[21] French embassy Warsaw to AE, Mar. 26, 1936, ibid., no. 506.

[22] See the memoranda of May 9 and June 16, 1936, and the agreement of July 18, AN, F^{30}/2005.

[23] Gamelin, *Servir*, II, 228-30; French embassy Warsaw to AE, Aug. 10, 1936, *DDF*, 2, III, 153; Gamelin memorandum, Aug. 24, AN, F^{30}/2485.

wrote that he had tried to persuade his government to make the
new loan conditional upon Beck's removal. His contemporary
telegrams, however, suggest the much more limited goal of
maintaining the Polish alliance in its present form. On August
16, after Gamelin's visit, he simply commented that he did not
think it possible to secure more specific commitments from Poland as long as Beck remained in charge. The next day, endorsing Polish requests for a loan, he stressed the need to meet
Polish wishes in order to maintain French influence: "To the extent that public opinion is attached to the French alliance, it
counts on France to facilitate the securing of war material. . . .
Whatever the reasons for our attitude, the Poles will be greatly
disappointed if our country does not furnish them with the material support which alone will allow them to regain confidence
in their future."[24]

When Śmigły-Rydz returned Gamelin's visit in September, the
French government entertained him at the president of the republic's chateau at Rambouillet. On September 6 the two governments agreed on a loan of 2 billion francs over the next four
years. This sum represented about ten times France's total imports from Poland during 1936. Only 800 million francs would
go for purchases of French arms; 200 million francs would go to
French firms for construction work in Poland; and most of the
remainder would be transferred immediately into Polish złotys
and used to finance domestic arms and railway construction.
The money was divided in this way for three reasons. First, the
slow pace of French rearmament ruled out any larger commitment of French arms for Poland; thus, Gamelin rejected Noël's
suggestion that the Poles be required to spend the entire loan in
France. Second, the Poles wanted to develop their own arms industry as a guarantee of their independence, despite the huge
cost involved. Lastly, the immediate transfer of much of the loan
into złotys would free some of the francs for service of previous
French loans.[25] Śmigły-Rydz still resisted any definite new com-

[24] Léon Noël, *L'Aggression allemande contre la Pologne* (Paris, 1946), pp. 139-40,
145-46; French embassy Warsaw to AE, Aug. 16, 17, 1936, *DDF*, 2, III, 153, 158.
Noël had previously warned that Poland might accept German arms in payment
of Germany's Corridor debt; French embassy Warsaw to AE, May 24, June 24,
DDF, 2, II, 238, 349.

[25] For the text of the agreement see *DDF*, 2, III, 259. On the Polish arms industry see Milan Hauner, "Die Rolle der Rüstungsindustrie in Osteuropa und
die Verteidigungsanstrengungen Polens bis 1939," and Georg W. Strobel, "Die

mitment to Czechoslovakia; he would say only that Poland would fulfill its League obligations should Czechoslovakia be attacked—obligations that of course did not include armed assistance—and that the construction of Czechoslovakian fortifications on the Polish-Czechoslovak border would be "a waste of money."[26]

Whether the French could have insisted on a stronger Polish commitment in return for the Rambouillet credit will never be known. Even had they done so, they might not have been able to insist on the fulfillment of such new commitments during 1938, for the simple reason that they themselves failed to live up to the terms of the credit. Bureaucratic lassitude, restrictive French laws, and, above all, slow French arms production combined to render most of the Rambouillet credit a dead letter. By 1938, French failure to observe its terms, especially those regarding the supply of arms, had become a new source of Polish resentment toward France. Poland had received virtually no arms deliveries by January 1938, at which time Paris officially informed Warsaw that the state of French arms production would not allow Paris to fulfill its commitments.[27]

Other administrative problems arose as well. In May 1937 the Polish government complained that the official French Assurance-Crédit agency, which insured French exports in much the same manner as the British Export Credits Guarantee Department, had refused to insure the credits for French exports provided for in the Rambouillet accord. The French Finance Ministry replied that under French law only exports by nationalized industries could be insured at 100 percent of their value; however, French nationalized industries could supply only a small portion of the Poles' wishes. This problem was not immediately resolved. In June, Śmigły-Rydz told Noël that further delays "would threaten to lose us the benefits of the [Rambouillet] accord within the army and among those Poles most determined to collaborate with France."[28] New problems emerged

---

Rolle der Rüstungsindustrie in Polen vor Ausbruch des Zweiten Weltkrieges," both in Forstmeier and Volkmann, eds., *Wirtschaft und Rüstung*, pp. 331-87.

[26] Delbos minute of Sept. 30, 1936, *DDF*, 2, III, 301.

[27] French embassy Warsaw to AE, Jan 20, 1938, *DDF*, 2, VIII, 11; AE departmental note, Jan. 31, ibid., 77.

[28] French embassy Warsaw to AE, May 5, 1937, Polish aide-mémoire of May 8, French embassy Warsaw to AE, June 28, *DDF*, 2, V, 402, 414, VI, 134. The documents do not show whether this difficulty was finally resolved.

in early 1938, after Paris officially backed out of its arms commitments. As Finance Minister Léon Blum informed the Quai d'Orsay on March 16, Poland had been promised 250 million francs to finance construction work by French firms within Poland under a provision of the *assurance-crédit* law that allowed credits for services up to a total of 25 percent of related credits for goods. Because France had withdrawn its 1-billion-franc arms credit, the 250-million-franc credit for services had become illegal. Paul-Boncour, who briefly served as foreign minister in March and April of 1938, first decided to suspend the credit because of Poland's questionable political attitude, but he reversed himself on March 26. His successor, Georges Bonnet, secured an exception to the law to permit the credit on April 15; France agreed to extend the credit in three installments over the next eighteen months. Thus most of the money arrived too late to be of any use.[29]

The abortive Rambouillet credit failed in its purpose. We shall see that Poland's equivocal attitude was a major factor in Paris's decision not to fight for Czechoslovakia in 1938. The French General Staff still attached the highest value to Polish assistance in the event of war, but the French government lacked the resources to rebuild the alliance.

During 1936 the Popular Front government also tried to strengthen the French alliance system in Southeastern Europe. Here, too, its motives were largely defensive; in the wake of the Rhineland crisis, French diplomats feared that the Danubian states, including Czechoslovakia, would no longer wish to maintain their ties to France. Increasingly fearful of both German and Italian intentions, the French government in late 1936 proposed to conclude a full defensive alliance with the Little Entente, provided that the Little Entente countries agreed to assist one another against aggression by *any* power rather than by Hungary alone. This plan foundered upon Yugoslav reluctance to become involved in a conflict with Germany or Italy and upon British opposition to closer French ties to Eastern Europe.

The French failure to contest the remilitarization of the Rhineland dealt a blow to French prestige among the Little En-

---

[29] Blum to Paul-Boncour, Mar. 16, 1938, *DDF*, 2, VIII, 463. In the fall of 1936 the French government had agreed to increase the total credit from 2.0 to 2.5 billion francs to compensate for the devaluation of the franc; see M. Baumgartner's Nov. 2, 1936, memorandum, AN, F^{30}/2485. See also *DDF*, 2, VIII, 482, IX, 55, 162, 190, 244, 526.

tente countries. Rumania and Czechoslovakia had stated their willingness to be associated with any action France might take, and French diplomats in all three countries subsequently reported that Paris's acquiescence in the German move had made a bad impression.[30] In July 1936, Victor de Lacroix, the French minister to Czechoslovakia, warned that the Czechoslovakian government might decide to come to terms with Germany. Czech President Beneš, he reported, had recently suggested that Britain would never go to war for Czechoslovakia; perhaps the new German-Italian entente and the recent German-Austrian agreement would force Prague to accept German offers of a new modus vivendi. The Czechs, Lacroix suggested, might survive their own surrender to German power, but France would not. "Will France, separated from Central Europe, remain a Great Power?" he asked. "Can she furthermore cease to be a great power without risking her very life?" Over the next two months Lacroix argued that France should conclude a defensive alliance with the Little Entente—a proposal that Beneš claimed to have discussed with Paul-Boncour during the latter stages of the Disarmament Conference.[31]

Paris responded slowly. The Blum government sincerely wished to explore possibilities for Franco-German reconciliation. Following London's lead, it patiently tried to secure German agreement to a new western pact to replace the Locarno Treaty. Blum privately discussed the chances of a settlement with Schacht in August.[32] By the fall, however, French attitudes were stiffening; German delays in negotiating the western pact rendered German motives increasingly suspect. The Italian intervention in the Spanish Civil War suggested additional dangers in the Mediterranean—dangers that the British refused to meet with France. On July 16, 1936, Delbos proposed to the British a multilateral Mediterranean pact to safeguard the status quo in the Mediterranean, but London, after putting off an official reply to the proposal for months, concluded its own gentlemen's agreement with Italy in November.[33]

In early October Lacroix again called for closer ties between

[30] DDF, 2, I, 309, 343, 360, 385, II, 84, 158, 168, 180.

[31] French legation Prague to AE, July 17, 1936, DDF, 2, II, 475; see also Lacroix's telegram of Aug. 26, ibid., III, 207.

[32] John E. Dreifort, Yvan Delbos at the Quai d'Orsay: French Foreign Policy during the Popular Front, 1936-38 (Lawrence, 1973), pp. 158-74.

[33] DDF, 2, II, 461, III, 147, 278, 314, 485, 489.

France and the Little Entente. Both Beneš and Czechoslovakian Foreign Minister Kamil Krofta had mentioned the possibility of a new German-Czechoslovakian agreement, and Lacroix did not believe this threat to be an idle one. Foreign Minister Delbos and Krofta had previously agreed that France and its allies should avoid provocative acts during the western pact negotiations, if only to avoid giving the Germans a pretext for wrecking the talks. Nevertheless, by October 22, Delbos was willing to entertain new proposals for stronger ties between France and its allies, either "to complete a reorganization of Europe," if talks with Germany succeeded, or to head off new German moves if they failed. On October 23, Delbos telegrammed new instructions. The Little Entente would have to widen the scope of its own alliance before the French government would begin negotiations; only after the Little Entente had been strengthened would France conclude new agreements.[34]

When Paris and Prague circulated their proposals in November, Belgrade quickly raised objections to any new agreement. Yugoslav Prime Minister Stoyadinovich initially refused to tighten the Little Entente before being assured of French assistance. The French quickly modified their position, agreeing to conclude a mutual-assistance pact with the Little Entente that promised French assistance to any of its members, provided that the other two members also came to the aid of the attacked power. Despite this concession, Stoyadinovich and Prince Paul characterized the new pact as a needless provocation that would encourage the formation of a firm German-Italian axis. Citing the dangers of German and Italian economic reprisals, they declined to run unnecessary risks or join in the formation of opposing blocs. French Minister Robert de Dampierre suggested that Stoyadinovich wanted to continue to profit from Yugoslavia's ambiguous position; at present, Germany, Italy, France, and Britain were all bidding for its favor to some degree.[35]

---

[34] French legation Prague to AE, Oct. 7, 14, 1936, *DDF*, 2, III, 320, 352; Delbos's telegrams, ibid., 391, 448.

[35] *DDF*, 2, III, 457, 467, 468, IV, 9, 57, 148, 156. Stoyadinovich and Prince Paul discussed the project with Blum's son Robert in December; see *DDF*, 2, IV, 180. The editors of *DDF* were unable to identify the author of this report, but a contemporary British diplomatic report, combined with references to Léon Blum in ibid., 180, leaves no doubt that it was he. See British legation Belgrade to FO, Dec. 15, 1936, FO 371/20436, R7570/1627/92.

The French government's only hope of securing Yugoslav assent to the new proposals seemed to lie in enlisting British help. British prestige in Yugoslavia remained high, and as early as November 18, Delbos had instructed Charles Corbin, the French ambassador in London, to ask the British to recommend the plan to Prince Paul. Corbin discussed the project with Eden on December 23 and reported that the foreign secretary was pleased to see France reasserting its leadership of the Little Entente. A different British attitude, however, emerged on January 21, 1937, when the French officially presented their proposals.[36]

Although, as we have seen, Foreign Office officials did not agree on the proper British response to a conflict in Eastern Europe, the new French proposals revealed unanimous opposition to any step that would increase the chances of French and British involvement in such a conflict. Rejecting the French request that London advocate the proposal in Belgrade, Owen O'Malley of the Southern Department argued that this step would "alienate moderate opinion in Germany," "shake the confidence reposed in us by the Yugoslav government," alienate Italy, and imperil Britain's European position.

> Our danger lies not only in the possibility that Germany will attack France, but also in the possibility that France might become involved in war with Germany by coming to the support of some Eastern or Central European power which might have been the victim of German aggression. It is therefore in our interest to limit French commitments in Central Europe as severely as possible.

Sargent decried the effect of the proposal on Franco-Italian relations. By this time, Paris and London had definitely split over the Italian question. Blum and Delbos were both suspicious of Italian motives and contemptuous of Italian abilities, whereas the British regarded good relations with Italy as an important element of their policy.[37] Sargent added that under the new plan "one of the Great Powers would once again be pledged to interfere in the internal quarrels of the Balkan States. We have consistently endeavored to prevent such a return to the old bad habits of the pre-war period." Such plans should be shelved until

[36] *DDF*, 2, III, 503, IV, 203.   [37] Dreifort, *Yvan Delbos*, pp. 151-58.

Czechoslovakia had settled its German minority problem and
the western pact negotiations had definitely failed. Britain's
guarantee to France entitled Britain "to exercise a definite control over [French] policy in the East of Europe," and France
should be advised against this step.

"I hope indeed we may do whatever may be possible to dis-
suade the French from this crowning folly," wrote Sir Alexander
Cadogan, a deputy undersecretary with responsibility for the
League of Nations. "I agree entirely with Mr. Sargent," Vansittart added. Eden, who had welcomed the plan in his earlier conversation with Corbin, changed his tune. "I agree also," he minuted, but he added that London must not take the blame for the
failure of the project.[38]

London's negative attitude ensured the collapse of the whole
project. On February 2 Eden told Corbin that Yugoslavia would
never agree to the project, and he echoed Yugoslav fears that it
would drive Italy into German arms. British pressure on behalf
of the pact would inevitably fail.[39] Some weeks later, on March
25, 1937, Belgrade dealt the death blow to the French plan by
signing a neutrality agreement with Italy despite French and
British protests. The two countries pledged to remain neutral
should either one become the victim of "unprovoked aggression" by a third party. London and Paris had to be content with a
declaration that the new pact did not contravene existing obligations.[40] In late March a conference of Little Entente foreign
ministers removed the question of the new pact from their
agenda. Delbos again broached the question of a strengthened
Little Entente during a tour of Eastern European capitals in late
1937 but made no major effort to secure agreement to it.[41]

The record of French diplomacy in Eastern Europe from
1935 through 1937 shows a strong connection between eco-

[38] Minutes by O'Malley, Sargent, Cadogan, Vansittart, and Eden, FO 371/
21136, R501/26/67.
[39] Ibid., R828/26/67; DDF, 2, IV, 404.
[40] On these negotiations, see Hoptner, Yugoslavia in Crisis, pp. 61-93, 301-3.
See also FO 371/21197, R318/224/92 et seq.; DDF, 2, IV, 395, 400, V, 59.
[41] For the Little Entente decision see French legation Belgrade to AE, Apr. 1,
1937, DDF, 2, V, 196; on Delbos's visits to Belgrade and Bucharest, see ibid., VII,
327, 349.

nomic and political developments; because the French government could not meet its eastern allies' economic needs, it found it increasingly difficult to maintain its political relations with them. In the case of Poland, it is doubtful whether even complete fulfillment of the Rambouillet agreements would have changed Beck's views, but it certainly might have strengthened pro-French elements within Poland and thereby influenced Polish policy during 1938. Within the Little Entente, Stoyadinovich's fear of losing German and Italian markets clearly contributed to his reluctance to strengthen ties to France. France's economic failure in Eastern Europe helped to erode its political prestige.

Two other factors also shifted the balance of power in the region against France: the French government's inability or unwillingness to act effectively against Germany in March 1936, and its continuing reliance on British diplomatic and military support. During the Rhineland crisis, Paris implicitly recognized that France was no longer a match for Germany and that France could no longer impose its will in Europe. The Polish government had begun to question French willingness to defend its eastern allies against Germany long before 1936, and French behavior during the Rhineland crisis did nothing to improve Paris's reputation. French consent to the remilitarization of the Rhineland in return for a British military commitment showed that the French still gave the British connection priority over all others, and the British impact on French negotiations with the Little Entente in 1936-1937 showed that London could exert an effective brake on French commitments in Eastern Europe. The French had begun to deemphasize their eastern alliances in order to maintain British support in 1925, and this trend continued during the 1930s.

Despite all these problems, Paris still professed fidelity to its eastern alliances at the end of 1937. Many government officials regarded these pacts as useful political and military assets; how they could be implemented in practice did not have to be specifically considered until Hitler posed this question in 1938. A new French government then decided not to fight to preserve the territorial status quo in Eastern Europe.

IX.

1938: Germany's Triumph

In 1938 the Anschluss of Germany and Austria and the German annexation of ethnically German Czechoslovakia—the so-called Sudetenland—established German hegemony in Eastern Europe. Hitler could draw freely upon the economic resources of the region, and no effective military resistance could be summoned to contain him there. Politically, Berlin prevailed over the western powers, who at Munich implicitly acknowledged Germany's ability to work its will in the east; economically, the creation of Greater Germany dramatically increased the German share of the trade of the successor states, leaving them with no alternative but to tighten economic relations with the Germans still further. In the wake of the Munich agreement of September 30, 1938, virtually no one disputed the fact of German domination of Eastern Europe.

After the Anschluss in March 1938, the British and French governments recognized that the fate of Czechoslovakia would decide the future of Eastern Europe as a whole. Nonetheless, both Paris and London decided not to go to war in defense of Czechoslovakia and allowed Hitler peacefully to dismember that country. In the meantime, some permanent officials in Paris and London had become concerned over Germany's growing economic influence in Eastern Europe in the wake of the Anschluss. They tried to improve their own countries' economic position in Eastern Europe during the spring and summer of 1938, but the denouement of the crisis over Czechoslovakia rendered their anti-German initiatives meaningless. Because Neville Chamberlain, Edouard Daladier, and Georges Bonnet handled political questions relating to Czechoslovakia while generally leaving economic policy to their subordinates, political and economic policies within London and Paris sometimes contradicted one another. In the end, the political leadership prevailed, leaving Germany supreme in Eastern Europe.

The sudden Anschluss of Germany and Austria in March
1938 took Europe by surprise. The crisis had not been carefully
planned; the most thorough scholarly studies of the episode
emphasize the role of chance in bringing it about, and Hitler
clearly did not control the events of February and March 1938.
During 1937 Austrian Chancellor Kurt von Schuschnigg had attempted to win over the Austrian Nazis to his regime. With the
help of German Ambassador Papen, he arranged a meeting with
Hitler for January 1938 to discuss German-Austrian relations.
The meeting was delayed when Hitler removed Generals Blomberg and Fritsch and Foreign Minister Neurath, creating a political crisis in Germany, but Hitler met Schuschnigg on February
12 at Berchtesgaden and concluded a dramatic new German-
Austrian agreement. Although Hitler tried to give the impression of having forced the agreement out of Schuschnigg, the
Austrian chancellor had already agreed to almost all of its provisions in previous negotiations with the Austrian Nazis. The
French government made a brief effort to preserve Austrian independence. On February 18 it suggested an Anglo-French declaration affirming that Austrian independence was "one of the
major interests of European peace" and opposing any "coup de
main" or act of war designed to alter the status quo in Central
Europe. However, Neville Chamberlain was counting on Mussolini to resist Hitler in Austria, and Eden also opposed a promise
of British help. On March 9 Schuschnigg announced an Austrian plebiscite designed to affirm the principle of Austrian independence. Hitler quickly replied with an ultimatum demanding that he cancel the plebiscite, Schuschnigg fell, German
troops entered Austria, and Hitler suddenly proclaimed Anschluss in Linz on March 13.[1]

The German annexation of Austria virtually encircled Czechoslovakia, which had come to be generally recognized as the last
real barrier to German eastward expansion. Hitler had to decide
how to take advantage of this new situation; the British and

[1] This brief summary of the Anschluss follows Gehl, *Austria, Germany, and the
Anschluss*, and Deutsch, *Hitler and His Generals*. Gehl treats the crisis largely from
the Austrian viewpoint, while Deutsch shows the connection between Anschluss
and the coincident political crisis within the German government. See also the
French memorandum of Feb. 18, CAB 24/274, CP 44 (38), and the cabinets of
Feb. 16, 18, CAB 23/92. Hitler referred to the Halifax visit during his Berchtesgaden talk with Schuschnigg, claiming that Halifax had said that Britain would
not mind if Germany absorbed Austria; see Nicolson, *Diaries*, p. 330.

French had to decide whether to resist him. While there is no room in this study for a narrative of the Munich crisis, German, British, and French policies toward Czechoslovakia show such consistency from March through September 1938 that there is no real need for one. The policies of these three governments can be discussed analytically, as their decisions at key points during the crisis fall into generally consistent patterns.[2]

Hitler had always had designs upon Czechoslovakia. Both his second book and Rauschning's subsequent testimony indicate that he had always planned to add the old Hapsburg provinces of Bohemia and Moravia (now the western part of Czechoslovakia) to the Reich. Significantly, he never seems to have distinguished privately between the so-called Sudetenland—the predominantly German areas along the Czechoslovak frontiers with Germany and Austria—from the rest of Bohemia-Moravia. A former Hapsburg subject himself, he knew that Czechs and Germans lived together throughout these two provinces, and he concerned himself only with the question of which would dominate the other.[3] Although he had explored a possible nonaggression pact with Czechoslovakia in 1936, the Hossbach memorandum confirms his designs upon that state as of November 1937.[4] By that time, Konrad Henlein, the leader of the Sudeten German party, was pressuring Hitler heavily to intervene on behalf of the Sudeten Germans, with a view to their eventual incorporation into the Reich. Until the Anschluss, however, Hitler

[2] The best comprehensive scholarly account of the Munich crisis is still Boris Celovsky, *Das Münchener Abkommen 1938* (Stuttgart, 1958). Others have contributed much in specific areas: Brügel, *Tschechen und Deutsche,* deals with the crisis from the standpoint of Czechoslovakian internal policy; Middlemas, *Diplomacy of Illusion,* is a useful study of British cabinet policy; Adamthwaite, *France and the Coming of the Second World War,* deals at length with French policy; and Murray, "Change in the European Balance of Power," is an excellent account of the military aspects of the crisis. A new study by Telford Taylor, *Munich: The Price of Peace,* appeared as this work was going to press. My analysis draws on these accounts and on my own reading of published documents and British Cabinet, Foreign Office, and Prime Minister's papers at the PRO.

[3] See above, Chapter III. See also *Hitler's Secret Conversations, 1941-1944,* trans. Norman Cameron and R. H. Stevens, with an introduction by Hugh Trevor-Roper (New York, 1953), for Hitler's attitude toward the Czechs. On feelers for a German-Czechoslovakian nonaggression pact see Gerhard L. Weinberg, "Secret Hitler-Beneš Negotiations in 1936-1937," *Journal of Central European Affairs,* XIX, no. 4 (1960), 366-74.

[4] See above, Chapter VI.

ignored Henlein's pleas for an interview; only an implied reference to the Sudeten Germans and a complaint that they had
been deprived of self-determination in his Reichstag speech of
February 20, 1938, signaled any change in his policy toward
Czechoslovakia.[5]

The Anschluss produced an outburst of Pan-German feeling
in Czechoslovakia, strengthened Henlein's position, and persuaded Hitler that the Czechoslovakia question was ripe for solution. The crisis of May 19-22, 1938, led to Hitler's decision to
attack Czechoslovakia within a matter of months. Meeting with
Henlein on March 28, Hitler expressed his intention "to settle
the Sudeten German problem in the not-too-distant future." He
did not specify the final solution he had in mind but agreed that
in negotiating with the Prague government for a new minorities
statute the Sudeten Germans "must always demand so much
that they can never be satisfied." In late April, Henlein announced his Karlsbad program, which included demands for
full autonomy for the Sudeten Germans that amounted to the
creation of a state within a state.[6] Evidence suggests that Hitler
had not yet decided to attack Czechoslovakia, but on May 19 the
Prague government, responding to intelligence reports of German troop movements along the border, called up some reserv-
ists. Worse, the British government, fearing an imminent German attack, warned Berlin that Britain would probably be
drawn into a general conflict. The crisis ended almost as quickly
as it had begun, but Hitler was furious at the world's impression
that British firmness had checked him in Czechoslovakia. He
immediately decided to destroy Czechoslovakia in the near future, using incidents in the Sudetenland to justify armed German intervention.[7]

[5] On Henlein see Brügel, *Tschechen und Deutsche*, pp. 238-59. In 1937 the
Prague government had begun an effort to alleviate the Sudeten Germans' few
valid grievances; they were in fact far better off than German minorities in Poland, Hungary, and Rumania. See Brügel, pp. 307-28, and Jacobsen, *Aussenpolitik*, pp. 521-28, 570-97. See also *The Speeches of Adolf Hitler, April 1922-August
1939*, ed. Norman H. Baynes, II (New York, 1942), 1405-6.

[6] *DGFP*, D, II, 89, 107; Brügel, *Tschechen und Deutsche*, pp. 340-44, 419-20.

[7] For conflicting views of the May crisis see William V. Wallace, "The Making
of the May Crisis of 1938," *Slavonic and East European Review*, XLI, no. 97 (1963),
368-90; D. C. Watt, "The May Crisis of 1938: A Rejoinder to Mr. Wallace," ibid.,
XLIV, no. 103 (1966), 475-80; Wallace, "A Reply to Mr. Watt," ibid., pp. 480-86.
Murray, "Balance of Power," pp. 315-16, argues that the German troops in ques-

From late May through September 1938, Hitler tried to arrange a successful military action against Czechoslovakia. Ultimately, his attempts failed. Despite his impressive diplomatic victory at Munich, overwhelming evidence indicates that he would have preferred a local war leading to the annexation of Bohemia-Moravia. He did not seek war with Britain and France; all his plans for the conquest of Czechoslovakia depended on their nonintervention. Up until the last minute, on September 28, he hoped to deter them, perhaps by the speed of his action, by the intervention of Hungary and Poland on Germany's side, by the internal disintegration of Czechoslovakia, or by the negotiation of a German-Italian-Japanese alliance. All of these plans miscarried, however, and with time running out, Hitler could not count on the western powers' disinclination to fight. Thus he finally agreed to a diplomatic solution to the crisis.

Hitler's apparent determination to attack Czechoslovakia despite the risk of Anglo-French intervention provoked bitter controversy within the German government during the summer of 1938. Army Chief of Staff Ludwig Beck submitted several memoranda to his chief, Army Commander Walther von Brauchitsch, arguing that France and Britain would intervene and defeat Germany. On August 15 Hitler met with senior officials and insisted that Chamberlain and Daladier would not intervene; Beck resigned a few days later.[8] Ernst von Weizsäcker, the secretary of state in the Foreign Office, warned of Franco-British intervention in several talks with and memoranda for Joachim von Ribbentrop, the new Nazi foreign minister. While affirming Germany's expansionist aims in the east, he argued that a new war would be disastrous both for Germany and for European civilization—a view shared, as we shall see, by high French and British officials. Even with Italian and Japanese help, he suggested on June 20, Germany would be defeated: "the common loser with us would be the whole of Europe, the victors chiefly the non-European continents and the anti-social powers." Ribbentrop insisted that he have faith in Hitler's genius.[9] A far-reaching anti-Hitler conspiracy ultimately

---

tion were returning to home stations from Austria. See also Hitler's May 30, 1938, directive, *DGFP*, D, II, 221.

[8] Robert J. O'Neill, *The German Army and the Nazi Party, 1933-1939* (London, 1966), pp. 151-60.

[9] *DGFP*, D, II, 259, 374. See also Bernd Jürgen Wendt, *München 1938. England zwischen Hitler und Preussen* (Frankfurt, 1965), pp. 58-71.

developed among army officers, diplomats, and prominent conservatives, including Beck, Weizsäcker, and Schacht. The con-
spirators tried to get the British government to warn Hitler that
Britain would intervene if Germany attacked Czechoslovakia,
but London, chiefly on the advice of British Ambassador Sir
Nevile Henderson, refused to do so. Plans to depose Hitler in
the event of a general war collapsed when Chamberlain offered
to visit Germany on September 13.[10]

During the summer, Hungarian and Polish assistance against
Czechoslovakia emerged as essential elements in Hitler's plans.
Göring tried to organize a common diplomatic and military
front against Prague but was only partially successful. Both Warsaw and Budapest demanded that their own ethnic minorities
within Czechoslovakia receive the same concessions given to the
Sudeten Germans, but neither government would commit itself
to armed action in the event of war. Hungary could not afford to
risk that Rumania and Yugoslavia would honor their Little Entente obligations to Czechoslovakia, and the Germans could not
guarantee that Belgrade and Bucharest would stand aside. Instead, on August 21, at the very moment that the Hungarian re-
gent, Admiral Miklós Horthy, was visiting Hitler, Hungary and
the Little Entente announced that Budapest had agreed not to
resort to force in pursuance of its revisionist claims in exchange
for equality of rights in armaments. Poland was equally reticent.
Beck hoped to secure the Czechoslovak province of Teschen for
Poland and apparently believed the disintegration of Czechoslovakia to be imminent, but he seems to have based his policy on
the belief that the crisis would be settled peacefully, and he refused to commit himself to war even after Göring vaguely offered cooperation against the Soviet Union in August.[11] German
economic power in Eastern Europe did not decisively influence
the course of events in 1938; despite Germany's economic
dominance there, Berlin clearly could not yet force the Eastern
European capitals to act as it wished.

Negotiations between the Prague government and the Sude-

[10] Wendt, München 1938, pp. 29-35, 58-71; Peter Hoffman, Widerstand,
Staatsstreich, Attentat. Der Kampf der Opposition gegen Hitler (Munich, 1969), pp.
69-130.
[11] Celovsky, Münchener Abkommen, pp. 230-34; Jorg K. Hoensch, Der ungarische
Revisionismus und die Zerschlagung der Tschechoslowakei (Tübingen, 1967), pp.
56-80; Wojciechowski, Polnisch-deutschen Bezienhungen, pp. 403-55. On Belgrade's attitude see DGFP, D, II, 412, 463.

ten German minority continued throughout the summer. The
climax of the crisis began on September 5, when Beneš agreed to
virtually the entire Karlsbad program. After the Sudeten Germans stalled for several days, Hitler, on September 12 at
Nuremberg, demanded self-determination for the Sudeten
Germans. Revolt began in the Sudetenland, and Henlein crossed
over into Germany and demanded self-determination himself
on September 15. The Prague government declared martial law
and quickly brought the situation under control, but Hitler continued to plan for an attack. Chamberlain's September 13 offer
to come to Germany to discuss the situation surprised him completely.[12]

At Berchtesgaden, on September 15, Chamberlain personally
accepted self-determination for any majority German districts of
Czechoslovakia and promised to put this proposal before the
British and French governments. In succeeding days, Hitler
worked feverishly for the dismemberment of Czechoslovakia
and the incorporation of Bohemia and Moravia into Germany.
On September 20, at Berchtesgaden, he sought promises of military action from Hungarian Prime Minister Béla Imrédy and
Foreign Minister Kálmán de Kánya and Polish Ambassador
Lipski. In his talk with the Hungarians he renounced interest in
both Slovakia and Ruthenia (the Ukrainian-inhabited eastern-
most part of Czechoslovakia) on condition that Hungary help to
destroy Czechoslovakia. Action by the army, he stated, was the
only satisfactory solution; he feared only that Prague would
submit to every demand. He then told Lipski that if Chamberlain met all his demands, thus leaving the Czechoslovakia question only partially resolved, he counted on Poland and Hungary
to begin hostilities to secure satisfaction of their claims. Both the
Hungarians and the Poles, however, contented themselves with
demands for equal treatment for their own minorities and refused to commit themselves to war. Hitler also worked for the
disintegration of Czechoslovakia from within, instructing the
Sudeten German leaders on September 19 to ask the Slovaks to
demand autonomy. This move came too late to produce results
during the September crisis, but Hitler successfully used it to destroy the rest of Czechoslovakia in March 1939.[13]

[12] Brügel, *Tschechen und Deutsche*, pp. 459-70; Celovsky, *Münchener Abkommen*,
pp. 311-14.
[13] *DGFP*, D, II, 487, 534, 554; Celovsky, *Münchener Abkommen*, pp. 388-91;

Thus, when at Godesberg on September 22 Chamberlain proudly told Hitler that both the French and Czechoslovak governments had agreed to the cession of the Sudetenland to Germany, Hitler presented the astonished prime minister with new demands. Germany must by October 1 occupy Czechoslovakia up to a specified line—clearly denying that country any possibility of independent existence—plebiscites must be held in additional areas, and Polish and Hungarian claims must immediately be satisfied. Otherwise, Germany would enforce a military solution and establish a "strategic" frontier—implicitly, one that would not leave a Czech salient between Germany proper and Austria. Hitler continued military preparations from September 23 through September 28. On September 26 he told Sir Horace Wilson, whom Chamberlain had sent on a personal mission, that Prague must accept his terms by 2 p.m. on the twenty-eighth, and that night in the Sportpalast in Berlin he repeated that he would have the Sudetenland by October 1. He made only one concession, offering to guarantee a rump Czech state after all minorities questions, including the Slovak question, had been settled. His plan for a local war miscarried, however. Poland and Hungary would not fight, and on September 27 Wilson delivered Chamberlain's warning that France would honor its treaty commitment if Germany attacked Czechoslovakia and that Britain would join France if active hostilities developed between France and Germany. On September 28, under heavy pressure from his generals and Göring and besieged with requests from President Roosevelt, Chamberlain, and Mussolini to call a con-

---

Hoensch, *Ungarische Revisionismus*, pp. 83-90. There is evidence that Hitler had the record of his Berchtesgaden conversation with Chamberlain altered so as to allow for further action against Czechoslovakia. Chamberlain's brief record of this conversation quotes Hitler to the effect that if the German, Hungarian, Polish, and Slovak minorities seceded from Czechoslovakia, "what was left would be so small that he would not bother his head about it" (*DBFP*, 3, II, 895). A fuller record prepared that evening by Paul Schmidt, Hitler's interpreter, contains no such disclaimer (*DGFP*, D, II, 487). Berlin then refused to send London a copy of Schmidt's record; see *DBFP*, II, 930, 931, 983, 985. After Munich, the Germans finally supplied a copy of Schmidt's notes, printed in ibid., no. 896, but this copy included a highly significant statement that had not appeared in Schmidt's original record. "Czechoslovakia," Hitler is reported to have said, "would, in any case, cease to exist after a time; for apart from the nationalities already referred to, the Slovaks were also trying with all their energy to detach themselves from that country."

ference, Hitler invited Chamberlain, Daladier, and Mussolini to meet at Munich the next day.[14]

The agreement reached at Munich late on the night of September 29 provided for German occupation of specified areas by October 1, an international commission to determine a provisional frontier by October 10, and German occupation up to that line on that date. Polish and Hungarian claims would be settled by negotiation or great-power arbitration; the four Munich powers would then join in an international guarantee of the remainder of Czechoslovakia. The ultimate frontier line differed little from the line on the map that Hitler presented at Godesberg.[15]

Hitler viewed the Munich agreement with mixed emotions. It obviously represented a major diplomatic victory; Czechoslovakia had been eliminated as a power in Eastern Europe. In addition, Hitler interpreted the Anglo-German agreement that Chamberlain pressed upon him on September 30 as a sign of British disinterest in Eastern Europe. But the Führer regretted his failure to march into Prague and solve the Czech question once and for all, and his surrender to his generals' and diplomats' pleas for a peaceful solution, implying that he had wrongly discounted Franco-British intervention, must have rankled.[16] His continuing determination to assert Germany's freedom of action in Eastern Europe made further crises almost inevitable; he could not possibly content himself with what he had already achieved.

Neville Chamberlain dominated British foreign policy throughout the crisis over Czechoslovakia. He kept a tight reign on policy, reaching decisions within the Foreign Policy Committee or the even smaller Committee on Czechoslovakia, pushing them through the cabinet, and sometimes taking initiatives on his own, particularly during his visits to Germany.[17] He sought

---

[14] On the Godesberg demands see *DBFP*, 3, II, 1033, 1048, 1053, 1057, 1068, and the map following p. 692. For Hitler's subsequent behavior see *Hitler's Speeches*, II, 1526, Celovsky, *Münchener Abkommen*, pp. 440-42, 451-60, and Alan Bullock, *Hitler: A Study in Tyranny*, rev. ed. (New York, 1962), pp. 464-67.

[15] Celovsky, *Münchener Abkommen*, pp. 483-85, includes the text of the agreement and maps.

[16] Bullock, *Hitler*, pp. 469-74.

[17] Middlemas, *Diplomacy of Illusion*, pp. 59-61. The Committee on Czechoslovakia, constituted in September 1938, included Chamberlain, Halifax, Simon, and Home Secretary Sir Samuel Hoare.

above all to prevent the outbreak of a general European war over Czechoslovakia, a war he regarded as needless and disastrous. He hoped to lay the groundwork for further Anglo-German agreements and a general settlement of European problems by arranging a peaceful settlement of the German-Czechoslovak dispute. He regarded the Munich agreement as a triumph for his efforts and hoped to move quickly toward the realization of his other goals as well.

We have seen that Chamberlain regarded either a new European war or a protracted arms race as disastrous. Determined instead to settle outstanding conflicts peacefully, he repeatedly argued, beginning in March 1938, that war over Czechoslovakia would be futile and unnecessary.[18] Throughout the crisis, Chamberlain and Halifax insisted to the cabinet and to the French government that France and Britain could not save Czechoslovakia; Germany would inevitably overrun it at the outset of a new war. To clinch the point—and perhaps to forestall analogies with the fate of Serbia after the First World War—they usually added that, whatever the outcome of a general war, it would be impossible subsequently to reconstitute Czechoslovakia within its present boundaries.[19] In discussions within the British government, Chamberlain also relied heavily on a March 21 Chiefs of Staff paper arguing that in a general conflict Germany would inevitably overrun Czechoslovakia and that Britain and France could not be sure of ultimate victory. In requesting this paper on March 16, Chamberlain had virtually ensured that its conclusions would be pessimistic by asking the chiefs to assume that France and Britain would become involved in war with Germany and Italy, that the risk of a hostile Japan was "consid-

[18] It would be hard to exaggerate Chamberlain's horror of a war over Czechoslovakia. On September 25, when war seemed imminent, he indicated that he might resign rather than go to war, and his September 27 broadcast also suggested that he might refuse to lead the British Empire into a conflict over Czechoslovakia. See Earl of Birkenhead, *Halifax* (London, 1965), p. 400, and Neville Chamberlain, *The Struggle For Peace* (London, 1939), p. 276. He apparently saw no British interest in the issue at hand. At Berchtesgaden he told Hitler: "Great Britain was not interested in the Sudeten German question as such. It was an affair between the Germans (or Sudeten Germans) and the Czechs. Great Britain was only interested in the maintenance of peace" (*DGFP*, D, II, 487).

[19] See for example the Foreign Policy Committee meeting of Mar. 18, 1938, CAB 27/623; Anglo-French conversations of Apr. 29, Sept. 18, 25, *DBFP*, 3, I, 164, II, 928, 1093; and Newton's Sept. 27 instructions, ibid., II, 1138.

erable," and that the Soviet Union, Poland, Rumania, Yugoslavia, Hungary, and Turkey would remain neutral. The report became a powerful weapon against dissenters in the cabinet.[20]

Chamberlain and Halifax recognized that failure to support Czechoslovakia would lead to German hegemony in Eastern Europe, but they denied that this development would have serious consequences for Britain and France. When in mid-March the Foreign Office prepared recommendations regarding Czechoslovakia for the Foreign Policy Committee, Sargent supported the organization of an anti-German coalition, and Vansittart argued that Britain and France should defend Czechoslovakia for the sake of the balance of power, provided that Prague made satisfactory concessions to its German minority. Cadogan, Gladwyn Jebb, and R. A. Butler, the parliamentary undersecretary of state, disagreed; they saw little danger to Britain in abandoning Czechoslovakia and acquiescing in German political and economic domination. Halifax echoed their views before the Foreign Policy Committee on March 18:

> Much of the argument for the need for a deterrent commitment rested on the assumption that when Germany secured the hegemony over Central Europe she would then pick a quarrel with France and ourselves. He did not agree with this argument. Secondly, the more closely we associated ourselves with France and Russia the more we produced on German minds the impression that we were plotting to encircle Germany and the more difficult it would be to make any real settlement with Germany. He [Halifax] distinguished in his own mind between Germany's racial efforts, which no one could question, and a lust for conquest on a Napoleonic scale which he himself did not credit.[21]

Similarly, when French Premier Daladier, who was in London for discussions of the European situation, argued on April 29 that Hitler would use the resources of Eastern Europe to attack

---

[20] CAB 27/627, FP (36) 57; Murray, "Balance of Power," pp. 287-94; Middlemas, *Diplomacy of Illusion*, p. 447. Chamberlain continued to argue that war over Czechoslovakia would have been disastrous even after the outbreak of the Second World War had demonstrated the impossibility of peace with Hitler.

[21] Sargent, Cadogan, and Jebb minutes, Mar. 18, 1938, FO 371/21674, C1855/132/18; Vansittart and Butler minutes, ibid., C1872; Foreign Policy Committee, CAB 27/623.

the western powers if allowed to destroy Czechoslovakia, Chamberlain denied that the time for armed conflict had come. He seemed to regard a war against Germany to preserve the balance of power, rather than a war in defense of French or British territory, as a "preventive war."

> In conclusion, Mr. Chamberlain had never excluded the possibility, for no one in his position could do so, that at some time we might be compelled to go to war . . . but he could only agree to go to war in the very last resort and could not envisage such a possibility as something to be undertaken lightly. He had himself seen war and had seen how impossible it was for anyone engaging in any war like the last war to come out of it stronger or happier. Therefore only dire necessity would ever persuade him to wage a preventive war. He was against preventive war.[22]

Precisely because he knew that Britain's ties to France could involve it in the war he feared, Chamberlain insisted on settling the crisis over Czechoslovakia peacefully. Throughout the crisis the French told London that they would honor their treaty commitment to Czechoslovakia if Germany attacked, and although the British government refused until September 26 to say what it would do in this case, Chamberlain and Halifax always recognized privately that if France became involved in war with Germany, Britain could not stand aside.[23] They therefore concluded that Prague must be forced to go to any lengths necessary to satisfy the Sudeten Germans and, ultimately, Hitler in order to avoid war—including, as a last resort, the cession of territory. As early as March 18, Halifax made it clear that he expected the Prague government to allow the Sudeten Germans to determine their fate by plebiscite, should this be necessary to avoid a conflict with Hitler. In mid-May Chamberlain suggested to American journalists that Czechoslovakia's frontiers should be revised, and after the May crisis Halifax repeated to the cabinet his suggestion of a plebiscite as a last resort.[24] Although the

---

[22] *DBFP*, 3, I, 164.

[23] See for example the Foreign Policy Committee meeting of Mar. 18, 1938, CAB 27/ 623; meeting of ministers, Aug. 30, CAB 23/94; cabinet of Sept. 25, CAB 23/95.

[24] In the Foreign Policy Committee on Mar. 18 Halifax suggested that Britain propose an international commission to resolve the Sudeten German dispute

British government did not officially endorse a plebiscite until Chamberlain visisted Berchtesgaden, London made it clear to Prague more than once that, in British eyes, the only significant test of new concessions to the Sudeten Germans was whether Henlein would accept them.[25] In July, Halifax also asked the French government to threaten to reconsider its treaty commitment to Czechoslovakia should the Prague government prove "unreasonable on the Sudeten question."[26]

London's insistence in July 1938 that the Prague government accept Lord Runciman as an impartial mediator represented another means of forcing Prague to yield to the Sudeten Germans' demands. The British government carefully refrained from committing itself to anything Runciman might recommend; London had no intention of standing behind any proposal before Henlein and Hitler had accepted it. Significantly, Runciman, who knew little about Eastern Europe, was accompanied by Ashton-Gwatkin, who had consistently sympathized with German penetration of the region. The denouement of Runciman's mission showed how impossible it was for the Prague government to please the British. Runciman ultimately termed Czech President Beneš's final offer a reasonable basis for settlement, but on September 16 Chamberlain, after returning from Berchtesgaden, brought Runciman to the Czechoslovakia Committee, where the mediator blamed Beneš for the breakdown in talks and helped Chamberlain to secure support for a plebiscite.[27]

After Hitler's September 12 Nuremberg speech and Henlein's

---

and that the government agree to stand by Czechoslovakia if Prague would accept the commission's verdict—provided that the commission reserved the right to recommend a plebiscite that would enable the Sudeten Germans to break away from Czechoslovakia. The Foreign Policy Committee rejected this intricate scheme, preferring merely to tell the French that Britain could not predict what it would do if France became involved in a war with Germany over Czechoslovakia while pressuring Prague to make concessions. See the meetings of Mar. 18, 22, CAB 27/623. For Chamberlain's statement see Celovsky, *Münchener Abkommen*, p. 199; press accounts of the briefing appeared on Mar. 14.

[25] See for example Halifax's instructions for Basil Newton, May 4, 1938, *DBFP*, 3, I, 171.

[26] In a July 7 memorandum Halifax noted with regret that Paris's latest démarche in Prague contained no such threat (ibid., 472).

[27] Celovsky, *Münchener Abkommen*, pp. 280-85; Middlemas, *Diplomacy of Illusion*, pp. 226-70; Runciman's Sept. 21, 1938, report, *DBFP*, 3, II, 675-79; Czechoslovakia Committee, Sept. 16, CAB 27/646.

flight from Czechoslovakia, Chamberlain moved quickly to avert war. On September 13 he asked to be received by Hitler; the next day, he secured the cabinet's authorization to propose a plebiscite. He personally agreed to self-determination at Berchtesgaden on September 15. The next day he restated the essence of his policy to the Czechoslovakia Committee:

> The Prime Minister said that he was satisfied that it was impossible to go to war in order to prevent self-determination, more especially now that Herr Henlein said that the Sudeten Germans wanted to go back to the Reich. The real question was, should that return be carried out in an orderly or disorderly manner.[28]

In London, on September 18, Chamberlain persuaded Daladier and Bonnet to agree to the cession of the Sudetenland to Germany, but the French ministers asked for a British guarantee of what remained of Czechoslovakia in return. Chamberlain and Halifax were not unprepared; they had recognized as early as June 16 that they might have to offer such a guarantee in return for the neutralization of Czechoslovakia. Since they refused to commit Britain to resist Germany in Eastern Europe, however, they had decided to square the circle by means of outright subterfuge. They had agreed to offer to participate in a "joint" guarantee—a wording that they interpreted to refer to a guarantee by several powers, which would come into effect *only if all of them agreed to implement it.* Germany, according to their original plan, would be included as a guarantor.[29] When at the September 18 meeting the French proposed an Anglo-French guarantee for the remainder of Czechoslovakia, Halifax first replied that Britain would require Prague to accept British advice in questions of peace and war; otherwise, Britain would be absolved of any new obligations. The French rejected this proposal. Chamberlain adjourned the meeting and

[28] Middlemas, *Diplomacy of Illusion*, pp. 333-36; Czechoslovakia Committee, Sept. 15, 1938, CAB 27/646. Chamberlain's reference to the Sudeten Germans going "back to the Reich" suggests that he may have actually believed that they had been citizens of the prewar German Empire.

[29] Foreign Policy Committee, June 16, 1938, PRO, CAB 27/624. A telegram to Paris suggesting revision of Czechoslovakia's alliances dropped the reference to a "joint" guarantee precisely because, as Chamberlain pointed out, questions as to the meaning of the phrase could prove embarrassing.

convened the Czechoslovakia Committee, which again agreed to participate in a "joint" guarantee, probably in conjunction with Germany. The Anglo-French plan submitted to Prague on September 19 included a British promise "to join in an international guarantee of the new boundaries of the Czechoslovak state"; the Munich agreement only reiterated this offer. The British did not explain to the French what their promise meant until November 24.[30]

Chamberlain's policy of securing a peaceful solution by convincing Prague and Paris to give in to all of Hitler's demands broke down after Hitler presented his new ultimatum at Godesberg on September 23. The British prime minister tried to get these new terms accepted, but his own government would not agree to them. Returning to London on the twenty-fourth, he told the Czechoslovakia Committee that Hitler's demand for immediate German occupation of the Sudetenland was "very difficult to deal with politically; but having once agreed to cession the sooner the transfer took place the better." Before the cabinet, he made every possible excuse for Hitler's behavior and reiterated all his old arguments against resistance. Halifax, prompted by Cadogan, shocked Chamberlain on September 25 by declaring that in his view there could be no peace until the Nazis were destroyed and by declining to recommend the Godesberg terms to Prague. Other important ministers took the same line.[31] In a sense, Chamberlain had a strong case; from the British standpoint, the effects of the Godesberg terms would differ little from those of the Anglo-French plan. The other ministers, however, refused to submit to further brutal demands.

Unable to insist upon the fulfillment of the Godesberg terms, Chamberlain secured a peaceful solution by threatening Hitler—a policy he had always regarded with extreme unease. He had warned on March 24, before the House of Commons, that Britain *might* become involved in a conflict arising out of

[30] Anglo-French conversations of Sept. 18, 1938. *DBFP*, 3, II, 928; Czechoslovakia Committee, Sept. 18, CAB 27/646; Anglo-French plan, *DBFP*, 3, II, 937; Anglo-French conversations of Nov. 24, ibid., III, 325.

[31] Czechoslovakia Committee and cabinet meetings of Sept. 24, 25, 1938, CAB 27/646, CAB 23/95; *The Diaries of Sir Alexander Cadogan, O.M.*, ed. David Dilks (London, 1971), pp. 103-5; Birkenhead, *Halifax*, pp. 400-401; Middlemas, *Diplomacy of Illusion*, pp. 370-80.

France's obligations to Czechoslovakia; he had told Daladier and Bonnet on April 29 that he would repeat this warning if a crisis arose; and British Ambassador Henderson had delivered this warning during the May crisis.[32] After that crisis, however, he generally accepted Henderson's view that this warning had angered Hitler, strengthened the "extremists" within the German government at the expense of the "moderates," and reduced the chances for further agreement. In early September, after first agreeing to repeat the warning, he accepted Henderson's appraisal that this step would "push Hitler over the edge" and make an attack on Czechoslovakia inevitable.[33] After he lost the support of his cabinet on September 25, however, he had no other options left. On September 26 he told Daladier that if France became involved in war with Germany as a result of fulfilling its obligations to Czechoslovakia, Britain would support France. He then sent Horace Wilson to Berlin to deliver this warning.[34]

Still Chamberlain did not give up hope of a peaceful solution. On September 27, without consulting the cabinet, he tried to press a compromise formula for German occupation of parts of the Sudetenland on Berlin and Prague. That evening, Wilson returned home and argued that the Czechs should be ordered to accept the Godesberg terms, but the Czechoslovakia Committee refused. Chamberlain appealed once more to Hitler for a peaceful solution, pledging to ensure that Czechoslovakia carried out

[32] *DBFP*, 3, I, 114, 164, 254. Henderson, who sympathized with German goals throughout the crisis, diluted the effect of the warning considerably by agreeing with Ribbentrop that the solution really lay in Prague. He did not, however, report this to London; compare ibid., 254, and *DGFP*, D, II, 186.

[33] Middlemas, *Diplomacy of Illusion*, pp. 320-26. On the issue of "moderates" and "extremists" see Wendt, *München 1938*, pp. 46-57. In British eyes, the moderates occupied the Foreign Office and the German army, while the extremists included Nazis like Ribbentrop and Himmler. Henderson wrote on May 25 that he believed Hitler, "in his saner moments," to be one of the moderates (*DBFP*, 3, I, 313).

[34] Cabinet of Sept. 26, 1938, CAB 23/95. Wilson left one loophole open in delivering his message to Hitler on Sept. 27; Britain would enter a war, he stated carefully, only if French forces "became actively engaged in hostilities with Germany." Twice he repeated, in response to Hitler's statements that Germany would not attack France, that his words were carefully chosen, and he added that he did not know *how* France would fulfill its obligations to Czechoslovakia (*DGFP*, D, II, 634). Chamberlain may have agreed upon this wording with French ministers; see below p. 243.

the terms of the Anglo-French plan.[35] He viewed Hitler's invitation to Munich as a personal triumph rather than as an admission that Germany, too, was not ready for war.[36]

Throughout the crisis, Chamberlain clung to the hope that a peaceful solution would lead to a broader European settlement. Thus, on September 24, in discussing the Godesberg terms with the cabinet, he claimed that he was on the verge of "a wonderful opportunity to put an end to the horrible nightmare of the present arms race."[37] On September 30, the day after the signing of the Munich agreement, he secured Hitler's assent to an Anglo-German declaration pledging to settle all matters of mutual interest through consultation, and he indicated both publicly and privately that he believed this agreement meant "peace for our time."[38] He summed up his view before the cabinet on October 3:

> Ever since he had been Chancellor of the Exchequer, he [Chamberlain] had been oppressed with the sense that the burden of armaments might break our backs. This had been one of the factors which had led him to the view that it was necessary to try and resolve the causes which were responsible for the armaments race.

[35] CAB 27/646; *DBFP*, 3, II, 1158.

[36] See, for example, the account of Harold Nicolson, who recorded Chamberlain's Sept. 28 announcement of his invitation to Munich in his diary: "The P.M., when he read out his final message this afternoon, had, it is true, a look of spiritual delight, but somewhere about it was the glow of personal triumph. I believe that he seriously imagines that Mussolini has made this gesture out of friendship for the Chamberlain family. He does not even now understand that what did the trick was the mobilization of the fleet and our proclaimed alliance with France and Russia. When all his supporters crowded round him to congratulate him afterwards, he showed great satisfaction and even greater self-satisfaction. Winston came up: 'I congratulate you on your good fortune. You were very lucky.' The P.M. didn't like that at all" (Nicolson, *Diaries*, p. 371).

[37] CAB 23/95.

[38] For Chamberlain's public statement on Sept. 30—often misquoted as "peace in our time"—see Chamberlain, *Struggle for Peace*, p. 303. On Oct. 3, in response to a suggestion by Lord Swinton, a former air minister, that Chamberlain had bought time for rearmament, the prime minister again indicated that he thought the Anglo-German agreement meant lasting peace; see Ian Colvin, *The Chamberlain Cabinet* (London, 1971), p. 169. At the conclusion of the House of Commons debate on Munich several days later, he suggested, however, that he had made his famous remark in a moment of extreme emotion and fatigue; Chamberlain, *Struggle for Peace*, p. 325.

He thought that we were now in a more hopeful position, and that the contacts which had been established with the Dictator Powers opened up the possibility that we might be able to reach some agreement with them which would stop the armament race.[39]

Although Chamberlain settled the German-Czechoslovak conflict peacefully, in the long run the crisis over Czechoslovakia doomed his policies. Hitler came away from Munich dissatisfied; his determination further to assert his will in Eastern Europe could only lead to further clashes with the western powers. More important, Halifax and Cadogan, two of Chamberlain's most important subordinates, had come to doubt the possibility of a lasting peace with Hitler, and they insisted upon a somewhat firmer policy after the occupation of Prague in 1939. Chamberlain himself finally recognized the failure of his policy after the outbreak of the Second World War. In the meantime, however, he helped to establish German hegemony in Eastern Europe.

From the standpoint of the French government, the crisis over Czechoslovakia involved the most fundamental questions of foreign policy. Given the equivocal attitude of Poland, Czechoslovakia was France's only remaining reliable ally in Eastern Europe; it possessed a well-trained, well-equipped army of thirty-four divisions and an important munitions industry. Czechoslovakian arms and capital held the Little Entente together; should Prague fall, the rest of the French alliance system would probably collapse. Failure to support Czechoslovakia would probably destroy the European balance of power, increasing German power beyond France's capacity to resist. Many Frenchmen, however, feared war with Germany, and London's equivocal attitude presented the chronic interwar problem of reconciling France's eastern alliances with its dependence on Britain. These questions divided the French government from March through September 1938; an important change of government in April determined how they would be answered.

Joseph Paul-Boncour returned to the Quai d'Orsay as a member of Léon Blum's second Popular Front government on March 14, 1938, after an absence of about four years. In his previous tenure he had begun negotiations for a Franco-Soviet Pact; now he returned to the task of containing Germany. He immediately

[39] CAB 23/95.

reaffirmed France's commitment to Czechoslovakia and tried to enlist British support. In instructions for Corbin, the French ambassador in London, he argued on March 21 that after the Anschluss it was no longer the fate of the Sudeten Germans or of Czechoslovakia that was at stake, but the fate of Europe. After Chamberlain refused on March 24 to commit Britain to aid Czechoslovakia, Paul-Boncour put the strongest possible interpretation on the prime minister's statements in a circular the next day, clearly hoping that London's attitude would stiffen as time went on. On April 6 he convened the French representatives to Poland, Czechoslovakia, Rumania, and the Soviet Union in Paris as a demonstration of French will.[40]

In the midst of Paul-Boncour's diplomatic activity, however, the Senate overthrew Blum's government. Edouard Daladier began the formation of a center-right government. He evidently considered retaining Paul-Boncour as foreign minister but finally dropped him in favor of Georges Bonnet, the erstwhile president of the Stresa conference of 1932. The intervention of the British ambassador, Sir Eric Phipps, may have been decisive. Phipps wrote Halifax on April 11 that after hearing that Paul-Boncour might be retained "I had Daladier and Paul Reynaud informed indirectly that Paul-Boncour's continuance at the Quai would be unfortunate, because of his wish to intervene in Spain and the need for France to be on better terms with Italy." Halifax warmly concurred in his reply two days later.[41]

Daladier and Bonnet did not openly reverse Paul-Boncour's policy. They saw no way openly to repudiate France's treaty commitment to Czechoslovakia, and their government included several relatively bellicose ministers.[42] In their talks with British ministers in April and September, they always began by citing the danger of German domination of Europe, the imminent establishment of Mitteleuropa, and the boundless extent of Hit-

[40] *DDF*, 2, IX, 3, 112; Celovsky, *Münchener Abkommen*, p. 63; Paul-Boncour, *Entre deux Guerres*, III, 93-94.

[41] PRO, FO 800/311, H/XIV/281-82.

[42] Adamthwaite, *France*, pp. 112-24, convincingly argues that the French cabinet divided into three groups: a hard-line group that included Paul Reynaud, Georges Mandel, and Auguste Charpentier de Ribes; a group favoring extreme concession, centered around Bonnet; and a larger middle group, which ultimately followed Daladier's and Bonnet's lead.

ler's ambitions, and they argued that Czechoslovakia must be defended.[43] On the whole, however, their behavior suggests that
they fired these opening salvos to show dissenters within the cabinet and the Quai d'Orsay that it was British weakness, not their
own, that rendered concessions to Germany inevitable. Unlike
their British counterparts, they seem to have accepted the need
for a European balance of power, but they did not believe that
France could afford the price of maintaining one. Thus they
struggled to find ways to avoid having to fulfill their commitment to Czechoslovakia, lacking even Chamberlains's optimistic
belief that a settlement of the present crisis would lead to lasting
peace.

In rejecting war on behalf of Czechoslovakia, Daladier and
Bonnet seem to have stressed three major considerations. First,
they clearly doubted that France was ready for war. The state of
the French air force particularly disturbed them; by early 1938,
the French had begun modernizing their air force, but new, up-
to-date types of aircraft would not come into production for
another year. On March 15 General Joseph Vuillemin, the Chief
of Staff of the French air force, told the Council of National Defense that in the event of war with Germany the French air force
would be wiped out in two weeks. Daladier and Bonnet cited
France's aerial weakness in order to persuade the cabinet on
September 19 to accept the Anglo-French plan for the cession of
the Sudetenland, and Vuillemin gave another very pessimistic
review of the air situation on September 26.[44] In addition, the
French government feared for its position on the ground; in a
general war, France would have to defend its eastern frontier
against Germany, its alpine frontier and North Africa against
Italy, and possibly even the Pyrenees against Franco. In March,
General Gamelin indicated that after troops were allocated
against Italy, France would lack the necessary forces for an offensive against Germany through Belgium, implying that
France would also lack the necessary forces to *defend* the Belgian
frontier if Germany turned west after overrunning Czechoslovakia. Gamelin could not promise to undertake any effective offensive against Germany should war break out. Although he

[43] *DBFP*, 3, I, 164, II, 928.
[44] *DDF*, 2, VIII, 446, IX, 377; *Les Carnets secrets de Jean Zay*, ed. Philippe Henriot (Paris, 1942), pp. 3-7.

often expressed doubt that Germany and Italy could fight a long war, his analyses were hardly optimistic.[45]

The equivocal attitude of Poland, combined with French distrust of the Soviet Union, also helped to convince Paris that 1938 was not an opportune moment for a trial of strength with Germany and Italy. Gamelin valued the Franco-Polish alliance very highly; in March 1938 he listed Poland as France's most important ally after Great Britain. Unfortunately, Warsaw steadfastly refused to promise to join France in a war over Czechoslovakia. Beck and Śmigły-Rydz stressed that action by France on behalf of Czechoslovakia would not bring the Franco-Polish alliance into play, and they even refused to promise in writing not to attack Czechoslovakia themselves. French Ambassador Noël reported that Warsaw believed that France and Britain would not fight for Czechoslovakia and that it hoped to receive the province of Teschen as its share of an eventual partition of that country.[46]

The Soviet Union was more forthcoming, but Paris shied away from collaboration with Moscow throughout the crisis. Shortly after the Anschluss, Litvinov reaffirmed Soviet obligations to assist Czechoslovakia if France did the same, and he even proposed a conference of Britain, France, Czechoslovakia, the Soviet Union, and the United States to discuss the maintenance of peace. Gamelin, however, doubted the value of Soviet help; Stalin's purges, he argued, had undermined the effectiveness of the Soviet army, and the harm that Soviet intervention would do by alienating Poland and Rumania would outweigh the help Moscow could provide. Bonnet apparently shared these views; from May to September 24 he repeatedly dodged Soviet requests for military staff talks. He frequently noted the refusal of Poland and Rumania to allow passage of Soviet troops or aircraft through their territory or airspace, ignoring Rumanian hints that Bucharest could do nothing to stop Soviet aircraft anyway should war begin.[47]

[45] See Gamelin's memoranda of Mar. 14, 29, 1938, *DDF*, 2, VIII, 432, IX, 73.

[46] Ibid., IX, 248, 302, 418, 458, 511, 525, 526, X, 15, 48, 132, 158, 219, XI, 315, 323, 327. See also Anna Cienciala, *Poland and the Western Powers, 1938-39* (Toronto, 1968), pp 71-78; Wojciechowski, *Polnisch-deutschen Bezienhungen*, pp. 421-25; Adamthwaite *France*, pp. 183-87.

[47] *DDF*, 2, IX, 144, 306, X, 6, 511, 534, XI, 93, 95, 165, 266, 267, 339, 367, 380, 416. See also Ministry for Foreign Affairs of the Czechoslovak Republic and

Lastly, Daladier and Bonnet shared Chamberlain's and Weiz-säcker's fear of the effects of a general war on European society, no matter who won or lost. Until war became imminent in September, they generally concealed these views from the British, but they stated them frankly and fully to the Germans. Thus, on May 1 Bonnet told Johannes von Welczeck, the German ambassador in Paris, that London and Paris would try to make Prague accommodating in the Sudeten German question. In Welczeck's words, Bonnet

> begged us most earnestly not to compel France, who always honored her obligations as an ally, to take up arms by reason of an act of violence in favor of the Sudeten Germans. . . . he considered any arrangement better than world war, in the event of which all Europe would perish, and both victor and vanquished would fall victims to world communism.[48]

Paul Reynaud, supposedly one of the more bellicose French ministers, told Welczeck on May 11 that a German attack on Czechoslovakia would lead to "the destruction of the civilized old world." Then, on May 22, as the May crisis was winding down, Daladier visited Welczeck at his home "to speak frankly as a French ex-serviceman to his German comrade."

> From our time in the trenches both of us knew the horrors of the last war, but the catastrophic frightfulness of a modern war would surpass all that humanity had ever seen, and would mean the utter destruction of European civilization. Into the battle zones, devastated and denuded of men, Cossack and Mongol hordes would then pour, bringing to Europe a new "culture." This must be prevented, even if it entailed great sacrifices.
> . . . The dilemma in which France found herself vis-à-vis her ally Czechoslovakia was not unknown to me [Welczeck]. He himself had not made the alliance, and was certainly not happy about. It did, however, exist and, if we attacked Czechoslovakia, the French would have to fight if they did not wish to be dishonored.[49]

Ministry for Foreign Affairs of the Union of Soviet Socialist Republics, *New Documents on the History of Munich* (Prague, 1958), no. 14; Celovsky, *Münchener Abkommen*, pp. 176-81; Adamthwaite, *France*, pp. 182-83, 203-4.
   [48] *DGFP*, D, II, 144.   [49] Ibid., 152, 192.

Daladier and Bonnet spoke in virtually identical terms to Curt Bräuer, the German chargé in Paris, during the first week of September.[50]

Lastly and most significantly, Daladier, in London on September 18, fell back upon the danger of war in indicating his agreement to the cession of Czechoslovakian territory and effectively renouncing France's commitments:

> The object of the French Ministers in coming to London was to see what could be done to preserve peace without destroying Czechoslovakia. He could not help recalling that not very long ago the British and French Governments had agreed on the principle of maintaining the unity of Czechoslovakia. He realized, however, that we must now take into account recent events. The problem therefore was to discover some means of preventing France from being forced into war as a result of her obligations and at the same time to preserve Czechoslovakia and save as much of that country as was humanly possible.[51]

Throughout the summer Bonnet desperately sought some means of avoiding war without openly repudiating France's treaty commitment to Czechoslovakia. In his efforts to pressure Prague into agreement with Henlein, he did not explicitly say that France *would* not honor its obligations, but he implied that it *could* not. It would be "extremely difficult," he informed Prague on July 17, for the French government to secure public support for war in a case in which France had not been attacked and in which Britain refused to support France. Although Daladier minuted that Bonnet had made this statement solely on his own authority, there is no evidence that he reassured the Czechoslovakian government.[52] Within the Quai d'Orsay, René Massigli, the political director and second-ranking permanent official, argued for standing by Prague; the fall of Czechoslovakia, he insisted in July, would lead quickly to a German drive westward. Secretary General Léger, however, apparently rejected war. On September 11—before Chamberlain's visit to Berchtesgaden—he proposed a conference of the French, German, British, and

---

[50] See their conversations of Sept. 2, 7, ibid., 422, 439.

[51] *DBFP*, 3, II, 928. This wording is confirmed by the French record, *DDF*, 2, XI, 212.

[52] *DDF*, 2, X, 222, 235, 238, 242.

Italian governments to settle the crisis, foreshadowing the eventual Munich conference. Daladier and Bonnet repeated this suggestion to London during the next few days, but Chamberlain decided to visit Germany himself instead.[53]

Although Chamberlain first officially accepted self-determination for the Sudeten Germans at Berchtesgaden on September 15, it is clear that the French ministers had decided to agree to cede Czechoslovakian territory in order to prevent war well before they went to London on September 18 to hear Chamberlain's report. On September 14 Bonnet told Phipps that he would accept a plebiscite as a last resort; two days later he told Czechoslovakian Minister Štefan Osuský that war would serve neither French nor Czechoslovakian interests and that France would not march without Britain.[54] Then, on September 17, Massigli submitted a memorandum implicitly recognizing that France would not fight to preserve Czechoslovakia. It proposed the cession of relatively small districts on the fringes of the Czechoslovakian frontiers, together with an exchange of populations—a solution that would preserve the Czechoslovakian fortifications intact and one to which President Beneš had already hinted agreement.[55] Daladier and Bonnet insisted upon the cession of territory rather than a plebiscite in their talks in London on September 18, but they also agreed that Prague must cede all districts that contained a German majority.[56]

Daladier and Bonnet defended the new Anglo-French plan before the French cabinet on September 19. For weeks Bonnet had been fishing for a definite British refusal to support France in a war over Czechoslovakia; now Daladier told the cabinet that Britain would go to war only if French territory were attacked. This was only a half-truth; the British had *promised* to fight only in this case, but they had never said that they definitely would not move in any other. The French cabinet agreed to put the

[53] For Massigli's attitude see his July 8, 1938, memorandum, ibid., 170. For Léger's proposal see *DBFP*, 3, II, 833, and Adamthwaite, *France*, pp. 210-11. See also Elizabeth R. Cameron, "Alexis St.-Léger Léger," in Gordon A. Craig and Felix Gilbert, eds., *The Diplomats, 1919-39* (New York, 1963), p. 394.

[54] *DBFP*, 3, II, 874; *DDF*, 2, XI, 177.

[55] *DDF*, 2, XI, 195. On Beneš's assent to such an arrangement see his Sept. 17 conversation with French Minister Lacroix and his secret communication for Daladier, ibid., 180, 192.

[56] Ibid., 212, 213. Daladier and Bonnet initially proposed an exchange of populations, but Chamberlain would not agree.

Anglo-French plan before the Prague government, reserving its attitude if Prague rejected it.[57] The Czechoslovakian government initially rejected the plan on the evening of September 20, but Prime Minister Hodža immediately told French Minister Lacroix that Prague would accept if Paris specifically stated that France would not come to Czechoslovakia's assistance if it persisted in its rejection. Bonnet and Daladier took the next step without consulting the cabinet; at 3 a.m. Lacroix gave Beneš a new démarche, stating that Prague's rejection would destroy Franco-British solidarity and, with it, the practical value of French assistance. "Thus Czechoslovakia is assuming a risk against which we have warned her. She should herself realize the conclusions that France has a right to draw if the Czechoslovak government does not immediately accept the Anglo-French plan." Prague gave in.[58]

Hitler's Godesberg demands split the French government as well as the British; Bonnet could swallow them, but Daladier could not. On September 26, in London, Daladier told Chamberlain that France would fight if Hitler attacked Czechoslovakia, receiving Chamberlain's pledge of assistance in return. However, while Wilson was delivering his warning in Berlin on September 27, Bonnet was making new attempts to avoid war. He had already written Daladier that the diplomatic and military situation made war impossible; he now told the French cabinet that France could not fight to prevent German entry into the Sudetenland on October 1 after having already agreed that the Germans should enter it on October 10. He suggested that France might somehow fulfill its obligations to Czechoslovakia without actually becoming involved in hostilities with Germany. This possibility apparently occurred to Chamberlain and Sir Horace Wilson as well. In his warning to Hitler, Wilson stressed that Britain would not join France unless actual Franco-German military conflict began, adding that he did not know how France would choose to fulfill its obligations. Bonnet failed to persuade the cabinet, but on the evening of the twenty-seventh he authorized French Ambassador François-Poncet to give Hitler a new plan that would allow German troops to enter certain Czechoslovakian frontier districts on October 1. François-Poncet met

[57] See the Bonnet-Phipps conversation of Sept. 10, *DBFP*, 3, II, 843; Zay, *Carnets Secrets*, pp. 3-7; Celovsky, *Münchener Abkommen*, pp. 351-53.

[58] *DDF*, 2, XI, 229, 232, 234, 249.

Hitler at 11:15 the next morning; during their conversation Hitler received Mussolini's telephone call asking him to delay military action for twenty-four hours.[59] Soon afterward, Hitler invited Mussolini, Daladier, and Chamberlain to meet with him at Munich.

Munich relieved Daladier and Bonnet of the choice between peace and war. Evidence suggests, however, that they had contemplated staying out of war even if Germany did attack Czechoslovakia and that they may even have discussed ways of doing so with Chamberlain in London on September 26. There is no record of Daladier's September 26 conversation with Chamberlain, during which the British prime minister declared that Britain would support France should France become involved in hostilities with Germany in fulfillment of its commitment to Czechoslovakia.[60] Chamberlain undoubtedly made this declaration. He repeated it to the cabinet that day, the British government made it public that evening, and Wilson repeated it to Hitler on September 22. Nevertheless, Chamberlain and Daladier might also have discussed ways in which France might fulfull its obligations *without* becoming involved in active hostilities with Germany—perhaps by holding troops on the frontier without fighting, more or less as they did in September 1939, and quickly making peace after Germany had overrun Czechoslovakia. Bonnet's discussion of such a step in the French cabinet, combined with Wilson's extremely careful language to Hitler, suggest that the two governments had discussed this possibility.

The French government must clearly take full responsibility for the surrender of Czechoslovakia; British pressure was not responsible for its decision not to fight. Léger proposed a four-power conference on Czechoslovakia on September 11, and Daladier and Bonnet apparently decided that Czechoslovakia must surrender territory in order to avoid war several days before September 18, when they went to London to hear Chamberlain's report of his Berchtesgaden conversations. Had they stood by Czechoslovakia, they could have dragged Britain in with them; as we have seen, Chamberlain and Halifax realized

---

[59] On Bonnet's activities see ibid., 390, 420, 426, Celovsky, *Münchener Abkommen*, pp. 426-27, and Adamthwaite, *France*, pp. 219-23.

[60] See Middlemas, *Diplomacy of Illusion*, pp. 387-88. It may also be more than coincidental that both the French and British prepared and submitted new proposals allowing Hitler to occupy some Czechoslovakian territory before Oct. 1.

throughout the crisis that Britain would have to join in a general war. After Munich, the French apparently concluded that French influence in Eastern Europe could not recover, and Bonnet moved to cut France's remaining alliance ties in Eastern Europe. The French, like the British, had abandoned the European balance of power. They reversed course in 1939 only after London had decided to resist further German aggression.

In the meantime, the Anschluss had also inaugurated a new struggle for economic influence in Eastern Europe. The annexation of Austria dramatically increased German economic power throughout the region, especially with respect to the four Danubian states and Poland. The disappearance of an independent Austria promised significantly to increase Germany's share in the region's trade. In 1937 Germany had taken between 13.7 and 24.0 percent of the exports of Czechoslovakia, Yugoslavia, Rumania, Hungary, and Poland, while supplying between 14.5 and 32.4 percent of their imports. If Austria's 1937 shares were added to these figures, Germany could expect to purchase between 19.4 and 41.0 percent of their exports and supply between 19.1 and 44.2 percent of their imports.[61] For Germany, the situation offered new opportunities; for France and Britain, perhaps the last real chance to resist German economic domination of Eastern Europe was at hand.

Despite these initial advantages, Berlin could not consolidate its economic gains in Eastern Europe until after the Munich agreement. Germany's share of the trade of Eastern Europe increased during 1938, both because of the Anschluss and because rearmament kept Germany relatively immune from the worldwide slump in foreign trade that began in late 1937. Berlin also concluded new trade agreements with Hungary and Poland—both of which had depended heavily on Austrian trade—providing for substantial increases in imports and exports.[62]

[61] LN, *ITS, 1937*, pp. 281-87, 303-9, *1938*, pp. 281-87, 303-9.

[62] The German-Hungarian agreement of May 7, 1938, doubled exports of many Hungarian products to Germany; see PA, Ha Pol, IVa Ungarn, Handel 13, Bd. 3. In negotiations with Poland the Germans refused to continue some Austrian preferences for Polish products dating from 1932 but agreed to increase trade generally; see *DGFP*, D, V, 35, and T-120/2040/446132-37. For the agreement of July 1 see ibid., 446139-43. The German trade balance suffered from the world recession, but imports fell relatively little. See Table A.1.

The Germans made no dramatic breakthroughs in Rumania and Yugoslavia, however. Emil Wiehl, who had replaced Ritter as head of the Wilhelmstrasse's Economic Department, noted on April 6 that Germany could not expect to retain all the concessions that Austria had enjoyed in trade with these countries. Having depended on Austria for foreign exchange, Bucharest and Belgrade would now attempt to divert more trade to hard-currency countries rather than accept more reichmarks. The uncertain political situation during the summer of 1938 also militated against any new, far-reaching, long-term commitments.[63] Until the Munich agreement, the Eastern European states generally hoped to avoid increased dependence upon German markets.

The Anschluss had complex economic effects upon Germany itself. In the short run, as contemporary reports by the Reich Statistical Office and the Economic and Armaments Office of the War Ministry noted, Germany secured useful stocks of various raw materials and vital foreign exchange. These reports suggested, however, that in the long run the Anschluss would worsen Germany's continuing food and raw-materials crisis. Like Germany itself, Austria depended on imported foodstuffs and raw materials; only further increases in German exports could pay for these goods. In addition, the integration of Austria into the German war economy would probably hurt Austrian export industries by diverting imports and production to fill the needs of German rearmament.[64]

Between March and September 1938 the French and British governments took steps to contain German economic influence in Eastern Europe and to increase their own. Elements within both governments recognized the imminence of German economic hegemony and feared the political implications of this development. In both cases, however, domestic interests stood in

[63] HPA meeting Apr. 6, 1938, T-120/4700/E227062-70. On the effects of the political crisis on German trade see the economic report of the Economic and Armaments Office, War Ministry, Oct. 1, 1938, T-77/126/856654-69.

[64] See the undated Reich Statistical Office memorandum on the effects of the Anschluss, T-71/102/603975-4069, and the Apr. 1, 1938, economic report of the Economic and Armaments Office, T-77/140/872728-34. See also the report of June 1 (ibid., 856718-24), which states that the incorporation of Austria had hurt the German trade balance, and the report of July 1 (ibid., 856697-716), which noted that Austrian import needs would increase as a result of Anschluss.

the way of effective economic help for Eastern Europe, and the surrender of the Anglo-French political leadership at Munich finally doomed these efforts. The German annexation of the Sudetenland, which included most of Czechoslovakia's important industrial districts, more than made up for the effects of any French or British economic initiatives during 1938.

Within the French government, Quai d'Orsay Political Director Massigli, the foremost advocate within the government of resistance to German designs upon Czechoslovakia, also led the fight for economic help for Eastern Europe. We have seen that at the time of the Anschluss the French government had been pushing for adoption of the Schüller plan, which would have eliminated exchange control within the Danubian states and, it was hoped, draw them out of the German economic orbit. In order to forestall increased German influence in the Danubian states, Massigli and Robert de la Baume, the assistant political director, proposed in late March that France transfer its old quotas for imports from Austria to Czechoslovakia and that Britain and France increase their purchases of those Yugoslavian and Rumanian products that Austria had formerly bought. On March 29 Foreign Minister Paul-Boncour and Premier Blum agreed in principle to oppose increased German economic influence in Southeastern Europe.[65]

The Quai immediately proposed joint action to the British Foreign Office but received a disappointing response. Some members of the Foreign Office favored British economic initiatives in Southeastern Europe, but most rejected joint Franco-British action as smacking too much of "encirclement" of Germany.[66] Daladier raised the issue again during the Anglo-French conversations of April 29, arguing that economic assistance for the Little Entente countries "would help towards European appeasement." Chamberlain replied that British investigations into the question had revealed "very great difficulties in the way," but he endorsed increased trade with Central and Southeastern Europe in principle and agreed to an experts' discussion. On May 7 Paris proposed an Anglo-French system of private clearings, which would exchange Danubian cereals and

[65] DDF, 2, IX, 47, 74.
[66] Minutes on FO 371/22341, R3269/94/67. For the French proposal of Mar. 30 see FO 371/21642, C2263/30/18.

British and French industrial products at high prices. E.M.B. Ingram, who had replaced O'Malley as head of the Southern Department, opposed "any Anglo-French organization," and the Board of Trade and the Treasury opposed the project on technical grounds. After dilatory consideration, London officially rejected the proposal on July 8.[67]

Massigli also encountered difficulties within his own government. The French Agriculture Ministry did not share his concern with French influence in Eastern Europe and concentrated instead on protecting French producers. In early June it refused to divert more than 60 percent of the Austrian timber quota to Czechoslovakia, Yugoslavia, Poland, and Rumania, preferring to leave the rest unused. When Massigli suggested buying more Yugoslav foodstuffs in May, permanent officials at the Agriculture Ministry argued that the 1936-1937 concessions to Belgrade had lacked economic justification, and they opposed extending them again. Paris did nothing for Belgrade until well after the Munich crisis, despite continuing pressure from French bondholders to increase imports from Yugoslavia. The French Commerce Ministry tried, but failed, to establish a central purchasing organization for Southeastern European products. Massigli's failure to arrange any major initiatives during the great political crisis of 1938 shows once again that in Paris, as in London, domestic economic considerations generally prevailed over foreign policy interests.[68]

The British government also reconsidered the question of German economic influence in Southeastern Europe after the Anschluss and eventually took some steps designed to combat it. These measures gave British policy a certain ambivalence during the crisis of 1938. Although Chamberlain had decided to sacrifice Czechoslovakia and accept German domination of Eastern Europe, if necessary, to satisfy Hitler, various high civil servants still feared Germany and wanted to resist German expansion economically, if not politically or militarily. Prodded by

[67] Afternoon conversation of Apr. 29, *DBFP*, 3, I, 164; French proposals of May 7 and Ingram's minutes, Waley to Foreign Office, May 19, Board of Trade memorandum of June 30, British reply of July 8, FO 371/22342-43, R4661/R4993/R6092/R6232/94/67.

[68] Massigli letter, May 19, 1938, Agriculture Ministry to AE, June 2, Agriculture Ministry memorandum, May 29, AN, F¹⁰/2163. See also the June 28 and July 12 memoranda by M Bolgert of the Bank of France, AN, F³⁰/2082.

public opinion and various interested members of Parliament, they formed the Interdepartmental Committee on Southeastern Europe to promote British trade with the region. The committee achieved almost nothing during 1938, both because of the government's determination not to antagonize Germany and because of longstanding prejudices against state intervention in international commerce. Finally, in September 1938, Chamberlain reversed the policy embodied by the committee when he decided to offer Germany special trading rights in Southeastern Europe as part of a general settlement.[69]

The Anschluss provoked an immediate, wide-ranging public debate within Britain on Germany's new position in Southeastern Europe and its consequences. Two journalists, Paul Einzig and Gerhard Schacher, especially stressed the dangers of the new German economic drive, or *Drang nach Südosten*. Einzig, the political editor of the *Financial News*, also had important political connections, including friendships with Hugh Dalton, the Labour party shadow chancellor of the Exchequer, and dissident Tories like Churchill, Harold Macmillan, and Robert Boothby. Articles on the imminence and the danger of German hegemony in Southeastern European trade appeared in the *Economist*, the *Spectator*, and the *Manchester Guardian*; in Parliament, Churchill stressed the danger of a reconstructed Mitteleuropa. Many linked the danger of British exclusion from trade in Southeastern Europe to the problem of Britain's generally slumping foreign trade and the continuing economic recession. During the spring Boothby and Macmillan also sent proposals for action to the Foreign Office and buttonholed Foreign Office officials.[70]

Foreign Office comments on proposals for action in Southeastern Europe in the weeks following the Anschluss revealed deep differences of opinion. Ashton-Gwatkin suggested that

[69] British initiatives in Southeastern Europe during 1938 have also been discussed by Bernd Jürgen Wendt in his *Appeasement 1938*, and his "Strukturbedingungen der britischen Südosteuropapolitik am Vorabend des Zweiten Weltkrieges," in Forstmeier and Volkmann, eds., *Wirtschaft und Rüstung*, pp. 296-307, and Gerhard Joseph Van Kessel, "The British Reaction to German Economic Expansion in Southeastern Europe, 1936-39" (Ph.D. diss., University of London, 1972).

[70] On the press campaign see Wendt, *Appeasement 1938*, pp. 39-68; on Einzig see Wendt, *Economic Appeasement*, p. 17. See also Boothby to FO, May 17, 1938, and Macmillan to FO, July 7, FO 371/22342, R5004/R5531/94/67.

nothing could be done to prevent Germany from becoming "the metropolis of Central Europe, composed of economic dominions"; this development, he argued, was "natural and constructive." E.M.B. Ingram dissented. "I think we should continue to examine if economically there is nothing to be done to stop the rot," he noted on March 30. But Permanent Undersecretary Sir Alexander Cadogan argued that any attempts at "the economic strangulation of Germany . . . would be as futile—and perhaps as undesirable—as are attempts at political and military strangulation."[71] Perhaps because of Cadogan's opposition, Ingram did not put forth specific proposals until May.

On May 12 the British cabinet approved a £16-million export credit guarantee to Turkey, including £6 million to finance warships. This step has been interpreted as the beginning of a broad British effort to resist German economic influence in Southeastern Europe.[72] But although the government established the Interdepartmental Committee on Southeastern Europe only a few weeks later, the two events should not be linked too closely. The Turkey credit stemmed from political and strategic preoccupations that did not apply to Southeastern Europe as a whole, and the government initially regarded it as the end, not the beginning, of resistance to the German drive to the southeast.

Within the British Foreign Office, Turkey was the responsibility not of the Southern Department but of the Eastern Department, which dealt with the region now known as the Middle East. The Foreign Office paper of May 7, 1938, that proposed the credit discussed the importance of Turkey primarily from a Middle Eastern perspective: "On account of her strategical position, Turkey's friendship or enmity is a vital factor for this country, above all, now that the implementation of the Balfour Declaration may inevitably cost us the friendship of the Arab countries which flank our communications with India." With regard to Southeastern Europe, the paper merely argued that after the Anschluss it was "difficult to see" what would stop the influence of Germany from spreading through Hungary, Yugoslavia, Rumania, and Bulgaria. "It is therefore not too much to say," it continued, "that Turkey has become not the main, but the only obstacle to the *Drang nach Osten*." The credit was neces-

[71] Minutes on proposals by Secretary-General of the League of Nations Joseph Avenol, FO 371/22341, R3269/R3319/94/67.

[72] Wendt, *Appeasement 1938*, pp. 69-86.

sary in part because the rest of Southeastern Europe seemed to be lost; since German influence could not be stopped in Europe, Britain must block it at the Straits.[73]

When the cabinet discussed this paper on May 12, Chamberlain made it clear that the new credit should not lead to others. "As the ex-Chancellor of the Exchequer, he naturally disliked the proposal and was apprehensive of the precedent which it would establish." Turkey, however, "was in a very special and exceptional position. She constituted a very real bulwark against German expansion in the Near and Middle East." Chancellor of the Exchequer Sir John Simon took definite steps to prevent the credit from establishing a precedent. Because £6 million of the credit would finance warships, the government had to amend the Export Credits Guarantee Act. Simon took care to provide for an exception to the act *in this case only*, rather than lift the general prohibition of credit guarantees for "munitions of war." The Foreign Office sought the elimination of this provision during the spring of 1938, but the Treasury, Board of Trade, and Department of Overseas Trade all continued to support it. It remained in force until after Munich.[74]

In early May, Lord Halifax's sudden assent to British economic initiatives in Southeastern Europe led to the formation of the new Interdepartmental Committee. The reasons for Halifax's decision are not completely clear. He seems to have been influenced by Harold Nicolson, a former Foreign Office official who had made an unofficial fact-finding tour of Eastern Europe during April. On May 2, in his report on his tour to Chief Diplomatic Adviser to the Government Vansittart, Nicolson emphasized that Rumania, Yugoslavia, and Bulgaria all hoped for help in resisting Germany: "Again and again did they ask me, 'Is there no point at which England will call a halt?' " They had abandoned hope of help from France but still hoped that Britain would realize "that a new Drang nach Osten is in progress and that the Balkan barrier must be fortified before it is too late." Passing this report on to Halifax, Vansittart argued that this call must be answered: "If we cannot find the answer, the future is bleak for the world—and *us*." Though generally loyal to Cham-

[73] CAB 24/276, CP 112 (38).
[74] Cabinet of May 12, 1938, CAB 23/93. On export credits see the Apr. 22, 1938, FO memorandum and succeeding documents on other departments' attitudes, FO 371/22501, W5214/4366/50.

berlain, Halifax was susceptible to the influence of his subordinates because of his inexperience in European affairs. Ingram noted on May 11 that the foreign secretary "is quite prepared to initiate a drive for the extension of British influence in the Balkans" and had asked his subordinates to prepare a memorandum for the cabinet discussing this question.[75]

Remarkably enough, Ingram's memorandum, which Halifax presented to the Foreign Policy Committee on June 1, directly contradicted what the foreign secretary had said just ten weeks earlier while arguing against any guarantee for Czechoslovakia. Using careful, tentative language, Ingram tried to persuade the government to resist German domination of Eastern Europe—something the ministers had explicitly conceded in March. He began by comparing the emerging German domination of Eastern Europe with the situation of 1917. Germany's increasing power, he continued,

> does not necessarily mean an extension of German territorial sovereignty; it does, however, mean an intensification of German economic and commercial influence, which in its turn means an extension of political dominance. This process, if it were allowed to proceed unchecked, would mean that Central and South-Eastern Europe would tend to become to Germany what, in many respects and with some obvious reservations, the Dominions are to the United Kingdom.

Ingram then argued for the maintenance of a European balance of power, while implicitly recognizing that some committee members rejected this policy.

> It has always been the traditional policy of His Majesty's Government to prevent one Power attaining a predominant position on the Continent. It is true that conditions change and that England no longer stands in exactly the same relation to Europe as she did either in the 18th or 19th centuries. Nevertheless it will no doubt be generally conceded that it remains very much to her interest—indeed, it will be argued in some

[75] Halifax-Comnène conversation, May 13, Nicolson's report and Vansittart's minutes, and Ingram's May 11 minute, FO 371/22342, R4857/R4737/R4755/94/67. For an entertaining account of Nicolson's journey see his *Diaries*, pp. 334-38. On Halifax's inexperience and his susceptibility to Foreign Office influence see Birkenhead, *Halifax*, pp. 417-21, and Middlemas, *Diplomacy of Illusion*, pp. 296-300.

quarters that it is vital to her interests—that Germany should not attain a virtual hegemony in Europe.

Given that Germany would eventually regain colonies and perhaps consolidate its influence in Spain, to counteract German influence in Eastern Europe was "highly desirable, if not vital." Ingram ended by trying to use the Turkey credit as a precedent—precisely what Chamberlain had hoped to avoid—and by denying that he envisioned an anti-German coalition, which of course the government had already rejected.

> That the situation is not hopeless is shown by the fact that we have already managed, so we hope, to prevent one power at least in this part of Europe from falling under German influence. This power is Turkey; and the success we have had in this direction leads us to hope that it may not be impossible to take similar action in respect of other minor European states. Even where it is not possible to prevent German influence playing a very large part, it might be all-important to convince the countries concerned that they are not completely abandoned by the Western Powers and that the latter still offer them a loop-hole of resistance to the German stranglehold which they dread. . . . In the meantime, it should be pointed out that our object is not, and should not have the appearance of being, to create an anti-German *bloc*. Such a *bloc* could in reality only be organized if this country and perhaps France were ready to grant military guarantees, which clearly they are not. Our object should rather be to endeavor to ensure that this area of Europe shall look specifically for leadership to this country and generally towards the Western Powers, rather than feel obliged in default of any other *point d'appui* to allow itself to be exploited by Berlin.

The memorandum concluded that the countries of Eastern and Southeastern Europe "would welcome any measure of economic assistance which would prevent them from being completely subservient to the German market, provided always that the adoption of these measures does not entail German hostility." It then recommended the creation of interdepartmental machinery to examine the possibilities for giving aid.[76]

[76] CAB 24/276, CP 127 (38); for an earlier draft see FO 371/22342, R5142/94/67.

In all probability, neither this memorandum nor the Interdepartmental Committee itself would ever have seen the light of day had not Ingram replaced Owen O'Malley, who had consistently sympathized with German economic expansion in Southeastern Europe, in late 1937. As it was, the memorandum directly contradicted Halifax's March 18 *denial* "that when Germany secured the hegemony over Central Europe she would pick a quarrel with France and ourselves," and it could hardly be reconciled with Chamberlain's policy of satisfying certain German goals in Eastern Europe as a prelude to an Anglo-German settlement.[77] When the Foreign Policy Committee discussed the memorandum on June 1, Chamberlain quickly questioned its assumptions, doubting both the imminence of German domination and the gravity of its consequences. Britain must beware of blackmail; the countries in question did not want to be dominated by Germany, yet they "were only too ready to use the argument that unless we were prepared to give them financial, economic and other tangible advantages, they must inevitably submit to be dominated by Germany." He seized upon the analogy with the British Dominions: "If this was the true position Germany might expect from time to time to be duly chastised by the small countries in much the same way as it had for some time been customary for the Dominions to chasten the mother country." When Halifax raised the specter of a German trading area from which British products might be excluded, Chamberlain retorted that the strengthening of the German economy might contribute to peace. The prime minister attacked the statement that Southeastern Europe should look to Britain for "leadership"; Halifax conceded that this "overstated the position," adding that London wanted only to give the countries in question another *"point d'appui."*[78]

Although ultimately accepting the proposal, Chamberlain in-

[77] CAB 27/623. An unsigned Foreign Office brief prepared for Halifax to use in presenting Ingram's memorandum argued that economic action must hold the line against Germany until 1940, when rearmament would be complete. Halifax did not use this argument, perhaps because he knew that Chamberlain hoped to make new agreements with Germany and Italy that would enable Britain to halt rearmament. See FO 371/22342, R5337/94/67.

[78] CAB 23/627. Halifax's private secretary, Oliver Harvey, commented on the committee's reaction to Ingram's plan: "The Foreign Policy Committee in the Cabinet can see nothing but difficulties. There is no spirit in them" (Harvey, *Diplomatic Diaries*, p. 149).

troduced a significant qualification: "The initiative in regard to all schemes to be considered by the Interdepartmental Committee," the Foreign Policy Committee's conclusions read, "should rest with the Export Credits Guarantee Department." Since the ECGD had to consider projects only on their economic merits, this provision would prevent political considerations from overriding economic ones. It also ruled out several important forms of assistance, such as loans or large-scale purchases of foodstuffs and raw materials. The Foreign Office secured the elimination of this provision on June 17, but economic considerations generally prevailed in the committee's discussions nonetheless.[79]

The appointment of Chief Economic Adviser to the Government Sir Frederick Leith-Ross to chair the new committee ensured that it would not pursue an aggressively anti-German policy. Leith-Ross shared Chamberlain's belief in an ultimate Anglo-German settlement and doubted that Britain could do much to increase trade with Southeastern Europe. Ingram, Ashton-Gwatkin, and Sargent represented the Foreign Office, and the committee also included representatives of the Treasury, the Board of Trade, the Export Credits Guarantee Department, and the Department of Overseas Trade.[80]

The Interdepartmental Committee on Southeastern Europe met twice during the summer of 1938, on July 1 and August 25.

[79] See the conclusions of June 1 and minutes, Cadogan to Leith-Ross, June 11, FO 371/22342, R5362/R5488/94/67; Foreign Policy Committee, June 17, CAB 27/624. Simon Newman, *March 1939: The British Guarantee to Poland* (Oxford, 1976), pp. 40-41, also discusses this meeting. He ignores almost everything that Chamberlain said, quoting only his suggestion that an improvement in Germany's economic situation might make Germany more peaceable, and he adds that "Chamberlain's comment should not be taken as evidence that he opposed the Foreign Office policy." But the evidence that Chamberlain *did* oppose this policy, both then and later, is overwhelming, and it completely contradicts Newman's more general argument that Chamberlain in 1938 showed an interest in Southeastern Europe that in some way foreshadowed his guarantee to Poland in March 1939.

[80] In a Mar. 25, 1938, letter to Lord de la Warr, Leith-Ross discounted the possibility of substantial British economic help for Southeastern Europe: "The best hope is that if we can arrive at an arrangement with Italy, Italy can build up an economic block with Yugoslavia and Hungary, by means of trade agreements similar to those which have recently replaced the Rome Protocols. This would make counterpoise in the Balkans without our having to come in" (FO 371/22341, R3318/94/67). On Leith-Ross's subsequent efforts at an Anglo-German settlement see below, Chapter XI.

It considered various schemes but did not put any into effect. Two major difficulties hampered its work. First, various specific proposals encountered all the traditional arguments against British economic intervention in Eastern Europe, including high Eastern European prices, British tariffs and quotas, and the general prejudice against state intervention in trade. Second, as the Czechoslovakia crisis worsened during the summer, the committee had to respect the government's fear of antagonizing Germany. At one time or another during the summer of 1938 the committee discussed increased purchases of Yugoslav and Hungarian turkeys, Rumanian oil and wheat, and Greek tobacco. It decided on July 1 to recommend reducing the duty on turkeys, but the Ministry of Agriculture rejected this proposal several days later. The committee asked the War Office whether it might divert some planned purchases of essential commodities, including food and oil, to Southeastern Europe, but the War Office replied that previous decisions to increase home and Dominions production ruled this out. In August, Sir Henry French of the Food Defence Plans department promised to look into purchases of Rumanian wheat. Plans to purchase Greek tobacco did not take concrete form until after Munich. Leith-Ross's preliminary draft of the committee's first interim report, prepared on October 14, noted that "For one reason or another none of the proposals considered has yet been found practical."[81]

The government's reluctance to offend Germany also affected the Interdepartmental Committee's work. Thus the government tried to keep the committee a secret rather than encourage the Southeastern Europeans by announcing it, and the Foreign Office was most unhappy when Paul Einzig published the news on June 13. Ingram refused to summon the British commercial attachés in Southeastern Europe for fear of creating an impression of "encirclement" of Germany, and he decided not to tell the French about the committee for the same reason. After news of the committee leaked out, the German press attacked it, and on July 8 Ingram, Ashton-Gwatkin, and Sargent urged Halifax to take advantage of a House of Lords debate on the Turkey

[81] See the Interdepartmental Committee meeting of July 1, 1938, War Office letter, July 16, Agriculture Ministry letter, July 18, Interdepartmental Committee meeting of Aug. 25, Leith-Ross's Oct. 14 draft, FO 371/22343-44, R6473/R6474/R6475/R7606/R8362/94/67.

credit to deny anti-German intentions in Southeastern Europe. Lord Stanhope, the president of the Board of Education, did so on July 18, denying German press reports that Britain wanted to eliminate Germany and Italy as customers in the Danubian and Balkan states and adding that the credit for Turkey "is not, of course, directed against any other country and is not part of any general policy such as that suggested in the newspaper articles to which I have referred."[82] The same fear of antagonizing Germany led London to refuse Rumanian Foreign Minister Tatarescu's June request that Leith-Ross visit Rumania to explore commercial opportunities. Ingram, Ashton-Gwatkin, and Sargent agreed that such a visit "would certainly be construed by the Geman government as part of a policy of encirclement" and "would raise hopes in Rumania that it would be impossible to fulfill." The Board of Trade concluded a new Anglo-Rumanian clearing agreement on September 2, to ensure continued service on British loans, but it dodged Rumanian proposals for large-scale, long-term British investments to develop Rumanian natural resources and industry.[83]

In September, events overtook the Interdepartmental Committee's leisurely deliberations. Prime Minister Chamberlain sought to bring British economic policy in Eastern Europe in line with his efforts to reach a settlement with Germany. Working with Sir Horace Wilson, he decided to concede to Germany a special position in Southeastern Europe as part of a general Anglo-German agreement. Wilson took the first step in this direction on August 23, during a conversation with Theodor Kordt, the German chargé d'affaires in London. After discussing Czechoslovakia, Wilson stressed the need to avoid an Anglo-German war. He then turned to Southeastern Europe.

A constructive solution of the Czech question by peaceful means would leave the way clear for Germany to exercise

[82] Leith-Ross to Cadogan, June 14, 1938, Farrar to FO, June 1, and minute by Ingram and Sargent, Ingram minute, June 2, FO 371/22342, R5703/R5362/R5389/94/67. On Stanhope's statement see the July 8 minutes by Ingram, Ashton-Gwatkin, and Sargent, ibid., R6233/94/67, and *PD*, Lords, 5th ser., CX, 401-3 (July 18, 1938).

[83] Leith-Ross-Tatarescu conversation and minutes, July 1938, FO to British legation Bucharest, July 6, FO 371/22457, R5760/R6040/94/67. See also the June 9 Rumanian government memorandum, FO 371/22456, R5428/223/37. On the negotiation of the clearing see FO 371/22457-58, R6376/R6663/R6885/R6933/R7391/223/37.

large-scale policy in the Southeast. He himself was not one of those who held the view that Germany wanted to organize Southeastern Europe and then to use its resources for the annihilation of the British Empire. In these areas he could see possibilities of action for Germany better than any that could be imagined. The Balkan countries were the natural buyers of German manufactured goods, and, on the other hand, were the natural sources of raw materials essential to Germany. There was no sense in sending a turkey from Budapest to London instead of to Berlin. Neither had Great Britain any intention of opposing a development of the German economy in a southeasterly direction. Her only wish was that she should not be debarred from trade there. There were a number of different products which Germany was not in a position to deliver to the Balkans. Britain wished to have her share in the Balkan trade in these commodities. The capital investments which Great Britain had recently made there were in no way intended as a weapon against German economy. Great Britain had realized that capital was needed in these countries, and it had been decided to divert capital there.[84]

Chamberlain decided to make a similar statement, if queried, while planning for his initial visit to Hitler. On September 10—days before the prime minister unveiled his plan to visit Hitler to the cabinet—Wilson wrote Cadogan, summarizing what Chamberlain planned to say. He included a prepared statement on Southeastern Europe, for use should Chamberlain be asked whether Britain's credit to Turkey meant "that you desire to block the extension of our economic development in Southeastern Europe."

Our offer of financial assistance to Turkey is in pursuance of our general policy of aiding the expansion of international

---

[84] *DGFP*, D, II, 382. The reference to Hungarian turkeys is striking; this was one of the concessions that the Interdepartmental Committee had discussed. Wilson did not report this conversation to the Foreign Office; there is evidence that he tried but failed to secure approval for an official statement along these lines. Thus, on Oct. 4, upon reading a preliminary report of Chamberlain's Sept. 30 conversation with Hitler, Vansittart commented: "I trust this is not a resurrection of Sir Horace Wilson's idea that we should give Germany some assurance in regard to Southeastern Europe which will lead all the countries concerned to think that we are morally abandoning them and recognizing a German preserve there" (FO 371/22344, R8003/94/67).

trade and whenever we find a good borrower our inclination is to facilitate international trade by the use of credit.

It must be obvious to everybody that the countries of South-eastern Europe to a very large extent form a natural market for the products of Germany just as Germany offers a natural market for the products of some of these countries. We should welcome an increase in the volume of trade between Germany and these countries. . . . There would of course be general objection to any attempt to intervene politically or militarily with these countries, but subject to this and to the maintenance of the "open door," we are ready to facilitate any increase in international trade in these regions.[85]

Even after Chamberlain's visit to Germany was announced, Cadogan did not impart this proposed declaration to his Foreign Office colleagues. Wilson also consulted Leith-Ross, who suggested that London offer to waive its treaty rights in Southeastern Europe "if at any time it appeared that our treaty rights in these countries hindered the development of their trade with Germany."[86] Before going to Berchtesgaden, Chamberlain did tell the cabinet that if Hitler asked about the Turkey credit he would deny any intention to hem Germany in: "other countries came to us and said that Germany had established a stranglehold over their trade. All these difficulties had arisen from the political situation and if only an understanding could be reached between the two countries, these matters could be easily settled."[87] Despite the routine practice of inserting relevant cabinet deliberations in Foreign Office files, the Foreign Office did not receive a copy of this statement.

Chamberlain made no such declaration at Berchtesgaden or Godesberg because Hitler did not mention the Turkey credit; instead, he insisted that the Czechoslovakia question must be settled before any other. In his private talk with Hitler in Munich

[85] Wilson to Cadogan, Sept. 10, 1938, PRO, PREM 1/265.

[86] On Sept. 30, after Ingram had learned of the proposed declaration, Cadogan wrote: "I regret that after the decision [for Chamberlain to visit Germany] was taken and had become known, I did not send this section of the paper to the Department." Ingram's minute of Sept. 29 quotes Leith-Ross's suggestion. Wilson or Chamberlain may have advised Cadogan not to inform his colleagues, knowing they would not agree; they almost certainly used this tactic with respect to subsequent initiatives by Leith-Ross. See FO 371/22344, R8044/94/67.

[87] Cabinet of Sept. 14, 1938, CAB 23/95.

on September 30, however, Chamberlain spontaneously raised
the question of "the relations between Germany and South-
Eastern Europe." "The suspicion that England desired not a military but an economic encirclement of Germany," he said, ". . .
was without foundation." He then asked whether Hitler had any
suggestions for improving international trade. Hitler in turn
noted the complementary nature of the German and Balkan
economies and, although postponing detailed discussion to an
indefinite future date, argued that the reconstruction of the
world economy depended on increased exchanges of goods, not
loans or tariffs. Chamberlain responded that loans would be
needed to facilitate trade between producers of primary products and producers of industrial goods.[88] Within a few weeks,
Leith-Ross would specifically offer Berlin more sterling with
which to increase trade with Southeastern Europe. Chamberlain
had agreed to form the Interdepartmental Committee under
pressure from Halifax. In his eagerness to reach a settlement
with Germany, he renounced its objective of containing German
economic power in Southeastern Europe.

Germany's annexation of the Sudetenland removed a crucial
military barrier to further German expansion eastward and
eliminated Germany's last major industrial competitor in Eastern European trade. Officials within the French and British
governments realized that Eastern Europe was lost. This conclusion emerged in deliberations within the British Foreign Office
in October 1938 and in Bonnet's attempts to loosen France's remaining alliances in Eastern Europe during the next few
months.

Members of the British Foreign Office had disagreed over the
policy that had led to Munich. Strang supported it, Cadogan
began to question it after Godesberg, and Collier and Vansittart,
though not major participants in the crisis, clearly opposed it. In
memoranda written in October in preparation for a presentation to the Foreign Policy Committee, all agreed upon its consequences: Eastern Europe was lost. "The Munich agreement and
what preceded it have laid Central and Southeastern Europe
open to German political and economic domination," Strang

[88] *DBFP*, 3, II, 1228.

wrote; this was now "inevitable and cannot be prevented by us, and in the economic sphere we should be ready not to stand on the strict letter of our rights." London should "try to maintain our position, both politically and economically, in Greece and Turkey. The Mediterranean and the Near East are of the first importance to us." Collier questioned the possibility of peace with Hitler, arguing that the Nazi regime would inevitably pursue expansion, but he added that Munich had made it impossible to organize a coalition that could restrain Hitler in Eastern Europe. "We must cut our losses in Central and Eastern Europe," wrote Cadogan; "let Germany, if she can, find there her 'Lebensraum,' and establish herself, if she can, as a powerful economic unit. I don't know that that necessarily worsens our commercial and economic outlook. . . . I know it is said that 'Mitteleuropa' will turn and rend us. But many things may happen before that." Although Cadogan wrote a memorandum embodying many of these conclusions, Halifax did not circulate it to the Foreign Policy Committee.[89] Nevertheless, he echoed these views in a November 1 letter to Phipps on future Anglo-French policy:

> One of the chief difficulties in the past has been the unreal position which France was occupying in Central and Eastern Europe. She claimed great influence in the policies of the Central European States in virtue of her system of alliances, but owing to the rising strength of Germany, and France's neglect of her own defences, she could no longer count upon being able to make her claims effective. At the same time, the fact of France making these claims was a continual irritant to Germany. With the conclusion of the Munich Agreement and the drastic change in French policy in Central Europe which that involves, Franco-German relations should have a fresh start.
>
> Henceforward we must count with German predominance in Central Europe. Incidentally I have always felt myself that once Germany recovered her normal strength, this predomi-

[89] For Cadogan's, Strang's, and Collier's memoranda, see FO 371/21659, C11471/42/18. They have been discussed in Donald Lammers, "From Whitehall after Munich: The Foreign Office and the Future Course of British Policy," *Historical Journal*, XVI, no. 4 (1973), 831-36. On Cadogan's views of Munich see Cadogan, *Diaries*, p. 114. His uncirculated memorandum of Nov. 8 is FO 371/21659, C14471/42/18.

nance was inevitable for obvious geographical and economic reasons.[90]

Georges Bonnet was already thinking along similar lines. On October 12 he told Phipps that he "contemplated shortly some revision of France's engagements towards Russia and Poland. . . . France, in a word, must no longer be exposed to the danger of being involved in a war on behalf of Soviet Russia or Poland as a result of circumstances over which she had no control." Bonnet discussed loosening or denouncing French obligations to Poland and the Soviet Union for several months, but French Ambassador Noël persuaded him that the potential value of Polish assistance in a Franco-German war ruled out such a drastic step.[91] In talks with Chamberlain on November 24, Bonnet downplayed the Franco-Soviet alliance, agreeing that a German-sponsored independence movement in the Ukraine would not bring it into play. During this conversation Daladier and Bonnet also agreed to the British proposal for a joint guarantee to Czechoslovakia, which would operate only if all the guarantors—including Germany—agreed to implement it.[92] Ribbentrop also raised the question of France's eastern alliances in talks with Bonnet in Paris on December 6, but we evidently shall never know exactly what Bonnet said. The German record of this talk states that after Ribbentrop said that Germany could no longer tolerate France's eastern alliances, Bonnet replied "that relations since Munich had fundamentally altered in this respect." The French record does not include this remark.[93] Bonnet ultimately decided against any definite step. He replied evasively on December 28 when Phipps asked him what France would do if Germany attacked Poland; three days later he told Phipps that he still wanted to "slacken" France's pacts with the Soviets and Poland but lacked the courage to make a new approach.[94]

[90] *DBFP*, 3, III, 285.
[91] British embassy Paris to FO, Oct. 12, 1938, FO 371/21612, C12161/1050/70; Georges Bonnet, *Defence de la paix*, Vol. II, *Fin d'une Europe* (Geneva, 1948), pp. 138-40; Noël, *Aggression allemande*, pp. 247-60.
[92] *DBFP*, 3, III, 325.
[93] *DGFP*, D, IV, 370; Adamthwaite, *France*, p. 291.
[94] British embassy Paris to FO, Dec. 28, 31, 1938, FO 371/21809, C16019/2688/55, FO 371/22912, C150/90/17. Bonnet, *Fin d'une Europe*, pp. 141-42, states

Obviously, 1938 did not see the end of great-power conflict in Eastern Europe. A new crisis broke out in March 1939 after the German occupation of Prague, and the Second World War began six months later when Germany attacked Poland. The French and British, however, could not resist German power in Eastern Europe after the war began; they had lost their last chance of doing so the previous year. War did not break out because of German attempts to establish hegemony in Eastern Europe. It began precisely because Hitler could not be satisfied with dominating the region peacefully and because the western powers finally recognized Hitler as a threat that they would have to deal with through war. The events of 1938 ensured that Hitler would fight the western powers with the resources of Eastern Europe at his disposal. As a result, he could only be defeated in a conflict fought on a world scale.[95]

---

that he continued to try to start discussions on revising the Franco-Polish alliance through March 1939, but without success.

[95] Murray, "Balance of Power, " argues provocatively that Britain and France would have defeated Germany had war broken out in 1938.

X.

Germany and Eastern Europe from Munich to War

The Munich agreement cleared the way for the establishment of a German-dominated sphere of influence in Eastern Europe.[1] With France and Britain in retreat, effective military resistance to Germany seemed impossible, and the annexation of the Sudetenland, and later of Bohemia-Moravia, made the region even more dependent on German industrial products and arms. Some within the German government, especially Helmut Wohlthat of the Four Year Plan, tried to take advantage of the situation by concluding new trade agreements with the successor states. Wohlthat hoped to stabilize German trade with Eastern Europe at an even higher level; he apparently regarded the creation of a new economic hinterland in Southeastern Europe as a possible solution to Germany's economic problems.

Such plans, however, could not succeed for two reasons. First, Eastern Europe simply could not supply Germany's economic needs. By 1939, German imports from that region had reached their upward limit. Second, Hitler himself was determined upon further expansion; he regarded the creation of the new Greater Germany as a prelude to the conquest of a huge land empire, and his policies militated against stabilization of trade with Eastern Europe. Rearmament continued to disturb normal trade, and the demands of the Wehrmacht limited arms exports. New territorial annexations and demands led in March 1939 to another confrontation with Britain and France, and in preparing for war with these two powers, Hitler had to look beyond Eastern Europe for essential supplies. Peacetime trade with Eastern Europe had helped to keep the German economy functioning for several crucial years, but such trade could play only a secondary role in the war that Hitler began in September 1939.

[1] Thus Felix Gilbert, in his "Mitteleuropa—The Final Stage," *Journal of Central European Affairs*, VII, no. 1 (1947), 58-67, noted that Hitler had seemingly attained Mitteleuropa after Munich.

German trade with Rumania was first to benefit from Germany's improved political position after Munich. Berlin valued trade with Rumania more highly than ever. In the summer of 1938 the Four Year Plan had adopted a new plan for meeting German petroleum needs. This plan, known as the Krauch plan after the IG Farben chemist who prepared it, foresaw that domestic synthetic production could not meet Germany's wartime needs and proposed to fill much of the gap with Rumanian imports. After Munich, Bucharest also showed interest in increasing trade; in October 1938 the German legation in Bucharest reported that the Rumanians were ready to stop diverting the maximum possible exports to hard-currency countries. Rumanian officials told German diplomats that a recent sale of 200,000 tons of wheat to Britain had been dictated only by the necessity of servicing foreign loans and that Rumania was ready to increase sales of cereals and oil to Germany. Negotiations began in early November and concluded one month later, after King Carol had visited both Britain and Germany. The agreement of December 10, 1938, called for total German imports from Rumania of 250.0 million RM for the twelve months beginning October 1, 1938—a significant increase over the total imports of 179.5 million RM in 1937 and 140.4 million RM in 1938. In order to secure 500,000 tons of desperately needed feed grains, the Germans contracted for 400,000 tons of less essential wheat and increased imports of Rumanian cattle, pigs, and timber. Bucharest undertook to subsidize these exports. The agreement again pegged oil exports at 25 percent of total German purchases through the German-Rumanian clearing, but it also provided for further exchanges of oil for German arms. After considerable bickering, the Germans agreed to an average clearing exchange rate of 41.0 lei to the reichsmark, compared with the 43.5 lei to the reichsmark that they had originally demanded. "The events of 1938 have led to a thoroughgoing change in Rumanian political conceptions," reported Carl Clodius of the Economic Department of the Foreign Office after concluding the negotiations in Bucharest. "The need for a measure of agreement with Germany has generally been accepted."[2]

[2] On the Krauch plan see Philippe Marguerat, *Le IIIème Reich et le pétrole roumain* (Leiden, 1977), pp. 18-21. On the negotiations see *DGFP*, D, V, 228, 231, 234, 236, 246, 247; for the agreement see T-120/7182/E527329-88; for Clodius's comment see T-120/2261/478818-22 (Dec. 13, 1938).

Three months later Berlin and Bucharest concluded a new agreement on the long-term development of the Rumanian economy. King Carol had first mentioned "systematic cooperation for the development of economic relations" to Göring in Leipzig on November 30, and Göring suggested the joint exploitation of Rumanian oil fields and other mineral deposits. Shortly thereafter, however, King Carol executed Corneliu Codreanu, the leader of the Rumanian fascist Iron Guard, and German-Rumanian relations cooled. In early February, after tension had eased, the king suggested that Wohlthat come to Bucharest to follow up his conversation with Göring. Carol received Wohlthat on February 13 and informed him that his government had prepared a program to link Rumanian economic development more closely to German needs. The program included consultation to tailor Rumanian agricultural production to fit German requirements, formation of a German-Rumanian oil company, joint exploitation of Rumanian mineral deposits and forests, cooperation between Rumanian and German industry, and German assistance in developing Rumanian arms production.[3]

Within the Wilhelmstrasse, Clodius and Wiehl doubted the ultimate value of these proposals. In their view, it was essential, above all, to ensure that promised oil deliveries took place as specified in the November 1938 agreement. Wohlthat, however, had more sweeping plans. An ambitious bureaucrat, given to overstating the importance of his work, he clearly hoped to make a name for himself as the economic reorganizer of Southeastern Europe. He indicated in a February 27 memorandum for Göring that he regarded a German-Rumanian treaty as the first step in a new, far-reaching policy:

> The present policy will secure us a predominant influence with specifically German methods without our having to revert to the old type of trade policy with unconditional most-favored-nation treatment and the gold standard. The stabilizing of exchange rates between the Reichsmark and the national currencies involved opens new possibilities for the international position of the Reichsmark. The financing of the harvests and the production of Southeastern Europe by diverting foreign capital, especially from the London market,

---

[3] Andreas Hillgruber, *Hitler, König Carol, und Marschall Antonescu. Die deutsche-rumänische Beziehunger, 1938-1944* (Wiesbaden, 1954), pp. 28-34; *DGFP*, D, V, 256, 293; German legation Bucharest to AA, Feb. 2, 1939, T-120/2261/478823.

via Berlin would open further possibilities for expanding the German transit trade. The raising of the living standard in Southeastern Europe would come about in direct relation to Greater Germany. The German position in the conflict with the economic interests of the British Empire and North America would be strengthened. The political development of the national states in Southeastern Europe will follow the German pattern to an increasing extent, while the influence of the western European democracies and the Soviet Union would be eliminated.[4]

Wohlthat returned to Bucharest on March 8 with instructions to conclude a new treaty. He reported on March 16 that Rumanian Foreign Minister Grigore Gafencu wanted to come to Berlin to sign a political agreement, under which Rumania would promise not to join any anti-German coalition in return for a guarantee of Rumanian frontiers. This initiative must almost certainly have been the inspiration for statements on March 17 by Viorel V. Tilea, the Rumanian minister to Great Britain, to the effect that Germany had demanded a monopoly of Rumanian exports in exchange for a guarantee of Rumania's frontiers. Although this rumor, which Gafencu quickly denied, disturbed the political situation, Wohlthat and the Rumanians signed an economic treaty on March 23 along the lines of the original Rumanian proposals for economic cooperation. It provided for joint planning and development of Rumanian agriculture, forestry, and oil resources and included a secret protocol promising a German credit of at least 200 million RM for arms and transportation and communications equipment.[5]

The German government took steps to implement this new treaty, particularly after London announced a commercial mission to Rumania led by Leith-Ross. Berlin and Bucharest concluded an agreement on the joint exploitation of Rumanian state forests on May 13 and signed a further agreement on July 20, under which the Rumanians promised to plan their agricultural production to meet German needs. Secret talks on the formation of a German-Rumanian oil company began during the summer

[4] *DGFP*, D, V, 294, 298, 306.
[5] Ibid., D, VI, 30, 78, 131; Gramsch memorandum, Mar. 16, 1939, T-120/2104/455796-97. On the rumors of a German ultimatum to Rumania see below, Chapter XI.

but did not bear fruit until November. As Wohlthat wrote Göring on March 30, he hoped to conclude similar long-term treaties with Yugoslavia, Bulgaria, Hungary, Greece, and Turkey: "On the basis of such a treaty system, I will propose to stabilize the rate of exchange between the reichsmark and the other currencies involved, to make possible a German-controlled clearing system extending over the whole of the Southeast."[6]

Under Göring's direction, the German government had already begun working on a major new agreement with Yugoslavia. In the fall of 1938 the Yugoslav clearing balance had reached 30 million RM, and Belgrade finally decided in early 1939 to purchase large quantities of German arms in order to reduce the balance. Göring's personal representative in Belgrade, Franz Neuhasen, reached a tentative agreement on a long-term credit of 200 million RM for land and air armaments in early February, but Foreign Minister Joachim von Ribbentrop delayed its conclusion for several months. Although Economic Department Director Emil Wiehl welcomed the opportunity to break into the Yugoslav arms market, Ribbentrop protested that the agreement had been concluded without his knowledge. He arbitrarily cut the credit in half, and when Yugoslav Foreign Minister Aleksander Cincar-Marković visited Berlin in late April, he tried to insist upon Yugoslav accession to the Anti-Comintern Pact as a condition of receiving it. After Cincar-Marković refused, Göring repeated his offer of a 200-million-RM credit, and Ribbentrop gave in. The two countries reached agreement in late June.[7]

Hungary also proposed a long-term economic agreement with Germany in early 1939, but in this case some of the problems inherent in Wohlthat's policies began to emerge. In January, Budapest proposed a ten-year treaty to plan the two countries'

---

[6] On the new agreements see: the interdepartmental meeting of Mar. 28, 1939, T-71/130/633818-20; German legation Bucharest to AA, May 13, and agricultural agreement of July 20, T-120/7182/E527495, 523-41; T-71/130/633824-961. Wohlthat's letter is T-120/1100/455752-59; clearly, he included Greece, Turkey, and Bulgaria in his definition of Southeastern Europe.

[7] German legation Belgrade to AA, Oct. 20, Dec. 10, 1938, T-120/5655/H007079-80; *DGFP*, D, V, 288, 290, 300, 307, VI, 262, 279, 573; AA to German legation Belgrade, Apr. 29, 1939, T-120/5570/398865-67; protocol of July 5, T-120/8045/E578364-67.

economies in a complementary manner. Wiehl replied in February that he saw no way of increasing the German share of Hungarian exports beyond the present 46 percent and that German exports to Hungary could increase only if the Hungarians limited their industrialization. This they steadfastly refused to do.[8] German trade with Hungary had reached its upper limit.

Obstacles to increased trade with Rumania and Yugoslavia also emerged during 1939. The German economy and German foreign trade had entered into a new crisis—a crisis leading inexorably to a choice between slower rearmament and war. Hitler's emphasis on rearmament was once again responsible. In October 1938 the Economic and Armaments Office of the War Ministry noted that accelerated rearmament and the construction of fortifications in the west had led to "overemployment" within the German economy. Labor shortages were becoming critical, reaching 1,000,000 workers in agriculture and 600,000 in industry by March 1939.[9] Moreover, world depression and the overexpansion of the economy was hurting Germany's trade balance. Imports exceeded exports during 1938 for the first time since 1934, and Göring suggested in mid-October 1938 that exports would have to increase by about 20 percent during the coming year. The annexation of Austria and the Sudetenland aggravated this problem; both territories had substantial import needs that Germany could not meet, and both lost exports as their productive capacity was diverted to meet internal German needs.[10]

In late 1938 Hitler rejected pleas from Schacht, Walther Funk, Göring, and Finance Minister Schwerin von Krosigk to slow down rearmament; instead, he dismissed Schacht from the Reichsbank in January 1939. In a January speech to the Reichstag he proclaimed, "We must export or die." Göring did what he could to increase exports during 1939, but the demands

---

[8] *DGFP*, D, V, 252, 272; Wiehl memorandum, Feb. 9, 1939, T-120/2452/D515347-55; Agriculture Ministry memorandum, Feb. 15, PA, Ha Pol IVa Ungarn, Handel 13a, Bd. 4; Clodius memorandum, Apr. 21, T-120/2999/D587651-53.

[9] Economic report, Economic and Armaments Office, War Ministry, Oct. 1, 1938, T-77/126/856654-69; meeting of Göring's Generalrat, Feb. 1, 1939, T-84/146/1449970-77 (National Archives series T-84 is cited series/reel [not serial]/frame).

[10] Göring memorandum, Oct. 15, 1938, T-77/131/863263-68; economic report, Economic and Armaments Office, Nov. 1, 1938, T-77/126/856621-33.

of rearmament made it difficult to expand normal exports, while the requirements of the German armed forces restricted arms exports.[11] The strategy of exchanging arms for Eastern European raw materials and agricultural products began to break down.

Arms deliveries emerged as a problem in German-Rumanian trade after the German occupation of Bohemia and Moravia in March 1939. Rumania had placed large orders with the Czech arms industry; if the Germans canceled these orders, the German trade balance with Rumania would suffer. On March 18, three days after the German occupation, the Rumanian government complained that large supplies of war materials had been held up at the border between Rumania and Czechoslovakia. Berlin authorized the shipments to proceed on March 23. When Rumanian Foreign Minister Gafencu visited Berlin in late April, the Germans promised that deliveries would continue, but King Carol complained on May 6 that this promise had not been kept. The Germans had requisitioned a great deal of material for themselves. "Having regard to the extensive requirements of the German Army itself," Clodius wrote on May 10, "possible deliveries [to Rumania] will be on a small scale." Bucharest promptly asked for late-model German aircraft as a condition of fulfilling the new German-Rumanian economic agreements and hinted broadly that further shipments of oil depended on German arms deliveries.[12] After discussing this issue with the Oberkommando der Wehrmacht (OKW), Wiehl wrote on July 3 that arms exports to Rumania would depend on three factors: Germany's own arms needs, the possibility of supplying other Balkan countries to a comparable extent, and Germany's need for "raw materials of military importance," specifically, oil. The third consideration prevailed. Clodius concluded a new agreement in Bucharest on July 8. In exchange for German aircraft, the Rumanians agreed to provide an additional

[11] Wendt, *Economic Appeasement*, pp. 533-36; Mason, "Innere Krise," pp. 160-62. On the problem of arms exports see the economic report of Nov. 1, 1938, T-77/126/856621-33, and the June 5, 1939, meeting of Göring's Reichsverteidigungsausschuss, T-77/131/863035-62. Desperation characterizes many of the internal discussions on the German economy in late 1938 and early 1939; see also the Reichsverteidigungsausschuss meeting of Nov. 18, 1938, T-77/131/863088-158.

[12] *DGFP*, D, VI, 31, 337, 354; German legation Bucharest to AA, May 13, 1939, T-120/2248/D515046, T-120/2661/478844-46.

30-million-RM worth of oil by the end of 1939, compared with 36-million-RM worth for the whole of 1938.[13]

In late July the issue of arms for Eastern Europe engaged the interest of Hitler himself. On July 22 the OKW informed interested ministries that Hitler did not approve of arms deliveries to "hostile countries or to States whose attitude in time of war was doubtful"; distant, friendly, or neutral countries, including South American states, the Baltic states, Norway, and Bulgaria, should have priority. Thus Hitler had canceled deliveries of late-model aircraft to Rumania and a shipment of Czech anti-tank guns to Yugoslavia. The vital importance of Rumanian oil led to the partial reversal of this decision; Wiehl argued that Germany would have to ration gasoline if the cancellation of the aircraft deliveries led to a stoppage of oil imports, and Göring authorized the aircraft shipments to proceed on July 30. Lacking an equally vital export, Yugoslavia did not fare as well. On July 30 Clodius informed the Yugoslav government that its promised arms deliveries would have to be reconsidered in light of German needs. Göring approved the previously agreed-upon deliveries on August 24, but on September 11—after Belgrade had declared neutrality in the war—he refused to commit himself to any specific delivery dates.[14]

Other problems in German-Rumanian trade suggest that Wohlthat's goal of stabilizing clearing exchange rates could not be achieved. Although the Rumanians had agreed to increase exports to Germany, they still needed hard currency to buy more raw materials, and in the spring of 1939 they again began juggling the value of the lei in order to encourage exports to hard-currency countries. In April, Berlin protested that Bucharest had effectively devalued the lei in relation to other currencies while leaving its relation to the reichsmark un-

[13] Wiehl memorandum, July 3, T-120/2104/455677; see also the OKW memorandum of June 24, T-120/5555/E395332-33. On the new agreement see *DGFP*, D, VI, 621, 632, 638, 639; for the figures of oil imports, *SJB, 1939-40*, p. 308.

[14] Memoranda by OKW and Wiehl, July 22, 1939, *DGFP*, D, VI, 703; AA to German legation Bucharest, July 30, T-120/2448/D515095; Marguerat, *Pétrole roumain*, pp. 137-38, 149-51; German legation Bucharest to AA, Aug. 19, 25, 28, T-120/2448/D515097-100, T-120/8449/E594905-7. Oil deliveries continued to lag behind German wishes. On Yugoslavia see AA to German legation Belgrade, July 30, T-120/5570/E398969, *DGFP*, D, VII, 240, 241, and Wiehl memorandum, Sept. 11, T-120/2162/470748-50.

changed; Rumanian prices had risen, and Rumanian products had become too expensive to Germany. The Germans asked that the lei be depreciated by about 20 percent in relation to the reichsmark. The Rumanians refused, and in June they once again began restricting cereals exports to Germany.[15]

Thus, despite Berlin's various new agreements, including further economic agreements with the Baltic states,[16] Wohlthat's plans to stabilize and increase German trade with Eastern Europe could not succeed. The successor states would continue, when possible, to divert exports to free-exchange countries, and the Germans could not maintain a steady supply of exports in return. Most important, Eastern European exports to Germany had reached their upper limit by 1939. The Mitteleuropäische Wirtschaftstag, an association of German industrialists established to foster trade with Southeastern Europe, succinctly discussed these problems in an August 12, 1939, memorandum for the German Economics Ministry entitled "Southeastern Europe as an Economic Complement to Germany."[17]

The memorandum began by noting that German trade with the agricultural states of Southeastern Europe had generally stabilized since 1938. Any new increase would depend on increasing German export capacity and improving Southeastern European production and transportation. German exports had never received sufficient attention; the expansion of German trade with Southeastern Europe had begun in 1934 as an "import campaign," not an export offensive. German imports had now reached the limit of Southeastern European productive capacity, and Germany could not supply enough exports in return. The absorption of Austria, the Sudetenland, and the rest of Bohemia-Moravia had not solved these problems but had instead increased the successor states' need to divert trade away from Germany.

[15] Clodius memoranda, Apr. 4, 12, 1939, Clodius letter, May 20, Clodius memorandum, June 17, T-120/7182/E526433-34, T-120/2661/478830-33, T-120/2104/455728, T-120/2103/455696.

[16] See the German-Estonian agreement of Oct. 31, 1938, PA, Ha Pol Vb Estland, Handel 13; German-Latvian protocol, Nov. 4, T-120/5920/E435261-64; German-Lithuanian protocol, May 20, 1939, T-120/9290/E659319-26. All three provided for across-the-board increases in the Baltic states' major exports to Germany.

[17] For the memorandum and accompanying tables see T-71/60/557727-979. On the founding of the Mitteleuropäische Wirtschaftstag see above, Chapter II.

Germany now cannot or will not supply a whole range of goods which the southeastern countries depend on, either because she needs them herself or must pay foreign exchange for them. This applies for example to cotton and wool and cotton and wool yarns, which the southeastern countries, prior to recent political changes, obtained from Austria, the Sudetenland, and Bohemia-Moravia. To obtain these goods the southeastern countries must attempt to place a certain portion of their exports in free exchange countries.

Customs or currency unions with these countries would serve no useful purpose;[18] Germany would have to supply their raw-materials needs at the cost of precious foreign exchange. In the future, more care would have to be taken to supply sufficient German exports and avoid familiar cases of "insufficient sales, false sales, or sales necessary because of clearing difficulties." Implicitly referring to the German labor shortage, the memorandum argued that Germany should concentrate on exports of goods for which worker productivity was very high; exports in labor-intensive industries, such as coal, had fallen or even ceased.

To what extent could Southeastern Europe supply a higher proportion of the foodstuffs that Germany imported? At present, the memorandum noted, Germany still imported most necessary agricultural products from Northern Europe and overseas; in 1937 the total agricultural exports of Southeastern Europe would have supplied only about one-third of German needs. Future increases depended on dramatic improvements in the productivity of Southeastern European agriculture, improvements that would take time. "The possibilities for German trade in the southeastern economic realm," the memorandum concluded, "can be very favorably estimated, insofar as it is possible to achieve the same increase in production per unit here as Northeastern Europe has already attained during the last one hundred years."

Thus, substantial increases in the Eastern European share of German trade, such as the increase to 25 percent that Wohlthat had proposed to Göring earlier in the year, would take years to

[18] Interestingly enough, a Nov. 22, 1938, memorandum by the Mitteleuropäische Wirtschaftstag had supported economic unions with southeastern states; see T-77/174/908653-77.

achieve and would also require some diversion of German productive capacity to normal exports. A substantial period of peace would thus be necessary. Hitler, however, had other ideas. By the spring of 1939, renewed territorial expansion in Eastern Europe had led to a new confrontation with Britain and France. The threat of war put Germany's economic problems in a new light.

Germany's new confrontation with France and Britain in March 1939—only six months after Munich—grew out of Hitler's attempts to dispose of several remaining territorial questions in Eastern Europe, including the return of Memel, the occupation of the remainder of Bohemia-Moravia, and the return of Danzig and the modification of the status of the Polish Corridor. To Hitler, all these changes followed logically from the western powers' recognition of the German people's right to self-determination and a German sphere of influence in Eastern Europe. Hitler interpreted the Anglo-German declaration of September 30, 1938, under which the two countries pledged to settle disputes through consultation and expressed their determination never to go to war again, as a British undertaking not to intervene against German expansion eastward. After visiting Paris in December 1938, Ribbentrop argued that Bonnet had also renounced interest in Eastern Europe.[19] Hitler therefore began rounding out the edges of the new Greater Germany, preparatory to the conquest of *Lebensraum* in the east.

The problem of Memelland was the simplest of the three remaining questions. The Memelland Germans were expecting their return to the Reich; elections scheduled for December 1938 would surely produce a heavily pro-annexationist Landtag. On December 1 a meeting of Wilhelmstrasse officials, Memel German leader Dr. Neumann, and officials of the Volksdeutsche Mittelstelle (VOMI), an SS organization dealing with Germans abroad, decided that the new Landtag would proclaim Anschluss with Germany on the basis of self-determination. Ribbentrop, however, suggested delaying any move until German-Polish relations had been settled; otherwise, Poland might demand compensation at Lithuania's expense. After the Germans

[19] On Ribbentrop's visit see above, Chapter IX.

won their election victory on December 11, the French and British governments offered Berlin their cooperation in ensuring that Lithuania respected the Memel statute. Ribbentrop indirectly replied that Memel was "an Eastern Question for Germany, that did not concern France and England at all."[20]

In December, Hitler personally told Neumann that the Memel question would be settled in late March or April 1939. Neumann requested instructions on February 23, 1939, noting that the new Landtag would meet no later than March 17. No orders seem to have been conveyed to the Memellanders through diplomatic channels, but they proclaimed incorporation into the Reich on March 15, after the German annexation of Bohemia-Moravia. They may have acted spontaneously, or they may have received instructions through the VOMI. On March 23 the Lithuanian government agreed to a treaty of incorporation, which included the promise of a free port in Memel and new German-Lithuanian economic arrangements.[21]

The complex issues surrounding the newly created rump state of Czecho-Slovakia may be studied in detail elsewhere.[22] Hitler had never expected the situation created by the Munich agreement, and it took him some time to determine his next move. On October 21 he asked the armed forces to prepare "to smash the remainder of the Czech State, should it pursue an anti-German policy"; on December 17 he issued slightly more precise instructions to prepare for the peaceful occupation of the remainder of the Czech state; and at some time in January he expressed his intention of falling upon the Czechs to SD leader Reinhard Heydrich. In early March he decided to force the issue.

On March 13 Hitler persuaded Slovak politicians with whom the Germans had long been in conflict to declare the independence of Slovakia, threatening them with Hungarian occupation if they did not. To conciliate Budapest, he apparently suggested the immediate occupation of Ruthenia. Then, on the night of March 14-15, Hitler received Czech President Emil Hácha in

[20] *DGFP*, D, V, 364, 369, 376, 378, 379. In mid-December Wiehl and Ritter discussed a possible German-Lithuanian customs union; see ibid., no. 380, and T-120/2142/468403-4.

[21] *DGFP*, D, V, 381, 394, 395, 399, 402, 403, 404, 405.

[22] See especially Jorg K. Hoensch, *Die Slowakei und Hitlers Ostpolitik. Hlinkas Slowakische Volkspartei zwischen Autonomie und Separation, 1938/1939* (Cologne and Graz, 1965).

Berlin. Hácha declared that Czechoslovakia could not continue to exist, and he pleaded for a new accommodation between Germans and Czechs. Hitler promised generous treatment but added that German troops would enter Bohemia-Moravia the next day, peacefully or otherwise. On March 15 Hácha "placed the fate of the Czech people and country in the hands of the Führer of the German Reich." Hitler created the protectorate of Bohemia-Moravia.[23]

In the meantime, new German-Polish negotiations had begun. Beck had initiated these discussions at the very height of the crisis over Czechoslovakia. Taking advantage of Germany's exposed position, he sought new guarantees for the German-Polish frontier in return for his cooperative anti-Czechoslovak attitude. Following instructions, Lipski met Ribbentrop on September 16 and proposed an extension of the German-Polish Non-Aggression Declaration, a new German declaration of respect for the Polish frontier, corresponding to Hitler's April 20, 1938, assurance to Italy regarding the South Tyrol, and an agreement to settle the status of Danzig without reference to the League of Nations. Lipski also tried to raise these points with Hitler on September 20 at Berchtesgaden after discussing Polish claims on Czechoslovakia, but Hitler cut him off.[24]

On October 24 Lipski met Ribbentrop to discuss the creation of a common Polish-Hungarian frontier—the key to Beck's plans for a "third Europe," which would include Poland, Hungary, Italy, and perhaps Rumania and Yugoslavia. Ribbentrop countered with new German demands: Danzig must return to the Reich, with Poland retaining its economic rights there; the two countries would recognize their respective boundaries, extend the nonaggression declaration to twenty-five years, and add a consultation clause; and Germany would build an extraterritorial road and railway across the Corridor. On the day before, Hitler himself had discussed this last provision with Fritz Todt, the director of German highway construction. "The traffic at present using the transit route on the basis of the Treaty of Paris," he noted, "involves considerable expenditures of foreign exchange and is greatly hampered by control measures."[25] Thus

---

[23] Ibid., pp. 208-24, 289-306; *DGFP*, D, IV, 99, 198, 199, 228, 229.

[24] Wojciechowski, *Polnisch-deutschen Beziehungen*, pp. 467-74; Cienciala, *Poland and the Western Powers*, pp. 105-19.

[25] Cienciala, *Poland and the Western Powers*, pp. 154-55; *DGFP*, D, V, 81, 86.

Germany's foreign-exchange shortage played a direct role in provoking the crisis that led to the Second World War.

Discussions of these proposals continued through March 1939. They spelled disaster for Beck, if not for Poland. Since 1934, Beck had based his policy on German friendship, often in the face of substantial domestic opposition. Beck delayed a definite reply for several months; Ribbentrop bribed and threatened. On January 9 Ribbentrop dangled German support for possible Polish designs upon the Ukraine before Beck; on January 26 he urged Beck to settle on this "extremely moderate basis," arguing pointedly that 99 out of 100 Frenchmen or Englishmen would support the return of Danzig and the entire Corridor to Germany. Discussions picked up after the German occupation of Bohemia-Moravia; Hitler's decision to assume the protection of an independent Slovakia disturbed Warsaw. Lipski gave Ribbentrop Beck's final reply on March 26. Warsaw would accept a joint German-Polish guarantee of an independent Danzig and improved transit facilities across the Corridor *without* extraterritoriality. Ribbentrop did not believe this to be Beck's last word.[26]

Hitler had not yet planned to attack Poland. In a March 25 military directive he denied any intention to "drive Poland into Britain's arms" by resolving the Danzig question by force or to solve "the Polish question." On the other hand, he referred to drastic, long-term plans for Poland, including German annexation and colonization of large areas of Poland—plans that could be realized under "especially favorable political preconditions." This statement, combined with the reference to Danzig, may have been the source of the rumors of an imminent Danzig coup that reached London on March 29. Two days later Chamberlain told the House of Commons that Britain would assist Poland militarily if Germany threatened Polish independence.[27]

Hitler reacted to Chamberlain's declaration in much the same way as he had responded to the May crisis in 1938. Abandoning his moderate attitude toward Poland, he decided to show all the interested parties that Britain and France could not thwart his will in Eastern Europe. On April 6 Ribbentrop told Lipski that Berlin's offer would not be repeated. Speaking to the Reichstag

---

[26] *DGFP*, D, V, 101, 112, 113, 119, 120, 126, VI, 61, 101.
[27] Ibid., VI, 99. On Chamberlain's decision see below, Chapter XI.

on April 28, Hitler publicly revealed this offer, announced that it had been withdrawn, and denounced both the German-Polish Non-Aggression Declaration of 1934 and the Anglo-German Naval Agreement of 1935. He had concluded the latter agreement, he stated, on the assumption that Britain and Germany would never again make war against each other; Chamberlain's declaration had destroyed that assumption.[28]

Germany now had to prepare for war with the western powers. Hitler was hardly more confident of the result of war with Britain and France in 1939 than he had been in 1938. In an April 11 directive he stated that Germany must isolate Poland before attacking it, and he told military leaders on May 23 that Germany alone could not fight Poland, France, Britain, and perhaps the Soviet Union.[29] Given Chamberlain's guarantee to Poland, Hitler could no longer pretend that Britian and France would not fight. The German government had to deter or break up the coalition that Hitler feared to face; it also had to solve the problem of sustaining the German economy in wartime. During the spring and summer of 1939 an accommodation with the Soviet Union emerged as the solution to the problems posed by the impending war.

In 1938, under the threat of war with Britain and France, various German government agencies had prepared studies of German access to vital raw materials in the event of war. During 1939 the Economic and Armaments Office of the War Ministry continued to receive such studies from various sources, including the Reichsamt für Wehrwirtschaftliche Planung, or Reich Office of War Economic Planning (a section of the Reich Statistical Office), the Wehrwirtschaftliche Forschungstelle, or War Economy Research Office, and private interest groups, including IG Farben. These studies generally assumed that Germany and Italy would find themselves at war with France, Britain, and perhaps the Soviet Union. Because the western powers would control the seas, Germany would have to depend on contiguous

---

[28] *DGFP*, VI, 167; *Hitler's Speeches*, II, 1623-26, 1628-33. At Berchtesgaden on Sept. 15, 1938, Hitler had told Chamberlain that the Anglo-German Naval Agreement would lapse if Britain undertook anti-German intervention (*DBFP*, 3, II, 896).

[29] *DGFP*, D, VI, 185, 433.

territories for foodstuffs and raw materials. Many of these studies dealt extensively with the importance of Eastern Europe to the German war economy.

In general, these reports suggested that although Eastern Europe could play an important role in supplying Germany's wartime needs, other sources of supply would be necessary. Some studies suggested that the Southeastern Europe states could supply Germany's total cereals needs, but only by diverting their entire export surpluses to Germany, thereby creating shortages in other parts of Europe.[30] Rumania's unexploited oil reserves might eventually fill Germany's oil requirements, but only German military occupation could ensure their exploitation and diversion to Germany on a sufficiently large scale. Yugoslavia and Hungary could contribute some bauxite, lead, and zinc, but many other vital imports, including oil seeds, iron ore, and other key metals, were not available in Eastern Europe at all.[31]

Other factors made Eastern Europe even less able to supply German needs in wartime than in peacetime. One RWP study noted that fully half of Germany's trade with Southeastern Europe traveled by sea through the Mediterranean and ultimately to German North Sea ports. It would be difficult or impossible to divert all this trade to river or rail routes during a war with Britain and France. An extremely significant IG Farben study, written during the summer of 1939, compared Southeastern Europe and the Soviet Union as sources of raw materials. The Soviet Union showed significant advantages. It contained more of the products Germany needed, and transport overland and through the Baltic Sea would remain secure in the event of war with Britain and France.[32] The memorandum foreshadowed the direction that German policy would take.

Significantly, German economic authorities had already rec-

[30] Wehrwirtschaftliche Forschungstelle study, "The State of Cereals and Flour Production in Greater Germany and the Greater Economic Sphere [Grossraumwirtschaft]," Dec. 8, 1938, T-77/405/1258957-89.

[31] Wehrwirtschaftstab study, "Die Mineralölversorgung Deutschlands im Kriege," April 1939, T-77/201/936950-7014; Reichsamt für Wehrwirtschaftliche Planung, "Die rohstoffwirtschaftliche Bedeutung des Südostraums für die deutsche Wehrwirtschaft," March 1939, T-84/80/1367771-860.

[32] Reichsamt für Wehrwirtschaftliche Planung, "Bedeutung des Südostraume"; IG Farben memorandum, "Der deutsche Rohstoffbezug aus der USSR and Südosteuropa," undated, T-84/80/1367890-912 (the T-84 index lists the date as "about 1939"; it seems to predate the Nazi-Soviet Pact).

ognized the importance of the Soviet Union. In November 1938 Göring noted the need to turn to the Soviets for supplies of vital raw materials. German-Soviet trade had run to hundreds of millions of reichmarks annually under the Weimar Republic but had fallen to trivial amounts since 1933. Berlin could no longer afford the ideological luxury of restricting it. In December 1938 Berlin asked Moscow for 300-million-RM worth of raw materials over the next two years, including feed grains, timber, and oil seeds, in exchange for long-term orders of German industrial products. One difficulty in dealing with the Soviets was that promised deliveries had to be made. Wiehl noted on December 1 that negotiators must consult carefully with German industry to ensure that promised products would be available. After some hesitation the Soviets in February 1939 offered 200-million-RM worth of raw materials over two years. On March 11, however, the HPA decided not to accept the offer; German industry, overworked as it was, could not promise to meet Soviet wishes. The Germans would keep the talks open, pursuing them more actively if German export capacity improved. Although Berlin tried to revive the talks after the occupation of Bohemia-Moravia, Molotov, who had replaced Litvinov as foreign commissar earlier in May, replied on May 20 that the two countries would have to establish a new "political basis" before economic discussions could resume.[33]

Molotov's meaning was not hard to discern. Despite his simultaneous alliance negotiations with Britain and France, he was offering Germany an accommodation, presumably on the basis of a delineation of interests in Eastern Europe. Such an accommodation would clear the way for war with Britain and France, but it would also require a reversal of German foreign policy. Thus, in his conversation with military leaders on May 23, Hitler stated that Germany would avoid war with Britain, France, and the Soviet Union but added that he planned to deter the enemy powers by concluding an alliance of Germany, Italy, and Japan. Negotiations for such an alliance—originally undertaken by Ribbentrop in June 1938—had been proceeding in earnest since January 1939. However, while Hitler counted on this alliance to

[33] *DGFP*, D, IV, 479, 482, 479, 490, 491, 492, 493, 494, 495, VI, 322, 424. For a detailed list of German desiderata in December 1938 see T-120/2092/ 452581-82.

intimidate Britain and France, the Japanese government consistently refused to promise to assist Germany in a war against these two powers. Although talks dragged on until August, by June it was clear that Tokyo would not accept this essential condition.[34]

Evidence suggests that Hitler then determined to solve his diplomatic and economic problems through accommodation with Moscow. In mid-June, Berlin proposed to reopen talks; in late July, German and Soviet officials began discussing specific political questions, including Poland, the Baltic states, and Rumania; by August 14, the Germans had offered to send Ribbentrop to Moscow to delineate spheres of influence in Eastern Europe. German and Soviet negotiators agreed on August 17 and 18 to an economic agreement, a neutrality or nonaggression pact, and a discussion of spheres of influence. On August 19 they signed an economic agreement calling for the delivery of 180-million-RM worth of Soviet foodstuffs and raw materials over the next two years, including feed grains, oil cakes, petroleum products, and timber. Finally, on August 23, Ribbentrop and Molotov signed a nonaggression pact in Moscow. A secret protocol defined spheres of interest in Poland, assigned Estonia and Latvia to the Soviet sphere of interest, and expressed German disinterest in the Rumanian province of Bessarabia.[35]

As Hitler told German military leaders on August 22, he could now attack Poland and risk war with Britain and France. His comments reflect the economic importance of the Nazi-Soviet Pact. They also suggest that Germany's economic situation inclined Hitler toward an immediate war:

> It is easy for us to make decisions. We have nothing to lose; we have everything to gain. Because of our restrictions

[34] *DGFP*, D, VI, 473. On the negotiations for a German-Italian-Japanese alliance see the excellent study by Theo Sommer, *Deutschland und Japan zwischen den Mächten 1935-40* (Tübingen, 1962), pp. 94-296; see also Frank W. Iklé, "Japan's Policies towards Germany," in James William Morley, ed., *Japan's Foreign Policy, 1868-1941* (New York, 1974), pp. 265-339. The Japanese army favored the alliance; the Foreign Ministry and the navy leadership opposed it.

[35] On the negotiations see *DGFP*, D, VI, 530, 543, 628, 642, 647, 685, 700, 729, 736, VII, 18, 50, 56, 105, 113, 131. For the economic agreement see ibid., VII, 135, and T-120/8379/E591220-21. After war began, new agreements provided for much larger Soviet deliveries of raw materials; see Philipp W. Fabry, *Die Sowjetunion und das Dritte Reich* (Stuttgart, 1971), pp. 155-219. For the political agreement see *DGFP*, D, VII, 228, 229.

[Einschränkungen] our economic situation is such that we can only hold out for a few more years. Göring can confirm this. We must act. . . . The East will supply us with grain, cattle, coal, lead and zinc.[36]

Although ready for war, Hitler still hoped that Britain might stand aside; in the same talk, he interpreted London's failure to lend Poland money as evidence that Chamberlain did not mean his guarantee seriously. He ordered an attack on Poland for August 26. But on August 25 he received two shocks: the signing of the formal Anglo-Polish alliance, and Mussolini's defection from war against Britain and France. Hitler had already sent Sir Nevile Henderson home to London with a proposal to guarantee the British Empire; now he postponed the attack on Poland. Although Göring pressured him heavily during the next few days to make a new deal with Britain, Hitler seems definitely to have renounced a peaceful solution of the Polish question. The new German offer to Poland that Ribbentrop read to Henderson on the night of August 30, which called for the return of Danzig and a plebiscite in the Corridor, was too generous to be meant seriously. That Ribbentrop read it only after the expiration of a German deadline for the arrival of a Polish negotiator in Berlin probably was not accidental. Hitler *hoped* to separate Britain from Poland, but he had decided on war.[37]

The attack on Poland began the conquest of *Lebensraum*. Although the end of the peacetime struggle for influence in Eastern Europe marks the close of this study, the course of German policy during 1938-1939, raises several additional questions that deserve some consideration. It is clear that Hitler had always planned a great war, but did he begin one in 1939 partly for economic reasons? If so, how did the course of the war ease Germany's economic problems? And what role did trade with Eastern Europe play in the new wartime context?

We have seen that a serious economic crisis had developed in Germany during 1938-1939, involving huge labor shortages, inadequate exports, and a generally overheated economy. In late

---

[36] *DGFP*, D, VII, 192.
[37] See Bullock, *Hitler*, pp. 534-35. For details of the final crisis see below, Chapter XI.

1938 Hitler had once again refused to solve these problems by slowing down rearmament. As early as November 1937, he had suggested that Germany's economic situation inclined him to begin a war of conquest by the early 1940s; on August 22, 1939, he referred to "bottlenecks" that threatened the German economy with collapse within a few years. To continue rearmament, Hitler had to find new sources of raw materials, food, and labor. The agreement with the Soviet Union helped to solve some of these problems; the war helped to solve others.

Although the economic costs and benefits of the German decision to begin war in 1939 have not been thoroughly studied, it is clear that Germany's conquest of Poland, Denmark, Norway, the Low Countries, and France significantly eased many of its economic problems. T. W. Mason argues powerfully that war enabled the Nazi leadership to impose greater burdens on German workers, burdens that Hitler feared to impose in peacetime.[38] Germany's conquests during the first year of war also gave it access to large quantities of food and certain raw materials, which the Germans could exploit without worrying about repayment. Most significant, perhaps, the war opened up a huge reservoir of foreign labor. By August 1940, about 1,000,000 foreign workers had been imported into Germany—650,000 Polish civilians and prisoners and 350,000 prisoners from the west.[39] War was not economically inevitable in 1939; Hitler could have eased the economic situation by slowing down rearmament and gradually reintegrating Germany into normal world trade. This, however, he would never do. Having insisted upon rearmament for the sake of conquest, he found himself in a situation where conquest was the only means of continuing rearmament. His belief that Germany must conquer a self-sufficient economic empire, rather than rely upon world trade, had become a self-fulfilling prophecy.

The long-term role of Eastern Europe in the German war economy has so far been studied only in relatively general terms; additional research is necessary to evaluate it fully. Here, as elsewhere, the presence of German military might enabled the

[38] In his *Arbeiterklasse und Volksgemeinschaft*, pp. 164-66, Mason discusses the economic benefits of war.

[39] Memorandum, Economic and Armaments Office, Aug. 13, 1940, T-77/33/745126-28.

Germans to plunder resources and run up clearing debts without worrying about repaying them.[40] It seems, however, that Eastern Europe continued to play only a secondary role in German trade. Statistics for German trade for 1940—the only wartime year for which comprehensive figures are readily available—show that although imports from Eastern Europe increased over 1939 levels, imports from Italy, France, the Low Countries, Switzerland, Scandinavia, and, above all, the Soviet Union increased much more.[41] The massive study of German wartime food and agriculture policy by Karl Brandt, Otto Schiller, and Franz Ahlgrimm confirms the relatively limited role of Eastern Europe. After the first year of war, France, Scandinavia, and occupied Soviet territories quickly outpaced Eastern Europe as suppliers of foodstuffs to Germany.[42]

Resources from Eastern Europe and the Soviet Union enabled Hitler to fight Britain and France; resources from Western and Northern Europe enabled him to turn against the Soviet Union. Hitler's triumph at Munich was the first of a chain of victories that continually allowed him to expand his war of conquest. The scope of his undertakings widened until other powers with greater resources at their disposal finally laid him low.

[40] See Berend and Ránki, *Economic Development*, pp. 319-341, for a general survey of the effects of the German war economy in Eastern Europe. They note that although clearing balances increased, military operations often disrupted local economies severely and cut production.

[41] For these figures see *SJB, 1941-42*, p. 321. It is of course possible that much of the increase in German imports from Italy and the Low Countries during 1940 actually represented imports from overseas that evaded the Anglo-French blockade by passing through neutral territory.

[42] See Karl Brandt, Otto Schiller, and Franz Ahlgrimm, *Management of Agriculture and Food in the German-Occupied and Other Areas of Fortress Europe*, II (Stanford, 1953), especially the summary tables, pp. 609-15. The same study includes tables on foreign workers and prisoners of war, of which the Soviet Union and Poland were the largest sources.

XI.

British and French Policy from Munich to War

British and French policy toward Eastern Europe changed in 1939. After Hitler occupied Prague in March, London and Paris reluctantly decided to declare war should Germany undertake further armed aggression in the region. This change, however, reflected a change in their view of how they must deal *with Hitler* rather than any new view of their interests *in Eastern Europe*. They still recognized that they could not resist Germany in Eastern Europe either economically or militarily; they failed to give the Eastern Europeans significant economic help, and they remained willing to permit further German expansion eastward, provided such expansion did not involve war. Peace remained their goal; they declared war only because they finally concluded that peace with Nazi Germany was impossible.

Interestingly enough, neither Paris nor London abandoned attempts to build up their economic influence in Eastern Europe in the months after Munich, despite renunciation of their political influence there. In London, bureaucratic momentum was largely responsible; in Paris, even Bonnet seems to have wanted to maintain some French influence in Rumania and Yugoslavia, in spite of his efforts to loosen the Franco-Polish alliance. Thus, on November 12, 1938, a French economic mission led by Hervé Alphand of the Commerce Ministry left for Rumania, Bulgaria, and Yugoslavia; Paris ultimately reached new economic agreements with Belgrade and Bucharest. French bondholders had been pressuring the government to increase purchases from Yugoslavia during the summer of 1938; the agreement of February 19, 1939, increased Yugoslav quotas for timber, corn, pigs, and sheep. Ultimately, it increased French imports from Yugoslavia by 70 percent over 1938 levels. The French Agriculture Ministry, however, blocked any concessions in the vital area

of wheat; during January 1939, even top-level ministerial meetings attended by Daladier and Bonnet could not overcome Agriculture Minister Henri Queille's opposition to Yugoslav wheat
imports.[1] Once again, domestic considerations prevailed over
foreign-policy interests.

During negotiations for a new Franco-Rumanian trade
agreement, which began in November 1938, Bucharest also
asked for substantially larger agricultural exports to France.
French imports from Rumania had dropped from 397 million
francs in 1937 to 215 million francs for 1938, and the Rumanians wanted to reach a level of 380 million francs for 1939. The
French had always respected the potential importance of
Rumanian resources to the German war economy; during the
Czechoslovakia crisis Daladier warned the British of the consequences of unrestricted German access to Rumanian raw materials.[2] When the Agriculture Ministry initially refused to raise
Rumanian quotas, Bonnet on December 3 wrote a strongly
worded letter stressing the danger that Rumania would be unable to service its foreign debts and would therefore fall completely into the German orbit. The Agriculture Ministry nevertheless continued to hold the line on quotas, particularly for
corn, and talks broke down in December. In February the Quai
d'Orsay, noting Wohlthat's latest visit to Rumania, warned that if
France did not buy Rumanian cereals, Germany would extort
increased oil deliveries from Rumania as the price of its cereals
purchases. Negotiators finally concluded a new Franco-Rumanian agreement on March 31, 1939, calling for larger quotas of
corn, soybeans, oil seeds, and timber, preferences for timber
and mutton, and substantial additional purchases of Rumanian
gasoline.[3]

[1] Adamthwaite, *France*, pp. 275-76; memoranda by M. Bolgert, Bank of
France, June 28, July 12, 1938, memorandum by M. Campion, representing
French bondholders, Nov. 16, letter of Henri Queille, Jan. 16, 1939, AN, F[30]/
2082. See also *AS, 1938*, p. 167, *1940-45*, pp. 218-19.

[2] See for example the Anglo-French conversation of Apr. 29, 1939: "He
[Daladier] thought it was clear that, if and when Germany had secured the petrol
and wheat resources of Roumania, she would then turn against the Western
Powers, and it would be our own blindness which would have provided Germany
with the very supplies she required for the long war she admitted she was not
now in a position to wage" (*DBFP*, 3, I, 164). For figures see Table A.3.

[3] Bonnet letter, Dec. 3, 1938, Agriculture Ministry to AE, Jan. 10, 1939, AE to
Agriculture Ministry, Feb. 24, accord of Mar. 31, AN,F[10]/2139.

In March 1939 Paris also introduced a new system to enable Rumania and Yugoslavia to take better advantage their corn import quotas. These quotas had proven largely meaningless because neither the quota system nor French tariffs applied to French colonies. By late 1938, Indochina had virtually cornered the French corn import market, even though the price of Indochinese corn exceded the world price, whereas Danubian corn was priced below it. In an effort to help Yugoslavia and Rumania, a French government decree of March 31, 1939, provided for tariff-free imports of Danubian corn equal to Indochina's total corn exports to third countries. Unfortunately, this system suffered from administrative difficulties and worked very slowly. Although Rumania and Yugoslavia made small gains at Indochina's expense during the first seven months of 1939, the two countries still exported only 16,000 tons of corn to France during this period, compared with more than 200,000 tons from Indochina. The new Franco-Rumanian agreement also proved a major disappointment; French imports from Rumania fell from 215 million francs in 1938 to 187 million francs in 1939.[4] French trade remained oriented toward the French Empire, leaving little room for Eastern European products.

In London, economic policy toward Eastern Europe continued to move in different directions on different levels. On the one hand, Chamberlain still hoped to concede to Germany a special position in the region as part of a general settlement. Leith-Ross and Ashton-Gwatkin approached German diplomats along these lines from October 1938 through February 1939. In addition, the Board of Trade encouraged cartel negotiations between British and German industry—negotiations that might have led to a territorial division of markets that would have left Eastern Europe to Germany. On the other hand, the Interdepartmental Committee on Southeastern Europe continued its work, and although it recognized that Munich had cut much of the ground from under its feet, it did help to arrange some concessions for Rumania during the fall and winter of 1938-1939.

On October 18, Leith-Ross proposed new steps to *increase*

---

[4] Agriculture Ministry memorandum, Dec. 30, 1938, Commerce Ministry to Agriculture Ministry, Sept. 18, 1939, AN, F^{30}/2082. See also *SMCF, 1939*, no. 7, I, 128, and Table A.3.

German trade with Southeastern Europe to Ernst Rüter, a German diplomat passing through London. Leith-Ross began by citing the need to follow up the Munich agreement with new economic agreements. He proposed an economic rapprochement among the four Munich powers, which would cooperate to resist the economic strength of the United States. He then turned to Southeastern Europe. Leith-Ross knew that the Southeastern European states did not want to increase their exports to Germany because they needed free exchange to buy raw materials on the world market, but while serving as chairman of the Interdepartmental Committee he had been skeptical of Britain's ability to buy more from them. He now proposed a triangular solution to this problem. Under Germany's payments agreements with Britain, France, and Holland, the Germans reserved a certain percentage of the proceeds of their exports to these countries to pay for purchases from them—in the British case, the exact figure was 60 percent—and used the rest for service of foreign loans and purchases on the world market. Leith-Ross proposed that these countries allocate to Germany more free foreign exchange—perhaps 25 percent more—which Germany could use to pay for additional imports from Southeastern Europe. As Chief Economic Adviser to the Government, Leith-Ross had direct access to Chamberlain. The prime minister, who publicly recognized Germany's special position in Southeastern Europe in the House of Commons on November 1, almost surely approved this new initiative.[5]

This proposal, which London reiterated in succeeding months, evidences a complete misunderstanding of Hitler's goals and of the significance of German trade with Eastern Europe. Doubtless, Berlin would have liked to have disposed of more of its foreign-exchange receipts freely, but it never would have used any for imports from Eastern Europe. Since 1934, German trade policy had aimed at accumulating the largest possible amounts of free exchange and using it to buy vital raw materials that could be acquired in no other way. Germany imported what it could from Eastern Europe, despite those countries' high prices, precisely because it could buy those products

[5] *DGFP*, D, IV, 257. See also MacDonald, "Economic Appeasement," p. 116. Presumably, by 25% more foreign exchange, Leith-Ross meant a total of 75% free exchange, not 85%. For Chamberlain's speech see *PD*, Commons, 5th ser., CCCXL, 79-80.

without foreign currency. By the winter of 1938-1939, Commercial Counsellor Magowan of the British embassy in Berlin realized that the Germans were using all their foreign exchange to speed rearmament, and he proposed the denunciation of the Anglo-German payments agreement. Instead, Leith-Ross wanted to sacrifice the interests of British exporters in the hope that the Germans would spend hard currency in Southeastern Europe.[6]

Leith-Ross did not report his talk with Rüter to the Foreign Office. Vansittart's reaction to the earlier revelation of Chamberlain's intention to go to Berchtesgaden with an offer to concede to Germany a special position in Southeastern Europe showed that it would have encountered strong opposition. However, he did confide in Ashton-Gwatkin, whose views harmonized with the proposal. Of all Foreign Office officials, Ashton-Gwatkin probably viewed the Munich settlement most favorably; in a memorandum of October 27 he recognized that German influence must now prevail over all of Central Europe, including Poland, but he emphasized its advantageous aspects:

> The way is now open for a development which should be economically advantageous for the world at large, though many people regard it as politically alarming, viz. the development of Eastern and South-Eastern Europe mainly by German enterprise and organization until these backward regions have attained something more nearly approximating a Western European standard of living. . . .

British capital, he argued, might assist this process; "if peace prevails," loans would ultimately promote British trade with Germany and with the increasingly prosperous Eastern European states.[7]

Leith-Ross repeated his proposal to Rüter on November 10, and Ashton-Gwatkin repeated it to a German embassy official in late November. In February, Ashton-Gwatkin went to Berlin to prepare for interministerial talks on economic questions. On the twentieth Wiehl finally told him that Germany would reject

[6] MacDonald, "Economic Appeasement," pp. 118-21, notes that Leith-Ross may have hoped that the additional sterling would flow from Germany to the Balkans, thence to the British Empire, and finally back to Britain.

[7] *DGFP*, D, IV, 267, 273, 316; Ashton-Gwatkin memorandum, Oct. 27, 1938, FO 371/21705, C13864/772/18.

Leith-Ross's proposal. Germany's foreign-exchange surplus in its trade with Britain, he argued, was not even high enough at present to service its financial obligations. Ashton-Gwatkin did not report Wiehl's rejection to the Foreign Office; clearly, he and Leith-Ross had decided to handle these talks alone.[8]

Leith-Ross's proposals represented one aspect of Chamberlain's efforts to improve the British economic situation through new agreements with Germany; proposals for Anglo-German cartel negotiations represented another. British exports were still suffering from the recession that had begun late in 1937, and during the winter of 1938-1939, both the Labour party and backbench Conservatives asked for expanded government intervention in international trade to meet German competition. The government, however, rejected attempts to fight Germany with its own weapons, such as subsidies or clearings; instead, it promised to solve British export problems through Anglo-German agreement. As Board of Trade President Oliver Stanley told the House of Commons, any new economic weapons the government might acquire would be designed, like military weapons, to encourage international agreement rather than to fight a war. Chamberlain also linked political and economic détente, stating publicly on February 22 that he hoped that a relaxation in Anglo-German tensions would help British trade.[9]

During the fall of 1938 the Board of Trade pressed for talks between the leading British and German industrial bodies, the Federation of British Industries and the Reichsgruppe Industrie. Brief conversations took place on March 15-16. In the meantime, Sir Laurence Collier of the Northern Department of the Foreign Office tried once again to persuade the government to take active steps to protect British trade. Collier renewed his campaign to get the government to assume the power to impose clearings to improve Britain's trade balances with other states; even the announcement that the government was considering the assumption of such powers, he argued, would be a useful weapon in commercial negotiations. The Board of Trade countered that the government would come under too much pressure from private interests to use these powers if it ever adopted

<hr />

[8] For Ashton-Gwatkin's report of his Feb. 20, 1939, conversation see FO 408/69, no. 84.

[9] Wendt, *Economic Appeasement*, pp. 481-524; MacDonald, "Economic Appeasement," pp. 121-24.

them, and Stanley even denied that clearings had brought Germany any major benefits "in the aggregate."[10] After Chamberlain publicly recognized Germany's special position in Southeastern Europe, Collier proposed that the prime minister publicly reaffirm British interest in the Baltic and Scandinavian markets, but Cadogan and Halifax refused to forward this suggestion. In early March, with cartel negotiations only weeks away, Collier complained that the trade departments had refused to give the Federation of British Industries any political guidance whatever. On March 8 the Board of Trade refused to do so, declining to mix politics with commercial questions.

It can be assumed that in negotiating cartel arrangements with Germany, the British industries will direct their attention to the development of those markets most likely to be profitable to them, and that in order to attain this end, they may find it worthwhile to yield ground in other markets. Interference by His Majesty's Government to promote a settlement of these arrangements otherwise than by reference to such industrial and commercial considerations would not merely discourage the industries concerned but might, in some cases, cause the industry to abandon its efforts altogether.[11]

The March 15-16 talks produced no results. The German government had instructed the Reichsgruppe Industrie not to discuss any division of third-country markets except within the rest of the British Empire. In the midst of the talks, the German occupation of Prague chilled Anglo-German relations and resulted in the cancellation of Oliver Stanley's planned visit to Berlin. London subsequently decided that further economic talks would have to await an improvement in the political situation, but the government clearly continued to prefer accommodation with Germany to competition.[12]

In the meantime, the Interdepartmental Committee on Southeastern Europe continued its work. Although in the wake

[10] Minute by Collier and Ashton-Gwatkin, Jan. 16, 1939, Halifax to Stanley, Jan. 28, Stanley to Halifax, Feb. 6, Stanley to Halifax, Mar. 7, FO 371/23653, N260/N702/N1308/64/63.

[11] Minute by Collier and Ashton-Gwatkin and comments by Cadogan and Halifax, Jan. 16, 1939, Collier minute, Mar. 7, Board of Trade to FO, Mar. 8, FO 271/23653, N260/N1261/N1262/64/63.

[12] DGFP, D, IV, 327; MacDonald, "Economic Appeasement," pp. 126-27.

of Munich it officially scaled down its objectives, it arranged significant assistance for Rumania.

In late September 1938, at the height of the crisis over Czechoslovakia, the Rumanian government offered 300,000 tons of wheat to the British government—specifically, to the Food Defence Plans Department, which was stockpiling essential commodities. Although the Rumanians offered the wheat at the world price, the Board of Trade argued that the purchase was uneconomic, and the Food Defence Plans Department refused to take more than 50,000 tons. The Rumanians desperately needed foreign exchange to service their foreign loans, and Vansittart, Sargent, and Ingram advocated a larger purchase. On October 6 they persuaded Halifax—whose conscience may have been bothering him following Munich—to suggest a purchase of 200,000 tons.[13]

At the cabinet Committee on Trade and Agriculture the next day, Halifax resorted to torturous reasoning reminiscent of the original memorandum advocating the establishment of the Interdepartmental Committee on Southeastern Europe. He conceded that the Rumanian purchase was "both uneconomic and unbusinesslike." "There was no question of our wanting to effect the economic encirclement of Germany or block her expansion, but it was very important at the present time that we should not appear disinterested in the Danubian countries." If nothing were done, a forthcoming visit to Rumania by German Economics Minister Funk might lead to the complete elimination of British trade in that country. Chancellor of the Exchequer Simon and Stanley insisted that Halifax secure Chamberlain's approval. Writing to Chamberlain on October 13, Halifax argued carefully that it would be worthwhile to maintain a small foothold in the Balkans, but he asked whether the prime minister might in fact regard the purchase as "a rather irritating and useless pinprick" to Germany. He pointed out that about one million tons of Rumanian wheat would still be available for export to Germany. Chamberlain agreed to the purchase the next day.[14]

[13] Ingram memorandum, Sept. 24, 1938, Ross memorandum, Oct. 5, Vansittart, Sargent, and Ingram minutes, Oct. 6, Stanley letter, Oct. 10, meeting of Oct. 12, FO 371/22459, R7947/R7989/R8197/R8230/223/37. Cadogan opposed the purchase; see Cadogan, *Diaries*, p. 121.
[14] CAB 24/279, CP 226 (38); letters of Oct. 13, 14, 1938, FO 371/22459, R8230/R8307/22/37.

For the first time during the 1930s, the British government had arranged a major purchase from Eastern Europe. However, the wheat deal did not herald any basic change in policy. Leith-Ross drafted the first interim report of the Interdepartmental Committee on Southeastern Europe in October and early November, and Halifax presented it to the Foreign Policy Committee on November 21. In a covering note, Halifax backed away slightly from the original objectives he had set for the committee in June. He still wanted to increase British influence, but he did not mean to do so at Germany's expense.

> It may be argued that recent events in Central Europe have rendered [the committee's objectives] Utopian; that owing to Germany's latest success we can no longer hope that the areas in question "shall look specifically for leadership to this country." But whatever view is taken, there will, no doubt, be general agreement that these countries should be actively encouraged that a possible *point d'appui* other than Berlin does exist, and that British interest in them, both political or economic, will be maintained and developed. Such an object is a moderate and reasonable one, but the counterpart, which should be clearly recognized, is that we must be ready, notwithstanding our efforts to safeguard this object, to permit Germany to obtain all she materially requires in these areas—indeed, we cannot very well prevent her from doing so.

More significantly, Halifax also narrowed the committee's area of interest. He largely discounted the possibility of effective initiatives in Hungary, Rumania, or Yugoslavia; only Turkey and Greece remained worthwhile fields of endeavor. This analysis, of course, reflected Halifax' broader conceptions of British foreign policy after Munich. As he told the Foreign Policy Committee on November 21: "As regards the general position, it seemed clear that we could not prevent Germany doing what she wished in Central Europe itself. We must, however, become as strong as possible and aim at securing the vital cord of the British Empire, namely our communications through the Mediterranean."

The Interdepartmental Committee report itself acknowledged that all the countries in question needed to divert trade to Britain in order to secure free foreign exchange, but the committee doubted that London could do much more than to suggest that they depreciate their currencies. It rejected any reductions in British tariffs, except those scheduled to come into force in 1940 under the new Anglo-American trade agreement, or any large government purchases. Only two other possibilities remained: the government might encourage private British "great combines" to purchase more Rumanian oil or Greek tobacco, or London might grant credits on a noncommercial basis.[15]

In December the government finally amended the Export Credits Guarantee Act to provide for noncommercial credits. The Board of Trade still resisted this step, but after Munich, acting partly on the advice of the Committee of Imperial Defence, it suggested a two-tier scheme for export credit guarantees, including a separate allocation of £10-million worth of credit guarantees for noncommercial purposes. The cabinet approved this measure on December 7, but further deliberations suggested that little of the money would go to Eastern Europe. The government asked the Committee of Imperial Defence to rank potential customers in order of their importance to British security. The committee's list, according to which the government planned to divide the projected £10 million in credit guarantees, ranked eligible countries according to their proximity to the British Isles and British trade routes: (1) Belgium and Holland; (2) Egypt; (3) Portugal and Turkey; (4) Iraq; (5) Greece; (6) Saudi Arabia; (7) Afghanistan; (8) Yugoslavia; (9) Rumania; (10) Bulgaria. In the eyes of the committee, the last three countries owed their importance to their coastlines on the Adriatic and Black seas.[16]

Given this list, it is unlikely that the Danubian states would have received any of the £10 million but for a state visit by King Carol of Rumania on November 15-18. When the visit had been arranged in midsummer, the Foreign Office had viewed it as part of the attempt to give the Danubian states "a *point d'appui*

---

[15] CAB 24/280, CP 257 (38); Foreign Policy Committee, Nov. 21, CAB 27/624. Simon Newman, *March 1939*, pp. 46-49, quotes the committee report in an effort to show a continuous British interest in Eastern Europe in 1938-1939. He neglects to mention Halifax's comments on Hungary, Rumania, and Yugoslavia and his emphasis on the Mediterranean.

[16] Board of Trade memorandum, Oct. 4, 1938, FO 371/22501, W11152/4366/50; cabinet of Nov. 9, CAB 23/96; Board of Trade memorandum, Nov. 4, CAB 24/280, CP 249 (38), 260 (38), 277 (38); cabinet of Dec. 7, CAB 23/96; Committee of Imperial Defence memorandum, Nov. 28, CAB 24/281, CP 289 (38). The memorandum lists Yugoslavia as an Adriatic power.

other than Berlin," but Sargent's November brief for the visit recognized the changed circumstances. He advised that nothing should be done to foster charges of encircling Germany and argued that London should consider only economically sound projects of assistance. Chamberlain, however—always susceptible to personal contacts—was evidently impressed by King Carol's presentation of Rumania's needs. "Something must be done for Rumania," he told Halifax. The Interdepartmental Committee examined the king's proposals for British economic help, which included credits to construct grain silos and a naval base on the Black Sea and to increase exploitation of Rumanian mineral resources.[17]

In an ironic reversal of roles, Chamberlain and Halifax pushed for action while Foreign Office officials expressed skepticism that anything could be done to keep Rumania from falling completely under German control. The Interdepartmental Committee supported credits for grain silos but rejected the naval base. Private interests, it noted, could expand the exploitation of mineral resources if only Bucharest would liberalize the Rumanian mining law; because that law reserved much of the proceeds of new finds for the government, Rumanian oil production had been dropping since 1936. In January 1939 an interdepartmental memorandum recommended that Rumania receive £1 million of the authorized £10 million in noncommercial credits.[18]

During the winter of 1939 London examined several new proposals for increased Anglo-Rumanian trade. Private interests suggested a holding company to finance purchases from Rumania, capitalized by £100,000 in export credit guarantees, but the Export Credits Guarantee Department replied that all guarantees must be tied to specific British exports. Rumanian proposals for British purchases of Rumanian goods for reexport moved slowly. In response to official Rumanian pressure, the government on March 2 authorized Leith-Ross to lead a com-

[17] Minute by Philip Nichols, June 7, 1938, FO memorandum, Nov. 14, conversations of Nov. 17, FO 371/22445, R5380/R9121/R9168/R9213/3/37. See also Leith-Ross's Nov. 28 memorandum, FO 371/22460, R9535/223/37, and Ingram minute, Nov. 21, FO 371/22345, R9305/94/67.

[18] Archibald Ross minute, Dec. 19, 1938, FO 371/23831, R211/113/67; Sargent minute, Dec. 22, FO 371/22345, R10352/94/67; Interdepartmental Committee meeting, Nov. 25, ibid., R9763/94/67; CAB 24/282, CP 1 (39). The memorandum recommended that Greece receive £2,000,000 and Yugoslavia and Bulgaria possibly £500,000 each.

mercial mission to Rumania, even though the Board of Trade insisted on postponing the announcement until after Stanley's visit to Berlin in mid-March so as not to antagonize the Germans. To help make the visit a success, the Export Credits Guarantee Department authorized £750,000 in guarantees for grain silos as a *commercial* credit, in addition to the £1,000,000 already authorized. But London refused to repeat the October grain purchase. British grain traders resented the government's previous intervention in their market, and, despite Foreign Office objections, Stanley promised them that the government would not make another such purchase until at least August 1, 1939.[19]

Thus, in the months from Munich until Prague, British economic policy toward Eastern Europe included several contradictory aspects. Chamberlain himself, although still willing to concede to Germany a special position in Southeastern Europe, had taken some interest in Rumania, and elements within the bureaucracy continued to disagree over various measures. The German occupation of Prague led to a dramatic change in British political and military policy toward Eastern Europe, but it did not resolve the various contradictions in the economic sphere.

When the new crisis over Czechoslovakia broke out in mid-March, neither Paris nor London planned any strong reaction. Bonnet told Phipps on March 13 that he had no intention of intervening in any way; Corbin and Halifax agreed on March 15 that at least their countries no longer had to face the "embarrassing commitment of a guarantee," which in fact had never been successfully arranged.[20] Chamberlain called the cabinet together on March 15 to discuss the statement he would make to the House of Commons later that day, but he did not hint at any basic change in policy. He still hoped for a general settlement

[19] On the new proposals and the commercial mission see FO 371/23831-32, R1208/R1470/R1495/R1559/113/37. On Stanley's promise, see Sir Henry French's minute of a Dec. 22 meeting that was attended by Stanley, Simon, and Halifax, among others, FO 371/22381/, R227/113/37. The new Rumanian minister in London, Viorel V. Tilea, submitted many new proposals; see Sidney Aster, *1939: The Making of the Second World War* (London, 1973), pp. 66-68.

[20] *DBFP*, 3, IV, 234, 280. On French reaction see also Adamthwaite, *France*, p. 301. Berlin had stalled regarding any commitment to guarantee Czechoslovakia.

with Germany and Italy; during February he had suggested privately that the combination of growing Anglo-French strength and German economic weakness would soon bring Hitler to the conference table. His March 15 House of Commons statement—in which he argued that since the Slovak Diet had proclaimed independence, "the state His Majesty's Government was to guarantee has ceased to exist"—recognized the new incident as a setback to his policy but closed by reaffirming his desire for new agreements to achieve peace.[21]

The prime minister, however, came under heavy pressure to respond more strongly to Hitler's new move, and within two days he decided to make a tougher statement. Halifax had doubted the possibility of peace with Hitler since Munich; by early February, influenced by many rumors of new German aggression, he had pressed the French to begin staff conversations. He and Cadogan regarded Hitler's violation of the Munich agreement and his incorporation of non-Germans into the Reich as revolutionary events, and they sought, with the zeal of converts, to make this new coup the occasion of a fundamental change in British policy. In addition, Chamberlain's Tory backbench supporters within the House of Commons, who had sincerely believed that Munich meant "peace for our time," evidently regarded the Prague coup as a humiliation both for Chamberlain and themselves. "The feeling in the lobbies is that Chamberlain will either have to go or completely reverse his policy," Harold Nicolson wrote in his diary on March 17. "Unless in his speech tonight [an address in Birmingham] he admits that he was wrong, they feel that resignation is the only alternative." That evening, Chamberlain obliged, repudiating his "cool and objective" statement of the fifteenth, asking whether the Prague coup was "in fact, a step in the direction of an attempt to dominate the world by force," and casting doubt on the wisdom of his would-be role as peacemaker. At the same time, however, he carefully swore off any new, indefinite commitments.[22]

[21] Neville Chamberlain to Hilda and Ida Chamberlain, Feb. 5, 12, 19, 26, 1939, Chamberlain papers; cabinet of Mar. 15, CAB 23/98; PD, Commons, 5th ser., CCCXLV, 435-40. The cabinet decided to cancel Stanley's planned visit to Berlin as a sign of disapproval.

[22] Birkenhead, Halifax, pp. 432-34; Cadogan, Diaries, pp. 155-63. Oliver Harvey wrote on Feb. 17, 1939, that Halifax's attitude toward Germany had already altered completely; see Harvey, Diplomatic Diaries, pp. 255-56. See also Nicolson, Diaries, pp. 392-93, Chamberlain, Struggle for Peace, pp. 413-20, and Aster, 1939, pp. 35-37.

Returning to London the next day, Chamberlain heard rumors of a new German coup. On March 16 Rumanian Minister Viorel Tilea had asked Sargent for a £10-million arms credit to make up for promised supplies from Czechoslovakia, which presumably were now lost. The next day, Tilea saw Halifax, repeated his request, and suggested that Germany would shortly move against Rumania. Referring to Wohlthat's negotiations in Bucharest, he stated that the Germans had demanded a monopoly of Rumanian exports and a halt to Rumanian industrial development in return for a German guarantee of Rumania's frontiers. Although Hungary's annexation of Ruthenia had produced tension along the Rumanian-Hungarian border, Tilea's story was clearly false; Wohlthat would never have made such an inflammatory demand, and we have seen that Bucharest, not Berlin, had suggested a political agreement. Tilea asked whether London would define its attitude toward German aggression against Rumania and suggested the formation of a new front in Eastern Europe. Halifax immediately asked British representatives in Paris, Warsaw, and Moscow to ascertain what their host countries would do in such a case.[23]

At a cabinet meeting of March 18, Chamberlain took the new rumor personally. He now believed, he said, that no further negotiations with the Nazi leaders were possible; their assurances were valueless. His Birmingham speech "was a challenge to Germany on the issue whether or not Germany intended to dominate Europe by force." If Germany accepted the challenge by moving against Rumania, "we had no alternative but to take up the challenge." He argued confusedly that a new German move against Rumania would be important not because Germany might improve its strategic position, but because "it raised the whole question whether Germany intended to obtain domination over the whole of South Eastern Europe"—something that the government in many ways had already conceded. Chamberlain secured agreement to seek the support of Poland, which he regarded as "the key to the situation," and said he would make some public statement to deter Hitler.[24]

After the British legation in Bucharest exploded Tilea's story later that day, Chamberlain quickly recovered his bearings and backed away slightly from his bellicose stance. As he wrote pri-

[23] *DBFP*, 3, IV, 287, 298, 395, 388, 389, 390.
[24] CAB 23/98.

vately on March 19, he wanted to combine a "bold and startling" plan for resistance to further aggression with an appeal to Mussolini to restrain Hitler. "As always, I want to gain time for I never accept the view that war is inevitable." In the cabinet the next day, Halifax more aptly characterized the plan as "not very heroic." It proposed a public undertaking by the British, French, Soviet, and Polish governments "immediately to consult together in the event of any action being taken" that appeared to threaten the independence of a European state. As Chamberlain put it, "although we did not tie ourselves down to do more than consult, the pronouncement had a definite implication, and people would expect consultation to be followed by action. While he was reluctant to take any step of this character, he was satisfied that nothing less would have any value."[25]

The cabinet approved this declaration. On the twentieth, however, when Chamberlain showed it to French Ambassador Corbin, Corbin complained that this declaration "would confirm the impression that the powers were not disposed to take any action and would only talk when threats arose." Chamberlain then altered it to provide for consultation "as to what steps should be taken to offer joint resistance" to any action constituting a threat to the independence of a European state.[26]

So far, the British had hardly consulted Paris. On March 21 Halifax met with Bonnet, who had accompanied French President Albert Lebrun on a state visit to London. The rumors of German designs upon Rumania had disturbed Paris, and the French had already tried to persuade Warsaw to commit itself to the defense of Rumania against Germany in return for French support over Danzig. Bonnet stressed the importance of securing Polish and Soviet help—in that order—for Rumania; Halifax replied that the question was one of checking German aggression, whether in the east or the west. In another conversation the next day, attended by Chamberlain, the ministers agreed to seek Polish help. Neither Chamberlain nor Bonnet, however, had decided that war was inevitable. Bonnet cautioned Halifax on March 23 that Britain must avoid charges of encirclement or ideological prejudice. Chamberlain told the House of Commons on the same day that Britain was determined to resist

[25] *DBFP*, 3, IV, 397, 399; Chamberlain letter, Mar. 19, Chamberlain papers; cabinet of Mar. 20, CAB 23/98.
[26] *DBFP*, 3, IV, 406; Aster, *1939*, p. 86.

any attempt "to dominate the whole of Europe and perhaps even to go further than that," but he also indicated his willingness to reopen the Anglo-German economic talks and denied any intention of setting up two European ideological blocs.[27]

Eager to secure Polish help, the British allowed Beck to deflect them from their original aim. Beck was determined not to offend Germany and Hungary by promising to assist Rumania, but he wanted British support regarding his continuing negotiations with Germany over Danzig. Because Britain was one of three League powers with special responsibilities for Danzig, Beck had already arranged to visit London in April. Thus, on March 24, Polish Ambassador to London Edward Raczynski rejected the British proposal for an Anglo-French-Soviet-Polish declaration; any declaration that included Moscow would be too provocative to Hitler. Instead, he proposed a confidential, bilateral Anglo-Polish undertaking to consult in the event of a threat to the independence of a European state. Although carefully refusing to promise to assist Rumania, Raczynski referred to action against Danzig as a case that would bring the declaration into play—provided that the action constituted a threat to Polish independence.[28]

Chamberlain and Halifax seized upon this proposal, presenting an even stronger version to the Foreign Policy Committee and the cabinet on March 27 and 28. Britain and France, they suggested, should confidentially undertake to support Poland and Rumania if they resisted a German attack. Halifax argued that if Hitler did attack Rumania or Poland, Britain could only stand aside at the price of an incalculable loss of prestige; Chamberlain suggested that because the understanding would be confidential, it would not increase the risk of war by provoking Hitler. Halifax, who had clearly given up most of his hopes for peace, also suggested that this understanding might deter Germany from embarking upon a two-front war. The cabinet approved this proposal on March 28.[29]

---

[27] *DBFP*, 3, IV, 402, 458, 484, 507. Although Poland and Rumania had a longstanding alliance, it committed them to mutual assistance only against a Soviet attack, not against a German one. For Chamberlain's statement see FO 371/22966, C3905/3356/18.

[28] On the genesis of Beck's visit see FO 371/23132, C92/92/55 et seq. See also *DBFP*, 3, IV, 405, 518.

[29] Foreign Policy Committee, Mar. 27, CAB 27/624; cabinet meeting, Mar. 28, CAB 23/98.

The very next day, chance intervened to change British policy once again. Ian Colvin, the former Berlin correspondent of the *News Chronicle*, came to the Foreign Office with a rumor of an impending German attack on Poland. Although there is no evidence that this rumor was any truer than Tilea's earlier reports, Halifax was sufficiently impressed to escort Colvin to 10 Downing Street, where Colvin told Chamberlain that Hitler would soon attack Poland and that he would ultimately turn upon the British Empire. Though not knowing quite what to believe, Chamberlain clearly feared being taken by surprise by Hitler once more. Two days later, on March 31, he told the House of Commons, after consulting the cabinet, that if Germany took action that "clearly threatened Polish independence," and if Poland resisted it, Britain would go to Poland's aid. When Beck came to London for conversations on April 4-5, Chamberlain agreed to a bilateral Anglo-Polish alliance.[30]

Having committed himself to a possible war with Germany, Chamberlain soon had to go further. Led by Daladier, the French government fell in line with London's new policy but demanded additional steps to make this policy effective. Daladier insisted upon a guarantee for Rumania, whose natural resources he still regarded as crucial. When in early April Chamberlain resisted such a step on the grounds that Britain would be unable to give Rumania effective help, Daladier forced him into it by threatening to guarantee Rumania unilaterally.[31] Still preoccupied with the balance of forces on land, the French also demanded repeatedly that London introduce conscription. After the Foreign Office, the War Office, and even the United States also advocated this step, Chamberlain, who had previously promised never to introduce conscription in peacetime, finally agreed in late April to do so.[32]

Much against his will, Chamberlain also agreed in April to open negotiations for some kind of alliance with the Soviet Union. Chamberlain's private profession of "the deepest distrust of Russia" is well known; he also doubted that Moscow could

[30] For accounts of the Colvin-Chamberlain meeting see Colvin, *Vansittart in Office*, pp. 303-10, and Chamberlain letters, Apr. 2, 1939, Chamberlain papers. See also cabinet of Mar. 31, CAB 23/98. On Beck's visit see *DBFP*, 3, V, 1, 2, 10, 16.

[31] Zay, *Carnets secrets*, pp. 64-66; *DBFP*, 3, V, 49, 53, 57, 58, 66; Foreign Policy Committee, Apr. 10, 1939, CAB 27/624; cabinets of Apr. 10, 13, CAB 23/98.

[32] *DBFP*, 3, IV, 440, 458, 507. See also Aster, *1939*, pp. 141-42.

provide effective help and, according to one account, even argued on March 31 that Poland would provide a sufficiently
strong second front to deter Germany from war. During April
and May the cabinet, the Chiefs of Staff, the parliamentary opposition, and the French forced the prime minister to begin and
to continue negotiations with Moscow. Chamberlain did not
conceal his attitude; an alliance with the Soviets, he believed,
would make a settlement with Germany impossible, and for him
this clearly outweighed the contrary danger of going to war
without Soviet help. Forced by the cabinet to continue the talks,
in late May he and Horace Wilson resorted to a subterfuge in
order to keep them as innocuous as possible.[33]

What precisely was the significance of the British guarantee to
Poland? London did not hope to prevent Germany from overrunning Eastern Europe militarily, and even though the British
cabinet hoped that the threat of a two-front war would deter
Hitler from beginning a conflict, they knew they could not save
Poland if he did attack. In addition, Halifax and Chamberlain
discounted any possibility of stopping the peaceable expansion
of German power in Eastern Europe. Halifax told the cabinet
that Britain would not resist German moves against Poland or
Rumania unless these countries did so themselves; Chamberlain
wrote privately on March 26 that should Germany successfully
impose upon Bucharest "a new 'commercial agreement' which in
effect puts Roumania at her mercy," Britain would have no op-
tion but to present Germany with an ultimatum. "We are not
strong enough ourselves and we cannot command sufficient
strength elsewhere to present Germany with an overwhelming
force. Our ultimatum would therefore mean war and I would
never be responsible for presenting it."[34] Why, if Chamberlain
could not hope to save Eastern Europe from Germany, did he
give the guarantees? His behavior during the second half of
March 1939 suggests that he wished above all to prevent Hitler

[33] Chamberlain letters, Mar. 26, 1939, Chamberlain papers. On the basis of
two sources, Aster, *1939*, p. 115, states that Chamberlain told Lloyd George on
Mar. 31 that the guarantee to Poland would deter Germany. On the talks and
Chamberlain's attitude see Aster, pp. 178-79, Chamberlain letters, May 21, 1939,
and Harvey, *Diplomatic Diaries*, p. 290. Chamberlain's and Wilson's subterfuge
consisted in tying British obligations to the Soviets to Article 16 of the League
Covenant, which Chamberlain expected shortly to be either amended or repealed; see Chamberlain letters, May 28.

[34] Foreign Policy Committee, Mar. 27, 1939, CAB 27/624; cabinet of Mar. 28,
CAB 23/98; Chamberlain letters, Mar. 26, Chamberlain papers.

from taking him by surprise with another coup; he may have concluded that neither British prestige nor his own would survive if he tolerated further German military expansion.

Doubtless such considerations influenced Chamberlain's sudden decision to guarantee Poland, but a careful analysis of his statements during 1938 and 1939 suggests that a change in his estimate of Hitler played a role as well. Chamberlain never accepted the need for a balance of power or the inevitability of conflict among nations, but he consistently maintained that Britain would resist attempts to dominate Europe or the world *by force*. During 1938 Chamberlain helped to arrange German domination over Czechoslovakia by international agreement. On September 27 he told the British people that "if I were convinced that any nation had made up its mind to dominate the world by fear of its force, I should feel that it must be resisted," but he indicated quite clearly that he was not yet convinced that such was Hitler's goal. We shall see that during 1939 Chamberlain frequently indicated willingness to discuss additional German demands and to make new concessions under appropriate circumstances, but he also stated repeatedly that Britain would oppose any attempt to dominate other countries *by force*. Oddly enough, Chamberlain sometimes seems to have cared less about exactly what Hitler wanted than about how he planned to achieve it. Even after guaranteeing Poland, he was willing to make new concessions at Poland's expense through negotiation but resisted Hitler's attempts to get what he wanted through intimidation or war. Knowing that he could not save Poland, Chamberlain made his guarantee a test of Hitler's intentions; he decided after Hitler attacked that peace with the German dictator was impossible. Even then, however, he counted on reason rather than force to achieve his aims. The German people, he hoped, would overthrow Hitler when they realized that they could not win the war, thus leading to an early and relatively painless end to the conflict.[35]

The British and French governments decided in the spring of 1939 to fight if Germany attacked Poland, but they did not re-

[35] Chamberlain, *Struggle for Peace*, p. 276. On Chamberlain's attitude toward Hitler after war began see Feiling, *Neville Chamberlain*, pp. 419-30.

verse their whole policy toward Eastern Europe in the months leading to the war. In the French case, we have seen that new steps to increase trade with Eastern Europe had mixed results. Despite Paris's respect for the importance of Rumania, French imports from that country did not increase during 1939. The record of British economic initiatives in Eastern Europe during 1939 is extremely uneven. Within the British and French governments, many doubted that Germany could be stopped in Eastern Europe, and some still worked for a new settlement with Germany involving further concessions. Specifically, London and Paris feared the outbreak of a German-Polish war over a relatively minor issue, and their efforts to settle German-Polish differences peacefully continued even after the Germans attacked.

As we have seen, Leith-Ross had been preparing his commercial mission to Rumania at the time the Germans occupied Prague. The immediate effect of that crisis on British policy was not what Bucharest would have hoped; on March 22 the Export Credits Guarantee Department *withdrew* its authorization for a £750,000 credit for silos on the grounds that changes in the political situation had made the project too risky. Contrary voices soon asserted themselves, particularly after the new German-Rumanian agreement became known; it was clearly a broad and general document whose significance would depend on its implementation. In early April, Leith-Ross and the Foreign Office suggested that the total of noncommercial export credit guarantees be increased from £10,000,000 to £20,000,000, including a total of £2,000,000 for Rumania and £2,000,000 for Yugoslavia.[36]

Halifax and Stanley supported this proposal at Foreign Policy Committee meetings on April 10-11, but Chamberlain and Simon showed skepticism. We have seen that the prime minister doubted Britain's ability to resist peaceful German penetration in Rumania; he now asked "why it was thought that we could effectively break down the economic dependence of these states on Germany by the use of a few millions of export credit guarantees." Nonetheless, he and Simon agreed to £5 million in credit

[36] ECGD to FO, Mar. 22, FO 371/23832, R1955/113/37; Leith-Ross letter, Mar. 22, ibid., R2055/113/37; FO memorandum, Apr. 1, FO 371/23990, W5054/436/50.

guarantees for Rumania to make Leith-Ross's mission a success. Leith-Ross also persuaded the Food Defence Plans Department to buy another 200,000 tons of Rumanian wheat.[37]

Leith-Ross arrived in Bucharest in late April and signed a protocol outlining Britain's new assistance on May 11. In return for the new credit guarantees and the new wheat purchase, Bucharest agreed to liberalize the mining law in order to encourage British oil companies to make new explorations. The British refused to finance a new Anglo-Rumanian trading company, and the implementation of the £5-million credit guarantee also proved difficult. In order to use the guarantee, the Rumanians had to contract for £5-million worth of long-term purchases of British goods; the guarantee did not represent a sterling credit that could be spent elsewhere. Bucharest wanted to use almost all of the guarantee for arms purchases, especially aircraft, antiaircraft guns, and antitank guns, but the British had few or none of these weapons to spare. Tilea pleaded for additional arms credits without success; ironically, while his March 17 démarche led to British guarantees for Poland and Rumania, he never received the £10 million in arms credits that he was after. Bucharest had not yet announced a new mining law by the time war broke out.[38]

Yugoslav calls for British help during the summer of 1939 met with less success. Belgrade did not want a British political guarantee; although the German occupation of Prague and the Italian occupation of Albania in April shook Yugoslav faith in accommodation with the Axis, the Yugoslav government still felt that a guarantee would be too provocative.[39] In an effort to strengthen British influence, the Foreign Office secured the al-

[37] Foreign Policy Committee, Apr. 10, 11, CAB 27/624; Sir Henry French to FO, Apr. 4, 1939, FO 371/23832, R2356/113/37.

[38] On Leith-Ross's mission and the resulting agreements see FO 371/23833-35. The May 11, 1939, protocol is R3943/113/37; the final July 12 agreement is R5700/113/37. On further Rumanian requests for arms see British legation Bucharest to FO, May 1, 1939, War Office to FO, May 2, FO to British legation Bucharest, May 4, Sargent minutes, June 8, and conversations with Tilea, July 19, FO 371/23833-36, R3529/R3573/R3633/R4878/R6000/113/37. On June 8 Tilea requested an audience with Chamberlain; it was refused. On the Rumanian mining law see British legation Bucharest to FO, July 29, FO 371/23848, R6155/529/27, et seq.

[39] British legation Belgrade to FO, Apr. 13, 1939, and Apr. 15 minutes, FO 371/23883, R2701/R2915/409/62.

location of £500,000 in political credit guarantees for Yugoslavia and sent Charles Stirling of the Economic Section on a commercial mission to Yugoslavia in May. Belgrade, however, considered this offer "derisory." The Yugoslav minister in London later told Ingram that this visit had done more harm than good because of its lack of results. London could not fill Yugoslav orders for British aircraft because of domestic and other needs. On August 15, 1939, Ingram passed a Yugoslav appeal for increased British purchases of Yugoslav bacon on to the Board of Trade. The Board's August 17 reply effectively summarized British trade policy toward Eastern Europe during the 1930s:

> As has been explained ad nauseum to the various Diplomatic Representatives in London and the itinerant Kings, Princes, and Cabinet Ministers of the Balkan States, we cannot regard the import quota system as a means to give favors to our friends, but as something which must be operated on m.f.n. principles impartially between all the supplying countries.[40]

In fact, by the spring of 1939 it was almost certainly too late for Britain seriously to contest German economic influence in Yugoslavia or Rumania or to make those states reliable allies against Germany. The case of Poland was somewhat different; no one could doubt Poland's will to resist should war come. Nonetheless, during the summer of 1939 London and Warsaw failed to agree on proposals for financial assistance for Poland. London's failure to accept Poland's terms reveals a great deal about the preoccupations of the British government during 1939.

Beck raised the question of a British loan in late April, and British Ambassador to Poland Sir Horace Kennard strongly supported him. The democracies, he wrote, "are supposed to be rich and generous—surely now is the time for the financial weapon to be used, and in full" to help Poland resist a German attack. When the Foreign Office raised the question with other interested departments, the Admiralty, the War Office, and the

[40] Stirling to BT, May 9, 1939, BT 11/1077; Ingram minute, July 7, FO 371/23881, R5534/325/92. On Yugoslav aircraft requests see FO 371/23879, R176/175/92 et seq. For Ingram's and the Board's letters see BT 11/1077.

Air Ministry all supported assistance in principle, but the Treasury quickly dissented on the grounds that Britain was not rich and could not afford to be generous. The Treasury's insistence on this point ultimately led to the breakdown of negotiations for a loan in late July.[41]

The Treasury refused to grant the kind of loan Warsaw wanted because of its concern with Britain's overall financial situation in the summer of 1939. The Poles wanted money for the immediate purchase of arms and raw materials, and they apparently realized that most of what they wanted would not be available in Britain. Thus, their requests, which they initially put at £60 million on May 13, could not be met merely with export credit guarantees; Britain would have to advance them sterling for purchases in the United States and elsewhere. Such purchases would increase Britain's foreign liabilities and could increase its gold drain. The Bank of England and the Treasury had recognized the British gold drain as a serious problem since mid-1938; after the Prague crisis, the drain had increased rapidly, averaging well over £10 million per month. During the winter of 1938-1939, the Bank of England had proposed various forms of intervention in financial markets to reduce the drain, but Simon and the Treasury refused to impose them. Upon hearing of Warsaw's request, Simon quickly wrote Chamberlain rejecting a sterling advance.

> This is a very serious situation. If we are to provide Poland with the means for paying for purchases in other countries, this can only be done by handing out gold. Again, if we are to put Poland in funds for the purpose of payments to be made inside Poland, this also can only be done by parting with gold. We simply cannot contemplate losing further large sums of gold for this purpose . . . of course, further depletion of our gold stocks means a reduction of the time for which we could feed our people during a war. My advisers regard the handing over of gold for Poland's necessities as really impossible.[42]

The Foreign Office failed to overcome the Treasury's objections. On May 20 the British government agreed to receive a

[41] *DBFP*, 3, V, 266; letters of May 5, 6, 8, 1939, FO 371/23144, C6997/C6999/1110/55.

[42] *DBFP*, 3, V, 508; undated Simon letter, PREM 1/357. On the gold drain and the reactions of the Treasury and the Bank of England see R. S. Sayers, *The Bank of England 1891-1944*, II (Cambridge, 1976), 562-67.

Polish delegation in London but stated that Britain could not provide assistance on the scale requested—£60 million—or allow any loan to be spent outside Britain. Polish Ambassador Raczynski asked for a reconsideration. On June 6 he met Chamberlain, asking for help to enable Poland to meet "the full burden that must inevitably rest upon her in the event of war." After refusing to promise Poland a cash advance, the prime minister spoke revealingly about the course that a future war might take.

> The Prime Minister said that we were fully alive to the force of everything the Ambassador had urged and were anxious to give every assistance that we could to the common cause in which we were both engaged. It must, however, be remembered that while it was very possible that the primary attack would fall upon Poland, this was not certain, and, even if it did, it was impossible for anyone to anticipate how long the war might last, and if it was a long war it was essential that this country should not have weakened its economic strength, on which in the last resort the prosecution of a war would largely depend.[43]

The implication that Britain should not waste money on Poland, which would certainly be overrun at the outset of a war, was virtually inescapable. In his own minute of the conversation Chamberlain wrote that Polish demands for cash to spend outside Britain presented "insuperable" difficulties.[44]

A Polish delegation arrived in London on June 13 with a request for an unrestricted loan of £24 million, and the Treasury, led by Leith-Ross, began negotiations. After weeks of talks, Simon on June 28 agreed to a £5-million cash advance but attached several conditions. Poland must accept unspecified controls over the use of the money; France must make a similar contribution; and Poland must make concessions to Britain in coal export markets. On June 30 the British also offered the Poles £8 million in normal export credit guarantees, but a Treasury official minuted that Britain would be able to supply only £3-million worth of arms and raw materials.[45]

The Polish delegation returned to Warsaw, and Leith-Ross

[43] DBFP, 3, V, 562, 725.
[44] Minute of June 7, 1939, PREM 1/357.
[45] Minutes of meetings, June 15, 19, 1939, Simon memorandum, June 28, aide-mémoire, June 30, FO 371/23145, C8361/C8377/C9260/C9244/1110/55. See also Waley memorandum, June 26, T 160/878/16062/2.

approached the French. Paris quickly agreed to add £3 million to a British loan of £5 million, but a joint Anglo-French note of July 16 communicating this proposal included three conditions: the Polish złoty must be devalued; Warsaw must agree not to convert the loan into gold but to hold it in sterling and francs "until drawn upon for purposes agreed with the British and French Governments"; and "the question should be examined of removing as large a proportion as possible of the gold reserves of the National Bank of Poland to centers where it would be available for use at any time." Simon told the cabinet on July 19 that he would refuse to allow the Poles to spend the money in America, and Leith-Ross wrote to the Foreign Office on July 17 that the Treasury "could only consider the question of allowing part of the money to be spent on purchases abroad in conjunction with a general review of the Polish financial situation," together with an appropriate adjustment of exchange rates. On July 20 the British finally agreed that Poland could spend some of the money in the United States, provided that it drew proportionally on its own gold reserves; they also insisted upon an immediate decision because of Parliament's impending adjournment. Warsaw rejected these terms on July 25, arguing that they would not bring about the immediate expansion of Polish armaments that Warsaw had sought.[46] The Poles had to content themselves with an August 2 agreement on £8 million in export credit guarantees.[47]

London failed to give Poland financial assistance partly because of accurate strategic considerations; Chamberlain realized that Poland would be overrun at the outset of a new war. In addition, the Treasury's objections illustrate the larger predicament in which the British found themselves in the summer of 1939. The Treasury believed that Britain faced a critical financial crisis. On July 5 Simon submitted a memorandum to the cabinet suggesting that Britain's continuing gold drain was reducing its ability to fight a long war. He argued that devaluation would not solve the problem and did not even mention other possible measures to halt the gold outflow. Instead, he noted

[46] Leith-Ross to FO, July 5, 1939, Anglo-French note, July 16, Leith-Ross to FO, July 17, FO note, July 20, FO 371/23145, C9805/C9966/C10053/C10288/1110/55. See also *DBFP*, 3, VI, 362; Koc to Leith-Ross, July 25, FO 371/23145, C10571/1110/55; CAB 23/100.

[47] FO 371/23141, C10881/521/55.

that the import of raw materials for rearmament was hurting the British balance of trade and suggested that a new limit on rearmament expenditures might be necessary. In essence, this July 3 memorandum confirmed Chamberlain's long-held view that Britain could afford neither a major war nor a protracted arms race. These considerations may partially explain London's continuing interest in a settlement with Germany during the summer of 1939.[48]

The British continued to sound out Berlin both publicly and privately. In a public speech on June 29 Halifax stated that Britain was determined to resist aggression but added that "if we could once be satisfied that the intentions of others were the same as our own, and that we all really wanted peaceful solutions"—something that could be done only with "deeds, not words"—London would discuss all issues of concern. He referred specifically to "the colonial problem, the problem of raw materials, trade barriers, the issue of *Lebensraum*, the limitation of armaments"—a list apparently drawn up with reference to Hitler's April 28 Reichstag speech.[49] In late July and early August, Sir Horace Wilson spoke similarly to Helmut Wohlthat, a frequent visitor to London during the 1930s, and to German Ambassador Herbert von Dirksen. As had Halifax, Wilson insisted that Germany would have to take concrete steps to demonstrate its peaceful intentions, including demobilization and an end to offensive press campaigns, before Britain could discuss a new settlement. He added, however, that if Berlin would join London in a renunciation of the use of force, Britain would drop its guarantees in Eastern Europe; "if it was once made clear by the German Government that there was henceforth to be no aggression on their part," he told Dirksen on August 3, "the policy of guarantees to potential victims *ipso facto* became inoperative." According to Wohlthat, Wilson also offered to recognize a special German trading position in Southeastern Europe, just as he had done one year earlier in his talk with Theodor Kordt.[50]

[48] Cabinet of July 5, 1939, and accompanying memoranda, CP 148 and 149 (39), CAB 23/100.

[49] Birkenhead, *Halifax*, p. 411. Aster, *1939*, pp. 223-24, dates the speech.

[50] For Wohlthat's contemporary record of his conversations with Wilson and Robert Hudson, the parliamentary secretary to the Department of Overseas Trade, see *DGFP*, D, VI, 716. Wohlthat subsequently admitted that he misrepresented his conversation with Wilson by stating that Wilson had given him a

In private letters, Chamberlain continued to hope that Hitler would abandon any plans for war and ultimately agree to a peaceful solution of the Danzig question.[51] The line the British had drawn in Eastern Europe was clearly not a firm one. The French government did not actively seek accommodation with Germany, although Bonnet made it clear in private that he hoped to revive this policy.[52]

Because neither the French nor the British government had yet concluded that war with Germany was *inevitable*, each feared the outbreak of war over a relatively minor issue and still hoped to keep the peace by making further concessions to Germany. Specifically, they regarded a German coup in Danzig as an inadequate *casus belli* and hoped to transfer Danzig peacefully to Germany as part of a new general settlement. Hitler's April 28 revelation of his previous offer to Poland disturbed Chamberlain and Halifax; they would have been delighted to see Poland remove the danger of war by accepting it. On May 20 Halifax and Corbin discussed the return of Danzig to Germany with appropriate safeguards for Polish economic rights, and Bonnet referred to this proposal on August 12 as a reasonable basis for settlement. Both governments sought to restrain Warsaw from taking precipitous action should Danzig incorporate itself into the Reich. This issue helped to delay the conclusion of a new Franco-Polish treaty of alliance until after war had begun.[53]

The British and French continued to pursue their dichotomous policies even after the Nazi-Soviet Pact had cleared the way for Hitler's attack on Poland. Both intended to meet war with war, but both hoped for a settlement even after the German attack began. On August 22 Chamberlain told the British cabinet that it was "unthinkable" that Britain would not fulfill its ob-

---

memorandum summarizing a program of Anglo-German negotiations; see Helmut Metzmacher, "Deutsch-englische Ausgleichungsbemühungen im Sommer 1939," *Vierteljahreshefte für Zeitgeschichte*, XIV, no. 4 (1966), 369-412. For Hudson's record of his conversation with Wohlthat and Wilson's records of his conversations with Wohlthat and with Dirksen see *DBFP*, 3, VI, 370, 354, 533. On the leak of the Hudson-Wohlthat conversation and reaction to it see Aster, *1939*, pp. 248-50.

[51] Chamberlain letters, July 2, 15, 23, 30, 1939, Chamberlain papers. He hoped for a peaceful settlement of the Danzig question after tensions died down.

[52] Adamthwaite, *France*, pp. 318-19.

[53] Aster, *1939*, pp. 188-215; cabinet of May 3, 1939, CAB 23/99; *DBFP*, 3, V, 569, VI, 80, 110, 111, 642; Adamthwaite, *France*, pp. 319-23.

ligations to Poland, and he sent a warning to Hitler that German aggression against Poland would mean war. The next day, the French Council of National Defense decided that France should fight now rather than allow Germany freely to secure the resources of Poland and Rumania. Neither government, however, gave up on a peaceful solution. Chamberlain's letter to Hitler also proposed a relaxation of tensions, direct German-Polish negotiations, and a new, internationally guaranteed settlement. The British government, it read, "would be ready, if desired, to make such contributions as they could to the effective operation of such guarantees." Chamberlain may well have planned to drop Britain's unilateral guarantee to Poland in the context of a general settlement. The French cabinet also wavered; at a meeting on August 24 Daliader, Bonnet, and others seemed to weaken in their support for Poland, and the government decided to pressure Warsaw to reach agreement with Berlin. The French asked Beck to take no precipitous action should Danzig incorporate itself into Germany.[54]

On August 25 Halifax signed the Anglo-Polish alliance, but he also suggested to Raczynski that Poland agree to modify Danzig's status in return for an international guarantee of "vital" Polish interests there. Later that day, Hitler gave Henderson his offer to guarantee the British Empire after the German-Polish question had been solved in some unspecified fashion. A divided British government took three days to compose its reply. On the night of August 25 Halifax dictated a reply suggesting that Poland agree to self-determination for Danzig in exchange for a German recognition of Poland's frontiers. Wilson and R. A. Butler, Halifax's parliamentary private secretary, weakened the British reply the next day at 10 Downing Street. Their draft offered to recommend Hitler's March offer to the Poles, provided that it could be secured by an international guarantee. That night, however, the cabinet rejected this wording. The final reply to Hitler on August 28 merely advocated an "agreement

---

[54] Cabinet of Aug. 22, CAB 23/100. Chamberlain's letter to Hitler is *DBFP*, 3, VII, 145. Significantly, immediately upon reading the passage regarding a guarantee on August 28, Beck asked for a clarification of it; see ibid., 420. He had received no reply by Aug. 31 (ibid., 609). On the French deliberations see *ESF*, II, 276-78, Bonnet, *Fin d'une Europe*, pp. 305-6, Zay, *Carnets secrets*, pp. 67-69; Ministère des Affaires Etrangères, *Le Livre jaune français. Documents diplomatiques 1938-39* (Paris, 1939), nos. 218, 226, 227.

between [Germany and Poland] on lines which would include the safeguarding of Poland's essential interests," adding that Hitler had recognized the importance of these interests in his April 28 speech—the speech in which he had revealed his earlier proposals. It further expressed the hope that a peaceful settlement would lead rapidly to measures "to enable the transition from preparation for war to the normal activities of peaceful trade to be safely and smoothly effected."[55]

On the evening of August 29 Hitler agreed to negotiate if a Polish plenipotentiary could arrive in Berlin on August 30, but he demanded the return of Danzig and the entire Corridor. Cadogan, Vansittart, and Sargent all argued that no settlement with Hitler was possible, but Halifax was not sure; Britain should work for a solution "on proper terms now." Bonnet urged the Poles to enter into direct conversations, but in London, questions of form and procedure decided the day. A cabinet meeting on August 30 showed sentiment for returning Danzig to Germany, but, as Chamberlain put it, Hitler's demand for the immediate presence of a Polish plenipotentiary represented "the old technique" and could not be accepted. London thus supported the Polish refusal to comply. On the night of August 31 Halifax, prodded by Sir Nevile Henderson, asked the Polish government at least to ask its ambassador in Berlin to receive the demands. The Germans attacked Poland before action could be taken on this telegram.[56]

Earlier, on the thirty-first, Mussolini had held out a last straw for the British and French to grasp at. Trying to repeat his triumph of the previous year, he proposed a conference to discuss revision of the Treaty of Versailles. Chamberlain, determined to avoid accusations of another Munich, insisted that de-

---

[55] For the Halifax-Raczynski conversation and Hitler's offer see *DBFP*, 3, VII, 309, 283. Cadogan, *Diaries*, p. 201, states that Halifax dictated a reply in the Foreign Office late on the night of Aug. 25. PREM 1/331a contains several drafts of the British reply, including one on Foreign Office stationery that is apparently the first draft. I infer that it is the one dictated by Halifax. Cadogan also reports that Wilson and Butler produced the subsequent draft at Downing Street; the numbering of paragraphs and certain penciled corrections make it clear that this draft is PREM 1/331a, pp. 454-58. The cabinet rejected this draft on the night of Aug. 26; see CAB 23/100. The final reply is in *DBFP*, 3, VII, 426.

[56] *DBFP*, 3, VII, 502, 608, 632; *Livre jaune français*, no. 291; CAB 23/100; Aster, *1939*, pp. 359-62.

mobilization must precede any conference and hinted strongly that Poland must be represented. In Paris, Bonnet argued for acceptance, but Daladier insisted that Hitler's word would in any case be worthless. Chamberlain continued to hope for a peaceful solution after the German attack on September 1 but insisted that German troops must withdraw from Poland before talks could begin. The British and French delayed their declarations of war until September 3, partly for military reasons, but also in the hope that something might happen to preserve peace.[57]

In March 1939 the British and French governments decided to fight if Hitler undertook further aggression; in September they declared war. They could not, however, escape the consequences of their refusal to fight in 1938. Having left Eastern Europe defenseless at Munich, they could neither contest Germany's economic position, build up an effective anti-German front, or prevent the conquest of Poland after war began. British attempts to conciliate Hitler with further negotiated, limited gains in Eastern Europe also failed. The ultimate effects of British and French policy toward Eastern Europe emerged in the spring of 1940, when Hitler, drawing on both Eastern European and Soviet resources, defeated France and drove Britain from the European continent.

It is of course theoretically possible that the British and French could have either deterred Hitler from making war or avoided their defeat in 1940 by concluding an agreement with the Soviet Union. We have seen that Hitler probably could not have begun war without the Nazi-Soviet Pact. Could Paris and London have outbid him and secured Moscow's help? Although the lack of any authoritative Soviet documentation rules out a definitive answer to this question, evidence suggests that the Anglo-French-Soviet negotiations, which dragged on from May through August of 1939, were probably doomed from the start.

The story of these negotiations need not be retold in detail here.[58] They split the British government. Halifax, like Daladier

[57] Aster, *1939*, pp. 373-89; Zay, *Carnets secrets*, pp. 78-82; Adamthwaite, *France*, pp. 344-52.

[58] See Aster, *1939*, pp. 152-87, 260-319, and Ulam, *Expansion and Coexistence*, pp. 269-79, for two accounts of these talks.

and Bonnet, argued that they were necessary in order to prevent an agreement between Moscow and Berlin; Chamberlain opposed the talks from the beginning, arguing that the Soviets could not provide effective help and that a deal between Stalin and Hitler was virtually impossible. In the course of the talks, the Soviets made a series of escalating demands regarding their right to resist German aggression against Finland, the Baltic states, Poland, and Rumania. They eventually demanded the right to intervene in these states in case of "indirect aggression," a phrase they defined so broadly as to give Soviet troops an almost arbitrary right to cross their western frontier. The British government initially resisted these demands but seemed willing to agree to them at the time that talks broke down. Stalin clearly feared war with Germany; his behavior during 1939 suggests that he was determined to establish a western buffer zone in which such a war could begin. One could argue that the British failure immediately to concede his right to occupy such a zone forced him to turn to Hitler, who respected his wishes in the Nazi-Soviet Pact.

Other evidence, however, suggests that Stalin would never have reached agreement with the British and French, even on these terms. The way in which the Soviets continually raised new demands as soon as London and Paris accepted their present proposals indicates that they were merely stalling until Hitler would submit a bid of his own.[59] Stalin may have wished to ensure not only that war with Germany would not begin on Soviet soil but also that it would not begin in 1939 at all.[60] No concession from Britain and France could keep him *out* of war with Germany, but an agreement with Hitler might give him a few years of peace. The alacrity with which Stalin concluded the Nazi-Soviet Pact, contrasted with the continual difficulties in the negotiations with Britain and France, also suggests that Stalin preferred an agreement with Hitler.

Had the British and French governments decided to fight for Czechoslovakia in 1938, they would have been assured of at least the benevolent neutrality of the Soviet Union. The vital role of

[59] Ulam, *Expansion and Coexistence,* p. 275, cites evidence that the Soviets had further, as yet unmentioned demands to make at the time that talks broke down.

[60] The situation in the Far East, where Japanese and Soviet troops had become involved in large-scale hostilities in the summer of 1993, must not be forgotten.

Soviet supplies in sustaining the German war effort in 1939-1940 suggests that even Soviet neutrality would have been a major asset. By 1939, however, London and Paris apparently could not secure Moscow's neutrality. Here again, the Anglo-French failure to resist Hitler in 1938 doomed their attempt to do so one year later.

XII.

Conclusion

In 1931 the German government, inspired by political goals, began an economic offensive in Eastern Europe. Under Hitler, German trade with Eastern Europe served the goal of rearmament for a war of conquest; beginning in 1937, agricultural imports from Eastern Europe played a key role in keeping the German people adequately fed until war could begin. The British and French, guided by other economic and strategic priorities, did little to contest Germany's economic offensive; in 1938 they acquiesced in German political and economic hegemony in the region. Economic diplomacy in Eastern Europe during the 1930s is interesting not only for its own sake but also for the light it throws on the different objectives, styles, and degrees of effectiveness of the German, British, and French governments and for its role in the overall development of European international politics during the twentieth century.

The most striking contrast that emerges between Germany on the one hand and Britain and France on the other is the German ability to link political goals and economic policy during the interwar period. A belief in the primacy of foreign policy was traditional in Germany; certainly it was strong under the Weimar Republic, when the Germans unanimously sought to overturn many provisions of the Treaty of Versailles. Thus, in 1931, the German cabinet ultimately accepted the preferential treaties with Rumania and Hungary and the customs union with Austria—projects of dubious economic benefit undertaken for political reasons. The primacy of political goals became even more apparent under Hitler, whose plans for a war of conquest increasingly shaped German economic policy during the decade. Paris and London were far less successful in tailoring economic policies to fit political goals. Neither government seems to have recognized the primacy of foreign policy; the British and French foreign ministries frequently failed to prevail over domestic or imperial economic concerns. The German government had emerged from the First World War preoccupied with international questions; the British and French never dealt successfully with a host of serious domestic economic problems—problems with important consequences for their foreign policy. Thus, for example, rearmament in Britain and France suffered from financial weakness and from relatively antiquated industrial plants. Their competitive position in the arms trade in Eastern Europe suffered, and France found itself in a potentially disastrous military situation in the crucial year 1938. Hitler's emphasis on rearmament to overturn the postwar European settlement, on the other hand, encouraged German arms exports and also kept domestic German demand at a high level, creating a market for imports of foodstuffs from Eastern Europe.

The German government profited from the economic weakness of the successor states both because of its political goals in Eastern Europe and because Germany lacked a colonial empire to distract its attention from European issues. Trade with Eastern Europe was never attractive on purely economic grounds; the region's relatively backward agriculture could not under normal circumstances compete with more advanced overseas producers. The depression and the rise of Hitler, however—themselves closely related events—established new priorities for German foreign trade. Hitler's rearmament program required huge quantities of foreign raw materials and overheated the German economy; thus Berlin had to maintain exchange controls and reserve hard currency to pay for raw materials. Purchases from Eastern Europe became attractive because the successor states' own economic weakness forced them, too, to impose exchange control and, specifically, to accept reichsmarks for their sales to Germany. Trade between Germany and the successor states grew during the 1930s, not because of the alleged complementarity of their economies, but because of the common weakness of the reichsmark, lei, dinar, and pengo on international exchanges. The British and French responded to the depression by increasing trade with their empires and ignoring the relatively underdeveloped parts of Europe; Germany freely exploited Eastern Europe while rearming to overturn the postwar European settlement once and for all.

The British and French decisions to increase trade with their empires during the 1930s reflected fundamental political miscalculations. Burdened by worldwide commitments, the British in particular abandoned the traditional basis of their foreign policy: the maintenance of a balance of power on the European continent. To paraphrase the Earl of Chatham, they forgot that an empire could be lost, as well as won, on the battlefields of Europe. The British and French failure to defend the status quo in Eastern Europe led to their military defeat in 1940, which in turn led directly to the loss of their Asian possessions in 1941 and helped to precipitate the loss of the rest of their empires after the war. In the meantime, the European balance of power was restored only by the intervention of the Soviet Union and the United States, which established European spheres of influence after the war was over. The consequences of the British and French failure to take responsibility for the development of Eastern Europe are with us to this day.

Appendix

TABLE A.1
Value of German Trade with Eastern Europe, 1928, 1933-1939
(In Millions of Reichsmarks)

	1928	1933	1934	1935	1936	1937	1938	1939
Austria								
Imports from	232.1	57.6	66.3	71.1	76.6	93.3	17.3	—
Exports to	425.7	120.7	106.7	107.9	108.5	122.7	29.0	—
Czechoslovakia								
Imports from	538.3	121.7	162.3	121.4	111.9	141.4	188.8	89.9
Exports to	649.4	160.1	148.4	130.0	139.0	151.0	161.6	86.9
Hungary								
Imports from	71.9	34.2	63.9	77.9	93.4	114.1	186.2	222.5
Exports to	154.0	38.1	39.6	62.9	83.0	110.5	146.4	228.7
Rumania								
Imports from	188.1	46.1	59.0	79.9	92.3	179.5	177.8	209.5
Exports to	173.0	46.0	50.9	63.8	103.6	129.5	168.6	216.7
Yugoslavia								
Imports from	66.6	33.5	36.3	61.4	75.2	132.2	172.2	131.5
Exports to	117.6	33.8	31.5	36.9	77.2	134.4	144.6	181.3
Poland and Danzig								
Imports from	377.9	77.1	78.1	75.5	74.0	80.8	140.8	97.8
Exports to	499.3	82.4	55.1	63.3	73.9	99.7	155.2	101.2
Estonia								
Imports from	33.3	8.4	8.2	13.1	13.8	23.7	24.3	28.3
Exports to	41.2	7.1	7.3	11.4	17.6	19.9	22.3	25.7
Latvia								
Imports from	66.3	17.5	21.1	31.1	33.2	45.7	43.6	44.1
Exports to	78.9	17.2	18.8	27.9	31.2	28.4	43.0	49.8
Lithuania								
Imports from	54.7	22.1	15.1	2.6	9.1	17.2	27.8	28.2
Exports to	52.6	19.7	14.7	6.7	7.3	20.4	24.3	29.3
Total German trade								
Imports	14,051.2	4,203.6	4,451.1	4,158.7	4,217.9	5,468.4	6,051.7	4,796.5
Exports	12,054.8	4,871.4	4,166.9	4,269.7	4,768.2	5,911.0	5,619.1	5,222,2

SOURCES: *SJB, 1929*, p. 234, *1936*, pp. 253-54, *1938*, pp. 280-82, *1941-42*, p. 321; Statistiches Reichsamt, *Monatliche Nachweise über den auswärtigen Handel Deutschlands*, April 1938 (Berlin, 1938), pp. 190-91.

TABLE A.2
Value of British Trade with Eastern Europe, 1928, 1933-1939
(In Millions of Pounds Sterling)

	1928	*1933*	*1934*	*1935*	*1936*	*1937*	*1938*	*1939*
Austria								
Imports from	2.16	1.21	1.61	1.64	2.15	2.56	1.63	—
Exports to	2.71	0.88	1.06	1.33	1.47	1.85	1.30	—
Czechoslovakia								
Imports from	7.80	2.74	3.55	4.18	5.66	7.03	6.67	3.09
Exports to	2.17	0.86	1.25	1.43	1.82	2.60	2.28	1.08
Hungary								
Imports from	0.49	1.39	1.30	1.76	2.17	2.35	2.32	1.92
Exports to	1.00	0.28	0.50	0.44	0.41	0.50	0.58	0.53
Rumania								
Imports from	1.68	4.05	3.50	3.08	6.06	4.35	3.75	4.77
Exports to	2.99	2.39	2.68	1.21	1.12	1.81	1.35	1.80
Yugoslavia								
Imports from	0.60	0.59	0.84	1.18	1.78	2.44	2.32	1.78
Exports to	1.27	0.60	0.82	0.93	0.89	1.00	1.24	1.03
Poland and Danzig								
Imports from	5.69	6.48	7.31	7.14	9.71	10.67	9.39	7.03
Exports to	5.25	2.74	3.00	3.79	4.86	5.70	5.37	4.17
Estonia								
Imports from	2.04	1.20	1.98	1.80	1.91	2.24	2.05	1.84
Exports to	0.60	0.37	0.44	0.68	0.73	1.29	0.94	0.75
Latvia								
Imports from	5.70	2.60	2.69	2.90	3.39	5.30	4.57	3.78
Exports to	1.29	1.00	1.16	1.12	1.25	1.69	1.68	1.35
Lithuania								
Imports from	0.35	1.94	1.82	2.24	2.92	3.21	3.03	3.34
Exports to	0.35	0.66	1.07	1.55	1.65	1.87	2.12	1.24
Total British trade								
Imports	1,075.32	625.94	680.17	700.73	786.98	952.69	858.98	885.52
Exports	723.58	367.91	395.99	425.83	440.60	521.39	470.76	439.54

SOURCES: *SAUK, 1924-38*, pp. 374-83; *TUK, 1939*, IV, 163-307.

TABLE A.3
Value of French Trade with Eastern Europe, 1928, 1933-1939
(In Millions of Francs)

	1928	1933	1934	1935	1936	1937	1938	1939
Austria								
Imports from	251	109	104	95	142	244	137	—
Exports to	202	69	85	81	95	150	125	—
Czechoslovakia								
Imports from	218	219	190	193	231	408	299	281
Exports to	199	191	231	199	264	421	405	181
Hungary								
Imports from	29	69	43	36	48	96	113	94
Exports to	46	49	28	13	17	28	46	43
Rumania								
Imports from	203	354	247	157	231	397	215	187
Exports to	147	129	167	106	114	212	347	360
Yugoslavia								
Imports from	121	50	32	29	59	97	101	170
Exports to	78	36	42	58	75	70	124	135
Poland and Danzig								
Imports from	210	204	177	153	205	400	444	441
Exports to	432	173	159	128	142	188	356	346
Estonia								
Imports from	23	23	17	11	18	41	33	28
Exports to	25	9	10	7	7	16	27	23
Latvia								
Imports from	105	31	17	14	13	29	45	38
Exports to	43	18	18	9	10	19	21	15
Lithuania								
Imports from	8	13	11	20	26	49	43	30
Exports to	13	10	18	8	21	62	45	24
Total French trade								
Imports	53,643	28,431	23,097	20,974	25,414	42,391	45,981	43,785
Exports	52,056	18,474	17,851	15,496	15,492	23,939	30,586	31,590

SOURCES: AS, *1930*, pp. 197-98, *1934*, pp. 195-96, *1935*, pp. 192-93, *1936*, pp. 194-95, *1937*, p. 175, *1938*, p. 167, *1940-45*, pp. 218-19.

TABLE A.4
Eastern European Shares of German Trade, 1928, 1933-1939
(In Percentages)

	1928	1933	1934	1935	1936	1937	1938	1939
Danubian States								
Total import share	7.7	7.0	8.6	9.9	10.7	12.1	12.2	13.6
Total export share	12.6	8.2	9.0	9.4	10.7	11.1	11.7	13.8
Austria								
Import share	1.6	1.4	1.5	1.7	1.8	1.7	0.3	—
Export share	3.5	2.5	2.6	2.5	2.3	2.1	0.5	—
Czechoslovakia								
Import share	3.8	2.9	3.6	2.9	2.7	2.6	3.1	1.9
Export share	5.4	3.3	3.6	3.0	2.9	2.6	2.9	1.7
Hungary								
Import share	0.5	0.8	1.4	1.9	2.2	2.1	3.1	4.6
Export share	1.3	0.8	0.9	1.5	1.7	1.9	2.7	4.4
Rumania								
Import share	1.3	1.1	1.3	1.9	2.2	3.3	2.9	4.4
Export share	1.4	0.9	1.2	1.5	2.2	2.2	3.0	4.2
Yugoslavia								
Import share	0.5	0.8	0.8	1.5	1.8	2.4	2.8	2.7
Export share	1.0	0.7	0.8	0.9	1.6	2.3	2.6	3.5
Northeastern States								
Total import share	3.7	2.9	2.8	2.9	3.1	3.0	3.9	4.1
Total export share	5.5	2.5	2.2	2.7	2.8	2.8	3.5	3.9
Poland and Danzig								
Import share	2.6	1.8	1.8	1.8	1.8	1.5	2.3	2.0
Export share	4.1	1.6	1.3	1.5	1.5	1.6	2.8	1.9
Estonia								
Import share	0.2	0.2	0.2	0.3	0.3	0.4	0.4	0.6
Export share	0.3	0.1	0.2	0.3	0.4	0.3	0.5	0.5
Latvia								
Import share	0.5	0.4	0.5	0.7	0.8	0.8	0.7	0.9
Export share	0.7	0.4	0.4	0.7	0.7	0.5	0.8	1.0
Lithuania								
Import share	0.4	0.5	0.3	0.1	0.2	0.3	0.5	0.6
Export share	0.4	0.4	0.3	0.2	0.2	0.4	0.4	0.5
EASTERN EUROPE								
Total import share	11.4	9.9	11.4	12.8	13.8	15.1	16.1	17.7
Total export share	18.1	10.7	11.2	10.9	12.5	13.9	15.2	17.7

For sources see Table A.1.

TABLE A.5
Eastern European Shares of British Trade, 1928, 1933-1939
(In Percentages)

	1928	1933	1934	1935	1936	1937	1938	1939
Danubian States								
Total import share	1.2	1.6	1.5	1.7	2.3	2.0	2.0	1.2
Total export share	1.3	1.4	1.7	1.2	1.2	1.5	1.5	1.0
Austria								
Import share	0.2	0.2	0.2	0.2	0.3	0.3	0.2	—
Export share	0.4	0.2	0.3	0.3	0.3	0.4	0.3	—
Czechoslovakia								
Import share	0.7	0.4	0.5	0.6	0.7	0.7	0.8	0.3
Export share	0.3	0.2	0.3	0.3	0.4	0.5	0.5	0.3
Hungary								
Import share	—	0.2	0.2	0.2	0.3	0.2	0.3	0.2
Export share	0.1	0.1	0.2	0.1	0.1	0.1	0.1	0.1
Rumania								
Import share	0.2	0.7	0.5	0.5	0.8	0.5	0.4	0.5
Export share	0.3	0.7	0.7	0.3	0.2	0.3	0.3	0.4
Yugoslavia								
Import share	0.1	0.1	0.1	0.2	0.2	0.3	0.3	0.2
Export share	0.2	0.2	0.2	0.2	0.2	0.2	0.3	0.2
Northeastern States								
Total import share	1.2	1.9	2.0	2.1	2.2	2.2	2.1	1.8
Total export share	1.0	1.3	1.5	1.8	2.0	2.0	2.2	1.7
Poland and Danzig								
Import share	0.5	1.0	1.0	1.0	1.2	1.1	1.1	1.8
Export share	0.7	0.7	0.8	0.9	1.1	1.1	1.1	0.9
Estonia								
Import share	0.2	0.2	0.3	0.3	0.2	0.2	0.2	0.2
Export share	0.1	0.1	0.1	0.2	0.2	0.2	0.2	0.2
Latvia								
Import share	0.5	0.4	0.4	0.4	0.4	0.6	0.5	0.4
Export share	0.2	0.3	0.3	0.3	0.3	0.3	0.4	0.3
Lithuania								
Import share	—	0.3	0.3	0.4	0.4	0.3	0.3	0.4
Export share	—	0.2	0.3	0.4	0.4	0.4	0.5	0.3
EASTERN EUROPE								
Total import share	2.4	3.5	3.5	3.8	4.5	4.2	4.1	4.0
Total export share	2.3	2.7	3.2	3.0	3.2	3.5	3.7	2.7

For sources see Table A.2.

TABLE A.6
Eastern European Shares of French Trade, 1928, 1933-1939
(In Percentages)

	1928	1933	1934	1935	1936	1937	1938	1939
Danubian States								
Total import share	1.5	2.8	2.7	2.3	2.8	2.9	1.9	1.6
Total export share	1.2	2.6	3.1	2.9	4.1	3.7	3.4	2.2
Austria								
Import share	0.5	0.4	0.5	0.4	0.6	0.6	0.3	—
Export share	0.4	0.4	0.5	0.5	0.6	0.6	0.4	—
Czechoslovakia								
Import share	0.4	0.8	0.8	0.9	0.9	1.0	0.7	0.6
Export share	0.4	1.0	1.3	1.3	1.7	1.8	1.3	0.6
Hungary								
Import share	—	0.2	0.2	0.2	0.2	0.2	0.2	0.2
Export share	—	0.3	0.2	—	0.6	0.1	0.2	0.1
Rumania								
Import share	0.4	1.2	1.1	0.7	0.9	0.9	0.5	0.4
Export share	0.3	0.7	0.9	0.7	0.7	0.9	1.1	1.1
Yugoslavia								
Import share	0.2	0.2	0.1	0.1	0.2	0.2	0.2	0.4
Export share	0.1	0.2	0.2	0.4	0.5	0.3	0.4	0.4
Northeastern States								
Total import share	0.6	0.8	1.0	0.9	1.0	1.2	1.3	1.2
Total export share	1.0	1.1	1.3	0.9	1.5	1.2	1.5	1.3
Poland and Danzig								
Import share	0.4	0.7	0.8	0.7	0.8	0.9	1.0	1.0
Export share	0.8	0.9	1.0	0.8	1.3	0.8	1.2	1.1
Baltic states								
Import share	0.2	0.1	0.2	0.2	0.2	0.3	0.3	0.2
Export share	0.2	0.2	0.3	0.1	0.2	0.4	0.3	0.2
EASTERN EUROPE								
Total import share	2.1	3.6	3.7	3.1	3.8	4.1	3.2	3.0
Total export share	2.2	3.7	4.4	3.8	5.6	4.9	4.9	3.5

For sources see Table A.3.

TABLE A.7
German, British, and French Shares of Eastern European Trade, 1928, 1933-38
(In Percentages)

	1928	1933	1934	1935	1936	1937	1938*
Austria							
Exports							
German share	18.5	15.1	15.9	15.6	16.1	14.8	—
British share	3.6	4.7	5.0	4.3	5.3	5.3	—
French share	2.4	4.1	3.8	3.6	4.5	4.3	—
Imports							
German share	19.9	18.7	17.1	16.6	16.9	16.1	—
British share	3.0	2.9	3.9	4.0	4.4	4.5	—
French share	2.8	2.6	3.0	2.9	2.9	2.8	—
Czechoslovakia							
Exports							
German share	22.1	17.7	21.5	14.9	14.5	13.7	20.1
British share	7.0	6.1	6.4	6.9	9.0	8.7	9.2
French share	1.3	5.5	4.1	4.0	4.3	3.8	2.5
Imports							
German share	24.9	19.8	19.4	17.3	17.5	15.5	19.1
British share	4.3	4.6	5.2	5.4	6.0	6.3	5.4
French share	4.3	6.2	6.4	5.6	6.0	5.3	4.7
Hungary							
Exports							
German share	11.8	11.2	22.2	23.9	22.8	24.0	45.9
British share	2.8	8.0	7.6	8.0	8.6	7.2	7.9
French share	0.8	4.5	3.4	2.3	1.9	2.0	1.9
Imports							
German share	19.5	19.7	18.3	22.6	26.0	25.9	40.8
British share	3.0	4.4	5.3	5.1	5.1	5.3	6.0
French share	2.6	5.6	2.9	1.2	1.0	0.9	1.5
Rumania							
Exports							
German share	18.4	10.6	16.6	16.6	17.8	19.2	26.5
British share	5.9	15.4	10.0	12.8	14.4	8.8	11.1
French share	4.8	12.4	9.7	4.0	8.1	5.7	4.7
Imports							
German share	23.7	18.6	15.5	24.4	36.1	28.9	36.8
British share	8.5	14.9	16.3	9.8	7.4	9.4	8.1
French share	6.4	10.5	11.1	7.2	5.9	6.1	7.7

* All German shares for 1938 include Austria.

TABLE A.7 (cont.)
German, British, and French Shares of Eastern European Trade, 1928, 1933-38
(In Percentages)

	1928	1933	1934	1935	1936	1937	1938
Yugoslavia							
Exports							
German share	12.1	13.9	15.4	18.6	23.7	21.7	42.0
British share	1.6	2.7	4.7	5.3	9.9	7.4	9.6
French share	3.8	2.2	1.3	1.6	2.0	5.4	1.5
Imports							
German share	13.6	13.2	13.9	16.2	26.7	32.4	39.4
British share	5.7	9.7	9.3	10.1	8.5	7.8	8.7
French share	4.5	4.2	5.0	4.3	2.5	1.7	2.9
Poland and Danzig							
Exports							
German share	34.2	17.5	16.6	15.1	14.2	14.5	24.1
British share	9.0	19.2	19.7	19.6	21.6	18.3	18.2
French share	1.7	5.5	4.2	3.5	4.3	4.1	3.8
Imports							
German share	26.9	17.6	13.6	14.4	14.3	14.5	23.0
British share	9.3	10.0	10.8	13.6	14.1	11.9	11.4
French share	7.4	6.8	5.8	4.9	4.3	3.2	3.6
Estonia							
Exports							
German share	25.9	21.2	22.5	24.4	22.5	30.5	31.4
British share	34.8	37.1	40.4	37.5	36.6	33.9	34.0
French share	1.3	7.0	4.2	2.7	4.7	3.2	2.7
Imports							
German share	30.3	22.5	21.2	26.3	29.8	26.1	31.3
British share	11.0	18.0	16.4	19.0	17.9	16.7	17.9
French share	3.9	5.4	5.9	3.4	2.0	2.2	2.7
Latvia							
Exports							
German share	26.4	25.9	29.5	33.5	30.8	35.1	33.7
British share	27.0	42.5	35.8	30.2	34.9	38.4	41.9
French share	3.5	5.3	3.1	1.8	2.2	1.8	2.2
Imports							
German Share	41.2	24.5	24.4	36.8	38.4	27.1	39.3
British share	9.4	21.9	22.6	20.4	21.4	20.7	19.3
French share	2.7	5.7	5.7	2.7	1.7	1.7	1.6

TABLE A.7 *(cont.)*
German, British, and French Shares of Eastern European Trade, 1928, 1933-38
(In Percentages)

	1928	*1933*	*1934*	*1935*	*1936*	*1937*	*1938*
Lithuania							
Exports							
German share	57.7	32.8	21.6	3.5	10.8	16.6	27.0
British share	20.4	44.7	42.6	45.6	48.4	46.4	39.4
French share	1.6	2.0	2.9	4.7	4.5	4.7	2.5
Imports							
German share	50.5	36.1	28.0	11.4	9.2	21.8	25.0
British share	6.6	17.1	25.3	37.2	36.5	27.9	30.9
French share	1.6	3.3	3.7	3.4	3.1	2.6	3.2

SOURCES: Ministère du Travail, de la Santé Publique et d'Assistance Sociale, *Annuaire statistique de la Roumanie 1933* (Bucharest, 1934), p. 259; LN, *ITS, 1927-29*, pp. 306-36, *1935*, pp. 302-33, *1938*, pp. 278-309.

Bibliography

UNPUBLISHED DOCUMENTS

France

Archives Nationales, Paris: Records of the Ministry of Agriculture, series F¹⁰.
Ministère des Finances, Paris: Records of the Finance Ministry, series F³⁰.

Germany

National Archives, Washington, D.C.: Records of the Economic Ministry (microfilm series T-71), the War Ministry (series T-77 and T-84), and the Foreign Office and Reich Chancellery (series T-120).
Politisches Archiv, Auswärtiges Amt, Bonn: Records of the Foreign Office.

Great Britain

Public Record Office, London:
  Records of the Board of Trade (BT 11) and Department of Overseas Trade (BT 59).
  Records of the Cabinet Office, including Cabinet minutes (CAB 23), Cabinet papers (CAB 24), and Cabinet committees, general series (CAB 27).
  Records of the Foreign Office, including General Correspondence—political (FO 371), confidential prints (FO 400 et seq.), and private collections (FO 800).
  Records of the Prime Minister (PREM/1).
  Records of the Treasury (T 160, T 188).
University of Birmingham Library, Birmingham: Neville Chamberlain Papers.

PUBLISHED DOCUMENTS

France

Les Evénements survenus en France de 1933 à 1945. Témoignages et documents recueillis par la Commission d'enquête parlementaire. 9 vols. *Rapport de M. Charles Serre, député au nom de la Commission d'enquête parlementaire.* Paris, 1947-1950.

Journal officiel de la République Française. Paris, various years.

Ministère des Affaires Etrangères. *Le Livre jaune français. Documents diplomatiques 1938-39.* Paris, 1939.

————, Commission de Publication des documents relatifs aux origines de la guerre 1939-1945. *Documents diplomatiques français (1932-1939).* Series 1: 1932-1935. Series 2: 1936-1939. Paris, 1963-1977.

Ministère des Finances, Direction Générale des Douanes. *Statistique mensuelle du commerce extérieur de la France.* Paris, various years.

Statistique Générale de la France. *Annuaire statistique.* Paris, various years.

Germany

Akten zur deutschen auswärtigen Politik 1918-1945. Aus dem Archiv des Auswärtigen Amtes. Edited by Hans Rothfels et al. Series B: 1925-1933. Göttingen, 1966-1968.

Kaiserliches Statistisches Amt (later Statistisches Reichsamt). *Statistisches Jahrbuch.* Berlin, various years.

Statistisches Reichsamt. *Monatliche Nachweise über den auswärtiger Handel Deutschlands.* Berlin, various years.

U.S. Department of State. *Documents on German Foreign Policy, 1918-1945, from the Archives of the German Foreign Ministry.* Edited by Raymond Sontag et al. Series C, Vols. I-V: 1933-1937. Series D, Vols. I-XIII: 1937-1941. Washington, D.C., 1949-1966.

Great Britain

Board of Trade. *Statistical Abstract of the United Kingdom.* London, various years.

Documents on British Foreign Policy, 1919-1939. Edited by E. L. Woodward et al. Series 2, Vols. I-XII: 1930-1938. Series 3, Vols. I-X, 1938-1939. London, 1946-1970.

Great Britain. *Parliamentary Debates.* House of Commons, House of Lords. London, various years.

————, Customs and Excise Department, Statistical Office. *Trade of the United Kingdom with Foreign Countries and British Possessions.* London, various years.

Miscellaneous Publications

International Military Tribunal. *Trial of the Major War Criminals before the International Military Tribunal, Nuremburg, 14 November 1945-1 October 1946.* 42 vols. Nuremburg, 1947-1949.

League of Nations. *Official Journal.* Geneva, various years.

——. *Publications.* Geneva, various years. (Includes the annual publications, *International Trade Statistics* and *Statistical Yearbook of the Trade in Arms.*)

——. *Treaty Series.* 205 vols. (Geneva, 1920-1946).

Ministère du Travail, de la Santé Publique et d'Assistance Sociale. *Annuaire statistique de la Roumanie 1933.* Bucharest, 1934.

Ministry for Foreign Affairs of the Czechoslovak Republic and Ministry for Foreign Affairs of the Union of Soviet Socialist Republics. *New Documents on the History of Munich.* Edited by V. F. Kločko et al. Prague, 1958.

U.S. Department of State. *Foreign Relations of the United States.* Washington, D.C., 1861-.

PERIODICALS

The Economist (London)

Institut für Konjunkturforschung. *Halbjahresbericht zur Wirtschaftslage* (Berlin)

PUBLISHED MEMOIRS, DIARIES, AND PERSONAL ACCOUNTS

Beck, Józef. *Dernier rapport, politique polonaise, 1926-39.* Neuchâtel, 1951.

Bonnet, Georges. *Défense de la paix.* Vol. I: *De Washington au Quai d'Orsay.* Geneva, 1946. Vol. II: *Fin d'une Europe.* Geneva, 1948.

Cadogan, Sir Alexander. *The Diaries of Sir Alexander Cadogan, O.M., 1938-45.* Edited by David Dilks. London, 1971.

Chamberlain, Neville. *The Struggle for Peace.* London, 1939.

Curtius, Julius. *Sechs Jahre Minister der deutschen Republik.* Heidelberg, 1948.

Eden, Anthony, Earl of Avon. *Facing the Dictators.* London, 1962.

Flandin, Pierre-Etienne. *Politique française, 1919-40.* Paris, 1947.

Gamelin, Maurice. *Servir.* 3 vols. Paris, 1946-1947.

Harvey, Oliver. *The Diplomatic Diaries of Oliver Harvey, 1937-40.* Edited by John Harvey. London, 1970.

Herriot, Edouard. *Jadis.* Vol. II: *D'une guerre à l'autre, 1914-36.* Paris, 1952.

Hitler, Adolf. *Hitler's Secret Conversations, 1941-1944.* Translated by Norman Cameron and R. H. Stevens. With an introduction by H. R. Trevor-Roper. New York, 1953.

——. *Hitlers zweites Buch. Ein Dokument aus dem Jahr 1928.* Edited by Gerhard L. Weinberg. Stuttgart, 1961.

——. *Mein Kampf.* Translated by Ralph Manheim. Boston, 1943.

——. *The Speeches of Adolf Hitler, April 1922-August 1939.* Edited by Norman H. Baynes. 2 vols. New York, 1942.

Hodža, Milan. *Federation in Central Europe*. London, 1942.

Laroche, Jules. *La Pologne de Pilsudski. Souvenirs d'une ambassade, 1926-35*. Paris, 1953.

Leith-Ross, Sir Frederick. *Money Talks: Fifty Years of International Finance*. London, 1968.

Lipski, Józef. *Diplomat in Berlin, 1933-1939: Papers and Memoirs of Józef Lipski, Ambassador of Poland*. Edited by Wacław Jędrezejewicz. New York, 1968.

Lukasiewicz, Juliusz. *Diplomat in Paris, 1936-1939: Memoirs of Juliusz Lukasiewicz, Ambassador of Poland*. Edited by Wacław Jędrezejewicz. New York, 1970.

Nicolson, Harold. *Diaries and Letters, 1930-39*. Edited by Nigel Nicolson. London, 1966.

Noël, Léon. *L'Aggression allemande contre la Pologne*. Paris, 1946.

Paul-Boncour, Joseph. *Entre deux guerres. Souvenirs sur la troisième république*. 3 vols. Paris, 1945-1946.

Rauschning, Hermann. *The Voice of Destruction*. New York, 1940.

Rosenberg, Alfred. *Das politische Tagebuch Alfred Rosenbergs aus den Jahren 1934/35 und 1939/40*. Edited by Hans-Günther Seraphim. Göttingen, 1956.

Schacht, Hjalmar. *76 Jahre meines Lebens*. Bad Wörishofen, 1953.

Simon, John Allsebrook, Viscount. *Retrospect: Memoirs of the Rt. Hon. the Viscount Simon*. London, 1952.

Speer, Albert. *Inside the Third Reich*. New York, 1970.

Thomas, Georg. *Geschichte der deutschen Wehr- und Rüstungswirtschaft (1918-1943/45)*. Edited by Wolfgang Birkenfeld. Boppard am Rhein, 1966.

Vansittart, Lord (Robert). *The Mist Procession*. London, 1958.

Zay, Jean. *Carnets secrets de Jean Zay*. Edited by Philippe Henriot. Paris, 1942.

SECONDARY WORKS

Adamthwaite, Anthony. *France and the Coming of the Second World War*. London, 1977.

Anderson, Edgar. "The British Policy toward the Baltic States 1918-20." *Journal of Central European Affairs*. XIX, no. 3 (1959), 276-89.

Aster, Sidney. *1939: The Making of the Second World War*. London, 1973.

Bankwitz, Philip C. F. *Maxime Weygrand and Civil-Military Relations in Modern France*. Cambridge, Mass., 1967.

Barnett, Correlli. *The Collapse of British Power*. London, 1972.

Basch, Antonín. *The Danube Basin and the German Economic Sphere*. New York, 1943.

Beckmann, Fritz, et al., eds. *Deutsche Agrarpolitik*. Vol. III. Berlin, 1932.

Bennett, Edward W. *Germany and the Diplomacy of the Financial Crisis, 1931*. Cambridge, Mass., 1962.

Berend, Ivan, and Ránki, György. *Economic Development in East-Central Europe in the 19th and 20th Centuries.* New York, 1974.

Birkenhead, Earl of. *Halifax.* London, 1965.

Boehme, Helmut. *Deutschlands Weg zur Grossmacht.* Cologne and Berlin, 1966.

Bracher, Karl Dietrich. *The German Dictatorship: The Origins, Structure, and Effects of National Socialism.* Translated by Jean Steinberg. New York, 1970.

————, Sauer, Wolfgang, and Schulz, Gerhard. *Die nationalsozialistische Machtergreifung: Studien zur Errichtung des totalitären Herrschaftssystems in Deutschland 1933/34.* Cologne, 1962.

Brandt, Karl, Schiller, Otto, and Ahlgrimm, Franz. *Management of Agriculture and Food in the German-Occupied Areas of Fortress Europe.* Vol. II. Stanford, 1953.

Broszat, Martin. *Nationalsozialistische Polenpolitik 1939-1945.* Stuttgart, 1961.

————. *Der Staat Hitlers. Grundlegung und Entwicklung seiner inneren Verfassung.* Munich, 1969.

Brügel, Johann Wolfgang. *Tschechen und Deutsche, 1918-1938.* Munich, 1967.

Bullock, Alan. *Hitler: A Study in Tyranny.* Rev. ed. New York, 1962.

Butterworth, Susan Bindoff. "Daladier and the Munich Crisis: A Reappraisal." *Journal of Contemporary History,* IX, no. 3 (1974), 191-216.

Carr, William. *Arms, Autarky and Aggression: A Study in German Foreign Policy, 1933-39.* London, 1972.

Carsow, Michel. *Quelques aspects du commerce impérial de la France.* Paris, 1935.

Celovsky, Boris. *Das Münchener Abkommen 1938.* Stuttgart, 1958.

Cienciala, Anna. "Poland and the Munich Crisis, 1938—A Reappraisal." *East European Quarterly,* III, no. 2 (1969), 201-19.

————. *Poland and the Western Powers, 1938-39.* Toronto, 1968.

————. "The Significance of the Declaration of Non-Aggression of January 26, 1934, in Polish-German and International Relations: A Reappraisal." *East European Quarterly,* I, no. 1 (1967), 1-30.

Clarke, Steven V. O. *Central Bank Cooperation, 1924-1931.* New York, 1967.

Colvin, Ian. *The Chamberlain Cabinet.* London, 1971.

————. *Vansittart in Office.* London, 1965.

Cowling, Maurice. *The Impact of Hitler: British Politics and British Policy, 1933-1940.* London, 1975.

Craig, Gordon A., and Gilbert, Felix, eds. *The Diplomats, 1919-1939.* New York, 1963.

Deutsch, Harold C. *Hitler and His Generals.* Minneapolis, 1974.

Doering, Dörte. "Deutsche Aussenwirtschaftspolitik 1933-35." Ph.D. diss., Free University of Berlin, 1969.

Dreifort, John E. *Yvan Delbos at the Quai d'Orsay: French Foreign Policy during the Popular Front, 1936-38*. Lawrence, 1973.

Ellis, Howard. *Exchange Control in Central Europe*. Cambridge, Mass., 1941.

Erbe, René. *Die nationalsozialistische Wirtschaftspolitik 1933-1939 im Lichte der modernen Theorie*. Zurich, 1958.

Fabry, Philipp W. *Die Sowjetunion und das Dritte Reich*. Stuttgart, 1971.

Feiling, Keith. *The Life of Neville Chamberlain*. London, 1946.

Feis, Herbert. *Europe, the World's Banker, 1871-1914*. New Haven, 1930.

Fischer, Fritz. *Germany's Aims in the First World War*. London, 1967.

———. *War of Illusions: German Policies from 1911 to 1914*. London, 1975.

Forstmeier, Friedrich, and Volkmann, Hans-Erich, eds. *Wirtschaft und Rüstung am Vorabend des Zweiten Weltkrieges*. Düsseldorf, 1975.

Fouchet, Jacques. *La Politique commerciale en France depuis 1930*. Paris, 1938.

Gehl, Jürgen. *Austria, Germany, and the Anschluss, 1931-1938*. London, 1963.

Geiss, Immanuel, and Wendt, Bernd Jürgen, eds. *Deutschland in der Weltpolitik des 19. und 20. Jahrhunderts*. Düsseldorf, 1973.

Gerschenkron, Alexander. *Bread and Democracy in Germany*. Berkeley, 1943.

Gilbert, Felix. "Mitteleuropa—The Final Stage." *Journal of Central European Affairs*, VII, no. 1 (1947), 58-67.

Gilbert, Martin. *The Roots of Appeasement*. London, 1966.

———, and Gott, Richard. *The Appeasers*. 2d ed. London, 1967.

Gruchmann, Lothar. *Nationalsozialistische Grossraumordnung. Die Konstruktion einer "deutschen Monroe Doktrin."* Stuttgart, 1962.

Hildebrand, Klaus. *Vom Reich zum Weltreich: Hitler, NSDAP und koloniale Frage 1919-1945*. Munich, 1969.

Hillgruber, Andreas. *Hitler, König Carol und Marschall Antonescu. Die deutsche-rumänische Beziehungen, 1938-1944*. Wiesbaden, 1954.

———. *Hitlers Strategie. Politik und Kreigführung, 1940-41*. Frankfurt, 1965.

———. *Kontinuität und Diskontinuität in der deutschen Aussenpolitik von Bismarck bis Hitler*. Düsseldorf, 1969.

Hoensch, Jörg K. *Die Slowakei und Hitlers Ostpolitik. Hlinkas Slowakische Volkspartei zwischen Autonomie und Separation, 1938/1939*. Cologne and Graz, 1965.

———. *Der ungarische Revisionismus und die Zerschlagung der Tschechoslowakei*. Tübingen, 1967.

Hoffmann, Peter. *Widerstand, Staatsstreich, Attentat. Der Kampf der Opposition gegen Hitler*. Munich, 1969.

Holt, John Bradshaw. *German Agricultural Policy, 1918-34*. New York, 1936.

Hoptner, J. B. *Yugoslavia in Crisis, 1934-41*. New York, 1962.

Hughes, Judith M. *To the Maginot Line: The Politics of French Military Preparations in the 1920's*. Cambridge, Mass., 1971.

Iklé, Frank W. "Japan's Policies towards Germany." In James Morley, ed., *Japan's Foreign Policy, 1868-1941*, pp. 265-339. New York 1974.

Jäckel, Eberhard. *Hitler's Weltanschauung: A Blueprint for World Power*. Translated by Herbert Arnold. Middletown, 1972.

Jacobsen, Hans-Adolf. *Nationalsozialistische Aussenpolitik 1933-1938.*. Frankfurt, 1968.

Jacomet, Robert. *L'Armement de la France, 1936-39*. Paris, 1945.

Jäger, Jorg-Johannes, *Die wirtschaftliche Abhängigkeit des Dritten Reiches vom Ausland dargestellt am Beispiel der Eisen- und Stahlindustrie*. Berlin, 1969.

Jarausch, Konrad H. *The Four Power Pact*, 1933. Madison, 1965.

Karsai, Elek. "The Meeting of Gömbös and Hitler in 1933." *New Hungarian Quarterly*, III, no. 5 (1962), 170-96.

Kindelberger, Charles P. *International Economics*. 3d ed. Homewood, 1963.

Kirk, Dudley. *European Population in the Interwar Years*. Geneva, 1946.

Klein, Burton H. *Germany's Economic Preparation for War*. Cambridge, Mass., 1959.

Kruszewski, Charles. "German-Polish Tariff War and Its Aftermath." *Journal of Central European Affairs*, III, no. 3 (1943), 294-325.

Kühl, Joachim. *Föderationspläne im Donauraum und in Ostmitteleuropa*. Munich, 1958.

Kuhn, Axel. *Hitlers aussenpolitisches Programm. Entstehung und Entwicklung, 1919-1939*. Stuttgart, 1970.

Kuisel, Richard F. *Ernest Mercier, French Technocrat*. Berkeley, 1967.

Lammers, Donald. "From Whitehall after Munich: The Foreign Office and the Future Course of British Policy." *Historical Journal*, XVI, no. 4 (1973), 831-56.

Lipgens, Walter. "Europäische Einigungsidee 1923-1930 und Briands Europaplan im Urteil der deutschen Akten." *Historische Zeitschrift*, CCIII (1966), 46-89, 316-63.

Long, Olivier. *Le Contingentement en France. Ses Incidences économiques*. Paris, 1938.

Lorenz, Robert. "The Essential Features of Germany's Agricultural Policy from 1870 to 1937." Ph.D. diss., Columbia University, 1941.

MacDonald, C. A. "Economic Appeasement and the German Moderates, 1937-93: An Introductory Essay." *Past and Present*, no. 56. (August 1972), 105-35.

Marguerat, Philippe. *Le IIIème Reich et le pétrole roumain*. Leiden, 1977.

Mason, Timothy W. *Arbeiterklasse und Volksgemeinschaft. Dokumente und Materialien zur deutschen Arbeiterpolitik 1936-39*. Opladen, 1975.

Mason, Timothy W. "Some Origins of the Second World War." *Past and Present*, no. 29 (December 1964), 67-87.

Metzmacher, Helmut. "Deutsch-englische Ausgleichsbemühungen im Sommer 1939." *Vierteljahreshefte für Zeitgeschichte*, XIV, no. 4 (October 1966), 369-412.

Meyer, Henry Cord. *Mitteleuropa in German Thought and Action, 1815-1945*. The Hague, 1955.

Middlemas, Keith. *Diplomacy of Illusion: The British Goverment and Germany, 1937-1939*. London, 1972.

Mitchell, B. R. *European Historical Statistics*. New York, 1975.

Morgan, O. S., ed. *Agricultural Systems of Middle Europe*. New York, 1933.

Mühlen, Norbert. *Der Zauberer. Leben und Anleihen des Dr. Hjalmar Horace Greeley Schacht*. Zurich, 1938.

Murray, Williamson. "The Change in the European Balance of Power, 1938-39." Ph.D. diss., Yale University, 1975.

Naudin, J. "La Politique douanière et les accords commerciaux." *Revue d'économie politique, La France économique*, 1931, 1029-47.

Newman, Simon. *March 1939: The British Guarantee to Poland*. Oxford, 1976.

O'Neill, Robert J. *The German Army and the Nazi Party, 1933-1939*. London, 1966.

Petzina, Dieter. *Autarkiepolitik im Dritten Reich. Der nationalsozialistische Vierjahresplan*. Stuttgart, 1968.

Pitts, Vincent J. "France and the German Problem: Politics and Economics in the Locarno Period, 1924-29." Ph.D. diss., Harvard University, 1975.

Pollard, Sidney. *The Development of the British Economy, 1914-67*. London, 1969.

Radant, Hans. "Die IG Farbenindustrie AG und Südosteuropa bis 1938." *Jahrbuch für Wirtschaftsgeschichte*, 1966, pt. 3, 146-95.

Recker, Marie-Luise. *England und der Donauraum, 1919-29*. Stuttgart, 1976.

Reichert, Günter. *Das Scheitern der Kleinen Entente, 1933-38*. Munich, 1971.

Rich, Norman. *Hitler's War Aims: Ideology, the Nazi State, and the Course of Expansion*. 2 vols. New York, 1973-1974.

Riekhoff, Harald von. *German-Polish Relations, 1918-33*. Baltimore, 1971.

Robbins, K. G. "Konrad Henlein, the Sudeten Question and British Foreign Policy." *Historical Journal*, XII, no. 4 (1969), 674-97.

Roos, Hans. *Polen und Europa. Studien zur polnischen Aussenpolitik, 1931-39*. Tübingen, 1957.

Ross, Dieter. *Hitler und Dollfuss. Die deutsche Österreich-Politik 1933-1934*. Hamburg, 1966.

Ruge, Wolfgang, and Schumann, Wolfgang. "Die Reaktion des deutschen Imperialismus auf Briands Paneuropaplan 1930." *Zeitschrift für Geschichtswissenschaft*, XX, no. 1 (1972), 40-70.

Sakwa, George. "The Franco-Polish Alliance and the Remilitarization of the Rhineland." *Historical Journal*, XVI, no. 1 (1973), 125-46.

Sauvy, Alfred. *Histoire économique de la France entre les deux guerres*, 4 vols. Paris, 1965-1975.

Sayers, R. S. *The Bank of England 1891-1914*. Vol. II. Cambridge, 1976.

Schacher, Gerhard. *Germany Pushes Southeast*. London, 1937.

Schoenbaum, David. *Hitler's Social Revolution: Class and Status in Nazi Germany 1933-1939*. Garden City, N.Y., 1967.

Schröder, Hans-Jürgen. "Deutsche Südosteuropapolitik 1926-1936. Zur Kontinuität deutscher Aussenpolitik in der Weltwirtschaftskrise." *Geschichte und Gesellschaft*, II, no. 1 (1976), 5-32.

———. "Südosteuropa als 'Informal Empire' Deutschlands 1933-39. Das Beispiel Jugoslawien." *Jahrbucher für Geschichte Osteuropas*, XXIII (1975), 70-96.

Schuker, Steven A. *The End of French Predominance in Europe*. Chapel Hill, 1976.

Schweitzer, Arthur. *Big Business in the Third Reich*. Bloomington, 1964.

Scott, William Evans. *Alliance against Hitler: The Origins of the Franco-Soviet Pact*. Durham, 1962.

Sering, Max, ed. *Die agrarischen Umwälzungen im ausserrussischen Osteuropa*. Berlin, 1930.

Seton-Watson, Hugh. *Eastern Europe between the Wars, 1918-41*. 3d ed. New York, 1962.

Skidelsky, Robert. *Politicians and the Slump: The Labour Government of 1929-1931*. London, 1967.

Sommer, Theo. *Deutschland und Japan zwischen den Mächten 1935-40*. Tübingen, 1962.

Stambrook, F. G. "The German-Austrian Customs Union of 1931: A Study of German Methods and Motives." *Journal of Central European Affairs*, XXI, no. 1 (1961), 15-44.

Stern, Fritz. *The Politics of Cultural Despair*. Berkeley, 1961.

Taylor, A.J.P. *English History, 1914-1945*. Pelican Edition. London, 1970.

———. *The Origins of the Second World War*. 2d ed. New York, 1966.

Teichova, Alice. *An Economic Background to Munich*. Cambridge, 1974.

Toynbee, Arnold, et al. *Survey of International Affairs 1936*. London, 1937.

Treue, Wilhelm. "Das Dritte Reich und die Westmächte auf dem Balkan." *Vierteljahreshefte für Zeitgeschichte*, I, no. 1 (1953), 45-64.

Trevor-Roper, Hugh R. "Hitlers Kriegziele." *Vierteljahreshefte für Zeitgeschichte*, VIII, no. 2 (1960), 121-23.

Turner, Henry A., Jr., ed. *Nazism and the Third Reich*. New York, 1972.
Ulam, Adam. *Expansion and Coexistence: The History of Soviet Foreign Policy, 1917-67*. New York, 1968.
Van Kessel, Gerhard Joseph. "The British Reaction to German Economic Expansion in Southeastern Europe, 1936-39." Ph.D. diss., University of London, 1972.
Vigrabs, Georg. "Die Stellungnahme der Westmächte und Deutschlands zu den Baltischen Staaten im Frühling und Sommer 1939." *Vierteljahreshefte für Zeitgeschichte*, VII, no. 3 (1959), 261-79.
Wallace, William V. "The Making of the May Crisis of 1938." *Slavonic and East European Review*, XLI, no. 97 (1963), 368-90.
———. "A Reply to Mr. Watt." *Slavonic and East European Review*, XLIV, no. 103 (1966), 480-86.
Wandycz, Piotr. *France and Her Eastern Allies, 1919-1925: French-Czechoslovak-Polish Relations from the Paris Peace Conference to Locarno*. Minneapolis, 1962.
Warner, Geoffrey. *Pierre Laval and the Eclipse of France*. London, 1968.
Watt, D.C. "The May Crisis of 1938: A Rejoinder to Mr. Wallace." *Slavonic and East European Review*, XLIV, no. 103 (1966), 475-80.
Weinberg, Gerhard L. *The Foreign Policy of Hitler's Germany: Diplomatic Revolution in Europe, 1933-1936*. Chicago, 1970.
———. "Secret Hitler-Beneš Negotiations in 1936-1937." *Journal of Central European Affairs*, XIX, no. 4 (1960), 366-74.
Wendt, Bernd Jürgen. *Appeasement 1938. Wirtschaftliche Rezession in Mitteleuropa*. Frankfurt, 1966.
———. *Economic Appeasement. Handel und Finanz in der britischen Deutschland-Politik 1933-1939*. Düsseldorf, 1971.
———. *München 1938. England zwischen Hitler und Preussen*. Frankfurt, 1965.
Wheeler-Bennett, John. *The Pipe Dream of Peace: The Story of the Collapse of Disarmament*. New York, 1935.
Wojciechowski, Marian. *Die polnisch-deutschen Beziehungen 1933-1938*. Leiden, 1971.
Wuescht, Johann. *Jugoslawien und das Dritte Reich*. Stuttgart, 1969.

Index

NOTE. Economic and trade relations between pairs of countries have been indexed in the following way: the economic and trade relations of France, Germany, and Great Britain with all other countries are indexed under France, Germany, and Great Britain. Economic and trade relations between other pairs of countries are indexed under the alphabetically preceding country, for example, Austria, economic and trade relations, with Poland. The same scheme has been used for foreign relations between pairs of countries.

Library of Congress Cataloging in Publication Data

Kaiser, David E   1947-
    Economic diplomacy and the origins of the Second
World War.

    Bibliography: p.
    Includes index.
    1. Germany—Commerce—Europe, Eastern.   2. Europe,
Eastern—Commerce—Germany.   3. Great Britain—
Commerce—Europe, Eastern.   4. Europe, Eastern—
Commerce—Great Britain.   5. France—Commerce—
Europe, Eastern.   6. Europe, Eastern—Commerce—
France.   7. Economic history—1918-1945.   I. Title.
HF3568.E35K34   382'.094   80-7536
ISBN 0-691-05312-X
ISBN 0-691-10101-9 (pbk.)